Africans Investing in Africa

Africans Investing in Africa

Understanding Business and Trade, Sector by Sector

Edited by

Terence McNamee
Deputy Director, The Brenthurst Foundation, Johannesburg, South Africa

Mark Pearson
Independent Consultant, Lusaka, Zambia

and

Wiebe Boer
Director, Group Strategy and Business Development, Heirs Holdings, Lagos, Nigeria

palgrave
macmillan

First published 2015 by
PALGRAVE MACMILLAN

Palgrave Macmillan in the UK is an imprint of Macmillan Publishers Limited,
registered in England, company number 785998, of Houndmills, Basingstoke,
Hampshire RG21 6XS.

Palgrave Macmillan in the US is a division of St Martin's Press LLC,
175 Fifth Avenue, New York, NY 10010.

Palgrave Macmillan is the global academic imprint of the above companies
and has companies and representatives throughout the world.

Palgrave® and Macmillan® are registered trademarks in the United States,
the United Kingdom, Europe and other countries.

ISBN: 978-1-137-54278-6

This book is printed on paper suitable for recycling and made from fully
managed and sustained forest sources. Logging, pulping and manufacturing
processes are expected to conform to the environmental regulations of the
country of origin.

A catalogue record for this book is available from the British Library.

A catalog record for this book is available from the Library of Congress.

Contents

Part I   Cross-Cutting Issues

Part II   Sectors with African Champions

Part III   Emerging Pan-African Sectors

List of Boxes

List of Figures

List of Tables

Foreword

Never have circumstances been more auspicious for African business. Rising disposable incomes, a young and talented population, rapidly improving infrastructure and an increasingly robust business climate have all combined to produce an emerging middle-class – poised to drive consumption, industrialisation and agricultural development. Global investor confidence in Africa is higher than it has ever been. Will the nations of Africa manage to capitalise on this period in history?

This was one of the key questions we sought to answer when the Tony Elumelu Foundation and the Brenthurst Foundation came together and conceptualised this joint project as part of our respective missions to create African thought-leadership around the continent's economic and social transformation.

For far too long, Africa's destiny was shaped by external influences and the self-interest of others more than by Africans themselves. In this age of globalisation and deepening economic integration, Africa must continue to integrate with the rest of the world, but not at the expense of strong economic ties between African nations. In order for Africa to live up to the prevailing narrative of 'Africa Rising', we must increase the depth and breadth of trade and investment between all its countries.

Through our respective experiences building businesses across Africa, we are both aware of the challenges of cross-border business operations on the continent. However, we have also both seen the incredible financial rewards to our respective commercial interests from such trade and, more importantly, we have seen the broader economic and social impact these activities create. This has shaped our agenda and created a focus on how to ensure more intra-African trade and other commercial flows.

In seeking to understand the profound changes under way in Africa's business landscape and how governments and entrepreneurs can open the way for more trade and investment by Africans, into Africa, the contributors to this volume have arrived at some vital – and often unexpected – conclusions.

While *Africans Investing in Africa: Understanding Business and Trade, Sector by Sector* can be read as a series of stand-alone chapters, together they represent an important manifesto for how intra-African commerce could help propel the continent to greater economic prosperity. The book illustrates why Africans must explore innovative ways to move beyond regional differences and competition, in order to forge lasting ties so that Africans at all levels become the primary beneficiaries of the continent's economic growth.

The purpose of this book is to demonstrate the diversity of sectors that are engaged in cross-border economic activity across the continent. The sectors covered in the various chapters use fresh case studies and in-depth analyses of African-led businesses that have successfully expanded internationally. Of course, due to Africa's vast diversity in tax, trade and customs regimes as well as in languages, cultures and social and business norms, challenges to further intra-African economic ties remain; many of which are discussed throughout this volume.

Over the course of this project, we have been particularly proud to engage a distinguished group of African thinkers and scholars from nine different countries, as well as non-African contributors – including one of the world's leading development experts, Paul Collier, who wrote the Introduction.

Both the Tony Elumelu Foundation and the Brenthurst Foundation believe that Africa's ability to effectively engage in intra-African business will be one of the key determinants of its future social and economic development. In this vein, we dedicate this volume to the next generation of pan-African investors who will carry what we started even further to the benefit of all Africans.

Tony O. Elumelu and Jonathan Oppenheimer

Acknowledgements

The editors wish to thank, firstly, Mr Tony Elumelu and the Oppenheimer family for their support in establishing the 'Africans Investing in Africa: Understanding Business and Trade, Sector by Sector' project. We are particularly grateful to the Tony Elumelu Foundation for hosting the initial pan-African philanthropy meeting, in December 2011, that led to this collaboration, as well as to Jonathan and Jennifer Oppenheimer for their kind hosting of the contributors' workshop in Johannesburg in March 2014.

A number of colleagues on both sides provided important insights at different stages of the project, which helped us refine our research questions and the key themes that appear in the book. They include: Peter Mombaur, Duncan Randall, Rudolf Dreyfus, Thomas Nziratimana, Samuel Nwanze, Owen Omogiafo, Moky Makura, Obinna Ufudo, Emmanuel Nnorom, Obong Idiong and Adim Jibunoh. We are also grateful for the insights and support of the Brenthurst Foundation's director, Greg Mills, as well as Leila Jack, Ghairoon Hajad, Wendy Trott and Leungo Motlhabane. From the Tony Elumelu Foundation, we recognize the contributions of David Rice, Serah Makka, Sesan Sulaiman, Maryamu Aminu, Desiree Younge, Claudine Moore, Eniola Shitta, Toyin Awesu and Somachi Chris-Asoluka. Special thanks to Tim and Jackie Sheasby, who assisted with graphs, figures and illustrations.

We are very grateful to the officials and experts who were interviewed by the contributors for their respective chapters. While too numerous to name individually, they gave generously of their time and their insights were crucial to the success of the project. A number of African governments as well as organisations and companies kindly permitted the contributors to use some of the data and tables found in this book, including Africa Practice, PPC, Dangote Cement, GIBS, MTN, McKinsey & Company, ICA and the Brenthurst Foundation.

Lastly, we thank our publisher, Palgrave Macmillan, in particular Liz Barlow and Kiran Bolla, for bringing this book to an international audience, as well as their anonymous reviewers, who provided such helpful comments.

Notes on Contributors

Wiebe Boer is Director, Group Strategy and Business Development at Heirs Holdings. He develops and refines the business, operational, philanthropic and communications strategy at the group, sector and subsidiary levels. Wiebe is a director of Mtanga Farms, East Africa Exchange and Avon Healthcare and also serves on the advisory board of several Nigerian public sector committees. Previously, he was inaugural CEO of the Tony Elumelu Foundation, an associate director in the Rockefeller Foundation's Africa office and a consultant for McKinsey & Company. He is from Jos, Nigeria and earned a PhD in History from Yale University.

Albert Butare, a former Minister of State for Infrastructure in the Republic of Rwanda, is a founder and CEO of Africa Energy Services Group Ltd. A winner of the UK based Ashden Foundation's International Award for Renewable Energies, Dr Butare has more than 20 years of energy, communication technology and water infrastructure experience in Africa. During his tenure as a minister, he participated in the installation of the first ever methane gas to electricity pilot plant, which to date serves as a study platform to all interested investors in gas. He is currently playing a key advisory role to governments in Africa and, in particular, the Eastern Africa region on matters related to energy and the environment as well as energy investment linkages within the region, where Independent Power Production, EPC contracts as well as PPP arrangements are the major focus. Dr Butare has extensive experience in high-level public sector policy and project development and implementation, engineering, social and economic development.

Jacqueline Chimhanzi is Senior Strategist at the Industrial Development Corporation of South Africa (IDC), a leading African development finance institution. Prior to IDC, she was Lead: Africa Desk with Deloitte South Africa assisting companies with their Africa growth strategies. Before that, she was a Manager with Deloitte Consulting leading project teams on diverse client engagements and interrogating and informing the strategies of major entities in power, oil and gas and steel. She is an Archbishop Tutu Leadership Fellow at Oxford University and serves as a Non-Executive Director on various boards. *Forbes* magazine featured her on their 20 Youngest Power Women in Africa 2012 list – women under 45 who are shaping the narrative of the continent's rising. She holds a BSc (Hons), MBA (with distinction) and a PhD (Strategic Marketing) from the University of Cardiff, United Kingdom. She has lectured and authored/co-authored papers in peer-reviewed leading academic journals. Her PhD research focused on enhancing companies' strategy execution capabilities.

Paul Collier is Professor of Economics and Public Policy at the Blavatnik School of Government; a Professorial Fellow of St Antony's College; and Co-director of the Centre for the Study of African Economies, Oxford. From 1998 to 2003, he took Public Service leave during which he was Director of the Research Development Department of the World Bank. Paul is currently adviser to the Strategy and Policy Department of the IMF, to the Africa Region, to the World Bank and to DfID. His research covers the causes and consequences of civil war, the effects of aid and the problems of democracy in low-income and natural-resources rich societies. In 2014, Paul received a knighthood for services to promoting research and policy change in Africa.

Stuart Doran is an independent scholar based in Johannesburg. He was previously employed by the Australian government as an official historian and diplomat and has more recently worked as a political advisor and consultant in Africa.

Tony O. Elumelu is an economist by training, a serial entrepreneur and philanthropist. Tony is the Founder and Chairman of Heirs Holdings, a privately held investment firm with interests in the power, oil and gas, financial services and hospitality sectors across Africa. He is Chairman of Transcorp, Nigeria's largest listed conglomerate, pan-African financial services group United Bank for Africa, and Seadrill Nigeria Limited.In 2010, Elumelu created The Tony Elumelu Foundation, which champions African entrepreneurship. In January 2015, the Foundation launched the US$100 million Tony Elumelu Entrepreneurship Programme to seed and support 10,000 African entrepreneurs over the next decade. The programme represents Tony's personal commitment to the economic philosophy of 'Africapitalism', a development model he propagated, that sees the African private sector as the catalyst ensuring Africa's sustainable social and economic development.Tony sits on numerous public and social sector boards, including the Global Advisory Board of the United Nations Sustainable Energy for All Initiative (SE4ALL), USAID's Private Capital Group for Africa Partners Forum (PCGA), and the Aspen Institute's Global Food Security Working Group. Tony also serves on the International Advisory Board of the Washington, DC-based think tank The Wilson Center, and as Vice-Chair of the National Competitiveness Council of Nigeria. In addition, Elumelu serves as an adviser to President Obama's Young African Leaders Initiative (YALI).

John Endres is the CEO of Good Governance Africa, a research and advocacy organisation established in 2012. He has also worked in business and as a lecturer, translator, interpreter and language coach and previously held the role of senior project officer at the Friedrich Naumann Foundation. John holds a PhD in Change Management from one of Germany's leading business schools.

Dianna Games is Chief Executive of Africa @ Work, an advisory company focusing on corporate trends, risk and development in Africa. She is a leading commentator on business issues and trends and writes extensively for the media, academic institutions and corporate publications. Dianna has been a columnist on Africa's political economy for leading South African newspaper *Business Day* since 2003. She is also the Executive Director of the South Africa-Nigeria Chamber of Commerce. Her book *Business in Africa: Corporate Insights*, published in 2012 by Penguin South Africa, is now in its second printing.

Eric Kacou is Co-founder and Managing Director of Entrepreneurial Solutions Partners (ESPartners), an advisory and consulting firm. ESPartners provides Intelligent Capital to entrepreneurs and leaders throughout Africa and the Caribbean. Author of *Entrepreneurial Solutions for Prosperity in BoP Markets*, Eric was honoured by the World Economic Forum as a Young Global Leader and by the African Leadership Institute as a Tutu Fellow. Eric earned his MBA at the Wharton School and his MPA at Harvard Kennedy School as a Mason Fellow.

Adrian Kitimbo is a visiting research fellow at the Centre for Dynamic Markets, Gordon Institute of Business Science, University of Pretoria. Previously, he was the Machel-Mandela intern at the Brenthurst Foundation, an economic development think tank based in Johannesburg. Adrian holds a bachelor of arts in International Relations from Whitworth University in Washington State and a master of science in Refugee and Forced Migration from the University of Oxford, where he was a recipient of the Queen Elizabeth House Scholarship.

Nicholas J.W. Kühne is Founder and Group-Managing Director of Wunderbrand; a pan-African brand consultancy. Nicholas has a BA Marketing Communications from the University of Johannesburg and is a Chartered Marketer. He is a regular lecturer at the University of Johannesburg and Wits Business School on marketing and branding in Africa. He has held senior marketing roles at Nando's, TBWA/Hunt Lascaris, MTV/VIACOM and Interbrand. He is passionate about building great African brands.

Terence McNamee is the Deputy Director of the Brenthurst Foundation. He was educated at universities in his native Canada and the United Kingdom, receiving his PhD in 2003 from the London School of Economics. He has been a writer and consultant on various projects in the areas of peace-building, post-conflict reconstruction and economic development, primarily in Africa. He has published in academic journals and newspapers, including the *New York Times* and the *Financial Times*. Other publications include *War Without Consequences: Iraq's Insurgency and the Spectre of Strategic Defeat* (ed.) (2008) and *On the Fault Line: Managing Tensions and Divisions within Societies* (2012, co-edited with Greg Mills and Jeffrey Herbst).

Muriuki Mureithi is an ICT consultant based in Kenya. He has spent more than 31 years in telecommunications industry. He consults in policy and regulatory and strategy evolution of ICTs in Africa. His work cuts across the UN agencies, governments, civil society, service operators and industry suppliers. He was a member of the UNECA High Level Working Group on ICTs that designed the African Information Society Initiative (AISI) in 1996. He holds an MBA in Strategic Management, a post-graduate certificate in Telecommunications Management from Stevens Institute of Technology, New Jersey, United States. He is currently pursuing a PhD focusing on ICT harmonization and integration in the East African Community.

Lite J. Nartey is an assistant professor in the Sonoco International Business Department, Darla Moore School of Business, University of South Carolina. Her research explores the relationships, contingencies and dynamics among multinational firms, governments and civil society actors and the implications on firm performance and societal value. Her focal industries are the extractive, telecommunications and finance industries, particularly within emerging markets. Her work has been recognized for several awards and nominations and published in top-tier academic journals. She holds a PhD from The Wharton School, University of Pennsylvania. She previously worked in the International Development arena and hails from Ghana.

Bitange Ndemo is the immediate former Permanent Secretary of Kenya's Ministry of Information and Communication. After his tenure with the government, he rejoined the University of Nairobi, where he is an Associate Professor at the Business School. He holds a PhD in Industrial Economics from the University of Sheffield, United Kingdom; an MBA from the University of St. Thomas, Minnesota; and a bachelor's degree in Finance from the University of Minnesota, United States. He is the immediate past Honorary Chair of the Alliance for Affordable Internet (A4AI) and an Advisor to the Better than Cash Alliance, a global initiative to digitize payments. He is a big data analytics and visualization enthusiast.

Moses E. Ochonu is Associate Professor of African History at Vanderbilt University, Nashville, United States. He is the author of three books: *Colonial Meltdown: Northern Nigeria in the Great Depression* (2009); *Colonialism by Proxy: Hausa Imperial Agents and Middle Belt Consciousness in Nigeria* (2014); and *Africa in Fragments: Essays on Nigeria, Africa, and Global Africanity* (2014). His articles have been published as book chapters and in several scholarly journals. Moses is a prolific commentator on African Affairs. His op-eds and commentaries have been published in *Chronicle Review/Chronicle of Higher Education, Tennessean.com, Pambazuka* and in Nigerian and African newspapers and web publications. He has appeared on National Public Radio (NPR) and on Voice of America (VOA) TV. Moses is a two-time recipient of the research fellowship of the American Council of Learned Societies (ACLS).

He has also received research grants and fellowships from the Harry Frank Guggenheim Foundation, the Social Science Research Council (SSRC), Rockefeller Foundation, Ford Foundation, National Endowment for the Humanities (NEH) and the British Library.

Jonathan Oppenheimer is a South African businessman who has spent most of his working life in Anglo American and De Beers. After leaving Anglo American in 2000, he has filled numerous senior roles within De Beers, including leading the strategic review of Debid (now Element Six) (2000–2001) after which he became Chairman until 2012; and most recently the Head of the Chairman's Office (2006–2012). He has also been actively involved in other aspects of the family's activities. Most notable of these has been the establishment of the Brenthurst Foundation and the formation of Tana Africa Capital, a joint venture between the Oppenheimer family and Temasek to pursue business opportunities across the continent in the consumer goods space.

Mark Pearson is an economist who has been living and working as a consultant to African governments, regional economic organisations, donor organisations and the private sector in Africa over the past 35 years, mainly in the Eastern and Southern Africa region but also with experience in West Africa and Sudan. He has been working on trade, transport, infrastructure and regional integration issues since the 1990s. He has managed large donor-funded projects and led multi-disciplinary teams of professionals working on infrastructure, trade facilitation and trade policy in a regional context. Mark is an Associate of the Brenthurst Foundation and his recent work has been on investment opportunities in infrastructure in Africa; value chains; trade facilitation and logistics; and trade policy in the context of the Tripartite and Continental Free Trade Areas.

David A. Rice is the Director of the Africapitalism Institute at the Tony Elumelu Foundation, a new pan-African think tank based in Lagos, Nigeria. Previously he was a professor at New York University where he taught graduate-level courses on Africa and ran a research program called the Development Dividend Project. Select prior positions include Visiting Faculty at the University of Nairobi; Africa Advisor to the Milken Institute; Executive Director of NYU's Development Research Institute under Professor William Easterly; contributing writer for *Fortune* magazine; and consultant to several African governments, global investment funds and multinational corporations. He has also worked for the World Economic Forum in Geneva and for Global Insight in London. David obtained his master's degree in International Development from Harvard University.

Daniella Sachs is a sustainable tourism economic development specialist, who has in-depth and multi-sector knowledge of the complexities of tourism in the context of Africa, at community regional and national scales. With a dual master's in both Architecture and Town and Regional Planning, Daniella works with destination stakeholders to develop integrated and effective local supply and value chains that are linked to regional and national cross-sectoral markets. Daniella has extensive expertise in developing scalable multi-stakeholder engagement projects and programmes that address environmental, socio-economic and cultural issues in relation to tourism. She is currently spearheading the Destination Alliance of Southern Africa regional initiative.

Lyal White is the Director of the Centre for Dynamic Markets (CDM) at the Gordon Institute of Business Science (GIBS), University of Pretoria, where he is also a senior lecturer in political economy and strategic thinking in Africa, Asia and Latin America. Previously, White was a Senior Researcher at the South Africa Institute of International Affairs (SAIIA) and a Visiting Scholar at the Centre for Latin American Studies (CLAS) at UC Berkley. He has also lectured at a number of universities, including University of Cape Town, Science Po–Bordeaux, France, Strathmore Business School, Kenya and Al Akhawayn University in Morocco. White completed his PhD in Political Studies at the University of Cape Town.

Editors' Note

This book is the outcome of a project conceived in 2011 by the Johannesburg-based Brenthurst Foundation and the Lagos-based Tony Elumelu Foundation. The foundations, drawing on their established record of scholarship and policy advice on issues impacting Africa's economic growth and development, agreed to undertake in-depth, case-study based research into why African-owned or/and African-based companies were still struggling to succeed across multiple geographies on the continent, despite Africa's impressive economic growth rates and overall improvements in macro-economic management. This crucial part of the 'Africa Rising' story had been largely ignored in the academic and policy-related literature. A 'foundational paper' for the project, authored by Jonathan Oppenheimer and Tony Elumelu, published in 2013, identified a number of under-examined factors – including cultural issues – which seemed to be seriously impeding cross-border trade and investment in Africa. The paper highlighted a clear need for further scholarly research into how these factors manifested and reinforced one another in practice – and how they could be ameliorated. A detailed research template, structured around several key questions relevant across all economic and business sectors under consideration, was devised and 15 case studies by leading academic and policy experts – affiliated to universities and institutions in the United States, Europe and Africa – were commissioned. Following their initial research and completion of draft papers, the case study authors were brought together for a day-long workshop in March 2014 in Johannesburg to engage in a structured critique of each of the papers, which were circulated to the workshop participants in advance. At the workshop, the papers were assessed on the basis of their originality, academic rigour and policy relevance. The case study authors were joined by a small number of distinguished external experts who also participated in the critique process. The workshop identified some key shortcomings and weaknesses in the initial research template, which were then adjusted to fit the realities of what the case study authors had encountered in the course of their research. Overall, the workshop revealed a welter of new insights and research findings that had not been anticipated at the outset of the project, though a few of the original case studies were eventually rejected on the basis of negative critiques and thus do not appear in this book. The workshop concluded with the appointment of the main editor, Mark Pearson, who helped mould the successful case studies into the final form found herein.

Introduction

Paul Collier

This is a timely book. Although for Africa the past decade has been economically benign, attention in the international business media has been narrowly focused. International investors have concentrated on the natural resource sector, due to high prices for its exports, and international consumer businesses have been attracted by the consequential scope for expanding imports of consumer goods. Yet Africa's economies have huge potential for growth that is more widely diffused across many sectors. Despite softer commodity prices, during the coming decade Africa will continue to catch up with the world economy.

Even in the natural resource sector, lower prices will be more than offset by the expansion in the volume of resources extracted, reflecting a decade of investment in prospecting. But the process of attracting further investment into the sector has become much more challenging now that the sector is on the wrong side of the super-cycle. Africa now has its own significant companies and these will more naturally continue to be focused on the region. Especially for these companies, as Chapter 12 discusses, governments will need policies that make investment secure and attractive, while ensuring that resource rents accrue as revenue.

From now on much of Africa's growth will come from harnessing the opportunities for investment and productivity across the economy. Sector by sector, this book discusses those opportunities and the constraints that will need to be overcome. To begin with a seemingly mundane example, as the income of more Africans rises above subsistence levels, discretionary consumption will increase disproportionately. This creates opportunities to revolutionize retail distribution, which in much of the region remains dominated by small scale and informality. The productivity gain from reaping the economies of scale and specialisation that come with malls, supermarkets and retail chains is enormous. This transformation is now happening across Africa, but, as Chapter 9 makes clear, it faces significant policy impediments. The successful management of scale and specialisation in retailing depends on professional expertise, and this is currently concentrated in relatively few African organisations. Yet as they bring their capabilities to new markets, they often meet resistance from politicians and bureaucrats who are suspicious of non-national companies. They also face logistical problems of moving products across borders: barriers, costs and delays can eliminate the potential productivity gains from organising supply chains regionally.

Further, with discretionary expenditures comes consumer concern for product quality and variety. Firstly, consider the need to respond to the demand for quality. Not only are informal modes of production and distribution unable to harness the gains of scale and specialisation, they are unable to build reputation with consumers. Informal products are not sufficiently standardised for consumers to be able to trust a product based on a past purchase, nor are good informal products legally protected from imitation by look-alike inferior ones. As discussed in Chapter 5, branding offers the solution to these problems, providing the scope for retailers and producers to build reputation with consumers free of the threat of imitation. But African firms are latecomers: international firms can offer African consumers established reputable brands and have the legal capacity to protect them through patents and copyrights. Establishing equivalent African brands urgently requires a phase of investment in advertising and legal expertise: without it, African business will miss the boat as new consumers, in their quest for quality, bond with international brands.

Probably the most important product whose quality urban African households want to upgrade is their housing: except in South Africa, years of neglect in housing investment have left most people living in shacks. People are often physically capable of improving their housing with their own labour, but the key input they need is cement. For decades, little cement was produced locally, and tapping into international supply was stymied by inadequate transport logistics, which are evidently particularly important for cement due to its low value-to-weight ratio. In the past decade, there has been a major expansion in African supply, but demand, driven by the desire for better housing, is also rocketing. As discussed in Chapter 8, it is important that the supply of cement is turned from a bottleneck to a driver of growth.

Now consider the quest for variety. People in poverty make their own entertainment, but one important use of discretionary spending is to widen horizons. The media provide the window onto the limitless emporium of modernity. But far more than in respect of products, the interface between people and information is mediated by culture, and cultures are specific to societies. A Chinese bicycle can be marketed to an African household more readily than a Chinese soap opera, let alone a Chinese newspaper. The expanding demand for information, discussed in Chapter 11, is a huge opportunity for an indigenous African media. On the base of meeting domestic demand, the industry can also meet the previously latent demand in the large African diaspora.

Scale and specialisation, the cornerstones of productivity, can take place only in large markets. Most African countries constitute small markets, and so trade with other countries is critical to rising prosperity. As the opening chapter makes clear, international trade is in Africa's blood: even in the twelfth century, African traders were exchanging goods over huge distances. Yet many countries are currently economically isolated due to a combination of inadequate transport infrastructure and bureaucratic impediments to the free flow of commerce. Being small and isolated is, in economic terms, a death sentence: people are trapped into the inevitable poverty of low productivity activities. While Chapter 1 demonstrates that the relationships that support long-distance trade are part of African tradition, Chapters 4 and 15 take up the associated themes of investment in transport infrastructure and transport logistics.

Africa has never had an infrastructure appropriate for its needs. During the colonial era, transport routes were overwhelmingly extractive: designed to move primary commodities to ports. During the half-century since, governments have seldom prioritised new investment in transport infrastructure. The lack of new investment was compounded by the systematic neglect of maintenance expenditures in budgeting. In consequence, in some respects, Africa's transnational transport infrastructure is even less adequate now than it was in the 1960s. There is, however, a new economic opportunity to finance transport infrastructure arising from the recent natural resource discoveries around the continent. Not only do governments have new revenues, they can be geared up by borrowing on sovereign bond markets: in conjunction with debt relief, credit ratings have improved dramatically. Rather than let new revenues and borrowings be allocated to infrastructure through the budget process, some governments have preferred to exchange the rights to resource extraction directly for the provision of new infrastructure, which typifies the Chinese resource deals. At their best, they provide a mechanism for political commitment of revenues to this important priority, and are much faster than negotiating a sequence of distinct transactions. At their worst, however, they result in opaque and disadvantageous deals.

The scope for big transport infrastructure projects has understandably gained political and media attention. However, while far less dramatic, the removal of bureaucratic barriers to trans-border trade, both at the border itself, through the harmonisation of 'behind-the-border' regulations, would yield even larger benefits to practical transport logistics at radically lesser cost. The two approaches are not alternatives: evidently, if transport infrastructure would lie unused because of bureaucratic impediments, it is not worth building.

The low priority that governments have given to transport infrastructure is a symptom of a wider problem: governments have taken exclusive responsibility for providing a wider range of infrastructure than they have been willing to finance. As Chapter 14 discusses, water is a stark instance of government insistence on a monopoly commitment for provision on which it has then defaulted. Politicians find it expedient to whip up popular resentment at commercial charges for water supplies by arguing that water is a 'basic right'. Yet other than in a few high-income districts, this is a 'right' that political leaders have repeatedly breached. The same phenomenon used to apply to telecommunications. African governments insisted on a monopoly on landlines for telephones and then failed to provide and maintain them. The transformation of telecommunications was not due to political enlightenment but to the happenstance of technological change. Fortuitously, mobile phones were classified as a sufficiently distinct product that they could be provided without infringing the public landline monopoly. For water, the nearest equivalent is water sold in bottles, which is not judged to breach the public monopoly on water provision. But unfortunately, bottled water is a less adequate substitute for a tap than is a mobile phone for a landline. However, the astounding take-up of mobile phones in Africa, discussed in Chapter 10, has the potential for a broader narrative to be accepted by ordinary citizens: where services can be well-provided privately, it is a breach of rights to insist on the retention of failing public monopolies.

The provision of security is an example of a public service which is technologically distinct from piped water and landline phones. It is invariably provided publicly, through police, because it enforces the rule of law, which is a basic duty of all government. However, while there is a duty of public provision, there is absolutely no technological need for such provision to have a monopoly. The private provision of security services did not need to await technological change analogous to the mobile phone, or labour under the disadvantage that delivering water in bottles is far more costly than delivering it through pipes: private security guards and police use a common technology. Nevertheless, as discussed in Chapter 13, without any technological impetus, private security services have expanded enormously across the region. Good security has repercussions beyond the obvious. As discussed in Chapter 16, one of Africa's best opportunities for diversifying exports beyond primary products is through the sale of tourist services. The continent clearly has huge advantages of natural endowments and proximity to major high-income markets. But an important deterrent to tourism to Africa is exaggerated fear: Ebola, though contained to three countries of West Africa, hit tourism across the continent. Similarly, security incidents anywhere on the continent hit tourism everywhere.

The underlying impetus for the expansion of private security provision is the same as that driving the exceptionally rapid expansion of mobile phones in Africa, namely, the poor quality of public provision. States have simply not got to grips with managing public services. The underlying reason derives from the nature of African politics, which has too often been about patronage rather than performance. In addressing African private investment, African politics is finally inescapable.

The economic implications of African politics appeared even during the liberation process: Africa's polities fragmented. One important economic consequence is that national markets are mostly very small. The only way to reconcile the need for economic scale with political fragmentation would have been to create strong supra-national political authorities, but whereas Europe succeeded in this endeavour, to date Africa has not. As Chapter 3 discusses, trans-national economic integration has lacked powerful champions. The most evident costs have been missed opportunities for shared infrastructure, such as transport routes and power generation, and the proliferation of beggar-thy-neighbour impediments to the flow of trade. But the lack of political energy behind integration has also had consequences for the flow of labour and capital.

Scale and specialisation, the engines of productivity growth, depend not only on cross-border flows of goods, but on the cross-border flow of skills. In politically fragmented markets, the same skill can become unwanted in one small market and yet be in high demand elsewhere. More subtly, people will be less inclined to acquire the specialist skills for which they have an aptitude, if they are restricted to a national market with only a few potential employers. The European Commission has long enforced the principle of the free movement of labour around all member countries, and for most of them movement across borders does not even require a passport. In contrast, as discussed in Chapter 6, movement across many African borders requires a visa with restrictions even more severe for fellow-Africans than for non-Africans. Employment of non-nationals is not only restricted, but in some countries restrictions are being tightened to the extent that even those long resident are being expelled. Even the possibility of such a tightening of policy discourages cross-border movement, and this in turn makes it more difficult for firms to find well-qualified workers. The upshot is that firms are discouraged from investments that would require such workers, and people are discouraged from acquiring specialist skills.

During the 1990s, most African countries liberalised their financial sectors and encouraged international banks to establish local businesses. The theory behind the welcome given to international banks was that their strong reputations would ensure that they remained financially robust, and that their global spread would enable them to diversify the risks inherent in local banks that were purely dependent on a small, volatile national economy. The global financial crisis disabused central bankers of these beliefs. Not only were international banks revealed as risk-prone, but finding that they needed to increase capital relative to liabilities in their core markets, they repatriated capital from their African businesses. This led to a credit squeeze in African markets that was entirely unrelated to African conditions. A lesson from this crisis is that a good way to reconcile diversification with a proper commitment to the local market is to encourage African banks to operate in several national markets. Such a strategy, discussed in Chapter 7, is not without challenges, because it requires prior agreement among African central banks as to how to manage the failure of either a branch in one country, or an entire banking group. But since the underlying structure of African banking operations is not complex, the task of policy coordination and cooperation is far less daunting than that faced by regulators in the OECD.

In combination, the pay-off to shared infrastructure, easier trade and unimpeded factor movements, is so large that the more purposeful sharing of sovereignty required for genuine regional integration is imperative. Africa has plenty of institutional structures for regionalism: the African Union, NEPAD, the African Development Bank and the RECs. Indeed, arguably, it has too many of them: some countries are simultaneously in several RECs which involve what might become incompatible commitments. To date, too much of this has been driven by the appetite for political theatre: prestigious meetings followed by portentous pronouncements on symbolic steps such as common currencies, but little action on issues that actually matter. What is needed in its place is a business-driven, practical agenda. African businesses need to become more vocal and themselves learn how to cooperate across borders in lobbying for change.

Yet African business has the potential to change African politics more fundamentally than through its lobbying. As Chapter 2 argues, until recently, the only feasible route by which indigenous Africans could become wealthy was through acquiring political power and then abusing it for personal gain. Now, while the political route to wealth has been discredited, Africa abounds in role models of business success. Gradually, this is changing the character of those who seek a political career. Those who aspire to wealth can seek it more productively, and with better chance of success, in business. This opens political opportunity for those who want to serve Africa rather than themselves. This is doubly important because African politics is set to change. Currently, the age gap between citizens and rulers is dramatically wider in Africa than anywhere else in the world. It will not remain so, and a younger generation of African leaders will have fresh priorities.

Part I
Cross-Cutting Issues

1
The Wangara Trading Network in Precolonial West Africa: An Early Example of Africans Investing in Africa

Moses E. Ochonu

This study focuses on the extensive business and trading empire that Mande-speaking merchants, trade brokers, and financiers built and ran across West Africa between the fourteenth and nineteenth centuries. The Wangara feature prominently in the economic and mercantile history of West Africa because they pioneered intra-regional long distance trading and investments. They faced and overcame obstacles to trade and investments in diverse cultural and political settings, leaving a legacy that is instructive for current discussions about Africans investing and trading across Africa.

For roughly five hundred years, these pioneers of regional intra-African investment with ancestral origins in the old Mali and Songhai empires (modern-day Mali) mastered a uniquely African brand of product distribution, arbitrage, financing, manufacturing, credit, mining, currency swaps, bartering and long-distance trading (see Figure 1.1).

Referred to in different sources as Wangara, Juula, Mandinka, Malinke, Mande, Mandingo and Djula, the Wangara merchants built a vast regional economic network extending from the Sahel in the north to the Akan Forest in the south and from the Senegambia and the Mano River Frontier in the west to modern Benin Republic and Northern and Western Nigeria in the east.

The West African commercial empire that the Wangara built connected territories in modern-day Mali, Senegal, Gambia, Guinea, Guinea Bissau, Cote d'Ivoire, Burkina Faso, Ghana, Benin and Nigeria.[1] This trading and brokerage system involved many goods, including gold, kola nuts, cloth, salt, natron, leather products and others. It also entailed a vast investment portfolio that spanned arbitrage, cottage manufacturing, services and mining.

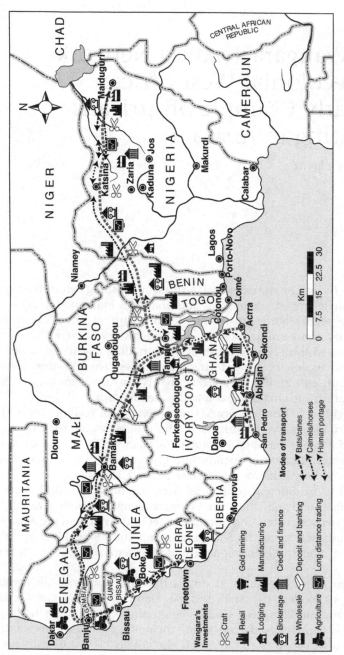

Figure 1.1 Trading routes and investments made by the Wangara

Source: Adapted by author from Longman School Atlas, 2000.

The Wangara were versatile investors, buying into economic endeavours that connected to or had the capacity to enhance their long-distance trading. The Wangara commercial network was large but was held together by a trust system that developed over many generations, by strategic appeals to political power when necessary and by the Wangara's skill in expanding the pool of participants in a growing trade system and its circuits of prosperity.

Wangara mercantile beginnings

The Wangara were a composite ethnic group comprising speakers of Mande languages (Malinke and Bambara) and a few speakers of the Azer dialect, a Soninke-derived 'commercial lingua franca in Western Sudan'.[2] Medieval historical sources ascribe many mercantile attributes to the Wangara. Beginning with early Arab travellers' accounts in the twelfth century through the mid-fourteenth century,[3] various narratives associated the Wangara with the supply of gold from the medieval gold mines of Bure and Bambuk in the kingdom of Mali.

Exchanged for salt mined at the edge of the Sahara and salt brought by Arab, Berber and Jewish traders,[4] gold was transported across the Sahara to North Africa. The Wangara then sold the salt, which was both a valued seasoning ingredient and a form of currency in several parts of West Africa, across a vast area in the kingdom of Mali, in Mossi country in present-day Burkina Faso, in the Guinea basin and in the Senegambia region. The Wangara organised and used camel-caravans to transport salt from the Saharan mines to Timbuktu, a major Wangara distribution hub, from where wholesale operations were coordinated. In Timbuktu, Wangara bulk purchasers bought blocks of salt to be caravanned to other West African commercial centres, from where the retail trade in salt took off in various directions.

By positioning themselves as the first link in the trade chain that transported West African gold to North Africa and distributed salt from Sahelian and North African salt producing areas to many parts of West Africa, the Wangara created a complex supply network that was a de facto monopoly. With this early, dominant involvement in commerce, the term 'Wangara' quickly became synonymous with 'trader' or 'long-distance trader', and vice versa, in much of West Africa. The process of mastering this trans-West Africa trade took time, but the spread of Wangara commercial influence from medieval Mali to other parts of West Africa was inevitable, given the importance of gold and salt to the economies of several states in West Africa.

Beginning probably in the late twelfth century, the Wangara began to expand their trading network to the Senegambia, to Guinea, and southwest to modern-day Ghana, Ivory Coast and eventually modern-day Nigeria. The logistics of this trading system became more complex as the Wangara sought out new commercial areas and invested in the extractive and manufacturing sectors. Some of the Wangara hired potters who carried salt and other

Sahelian and North African goods on their heads; some relied on the familiar camel-caravan system. Others employed both means. After about 20 days of travel, the traders would arrive in either the forest states of modern Ghana or in Senegambia.[5] As they made their way south and west, they would sell salt and other goods along the way to defray expenses and buy other trade goods from communities on the trade routes.

Over the next three centuries, the Wangara perfected this trading system and not only opened up a set of recognised trade routes connecting the Sahara to multiple West African hinterlands (see Figure 1.2), but also established permanent trading centres in the various areas of West Africa with which they conducted trade. At the peak of the Wangara's commercial ascendance, their economic activities and investments encompassed product distribution, arbitrage, financing and credit, lodging, mining, manufacturing, bartering, brokerage and long-distance trading.

Overview of the Wangara trading and investment network

To the west of the Wangara's Mali heartland lay the vast territory comprising the modern states of Senegal, Gambia, Guinea and Guinea Bissau. Given the contiguity of this region to Mali, the Wangara were very active here, setting up the social, political and economic infrastructures to support their lucrative commercial activities. Many Wangara migrated to this region, helping to found small city-states and to consolidate kingdoms like Kaabu.[6] Many of the migrants were itinerant traders, going between east (Mali) and west and carrying goods back and forth.

A product of this commercial and political influence of the 'Wangara [trade] Diaspora'[7] in the Senegambia region was a strong kinship network that produced an ever-expanding circuit of confidence, which in turn facilitated business transactions and credit. Furthermore, some of the Wangara traders who settled permanently in the Senegambia region took to artisan pursuits, becoming cobblers and blacksmiths, manufacturing and supplying footwear, accessories and weapons to Wangara and non-Wangara warriors, political leaders, priests and long-distance traders. This group of Wangara artisans became valuable auxiliaries in the expanding trading system, supplying footwear, weapons and other products integral to professions like long-distance trading, which involved constant mobility in rough terrain.[8] The trade system in turn sustained the Wangara artisans by keeping them employed. A small number of the Wangara may have also invested in agriculture, the product that catered to the commercial classes, supplying long-distance merchants with specially preserved foods.[9] Wangara merchants and artisans in this region built a vast reciprocal system of exchange and trade and catered to the commercial demands of many communities in this region. In this way, they drew in several non-Wangara peoples into the emerging Wangara economy.

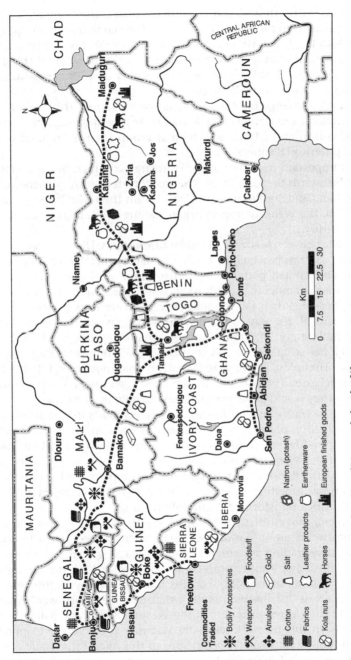

Figure 1.2 Trading routes and commodities made by the Wangara

Source: Adapted by author from Longman School Atlas, 2000.

In the late sixteenth and seventeenth centuries, the Wangara's trading activities spread even further to the north of the Gambia river and probably all the way to the Lower Guinea Coast. This was probably due to increased Wangara out migration as a result of the decline and eventual collapse of the Songhai Empire. The Wangara began to broker trade in European manufactured goods between the Portuguese and Africans and to sell gold to the Portuguese in exchange for manufactured goods during this period.[10] The Wangara traders from Gambia and Sierra Leone met at Badoora to exchange kola nuts, cotton and fabrics, which each group then distributed over its commercial territorial sphere.

Another important trajectory of the Wangara's commercial expansion was southwards towards the Akan forest, the vast forested territory encompassing modern Ghana and Southern Ivory Coast. From their Middle Niger base in modern Mali, the Wangara traders began trading south as early as the early fifteenth century.

In the trade between Mali and the Akan forest states, Djene served as a hub. From Djene, salt was broken into smaller tradable units that could be carried by camels and human porters for the two–three weeks' journey spanning some five hundred miles to the vast Akan goldfields.[11] In the Akan goldfields, the Wangara traded their salt for gold over a vast territory corresponding to modern Ghana all the way to the coastal region encompassing the famous European trading port of Elmina.[12] After exhausting their stock of Saharan salt through bartering, the traders commenced the return journey to Djene, and then to Timbuktu, where they sold Akan gold to Arab and Berber trans-Saharan merchants. The Wangara traders then used the proceeds to buy salt with which they would purchase their next supply of Akan gold.

The Wangara traders' expansion to, and investments in, the alluvial gold mining production of the Akan region represented another strand in their fast-growing trading and investment repertoire. It was no accident that the extension of the Wangara's trading network to the Akan region occurred in tandem with 'the development of new centers of gold production'.[13] Wangara capital investments, credit and the thriving Wangara gold trade with North Africa transformed Akan gold mining.

The Wangara's investment in the Akan goldfield expanded in the subsequent centuries as more Mande-speaking traders moved south to partake in this lucrative trading system.[14] By building a vast distribution network connecting the major West African centres of gold and salt production, and by creating a virtual monopoly over this trade, the Wangara 'became...the first link in a vast distributive network that extended northward from the goldfields to the greater entrepots of the Western Sudan and Sahel'.[15] Being the first link in this network gave the Wangara the leverage to put their imprimatur on the subsequent expansions of this Akan-Sahel trade.

Another factor that gave the Wangara traders preeminence in the trade of the Akan zone is kola nut, a stimulant grown almost exclusively in the

Akan forest,[16] which enjoyed and still enjoys widespread recreational and ritual-use demand across West Africa and the Maghrebian lands north of the Sahara. This trans-West African and trans-Saharan market for kola nut and the Wangara's tentacles and settlements in regions that produced it gave the merchants an opportunity to expand and consolidate their dominance over long-distance trading in West Africa.

Ever with an eye for emerging demands and new trading opportunities, Wangara traders were quick to spot the vast kola nut export potential that lay in the Akan forest and to correlate this to demand for the product across West Africa. Given the fact that 'long-distance traders were usually in the best position to respond to new opportunities',[17] the Wangara were in a unique position to develop a new trade in kola nut. They leveraged their existing gold and salt trade infrastructures to add kola nut export to their trading portfolio. The ensuing trade in kola nut gave the Wangara another opportunity to establish more trading outposts and settlements along new trade routes that they helped pioneer to support the new kola nut economy.

The Wangara-controlled kola nut trade opened up new trading routes, and with them new Wangara settlements and trading diasporas in present-day Benin Republic, Niger and Nigeria. Trading under the corporate identity of Wangara, Mande-speaking merchants began to trade in kola nut obtained from the Akan forest region to Hausaland (in modern Niger and Nigeria) probably as early as the middle of the fourteenth century or the early fifteenth century.[18]

One of the most popular routes in this new trade was a fairly simple one, given the territorial contiguities that facilitated the journey. The Ghonja-Nikki-Borgu-Hausaland route became a natural trajectory for Wangara merchants. This direct kola nut trade between the Akan forest region and Hausaland exploded in the eighteenth century, when there was 'an upsurge in the demand for kola nuts in Hausaland, thus motivating the Wangara to obtain the commodity in large quantities from Gonja'.[19]

Once introduced to Hausaland and other Islamic polities like Bornu, kola nut became the recreational stimulant of choice for many communities in the hinterlands of the Sahara and of the rivers Niger and Benue. Connecting this vast demand with the source of supply in the Akan region was another instance of the Wangara's adroitness in identifying arbitrage opportunities and moving in to create new trading activities around them.

Travelling in convoys carrying kola nuts, gold and manufactured wares obtained from the coastal parts of the forest region of the Middle Volta, the Wangara traders usually set off from Ghonja, an Akan principality. The caravans then crossed territories in modern Togo into Nikki and other Borgu towns in modern Benin Republic. Next, they crossed into Yorubaland, to Nupe and Baatonu or Bariba land, as well as Bussa in the Borgu confederacy.[20] Many Wangara traders ended their journey in Baatonu land, selling their wares to Hausa or Wangara retailers who then took the goods to Hausaland, only a few days' journey away. Others made the trip into Hausaland themselves because they were interested in purchasing leather and other products from Hausaland for trade.

Over time, in the course of the eighteenth century, the range of goods flowing into and through Borgu to Hausaland on Wangara trade caravans increased to include horses, natron, salt, earthenware and European manufactured products such as jugs, brass, cotton cloth, processed wool products and copper dishes.[21]

Many Wangara merchants who operated in the Borgu sector merely used the area as an intermediate point or springboard in their quest for the big markets of Hausaland. Such was the Borgu-Hausaland connection in the expansion of the Wangara commercial influence in Central Sudan that many Wangara merchants continued to frequent Hausaland from Mali and Borgu even after the collapse of Songhai in the late sixteenth century.[22]

In Hausaland, Wangara traders invested in a wide variety of commercial activities, seeking a stake in the most lucrative cottage craft industries of sixteenth- and seventeenth-century Hausaland. The development of Hausaland's famous leather industry, which manufactured bags, pouches, shoes, straps, amulet holders, cushions, fans, wearable leather and other valued leather products, was made possible partly by Wangara investments.[23] The Wangara merchants invested in the manufacture of these leather goods as well as in the processing of rawhide, and then exported these products across the Sahara to North Africa, especially Morocco, where Mediterranean and European buyers mistakenly identified them as Moroccan leather. A popular leather brand throughout Europe, 'Moroccan leather' had origins in Hausaland and was introduced to the world by Wangara merchants and investors.

Colonialism and the demise of the Wangara trading network

By the mid-to-late nineteenth century, the Wangara merchants' influence was waning in Hausaland, as was also the case in Borgu, Senegambia and the Akan area. Given the profound impact it had on many economies across West Africa, the decline and demise of the Wangara's pan-West African trading empire deserves to be understood in the context of multiple factors that interrupted what seemed like the early signs of a trade-driven regional economic integration.

By the late eighteenth and early nineteenth centuries, some of the Wangara's commercial dominance had become brittle because states, kingdoms and empires were trying to directly carry on trade with an increasingly ubiquitous group of European traders. Hinterland states like Asante and the Sokoto Caliphate, after it emerged in the first decade of the nineteenth century, began to imagine their commercial destinies outside the Wangara system and increasingly sought to cultivate their own direct trade ties to Europeans at the coast.

The Europeans who extended their trading networks from the coastal parts of West Africa to the interior in the eighteenth and nineteenth centuries were more efficient traders and could thus offer their African trade partners more generous trade terms than the Wangara could. Their ships carried more goods than the Wangara managed to carry around with their portering, caravanning and canoeing system of transporting and distributing goods. And the Europeans could sometimes fill demands for manufactured goods and buy African products more efficiently than the Wangara could. The Europeans were also better financed and could extend more credit at better terms than the Wangara. All of this meant that Europeans could increasingly offer better terms of trade to African communities that relied on Wangara traders for several centuries. The Europeans, moreover, had a more diverse offering of goods, not only supplying their African clients with consumables but also instruments of war and defence. The Wangara had no capacity to supply military hardware, which was much in demand in the turbulent period of the late eighteenth to mid-nineteenth century. African communities, rational economic actors that they were, naturally gradually gravitated away from the Wangara and toward the expanding European trading relays that extended from the coasts to the interiors.

Furthermore, European merchants, especially those not so well financed, preferred to bypass middlemen like the Wangara and deal directly with the sources of supply of groundnuts, palm produce, cocoa, cotton and other goods they desired – and to sell their goods directly to African consumers. These sources and markets were located in hinterlands controlled by states that were now using these resources as leverage to exact profits and strategic goods from European merchants. Commercial agreements and contracts between European merchants and powerful West African states became common in the nineteenth century. These commercial and political treaties began to take on the looks of quasi-colonial accords in which European companies like the Royal Niger Company and the French companies operating in the Lower Niger area increasingly acted on behalf of the British and French governments, respectively.[24] The manoeuvres of European merchants who wanted to avoid African trade brokers in order to minimise cost and maximise profit gradually marginalised African traders and brokers like the Wangara.

All of these developments and the increased European commercial penetration that resulted from them had a profound impact on the consumption patterns of West Africans. To put it simply, Africans acquired a taste for European goods, which gradually acquired a cultural cache as status enhancers, to the detriment of Africa-originated goods traded by the Wangara – many of which were now seen as low-status commodities. To further isolate the Wangara, the Portuguese and British began to trade internally within West

Africa, using their naval skills to navigate West Africa's ocean shorelines and rivers, buying gold and kola from one area and selling them in other areas, a much faster transportation process than the method of mobility employed by the Wangara. Because they had more capital than the Wangara, and because European-denominated currencies were replacing local ones, the Europeans were on the ascendance commercially while the Wangara were caught flatfooted, unable to compete or adapt.

With the advent of informal imperial arrangements in the mid-to-late nineteenth century, European states, invoking treaties and territorial claims as part of the scramble for Africa, began to use military might and their state-backed monopoly trading companies to decimate African trading networks, commercial groups, middlemen and trade brokers. As the alliance of European commercial and political interests moved more aggressively to capture and monopolise African trade within increasingly defined and protected territories, the commercial empire of the Wangara was squeezed and began to disintegrate. Moreover, the increased emphasis on, and policing of, imperial territorial sovereignties struck a blow at one of the foundations of the Wangara trading system: easy trans-West Africa movement.

The ability to move freely by simply observing some traditional protocols required of strangers and visitors in a new land had been central to the commercial success of the Wangara. Territorial barriers defined first as European commercial spheres and later as colonial possessions limited free movement over long distances across West Africa. At the heart of the colonial enterprise was a protectionist economic ethos, which contradicted the free, franchised trading enterprise of the Wangara. Protected markets and fenced in territorial zones of arbitrage and production – the very hallmarks of colonial economic management – violated the essence of the Wangara commercial system of trans-regional free movement of goods and people. This new regime of colonial protectionism, along with several emerging colonial realities, broke up the Wangara trading network.

One of these emerging colonial realities was taxation. In both the French and British sectors of West Africa, the first colonial business after conquest was the quest for revenue, which led to the imposition of taxation. Taxation had to be paid in colonial currency. The introduction of taxation had a negative impact on the Wangara trading network in several ways. Firstly, colonial taxation and its dependence on new colonial currency systems undermined the commercial provenance of bartering, which had been an essential part of Wangara trading. Secondly, it made local currencies like cowries, gold and salt lose their power as legal tender, again undermining the monetary system central to the Wangara network. Finally, taxation by the colonial government forced many Wangara – ethnic Soninke-, Bambara- and Mande-speaking peoples – out of trading and into professions in which they could earn the colonial currency, since that was the only currency acceptable for colonial tax payment.

With long-distance trading losing its appeal as a result of the new logistical, security and monetary problems, some Wangara continued to trade but only within specific locales. In the French zone, many Wangara became migrant labourers, working for wages in the French Navy as laptots, as boat hands for French merchants, as porters, as agricultural hands in the growing colonial export crop industry and as workers in other new colonial enterprises in distant African lands.[25] This was a dramatic reversal of fortunes for the Wangara.

Insights and lessons from the rise and fall of the Wangara trading empire

Lasting for over five hundred years, the trading network built by the Wangara confronted and overcame many obstacles, some of which are analogous to the obstacles faced by Africans who desire to invest across African borders today. The Wangara utilised the advantages of scale, of logistical nimbleness and of versatility to overcome disruptions and fluctuations in trade and production. Even so, the Wangara trading system fizzled out rather rapidly beginning in the late eighteenth century because, faced by better capitalised, more efficient and politically aggressive European merchants, the network could not adapt. Both the Wangara's earlier successes and their failure to adapt to changing economic and mercantile circumstances hold important lessons and insights for trans-regional investments in Africa. We now turn to these lessons.

Foresight, vision and nimbleness

The Wangara's ability to spot market opportunities and emerging demands and their investment in mechanisms for satisfying these demands gave them control over the long-distance trade in several commodities. It also enabled them to invest widely across multiple value chains in production, mining, manufacturing, distribution and arbitrage. The Wangara saw West Africa as a vast, interconnected zone of trade and investments. Their investment in trade, in the extraction industry and in artisanal manufacturing helped to commercially integrate the region and to dissolve political, cultural and economic barriers to trade. In several of the commercial and investment theatres in which the Wangara operated, the ability to spot opportunity in production, distribution and arbitrage was central to their success. This ability to see beyond existing trade patterns was crucial for the Wangara's commercial ascendance and is instructive for African merchants today.

In the Akan sector, for instance, the Wangara's investments and interventions were instrumental in transforming a localised gold mining operation with limited distribution into an export-oriented multi-national industry. It also was responsible for starting and building a pan-West Africa kola nut trading system. Connecting the nodes of kola nut supply in Akan country (modern Ghana) and of demand in the Yoruba-Borgu-Hausaland axis (modern Nigeria), on the visionary premise that demand for the stimulating and ritual utility of kola nut would grow, produced one of the most lucrative commodity trading system in precolonial West Africa. This ability to see into the future and to invest in the prospect and promise of good returns entailed educated risk taking and is an example for today's ambitious African investor.

The Wangara traders showed a remarkable capacity for nimbleness and adaptability, using their trade towns across West Africa, their name recognition – an early form of branding – their control of credit, their reputation for honesty and their political goodwill to move creatively within and between different sites in their vast commercial network as occasion demanded. When one sector of the network became challenged, the Wangara simply moved to a different sector. An example was a case in the mid-sixteenth century when conflict in Akan coastal states reduced access to the coast and disrupted the Wangara's hinterland-coast operations. Many Wangara traders diverted their gold from Elmina and other southern coasts to the Gambia River and its extensive network of Wangara trading centres. The advantages of scale and of logistical nimbleness helped the Wangara to overcome potentially devastating disruptions to trade.

The preeminent lesson here is that versatility confers flexibility, which in turn can both enhance commercial expansion and give merchants a platform to escape the risks of large-scale trading.

Political savvy in the service of enterprise

Exchange of information regarding trade and commercial opportunity within the Wangara network was crucial to the ability of traders to spot new demand, markets and niches and to move to satisfy them with goods and services.[26] Information came through political contacts and insiders and through participation in the politics of host communities. The Wangara were adept at cultivating political ties and relationships in the interest of more trade liberalisation.[27] Realising the crucial interconnections between politics and business, the Wangara traders stationed commercial envoys in host communities, trade representatives 'who served as ambassadors in many nations, and do this to make commerce'.[28] In the process, the Wangara built what one might call an early example of an African private-public partnership in the interest of commercial consolidation and expansion. The Wangara trade consuls supervised trade, smoothed over political challenges to trade, helped resolve commercial disputes and generally worked the political system in favour of business or to undermine political decisions and processes harmful to Wangara trade.

In all the regions where they operated, Wangara traders and investors recognised the important entwinements of the business and political realms and worked hard to dissolve antagonism between the two and to bring them into a productive, cooperative relationship. In the polities where the Wangara established trading communities and supply chains, they designated Wangara merchants and trade consuls to lobby the host political establishment. This lobbying activity was instrumental in securing trade, getting a set of uniform trade rules enforced and opening up new markets. This strategy of the Wangara is particularly relevant today, since today's African investor has more rigidly defined political entities to appease and boundaries to negotiate in embarking on regional commercial expansion and regional investments.

Trading settlements as auxiliary support

To consolidate their long-distance trade in this area, the Wangara traders established many rest stations (*ribats*) along their trade routes, which later morphed into vibrant commercial centres 'to which [traders] flocked from all sides'.[29] In the Senegambia area, these trade settlements served as links to other commercial and mining centres in Mali, Fouta Djallon, and as far as Casamance in modern Southern Senegal.[30] One of the most prominent of these Wangara trade towns in Senegambia was Bijini. As stated earlier, trade settlements were also crucial to Wangara trade and investments in Borgu and Akan.

The Wangara trading settlements solved some logistical challenges and enabled the Wangara to establish a commercial foothold and to eventually dominate key trades. A good example of this is the Akan area. Here, the Wangara traders were not content with buying and selling gold across this vast long-distance route. They wanted to ensure an uninterrupted supply and production of gold in the Akan goldfields. This led them to establish, as they did in the Senegambia region, several trade settlements on the northern frontiers of the Akan area, where Wangara kinsmen settled to coordinate exchange and smooth over challenges. Wangara trading settlements such as Bitu, Baha and Banbarranaa morphed fairly quickly into self-contained commercial hubs,[31] with their own distinctly Wangara political and cultural traditions in the Northwestern sectors of the vast Akan country.[32] The Wangara trading diaspora spread throughout the Akan hinterland, as far as modern-day Ivory Coast.[33]

The trade settlements were a pillar of support for Wangara business activities in four specific ways. Firstly, being situated in the local Akan milieu, the Wangara settlers provided the itinerant Wangara gold and salt merchants with lodging and logistical services during their trading trips. Secondly, the settled Wangara provided brokerage and mediation services to both Akan gold producers and Wangara gold and salt traders. Their linguistic and cultural existence in both the Akan and Mande diasporic commercial worlds placed them in a unique position to play this role. Thirdly, the settled Wangara provided security for the itinerant traders and their goods, helping with safe depositing of gold and other valuables for a commission. In that sense, they provided deposit and safeguarding services analogous to modern banking services. Finally, when the Wangara identified the European coastal demand for gold, they used Wangara trade towns as platforms to extend their trading empire to the Cape Coast, increasingly becoming middlemen in the trade between several Akan communities and European merchants on the coast.

Rest stations and trade settlements formed the nucleus of a social support system that enhanced trade through the provision of credit, safe deposit services, lodging, travel supplies and brokerage. The lessons here are apparent: auxiliary social supports for long-distance trading and investment activities are crucial to the success of those activities. Given the sensitivity of migration as a phenomenon and the current restrictions of national borders, today's African investors may no longer be able to recreate the types of support communities that the Wangara built along their trading and investment routes. However, the possibilities exist for building a community of support businesses, services and auxiliary activities that can enhance and add value to an investor's primary economic activity.

Branding

The Wangara recognised the power of brand building, to use a contemporary business terminology. Trading in multiple political and cultural contexts, they gave stakes to non-Wangara traders in several polities, allowing the latter to buy into the Wangara franchise and to parlay the commercial, social, cultural and political capital associated with that name into primary or secondary trading activities. The Wangara thus built a brand that was permissive, pan-ethnic and pan-West African. They saw local merchants as partners and potential distributors of their goods rather than as competitors. This attitude further enhanced the reputation of the Wangara trading network and made it attractive to more West African groups of traders.

This branding effort was a feature of Wangara enterprise in the Akan and Borgu areas, but it was at its most elaborate in Senegambia. It was there that the phenomenon of non-Wangara buying into the brand was most clearly realised. As the Mande commercial empire flourished and expanded from the Sahel to the Gambia river and to the Atlantic, connecting Sahelian and hinterland West African peoples to the markets of North Africa and to European Atlantic products, Mande became a brand that ambitious commercial investors who were not ethnic Mande came to embrace in an honorary capacity in order to tap into the economic, social and political capital of the Mande-speaking traders. In this process, a pan-West Africa merchant brand emerged, attracting many peoples and further extending the frontiers of the Wangara commercial monopolies and trading networks.

In a multi-ethnic region, the Wangara trading network created 'a common [commercial] identity which transcended mere parochial interests' and gave everyone – host or settler, sedentary or nomadic – a stake in the commercial prosperity of the region.[34] This provides profound insights for today's African investor. For while the Wangara were a composite ethnic group and shared certain traits, the commercial brand they build was multi-ethnic, permissive and cosmopolitan. Given Africa's bewildering ethnic, cultural and religious plurality, the business of brand building and of establishing trans-regional trading networks should mirror the continent's demographic diversity. Even businesses that begin from a particular ethnic or geographical space, where familiarity can enhance confidence and credit, would sooner or later have to find a way to broaden their appeal to ethnic Others if their brands are to transcend their parochial ethnic beginnings

Diversification

The Wangara succeeded through a conscious diversification of their investment portfolios. They invested their capital and knowledge across the economic chain – in manufacturing, wholesale, retail, distribution, consultancy, support professions and crafts, and in cultivating political economic ties for the benefit of business. Diversification gave the Wangara more economic leverage. Their forward and backward linkages and processes gave them a unique and dominant foothold in the long-distance trade sector. The much discussed trade monopoly of the Wangara was thus *de facto* and not *de jure*, a product of the ability to spread investments across multiple points of a value chain.

Diversification in the Wangara's commercial activities increased their forward and backward integration, which cut operational costs. It also increased their ability to move from one node of the supply and manufacturing to the other. In turn, this enhanced the Wangara's resilience and their ability to weather downturns in trade and in the broader economy. Furthermore, multi-product arbitrage gave the Wangara a greater share of markets and an opportunity to spread their trading capital around, thereby minimising losses due to fluctuations in prices and demand.

Diversification also entailed the embrace of multiple modes of transport in different sectors and as part of the same relay system on a particular trade route. As shown in the first section of this chapter, the Wangara used multiple means of transportation, employing whichever ones proved more efficient for a particular region, set of goods or season. A diversified transportation infrastructure cut the time of travel, reduced operating expenses and enabled Wangara traders to avoid disruptions to trade caused by conflicts and banditry along certain routes or rivers. It also provided an opportunity to alternate between different transportation modes as these modes became scarcer, more expensive, more available, or cheaper. Diversification produced flexibility and a system of constantly evolving trade logistics.

Credit

A major obstacle to long-distance multi-state commerce is currency and credit differences and policies. As gold traders and connoisseurs, the Wangara overcame this problem by spreading the adoption of gold as the standard of value in many places. Although they adapted to the varieties of currency used for exchange in the many polities in which they operated and participated in bartering operations where necessary, they introduced the gold standard of value to commerce in many regions of West Africa. This form of standardisation helped the Wangara to invest and trade in multiple cultural and geographical contexts without their commercial empire being undermined by the problem of monetary differentiation.

The Wangara also developed a system of credit that helped many West African groups to trade with, or for, them as retailers and partners in localised areas. Much of this credit system was based on a system of trust, which itself was cultivated over long periods of repeated transactions. This early example of the benefits of standardisation and monetary linkages holds particular lessons for how pan-regional investments and business operations can lay foundations from below for the much talked about West African monetary union.

Lessons of failure

Despite its successes and commercial creativity, the Wangara trading and investment network was overwhelmed by European commercial and political incursions into West Africa in the nineteenth and early twentieth centuries. The network could not adapt to changing tastes, changing consumption patterns, changing demands and, of course, the restrictions and protectionist policies of colonial regimes.

One example of this failure to adapt is that the Wangara could not match the speed with which Europeans delivered products to the West African interior and bought African products from the same sources. One of the Wangara's earlier strengths was their ability to compress time and distance by using multiple means of transportation to get goods from source to destination. The Wangara used porters, camel and donkey caravans, canoes on rivers and horse rides to reduce the amount of time it took to transport goods between different regions. But when European trading ships began to navigate West Africa's rivers to reach deep into hinterlands, the Wangara had no answer and were marginalised as a result.

The expansion of the Wangara commercial and investment empire and the strategies that underpinned this expansion demonstrate the possibilities of intra-Africa trans-national investments. However, its rapid collapse also holds valuable lessons. At its peak, the Wangara's investment portfolio was diverse and balanced, embracing multiple sectors, benefitting from the economies of scale and tapping into a vast reservoir of demand, supply and latent production capacity. These same opportunities exist today for African individuals and groups desirous of building a trading and investment portfolio similar to that of the Wangara. On the other hand, the Wangara simply could not compete with better-financed traders who could offer cheaper and more efficiently manufactured goods. The failure to adapt to changes brought on by external factors – changes over which an African business actor has no control – is a recurring aspect of business stagnation and failure in Africa today. The Wangara faced a problem analogous to the challenges faced today by African investors in the era of globalisation, as cheaper and more efficiently manufactured goods flood African markets and as the foreign traders and manufacturers pushing these goods leverage their superior financing to offer better terms to African retailers and consumers. When European merchants and their African allies began to challenge the trade monopoly of the Wangara, they revealed a new dynamic. Overwhelmed, the Wangara could not adapt. As imperial control made the influx of foreign goods possible, and as the Wangara lost political allies who could protect their trading rights and limit European commercial incursions, they buckled. African investors today face a similar problem. Political forces, international and bilateral treaties, agreements, arrangements and free trade globalisation can suddenly over-whelm the local market in which an African investor operates. Without fore-thought and prior planning for such events, and without the ability to be nimble and to adapt, the fate that befell the Wangara becomes inevitable.

In the era of European commercial and imperial expansion in West Africa, the Wangara also faced another problem, which today's African investors also face: they suddenly came up against a perception that foreign goods, manufactured or not, were superior to and thus better markers of status than locally manufactured or locally sourced products. This problem was particu-larly acute in the so-called period of legitimate trade from the early to late nineteenth century. These perception problems persist to date and hamper some African investors in certain sectors.

The Wangara traders were helpless in the face of this perception of them as peddlers of inferior, locally sourced goods. Many African traders and local manufacturers today also appear helpless and complain about this perception, as several studies in this volume show. These perceptions took the Wangara by surprise and they could not counter it effectively. Today, however, given how familiar the perception is to many African investors, it is possible to counter it and retain and even grow an investor's market share through conscious branding, rebranding, creative advertising and even commercialised nationalist appeals to the sentiment of 'buying local'.

Another insight into the collapse of the Wangara commercial system turns on the fact that, in spite of investing in several sectors and trading in a diverse array of products, the Wangara were incapable of meeting certain demands. The Wangara neglected, for instance, to invest in the technology and manu-facture of firearms despite soaring demand for them during the late eight-eenth century and in the long nineteenth century. Despite the Wangara's well-deserved reputation for spotting emerging demands and markets and for being able to forecast changing patterns of need, they failed to identify this growing demand for, and increased valuation of, firearms. By the early nineteenth century, the firearm trade was, aside from the waning Atlantic slave trade, the most lucrative commercial activity in many regions of West Africa. By failing to see that times were changing and by failing to adapt to these changing times and their mercantile implications, the Wangara missed out on a new lucrative trade, a loss which further weakened their financial position in relation to European competitors, who were all too eager to become major suppliers of arms to West African polities.

Conclusion

The lessons of the rise and decline of the Wangara trading network conduce to one salient point: whether one is thinking in sectoral terms or in terms of trans-national economic concepts and institutions, the history of intra-African trade and investments reveals the opportunities and problems of imagining and acting out investment and commercial strategies across Africa's formal and informal borders. While some of the strategies deployed by the Wangara can be effective today, others may serve as a cautionary warning for today's African investors in ICT, media and entertainment, telecoms, cement and lumber, and in the forging of regional markets.

This chapter thus serves as an appropriate framework for the other studies in this project in that historical issues from the Wangara's long-distance trading and investment experience continue to reoccur to both challenge and enable trans-Africa entrepreneurship. As African economic and physical boundaries continue to collapse under the weight of regional economic cooperation, trans-national trade and the Africa-focused investment strategies of African entrepreneurs, and as Africans carve out, identify and pursue demand and supply nodes across the continent or its sub-regions, the issues, challenges and opportunities that the Wangara grappled with, mastered or succumbed to will resonate across all the sectors covered by the 'Africans investing in Africa' project.

Notes

1. Andreas W. Massing, 'The Wangara, an Old Soninke Diaspora in West Africa?', *Cahiers d'etudes africaines* (Vol. 158, 2000), p. 281.
2. Ghislaine Lydon, *On Trans-Saharan Trails: Islamic Law, Trade Networks, and Cross-Cultural Exchange in Nineteenth-Century Western Africa* (Cambridge: Cambridge University Press, 2009), p. 64.
3. Ivor Wilks, 'Wangara, Akan and Portuguese in the Fifteenth and Sixteenth Centuries I, the Matter of Bitu', *Journal of African History* (Vol. 23, No. 3, 1982), p. 333.
4. Lydon, *On Trans-Saharan Trails*.
5. E.W. Bovill, 'The Silent Trade of Wangara', *Journal of the Royal African Society* (Vol. 29, No. 113, 1929), pp. 27–28.

6. *Tarikh Mandinka de Bijini/La Memoire des Madinka et des Sooninkee du Kaabu* (Introduction, notes, and commentaries by Cornelia Giesing and Valentine Vydrine) (Translated from French to English for this project by Carolyn Taratko). Hereafter *Tarikh Mandinka* (Leiden and Boston: Brill, 2007), pp. 161–162.

7. Paul Lovejoy, 'The Role of the Wangara in the Economic Transformation of the Central Sudan in the Fifteenth and Sixteenth Centuries', *Journal of African History* (Vol. 19, No. 2, 1978), pp. 173–193.

8. *Tarikh Mandinka*, p. 173.

9. *Tarikh Mandinka*, p. 242.

10. A.A. de Almada, *Tratado Breve dos Rios de Guine do Cabo Verde* (Leitura, Introducao e Notas de Antonio Brasio) (Lisboa: Edotial L.I.A.M., 1964 [1594]), cited in *Tarikh Mandinka*, p. 231.

11. *Tarikh Mandinka*, p. 340.

12. Ibid., p. 337.

13. Ivor Wilks, 'The Juula and the Expansion of Islam into the Forest', in Nehemiah Levitzion, *The History of Islam in Africa* (Athens: Ohio University Press, 2000), p. 94.

14. Wilks, 'Wangara, Akan, and Portuguese I', pp. 339–343.

15. Wilks, 'The Juula and the Expansion of Islam', p. 94.

16. Wilks, 'Wangara, Akan, and Portuguese I', p. 343.

17. Lovejoy, 'The Role of the Wangara', p. 173.

18. Ibid., p. 174; and Julius Adekunle, 'Borgu and Economic Transformation 1700–1900: The Wangara Factor', *African Economic History* (Vol. 22, 1994), p. 4.

19. Adekunle, 'Borgu and Economic Transformation', p. 8.

20. Ibid., p. 1.

21. Ibid.

22. Lovejoy, 'The Role of the Wangara', p. 176.

23. Ibid.

24. See J.E. Flint, *Sir George Goldie and the Making of Nigeria* (London: Oxford University Press, 1960), pp. 9–33. Flint discusses the United Africa Company's frantic and aggressive acquisition of French competitors in the Niger trade.

25. Flint, *Sir George Goldie*, pp. 74–84.

26. Ibid., p. 174.

27. Ibid., p. 230.

28. Manuel Padre Alvares, *Etiopia Menor e descricao geografica da Serra Leoa* (1916 [1616]), Texte dactylographique a la Bibliotheque du Centre de Recherches Africaines, (C.R.A) Universite de Paris I (Copie du Manuscript MS 141-C-1 a la Societe de Geographie de Lisbonne). Cited in Flint, *Sir George Goldie*, p. 249.

29. Manuel Padre Alvares, in Flint, *Sir George Goldie*, p. 249.

30. Ibid.

31. John Blake, 'Europeans in West Africa, 1540–1560: Documents to Illustrate the Nature and Scope of Portuguese Enterprise in West Africa', *Hakluyt Society* (Vol. I, 1942), pp. 65–68.

32. See Wilks, 'Wangara, Akan and Portuguese I', p. 344. So profound was this Wangara commercial-demographic penetration of Akan country that many Muslim communities in this region of modern-day Ghana claim Wangara, Juula, Mande origins.

33. Wilks, 'Wangara, Akan and Portuguese I', p. 344.

34. Lovejoy, 'The Role of the Wangara', p. 173.

2
Why Governance Matters for Investment

John Endres

After decades of decline, per capita incomes in Sub-Saharan Africa started rising from 1995 onwards. By 2008, they finally passed their previous peak of $941, seen 34 years previously, in 1974. Since then, they have continued rising, reaching a level of $1,016 in 2013, the latest data available.[1]

These changes in the averages are encouraging and have played a large part in sparking the 'Africa rising' story, but they represent only a tiny sliver of how Africa has changed over the past two decades. There have also been dramatic changes at the very top end of the scale, namely, in the wealth and identity of Africa's most prosperous citizens.

In the past, the principal path to fabulous wealth, and often the only one, was through political power or strong connections to people in political power. Being the president meant that you could build up a tidy nest egg by controlling the treasury and by charging for access to state and natural resources. In this way, leaders such as Mobutu Sese Seko of Zaire, Teodoro Obiang of Equatorial Guinea and Eduardo dos Santos (not forgetting his daughter Isabel, one of Africa's wealthiest women) of Angola managed to become not just dictators, but dollar millionaires and in some cases even billionaires, according to Forbes magazine.[2]

Not only did this represent illicit self-enrichment on a staggering scale, it usually also resulted in large amounts of money leaving the country, spirited away to be deposited in secret bank accounts and tax havens. According to Global Financial Integrity (GFI), a research organisation based in Washington, DC, an estimated $854 billion to $1.8 trillion were taken out of Africa in the form of unrecorded, illicit financial outflows between 1970 and 2008.[3]

This figure is comparable to the entire continent's annual GDP at the end of that period ($1.6 trillion in 2008),[4] and dwarfs the annual

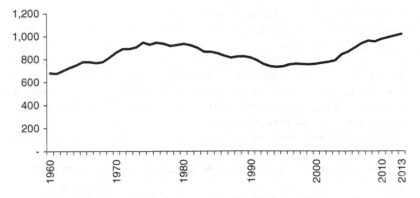

Figure 2.1 Per capita incomes in Sub-Saharan Africa (in US$)
Source: World Bank, *World Development Indicators*, http://databank.worldbank.org.

financial inflows. In fact, the total amount of money thought to have been removed from the continent implies that the continent is a net creditor to the rest of the world[5] – and the figures do not include most proceeds from drug trafficking, human smuggling and other criminal activities, which are often settled in cash. For a capital-deficient continent with a capital spending backlog, dependent on the charity of strangers in the form of foreign aid, this diverted money spells decades of missed opportunities for development. The funding gap came about as a direct result of fraud, theft and trade mispricing enabled by bad governance.

Now contrast the wealth of Africa's dictators with that of the developed world's most successful businessmen. Few Africans managed to become the Bill Gates or Warren Buffet of their countries after decolonisation, and no wonder: success would immediately have attracted the covetous attention of the political elite. Therefore, the choice was between giving up one's grand ambitions or being co-opted into the system. The prospects for making a fortune without controlling the state's lever of powers, or having privileged access to those who controlled them, were slim. Many businessmen concluded that it was safer to pretend to stay small and hide whatever successes they could achieve.

This has changed over the past decade. Since 2011, it has become worth Forbes's while to compile a list of the wealthiest Africans, who, although often politically well connected, managed to build their fortunes through trade and business rather than by exercising power.[6] Notably, some extremely successful African businessmen have built their fortunes not in the usual sectors such as oil or mining, but in communication, financial services or building materials. In other words, fortunes are now being made based on offering value to customers, rather than on skimming rents from resources.

This is an important and welcome change. The emergence of extremely wealthy entrepreneurs indicates that space is beginning to open up for ordinary citizens to generate wealth. It means that more people are deciding to keep some of the fruits of their labour within Africa, reinvesting to reap the benefits of fast-growing economies.

Rising GDPs and the bulging net worth of wealthy individuals reflect a change in the economy. But what about politics and governance? Have improvements in one area been accompanied by improvements in the other?

Here, the picture is mixed. The World Bank's key measure of governance, the Worldwide Governance Indicators, for instance, shows that just three mainland African countries, Botswana, Namibia and South Africa, as well as three island nations, Mauritius, Seychelles and São Tomé and Príncipe, managed to achieve positive governance scores in 1996, the first year that these statistics were collected. By 2012, the latest year for which figures are available, only a single mainland country, namely, Ghana, had joined the group. Apart from some islands (Cape Verde, Mauritius, Réunion and Seychelles), all other countries remain stuck in negative territory.[7]

However, it is also worth taking a look at which countries showed improvements over the same period. The result inspires slightly more hope: 25 countries, almost half of the total, improved their scores. If they manage to stay on this path, there will soon be many more countries with positive governance scores. And this may be the more significant observation: although most countries have not yet managed to break into positive territory, the fact that they are getting better may be enough to give African investors enough confidence to keep their money on the continent.

A further factor inspiring confidence is that most African countries have abandoned their earlier dalliances with socialism and its derivatives. The experiences of the former East Bloc countries have thoroughly discredited this political philosophy. A belief in democracy and free enterprise has supplanted it – conditions much more favourable for nurturing successful entrepreneurs and growing economies.

The end of the Cold War, and with it the ending of the proxy wars and ideological battles, has also given a different character to African business identity. African business and political leaders seek to speak to their peers from other continents at eye level, rather than being seen as the permanent underdog or supplicant, as in the past. The wealth of Mobutu

Sese Seko and the glittering trappings of Emperor Jean-Bédel Bokassa's power, for instance, may have impressed onlookers and inspired fear and deference, but not respect. The next generation of Africans wants to bask in earned respect, not deference.

But this process of economic improvement is still at its very beginning, and fragile. Africa now finds itself at a fork in the road: the low road beckons with corruption and indifferent (at best) governance. The political elites continue to enrich themselves, while ordinary citizens start becoming poorer again, as in the past. What's more, it is by no means certain that demand for Africa's commodities, as well as the prices of those commodities, will remain as high as they have been over the past decade and a half. Instead, scenarios like a slow-down in China's economic growth and increasing reliance on alternative energy sources like renewables and shale gas may cause demand for African resources to flag.[8] Combined with a rapidly growing population unable to produce the goods and services that consumers throughout the world want, the result is frustration, impoverishment and instability, leading to further declines in governance quality, greater poverty and a widening gap between Africa and the rest of the world.

By contrast, there is a high road that leads to a virtuous cycle. In this scenario, better governance enables stronger business growth. Higher economic growth lifts millions out of poverty and allows an increasingly assertive middle class to emerge, which clamours for further improvements in governance, such as more transparency, more accountability, more political freedoms and better service delivery. If such a cycle is set in motion, the countries participating in it may find themselves transformed within a generation, much as Asia's tiger economies did.

Although it may be true that better governance leads to higher growth, better governance is not cheap – which may explain why wealthier countries often have better governance, as Mushtaq Khan, an economist at the School of Oriental and African Studies in London, pointed out in a 2007 paper.[9] Developed economies have the resources needed to create and enforce property rights, uphold the rule of law, reduce corruption and provide public goods and services transparently, accountably and in response to democratically expressed preferences. For African countries that have benefitted and continue to benefit from demand for their resources, the implication is that they should make an effort to employ the windfall revenues to improve governance.

There is a further noteworthy aspect to the link between governance and growth: better governance also means formalising the economy by registering, regulating and taxing companies operating in the informal sector. The benefits for the state are obvious: apart from additional income for the state coffers, formalisation also allows statistical offices to gain a more accurate understanding of economic activity in the country. Although empirical evidence suggests that formalisation correlates with higher per capita incomes, there is a risk in poorly governed countries that tax revenues go straight to corrupt officials rather than to the state coffers, as well as opening up more scope for kickbacks or extortion.[10]

For informal enterprises, getting caught in the net of state surveillance and taxation may seem like a bad deal, but it has its upside: informal businesses are often destined to remain small because they have to remain inconspicuous to avoid the state's attentions and because they find it harder to access funding for expansion from banks and investors. Becoming formally registered removes these impediments, allowing enterprises to grow to much larger sizes. Larger enterprises are able to benefit from economies of scale and greater division of labour, making them more efficient and able to offer better products and services to consumers.[11]

Although most people detest being coerced into making involuntary contributions to the state coffers, taxes have an important role to play in governance. The more a state depends on taxes from individuals and companies, the more accountable it has to be to both. Those paying the bill are more likely to question what is being done with the money when they are citizens than when they are foreign governments (in the case of development aid) or large concerns exploiting natural resources, eager to maintain friendly relationships with the host country government.[12]

Africa still faces enormous challenges. Corruption is pervasive, physical infrastructure lacking or insufficient and states appear incapable of delivering the services that many citizens need or desire.[13] Poverty remains shockingly high and the high population growth rates raise the spectre of enormous masses of young, frustrated people finding ways to express their outrage destructively. Violent extremism is on the rise in east and west Africa, and some regions, like South Sudan and the Central African Republic, are descending into violent anarchy.

Yet many of these problems have existed, in one form or another, for decades. It is only in the past 10–15 years that the prospect has emerged, however slim its chances, of a change in this situation. It is not just because there has been some economic growth where previously there was very little. It is also because all African countries now conduct elections, most allow multiple parties to participate (or at least pretend to) and several have experienced a change of leadership by means of elections. Governance, though far from perfect, is beginning to improve. International relations do not need to focus inexorably on the former colonisers in the Western world, but can be built with countries such as Brazil, China and India in the global south.

In other words, in the political realm as much as in the economic, the idea is beginning to take hold that things can get better. Instead of stagnation and decline being inevitable, growth and rising prosperity are seen to be possible. From seeing that these things are possible, it is a small step to demanding that they be made true. And this is essential: Africa cannot be improved from the outside. It has to be done from the inside, by Africans who want it to be done and are ready to make sure that it is done. Africans investing in Africa is both an expression of this increasing assertiveness and a driver of ongoing improvements.

Notes

1. World Bank, *World Development Indicators,* http://databank.worldbank.org (accessed 27 August 2014). Figures are constant 2005 US dollars, corrected for the effects of inflation.
2. Forbes, *How Dictators Manage Their Billions,* http://www.forbes.com/2000/06/ 22/feat.html; *Who Were Africa's Richest Dictators?,* http://www.forbes.com/ sites/mfonobongnsehe/2011/11/08/who-were-africas-richest-dictators/; *Daddy's Girl: How an African 'Princess' Banked $3 Billion in a Country Living on $2 a Day,* http://www.forbes.com/sites/kerryadolan/2013/08/14/how-isabel-dos-santos-took-the-short-route-to-become-africas-richest-woman/ (all accessed 27 August 2014).
3. Global Financial Integrity, *Illicit Financial Flows from Africa: Hidden Resource for Development* (March 2010), http://www.gfintegrity.org/storage/gfip/ documents/reports/gfl_africareport_web.pdf, p. 5.
4. World Bank, *World Development Indicators,* http://databank.worldbank.org (accessed 27 August 2014). The figure given is in current US dollars. Africa's GDP was given as $2.3 trillion in 2013.
5. Global Financial Integrity and African Development Bank, *Illicit Financial Flows and the Problem of Net Resource Transfers from Africa: 1980–2009* (March 2013), http://www.gfintegrity.org/storage/gfip/documents/reports/ AfricaNetResources/gfi_afdb_iffs_and_the_problem_of_net_resource_transfers_ from_africa_1980-2009-web.pdf, p. 1. Quote: 'Results indicate that Africa was a net creditor to the world, as measured by the net resource transfers, to the tune of up to US$1.4 trillion over the period 1980–2009, adjusted for inflation'.
6. Forbes, *Number of African Billionaires Surges to 27,* http://www.forbes.com/ sites/kerryadolan/2013/11/13/number-of-african-billionaires-surges-to-27-up-two-thirds-from-2012/ (accessed 27 August 2014).
7. World Bank, *Worldwide Governance Indicators,* http://info.worldbank.org/ governance/wgi/index.aspx#home (accessed 27 August 2014).
8. Deloitte University Press, *The Boom and Beyond: Managing Commodity Price Cycles,* http://dupress.com/articles/global-economic-outlook-q1-2014-the-boom-and-beyond-managing-commodity-price-cycles/ (accessed 27 August 2014).
9. Mushtaq H. Khan, *Governance, Economic Growth and Development since the 1960s,* http://eprints.soas.ac.uk/9921/1/DESA_Governance_Economic_Growth_ and_Development_since_1960s.pdf.

10. Christopher Woodruff, *Registering for Growth: Tax and the Informal Sector in Developing Countries* (July 2013), http://www2.warwick.ac.uk/fac/soc/economics/research/centres/cage/onlinepublications/briefing/chj854_cage_woodruff_bp_09_07_13_web.pdf. 'Increasing the formalization rates of small firms is unlikely to offer governments a substantial new source of revenue in the short run' (p. 10).
11. On the benefits of business formalisation, see USAID, *Removing Barriers to Formalization: The Case for Reform and Emerging Best Practice* (March 2005), http://www.oecd.org/dac/povertyreduction/38452590.pdf.
12. OECD, *Citizen-State Relations: Improving Governance through Tax Reform* (2010), http://www.oecd.org/dac/governance-development/46008596.pdf.
13. Afrobarometer, *Governments Falter in Fight to Curb Corruption: The People Give Most a Failing Grade* (November 2013), http://www.afrobarometer.org/files/documents/policy_brief/ab_r5_policybriefno4.pdf; *What People Want from Government: Basic Services Performance Ratings, 34 Countries* (December 2013), http://www.afrobarometer.org/files/documents/policy_brief/ab_r5_policy-briefno5.pdf.

3
Regional Economic Communities

Jacqueline Chimhanzi

There is, arguably, no greater topical issue in Africa than that of regional integration – a concept whose time has definitely come but whose operationalisation is still in the making and upon which Africa's massive unrealised potential lies. Central to the importance of Regional Economic Communities (RECs) is their cross-cutting nature that transcends virtually all economic activity and sectors – from manufacturing, energy, infrastructure and financial services to tourism – underpinned by a very simple rationale – that there is strength in numbers. Given the transformative potential of regional integration, the integration discourse is actually best located in the broader context of development and economic transformation – beyond merely 'fixing borders' as an end in itself. Marcelo Giugale, the World Bank's Africa Director for Poverty Reduction and Economic Management, aptly expressed it as follows: 'The final prize is clear: ... Africans trad[ing] goods and services with each other. Few contributions carry more development power than that'.[1]

Despite this recognition of the salience of regional integration, it is not happening fast enough and undermines Africa's continued 'rising' and competitiveness. The African market is highly fragmented. With a similar population size to China and India, Africa is, in comparison, 54 markets, China 1 and India 1, and therein lies the challenge for companies – both international and African – wanting to access African opportunities and do business on the continent. Africa's intra-trade levels remain low compared to other regions in the world.

The chapter opens with the rationale and context for the need for RECs on the African continent followed by an overview of the state of play in the development of African RECs. There will then be a focus on attempting to understand the underlying issues accounting for low intra-regional trade. This is followed by a specific focus on the East African Community (EAC), deemed one of the better performing and most dynamic RECs. Justification, along different performance metrics and indicators, is provided for with the selection of the EAC as a focal case study. The experience of the MeTL Group based in Tanzania and recognised as a leading East African industrial conglomerate is used to illustrate the realities of operating within the realm of the EAC legislative framework. In a departure from Africa, the case of Airbus, touted as a 'pragmatic' approach and presenting a different architecture to regional integration, is examined. Insights and learnings are drawn from both the East African and Airbus experiences, and the chapter closes with policy recommendations for African RECs.

The need for Regional Economic Communities

It is observed that 27 of Africa's 54 countries are small, with national populations of fewer than 20 million and economies of less than US$10 billion.[2] Infrastructure systems, like borders, are reflections of the continent's colonial past, with roads, ports and railroads built to facilitate the export of raw materials, rather than to bind territories together economically or socially.[3] The Economist,[4] in a seminal piece titled 'Aspiring Africa', boldly challenged African leaders: 'Why not rekindle pan-Africanism by opening borders drawn in London and Paris?' In short, decades after the end of colonialism, African countries continue to be doubly challenged by size and connectivity[5] and are unable to compete on favourable terms on the scale that is required for competitiveness. According to Mohammed,[6] this is more so the case where exports are specialised, making them yet more vulnerable from a scale perspective. Against this backdrop, is increasing globalisation with cost-efficient producing countries, such as China, presenting a new form of competition for Africa?[7] The net impact has been Africa's deindustrialisation, as evidenced by the share of manufacturing in African GDP falling from 15 per cent in 1990 to 10 per cent in 2008.[8] The implications of this trend for intra-African trade and how African countries can rebuild their productive capacities and attain competitiveness should strongly form part of the new regional agenda to boost intra-African trade.[9]

The World Economic Forum's (WEF) Global Competitiveness Report 2014–2015 defines competitiveness as "the set of institutions, policies and factors that determine the level of productivity of a country." (WEF, 2014:4). The index is based on a composite score that ranks countries on 12 pillars of competitiveness. According to this ranking, seven of the ten least competitive countries are African. Strikingly, on the contrary, seven African countries feature on the list of the ten fastest growing economies in the world, in the period between 2011 and 2015: Ghana, Ethiopia, Tanzania, Zambia, DRC, Nigeria and Mozambique (The IMF/Economist 2010 in The Economist, 2011). In juxtapositioning these two sets of statistics and realities – pertaining to a continent whose countries occupy the lowest positions on competitiveness rankings whilst also simultaneously occupying the highest rankings on the world's fastest growth index – a powerful message emerges: that Africa has significant growth potential which, however, can only be further unlocked and sustained through regional trade and the resultant competitiveness. Indeed, whilst the African narrative has shifted from 'The Hopeless Continent'[10] to 'The Hopeful Continent: Africa Rising',[11] the case for regional integration has never been more compelling even as the new face of Africa is celebrated. A lack of integration represents the biggest threat to Africa's continued rising.[12]

It against the backdrop of this recognition for the need for integration that the notion of an African Economic Community (AEC), comprising eight regional economic communities, was conceived. The ultimate aim of the AEC is continentally uniform economic, fiscal, social and sectoral policies and the creation of a 'single competitive market' that increases the interconnectedness of African economies.[13] The Sirte Declaration, signed in 1999, called for the formation of the African Union and the speeding up of the provisions of the Abuja Treaty to create an African Economic Community. The Abuja Treaty signed in 1991 had defined the migration path for how the AEC would be achieved via a six-stage process over a 34-year period[14] ending in 2028 (see Table 3.1).[15]

There are a total of 14 RECs on the continent though only 8 are recognised by the African Union (see Table 3.2). Six African countries are members of only one REC, 26 are members of two RECs and 20 are members of three RECs, while only 1 country belongs to four RECs. The main reason provided for membership of more than one REC is that countries believe this enhances their political and strategic positioning.[16] However, practically, it is challenging as it has led to 'duplication and overlapping protocols, structures and mandates'.[17]

Table 3.1 Six stages of the establishment of the African economic community

Stage	Goal	Time Frame
1	Creation of regional blocs in regions where such do not yet exist	Was to be completed in 1999
2	Strengthening of intra-REC integration and inter-REC harmonisation	Was to be completed in 2007
3	Establishing of a free trade area and customs union in each regional bloc	To be completed in 2017
4	Establishing of a continent-wide customs union (and thus also a free trade area)	To be completed in 2019
5	Establishing of a continent-wide African Common Market (ACM)	To be completed in 2023
6	Establishing of a continent-wide economic and monetary union (and thus also a currency union) and Parliament	To be completed in 2028
	End of all transition periods	2034 at the latest

Source: Abuja Treaty, Article 6.

Table 3.2 African states' REC memberships

Regional Economic Community	Member States	Formation Year	Headquarters
CEN-SAD (Community of Sahel-Saharan States)	Benin, Burkina Faso, Cape Verde, Central African Republic, Comoros, Côte d'Ivoire, Chad, Djibouti, Egypt, Eritrea, Gambia, Ghana, Guinea-Bissau, Guinea, Kenya, Liberia, Libya, Mali, Mauritania, Morocco, Niger, Nigeria, São Tomé and Príncipe, Senegal, Sierra Leone, Somalia, Sudan, Togo, Tunisia.	1994	Tripoli, Libya
COMESA (Common Market for Eastern and Southern Africa)	Burundi, Comoros, Democratic Republics of Congo, Djibouti, Egypt, Eritrea, Ethiopia, Kenya, Libya, Madagascar, Malawi, Mauritius, Rwanda, Seychelles, Sudan, Swaziland, Uganda, Zambia, Zimbabwe	1994	Lusaka, Zambia
EAC (East African Community)	Burundi, Kenya, Rwanda, Tanzania, Uganda	1966–1977 then 2000–present	Arusha, Tanzania
ECCAS (Economic Community of Central African States)	Angola, Burundi, Cameroon, Central African Republic, Chad, Democratic Republic of Congo, Equatorial Guinea, Gabon, Republic of Congo, São Tomé and Príncipe	1983	Libreville, Gabon
ECOWAS (Economic Community of West African States)	Benin, Burkina Faso, Cape Verde, Côte d'Ivoire, Gambia, Ghana, Guinea, Guinea-Bissau, Liberia, Mali, Niger, Nigeria, Senegal, Sierra Leone, Togo	1975	Abuja, Nigeria
IGAD (Intergovernmental Authority on Development)	Djibouti, Eritrea, Ethiopia, Kenya, Somalia, Sudan, Uganda	1996	Djibouti, Djibouti
SADC (Southern African Development Community)	Angola, Botswana, Democratic Republic of Congo, Lesotho, Madagascar, Malawi, Mauritius, Mozambique, Namibia, Seychelles, South Africa, Swaziland, Tanzania, Zambia, Zimbabwe	1980	Gaborone, Botswana
UMA	Algeria, Libya, Mauritania, Morocco, Tunisia	1989	Rabat, Morocco

Source: UNECA (http://www.uneca.org/oria/pages/history-background-africas-regional-integration-efforts).

Consequently, countries are stretched with resources being inefficiently used[18] and RECs grappling with 'existential and credibility issues'.[19]

The streamlining and consolidation of RECs in different regions remains a key challenge for the realisation of both regional and pan-African economic integration. In the interim, in the process of migrating towards the AEC, there is a 'milestone' – Stage III – to form free trade areas and customs unions. The Tripartite Free Trade Area (TFTA), for example, comprising the Common Market for Eastern and Southern Africa (COMESA), the East African Community (EAC) and the Southern African Development Community (SADC) regional bodies, will encompass 26 African countries, representing more than half of the AU membership, with a combined population of 530 million (57 per cent of Africa's population) and a total GDP of $630 billion or 53 per cent of Africa's total GDP.

Assessment of the performance of RECs against their mandate

In light of the aforementioned strategic context outlining the mandate and scope of RECs, what is the state of play of African integration? There would appear to be consensus that, overall, the implementation of the Abuja Treaty has not been satisfactory. The progress attained, thus far, by the RECs has been described as 'mixed',[20] 'slow and partial'[21] and as being 'punctuated by periods of stagnation or blighted by reversals, with modest achievements, at best, in a few instances'.[22] The net impact of these varying levels of maturity in the development of RECs is that Africa has integrated with the rest of the world faster than with itself. Levels of intra-Africa trade remain extremely low at 11 per cent, whilst 40 per cent of North American trade is with other North American countries, and 63 per cent of trade by countries in Western Europe is with other Western European countries as depicted in Table 3.3.

Specifically regarding free trade and customs unions, limited progress is recorded in four of the eight RECs, namely, UMA, ECCAS, CEN-SAD and IGAD, whilst important progress has been achieved in COMESA, EAC, SADC and ECOWAS (see Table 3.4). Given the uneven progress, the overall present state of African economic integration is insufficient to support achievement of the African Common Market.

Explanations for low levels of regional integration

The large disparity among regional groupings in terms of intra-regional trade is clearly attributable to their differentiated levels of progress in implementing the structured set of modalities designed to eliminate trade barriers and non-tariff barriers (NTBs). Tariff barriers emanate from taxes and duties

Table 3.3 Comparisons of different continents' intra-regional trade levels

Region	2000 (in per cent)	2009 (in per cent)
Africa	9.2	11.7
Asia	49.1	51.6
CIS	20.1	19.2
Europe	73.2	72.2
Middle East	8.7	15.5
North America	55.7	48.0
South and Central America	25.6	26.1

Source: WTO Secretariat.

Table 3.4 Estimated value and share of intra-REC trade, 2009

REC	Value of Intra-REC Exports (US$ Billions)	Share of Intra-REC Exports (in per cent)
AMU	3.9	4.6
CEMAC	0.1	0.5
COMESA	6.4	6.8
EAC	2.4	23.0
CEEAC	0.2	0.3
ECOWAS	7.7	9.7
SACU	2.9	4.2
SADC	16.0	12.2
UEMOA	2.7	14.5

Source: WTO Secretariat and UN Comtrade.

that undermine trade while non-tariff barriers refer to non-tariff related trade restrictions resulting from prohibitions, conditions or specific requirements that render the importation and exportation of goods difficult or expensive.[23] These include red tape and bureaucracy, inefficient customs and border posts and poor infrastructure for the movement of goods between countries. Also, licensing rules, import permits and standards, including their implementation, fall within this category.

A key challenge militating against effective regional trade relates to the delays in moving goods across borders within and between regions. Delays in terms of crossing borders are, on average, longer than in the rest of the world: 12 days in Sub-Saharan countries compared with 7 days in Latin America, less than 6 days in Central and East Asia, and slightly more than 4 days in Central and East Europe.[24] These delays add a tremendous cost to importers and exporters and increase the transaction costs of trading among African countries. For food and other perishable goods, such delays can be devastating.

According to Brenton and Gözde,[25] 'thickness of borders' (2012:8) is a proxy for ease of access; thus, the denser the border, the more the country limits trade, travel and the flow of factors of production. A World Bank survey found that African borders are very 'thick' relative to other parts of the world. This was highlighted by President Mahama of Ghana, on a World Economic Forum panel in Davos in 2014, who noted that goods being transported from Nigeria to Ghana need to go through six border posts paying both 'official and non-official' fees. In yet another example, the Chirundu One Stop Border Post, between Zambia and Zimbabwe located on either side of the Zambezi River, often touted as an example of progressive border post management on the continent, is beset by a number of challenges. Anecdotal experiences of using this border post suggest that whilst processing times have been reduced, the border post is not fully realising what it was set up to achieve.

Another key constraint relates to the high volume of paper-work to be processed owing to rules of origin. By determining the origin of goods, rules of origin is the instrument used to prevent trade deflection, to ensure that only the member states of a preferential trade arrangement benefit from the negotiated tariff preferences. It is, however, deemed that SADC rules of origin are particularly stringent as they are based on sector or product-specific requirements. The experience of Shoprite, the largest retailer on the African continent, is illustrative of this form of trade barrier. In a report examining the barriers that stifle cross-border trade within Africa, the World Bank revealed that the retailer spends US$20,000 a week in import permits to transport meat, milk and other goods to its stores in Zambia alone. Approximately 100 single entry import permits are applied for every week, and this figure could rise up to 300 per week in peak periods. On average, according to the World Bank, there can be up to 1,600 documents accompanying each truck the retailer sends with a load that crosses a border in the region.[26]

For garments, the rule is even stricter and requires that two stages of transformation take place in a SADC member state for the garment to qualify for SADC preferences. This means that either the fabric, the yarn or the garment has to be manufactured in a SADC member state. With very little textile manufacturing in this region, the rules effectively limit the trade of garments in this region.[27] The administrative requirements for certificates of origin can account for nearly half the value of the duty preference. Shoprite, therefore, opts not to claim SADC preferences in sending regionally produced consignments of food and clothing to its franchise stores in non-SACU SADC markets. Instead, it pays full tariffs.

While rules of origin can be used, just as import tariffs, to protect domestic industry from import competition, a balance needs to be struck so that companies are not over-burdened by being obliged to use inputs from specific sources and having to adapt production processes to meet the rules of origin requirements to qualify for preferential market access. As stated by the World Bank in their seminal annual *Doing Business* reports and with great relevance here: It is 'about smart business regulations, not necessarily fewer regulations'.[28] Reforms to minimise costs could come from two sources: reforms in the rules of origin itself in the form of simplification and easing of standards, and reforms in the administrative procedures, particularly the certification process. A complex ROO regime accompanying a free trade agreement can further complicate rather than facilitate trade in the region. There is the need for the streamlining of customs procedures and simplification of customs clearances, including the introduction of paperless trading with the objective of minimising documentation costs.[29]

Underlying these barriers are issues of leadership and political will. In superimposing various states' memberships, a complex and convoluted picture emerges (see Figure 3.1) which provides explanations for the slow progress towards integration. While the REC is the unit of analysis and the explicit focus of this chapter, there is recognition of the tensions that are inherent in how individual countries interact with their REC(s) as well as how the different RECs themselves align in evolving to become a single monolithic

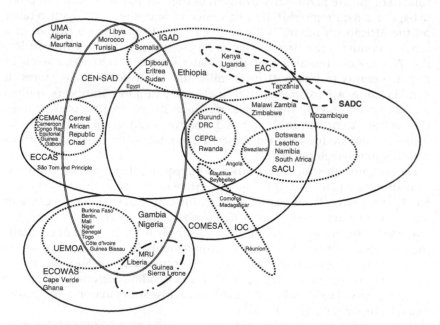

Figure 3.1   Overview of overlapping African countries' REC memberships

Source: Economic Commission for Africa, 2006, in ECA, AUC and AfDB (2010). Assessing Regional Integration in Africa IV. Enhancing Intra-African Trade. United Nations publication. Sales No. E.10.II.K.2. Addis Ababa.

free trade area. The African REC, therefore, straddles both national and supranational contexts and therein lies the complexity in operationalising the regional trade mandate.

At the opening session of the 2013 African Development Bank's Africa Economic Conference, South Africa's then finance minister, Pravin Gordhan, acknowledged this collaboration/competition tension stating that treading this fine balance requires a 'special kind of leadership' that appreciates sovereignty yet relinquishes aspects of it for the greater regional good. A particularly fitting illustration of this is how African states continue to negotiate as individual countries and not as RECs, thus losing the opportunity to leverage scale. By mid-2010, for example, African countries had signed 748 bilateral investment treaties, 140 of which were with other African countries.[30] Whilst, for instance, a singular negotiator, the European Commission, carries out negotiations on behalf of the European Union, no REC Commission or Secretariat negotiates on behalf of their member countries.

Integration continues to be viewed as threatening whereas it should be viewed as a win-win policy and not as a zero-sum game. In similar vein, UNCTAD[31] finds it difficult to understand why countries are reluctant to adopt common standards and regulations from which they are all likely to gain. This points to the need to actively manage the soft side of integration. Fears of sovereignty being undermined need to be mitigated against as they are unfounded. Empirical evidence points to the potential benefits of integration. In a study by TradeMark Southern African, the potential benefits of a successful TFTA were outlined in the impact study, 'General Equilibrium Analysis of the COMESA-EAC-SADC Tripartite FTA'. The report considered eight TFTA simulator scenarios and found that net real income gains would accrue to members of the TFTA generating annual welfare gains of $518 million.[32] It is perhaps due to this perceived loss of sovereignty that African governments have not successfully managed to mainstream and integrate regional trade mandates into national policies. It would appear that countries have not 'internalised' regional trade imperatives as planning for the state and for the region continue to happen in parallel, not concurrently nor in an integrated manner. On this, Rwanda's experience is instructive. The country is embarking on socio-economic transformation that is to be attained via regional integration. This aspiration has, subsequently, been enshrined in the country's Vision 2020.

While the AU has set up the Conference of Ministers in Charge of Regional Integration to holistically look into the implementation of protocols, harmonisation of policies and programmes and co-ordination between RECs, there is a 'hearts and minds' aspect that cannot be addressed by policy instruments. Winning hearts and minds could be the basis for building the necessary political will.

Regional Economic Communities and private sector development: towards a new paradigm

There is a compelling case for the reinvigoration of the African integration agenda. There is a need to locate the issue of intra-Africa trade in the broader context of private sector development (PSD) and the development discourse, which transcends 'fixing borders'.[33] This is corroborated by UNCTAD[34] in stating that although inefficient customs and regulatory procedures certainly hamper trade in the region, experience has demonstrated that the main barriers to increasing intra-African trade are often not found at the border. Trade facilitation needs to be an integrated part of development strategies in most African countries because it is a catalyst for further progress in areas beyond trade and export expansion.[35] It is only in this broader context that the import of regional integration can be effectively conveyed. Rippel[36] illustrates how trade facilitation across borders can contribute to reaching development goals (Figure 3.2).

UNCTAD[37] proposes a shift in paradigm from a linear and process-based approach to integration. They view the current paradigm as having an undue focus on the elimination of trade barriers and subscribe to a more development-based approach to integration, which pays as much attention to the building of productive capacities and private sector development as to the elimination of trade barriers. It is contended that the current integration paradigm does not address adequately the fundamental supply side constraints – a weak private sector, poor labour productivity, lack of access to finance, inadequate infrastructure, low institutional capacity and low access to technology and innovation. These collectively constitute an ecosystem and in its absence, companies cannot achieve manufacturing and productive capacities to ensure that there are goods and services to be had for regional trade, in the first instance. African countries will struggle to compete favourably against growing global competition without an outward reorientation of their trade policies.

On labour productivity specifically, Rankin, Söderbom and Teal (2006) conducted a study comprising 1,012 firms spanning the period from 1992 to 2003 in five countries: Ghana, Kenya, Nigeria, South Africa and Tanzania. The key conclusion drawn from the findings is that firms with higher labour productivity are more likely to export than those with lower labour productivity. Moreover, African manufacturing firms generally have lower labour productivity than firms on other continents. Thus, if African governments want to boost intra-African trade, they will have to enhance the export competitiveness of African manufacturing firms by addressing these obstacles to productivity growth.[38]

UNCTAD[39] attributes poor regional integration outcomes, in part, to the limited role of the private sector in regional integration initiatives and efforts. In a telling 2012 UNECA survey,[40] 31 per cent of respondents stated

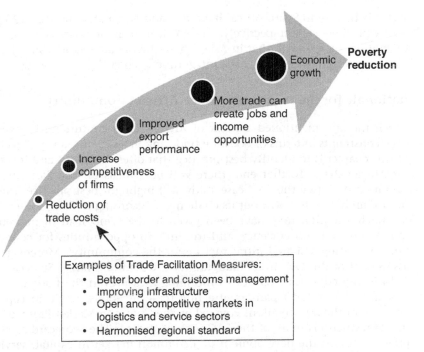

Figure 3.2 How trade facilitation can contribute to reaching development goals

Source: Rippel, B., "Why Trade Facilitation Is Important for Africa," in World Bank 2012: "De-Fragmenting Africa: Deepening Regional Trade Integration in Goods and Services".

political motivations for joining a REC, 39 per cent cited economic reasons, 16 per cent cited geographic reasons, 6 per cent historical and 8 per cent cultural. This further supports the assertion that even for those RECs with a trade agenda, trade is not always their overarching priority despite all their pronouncements. While trade agreements are signed by governments, it is the private sector that understands the constraints facing enterprises and is in a position to take advantage of the opportunities created by regional trade initiatives. While there are business councils, governments remain the only active drivers of regional integration in Africa and the private sector remains a passive participant in the process. If African governments want to achieve their objective of boosting intra-African trade, they have to create more space for the private sector to play an active role in the integration process. But more importantly, the African private sector must be able to occupy that space. Evidence, however, points to a weak African private sector with limited capacity. For instance, most African private sector jobs are in the informal sector with only 2–10 per cent of African workers occupying permanent/ formal wage employment. Permanent formal employment in the private sector is highest in South Africa, Botswana and Egypt at 46 per cent, 23 per cent and 18 per cent, respectively.[41] The African scenario, as depicted, is said to contrast sharply with that in Asia, where the private sector is strong and plays a crucial role in shaping the integration agenda.[42]

Rationale for the focus on the East African Community

Given the aforementioned context of African RECs continuing to experience constraints in terms of boosting trade and investments, a key objective of this chapter is to identify best practice that offers learnings and insights for African RECs. To that end, there will be a focus on the East African Community. While the EAC case study will highlight best practice, this is not to imply that it is without its challenges. According to Paul Collier, '[T]oo much attention may have been given to the symbolism of monetary union and common currency, and too little to opportunities for cooperation in creating a shared infrastructure for the community'. Moreover, an assessment of the EAC in its inaugural EAC Common Market Scorecard of 2014 identified at least 63 non-conforming measures in the trade of services and 51 non-tariff barriers affecting trade in goods, while in capital, only two of the 20 operations covered by the Common Market Protocol are free of restrictions in all of the EAC partner states.[43] The Scorecard assesses progress toward the development of a common market in capital, services and goods across the Partner States of the EAC and in terms of commitments made by the Partner States, outlines progress in removing legislative and regulatory restrictions to the Protocol, and recommends reform measures. Member states are assessed for compliance with 683 laws and regulations relevant to the common market – 124 in Capital, 545 in Services and 14 in Goods. Notwithstanding the indictment according to the Scorecard findings, the EAC is still lauded as the top performing African REC on a number of indices and metrics (see Figure 3.3). Table 3.4 depicts the EAC as having had the highest levels of trade with intra-REC exports accounting for 23 per cent of all exports in 2009. This is in stark contrast to CEMAC's 0.5 per cent and SADC's 12.2 per cent. Implementation of the Customs Union Protocol in 2005 has had a positive impact on intra-EAC trade which has grown from $US2 billion in 2005 to $US5.5 billion in 2013, a growth of 36 per cent.[44]

Regarding, specifically, the export of services, Africa has experienced growth at an average annual rate of 14.2 per cent in the period 2000–2008 with significant variations in services export growth among African RECs.[45] Again, on the basis of this metric, the EAC recorded the fastest average annual growth at 17 per cent, while COMESA and SADC services exports grew at 14 per cent, and ECCAS and ECOWAS services exports grew at 10–11 per cent, lower than the average for Africa.

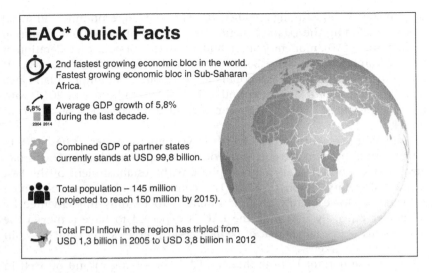

EAC* Quick Facts

2nd fastest growing economic bloc in the world. Fastest growing economic bloc in Sub-Saharan Africa.

Average GDP growth of 5,8% during the last decade.

Combined GDP of partner states currently stands at USD 99,8 billion.

Total population – 145 million (projected to reach 150 million by 2015).

Total FDI inflow in the region has tripled from USD 1,3 billion in 2005 to USD 3,8 billion in 2012

Figure 3.3   EAC quick facts

Note: *The East African Community (EAC) is the regional intergovernmental organisation of the Republic of Burundi, Kenya, Rwanda, the United Republic of Tanzania, and the Republic of Uganda, with its headquarters in Arusha, Tanzania.

Source: Africa Practice (2014), "East Africa Integration: State of Play," Africa Practice InDepth.

The very establishment of the Scorecard itself, in the first place, and less so the outcomes of the scoring exercise, is indicative of the EAC's commitment to a functioning REC. The Scorecard has established a starting point for continuous improvement based on a quantifiable basis.

Background to and context of the East African Community

There has been a long history of cooperation under successive regional integration arrangements in the region. Kenya, Tanzania and Uganda have participated in regional integration arrangements dating back to 1917, starting with a Customs Union between Kenya and Uganda in 1917, which the then Tanganyika (Tanzania) joined in 1927; the East African High Commission (1948–1961); the East African Common Services Organization (1961–1967); the East African Community (1967–1977); and the East African Co-operation (1993–2000). The relative success of the EAC is often attributed to the community having transitioned through many phases and, as a result of the failures and collapses, for example, in 1977, it is stronger.

The second iteration of the EAC was established in 2000 by Kenya, Tanzania and Uganda while Burundi and Rwanda joined in 2007. Its objectives are to deepen cooperation among member states in political, economic and social fields – including the establishment of a customs union (2005), common market (July 2010), monetary union and, ultimately, a political federation of East African States (see Figure 3.4). Burundi and Rwanda joined the customs union in 2009. The EAC has a population of about 133 million, a land area of 1.8 million square kilometres and a GDP of $99 billion as of 2014, with Kenya, the largest economy, accounting for approximately 40 per cent of that.

The EAC is, currently, in the fourth Development Strategy phase (2011–2016) with a focus on the deepening of the integration process. The immediate and key objective of the new phase is the establishment of the East African Monetary Union (EAMU). The common market protocol, which entered into force in July 2010, is intended to be fully implemented by December 2015. By that time the EAC is expected to have achieved the '4 freedoms' – free movement of people, goods, services and capital within the common market.

It is also important to note that the EAC is evolving in and of itself in terms of intra-REC integration but also, in pursuance of a parallel mandate, in adapting to meet the inter-REC integration necessitated by the Tripartite Free Trade Area integration of SADC, COMESA and EAC.

Learnings from EAC: how is the EAC facilitating cross-border trade and investment?

As mentioned earlier, the EAC is the better performing of the African RECs. However, closer examination reveals that integration is neither consistent nor wholesale. Rather, integration in the EAC manifests in three of the following ways:

- at an EAC level with *all* members;
- at an EAC level with only *some* members, known as the 'Coalition of the Willing';
- *individual country efforts* that, however, augur well for the EAC and are often misconstrued to be efforts at an EAC level.

The EAC is characterised by a fissure in its membership with a feet-dragging element and a fast-tracking one commonly referred to as the 'Coalition of the Willing' but officially known as the 'Tripartite Initiative for Fast Tracking the East African Integration'.[46] Accordingly, EAC progress regarding a number of regional initiatives to promote regional trade and investment can be drawn along the lines of these two groupings.

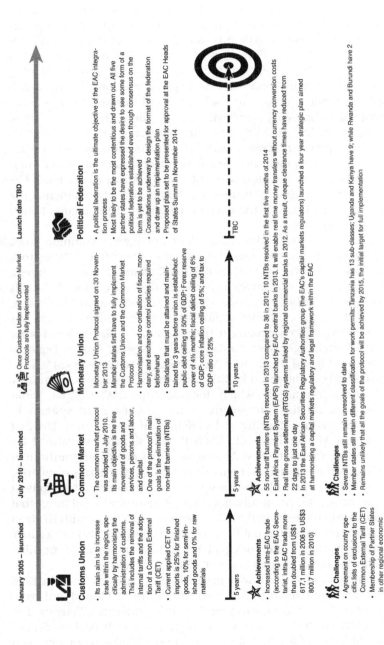

January 2005 – launched **July 2010 – launched** Once Customs Union and Common Market **Launch date TBD**
Protocols are fully implemented

Customs Union

- Its main aim is to increase trade within the region, specifically by harmonising the administration of customs. This includes the removal of internal tariffs and the adoption of a Common External Tariff (CET)
- Current applied CET on imports is 25% for finished goods, 10% for semi-finished goods and 0% for raw materials

Common Market

- The common market protocol was adopted in July 2010. Its main objective is the free movement of goods and services, persons and labour, and capital
- One of the protocol's main goals is the elimination of non-tariff barriers (NTBs)

Monetary Union

- Monetary Union Protocol signed on 30 November 2013
- Member states first have to fully implement the Customs Union and the Common Market Protocol
- Harmonisation and co-ordination of fiscal, monetary, and exchange control policies required beforehand
- Standards that must be attained and maintained for 3 years before union is established: public debt ceiling of 50% of GDP; Forex reserve cover of 4½ months; fiscal deficit ceiling of 6% of GDP; core inflation ceiling of 5%; and tax to GDP ratio of 25%

Political Federation

- A political federation is the ultimate objective of the EAC integration process
- Most likely to be the most contentious and drawn out. All five partner states have expressed the desire to see some form of a political federation established even though consensus on the form is yet to be achieved
- Consultations underway to design the format of the federation and draw up an implementation plan
- Proposed plan set to be presented for approval at the EAC Heads of States Summit in November 2014

5 years   5 years   10 years   TBC

⭐ **Achievements**

- Increased intra-EAC trade (according to the EAC Secretariat, intra-EAC trade more than doubled from US$1 617.1 million in 2006 to US$3 800.7 million in 2010)

⭐ **Achievements**

- 55 non-tariff barriers (NTBs) resolved in 2013 compared to 36 in 2012. 10 NTBs resolved in the first five months of 2014
- East Africa Payment System (EAPS) launched by EAC central banks in 2013. It will enable real time money transfers without currency conversion costs
- Real time gross settlement (RTGS) systems linked by regional commercial banks in 2012. As a result, cheque clearance times have reduced from 22 days to just one day
- In 2013 the East African Securities Regulatory Authorities group (the EAC's capital markets regulators) launched a four year strategic plan aimed at harmonising a capital markets regulatory and legal framework within the EAC

👥 **Challenges**

- Agreement on country specific lists of exclusions to the Common External Tariff (CET)
- Membership of Partner States in other regional economic communities (RECs) that have different CET rates

👥 **Challenges**

- Several NTBs still remain unresolved to date
- Member states still retain different classification for work permits: Tanzania has 13 sub-classes; Uganda and Kenya have 9; while Rwanda and Burundi have 2
- Remains unlikely that all the goals of the protocol will be achieved by 2015, the initial target for full implementation

Figure 3.4 Overview of the EAC integration process: key phases and milestones

Source: Africa Practice (2014), "East Africa Integration: State of Play," Africa Practice InDepth.

Integration efforts at an EAC level with all members

The EAC's approach to integration can be said to be consistent with the tenets of the new developmental regionalism approach that lays emphasis on addressing supply side constraints and not just 'fixing borders'. For example, the current EAC development strategy, covering the period 2011/12 to 2015/16, has an explicit focus on deepening and accelerating integration and particularly prioritises the expansion of productive capacities to facilitate product/service diversification and infrastructure network development for enhanced connectivity within the region. Examples of these ongoing efforts include an East African transport strategy and regional road sector development programme; an East African railways master plan; and the ongoing development of a regional power master plan and interconnection code, in collaboration with the Eastern Africa Power Pool. The EAC has also been successful in securing funding from investors such as the African Development Bank for the operationalisation of these cross-border infrastructural programmes.

Regarding capital markets, the region does not have a common stock exchange although plans are under way for the integration of the stock markets in Kenya, Uganda, Tanzania and Rwanda. Burundi does not have a stock exchange. The East African Securities Exchange Association (EASEA) is working with the Securities Exchanges of each member country to achieve integration. In 2012, the combined capitalisation of the four exchanges was estimated at US$31 billion, making it the continent's third largest bourse if the EAC stock exchanges were combined, after Western African Regional Stock Market (BRVM) and the Central African Stock Exchange (BVMAC).

Integration efforts commenced in 2010 with the East African Community Monetary Policy Committee, which includes the EAC Central Banks commencing work on the interlinking of the EAC payment systems in order to facilitate trading, clearing and settlement infrastructures. The East African Common Market Protocol (EACMP) was signed and ratified on 1 July 2010. Furthermore, the East African Securities Regulatory Authorities (EASRA), which is the regional umbrella body for capital markets regulators, is drafting legislation that will allow companies in the four countries to float bonds within the region. Harmonisation of legal frameworks will mean that a single information memorandum will be required to comply with the laws in each market. Also, an initial public offer of securities will also use a single set of disclosure standards. It is anticipated that these changes will considerably ease and raise levels of cross-border trading by investors.

While the number of African stock markets has increased from 5 in 1960 to 29 in 2014,[47] they remain highly fragmented, small, illiquid and technologically weak, this severely affecting their informational efficiency. The total value of African stocks outside of South Africa was only 0.94 per cent of world stock market capitalisation, and 2.14 per cent of all emerging markets stocks at the end of 2011.[48]

It is further contended that African stock markets are also small compared with the size of their own economies.[49] For example, market capitalisation of the Mozambique stock exchange is only 4.7 per cent of nominal GDP, whilst Nigeria, Uganda and Tunisia's capitalisations are between 31 and 63 per cent.[50] This compares unfavourably to the UK's 145.6 per cent and the USA's 122.8 per cent and even to emerging economies with Malaysia at 183.7 per cent and India at 172.5 per cent. The case for the integration of African stock markets is, therefore, self-evident with a number of benefits cited which include increased visibility due to scale;[51] increased liquidity and cheaper cost of capital resulting in the expansion for trading volumes;[52] and finally, greater financial deepening.[53]

The East Africa Exchange (EAX), established by Heirs Holdings in 2013, heralds progress towards a common market. Launched in 2013, the commodity exchange 'has the capacity to facilitate cross-border trading of commodities within the EAC, providing a central marketplace, connecting buyers and sellers throughout the region', according to Dr. Frazer, the Chairman of the Board.[54] It will link smallholder farmers to agricultural and financial markets, to secure competitive prices for their products, and to facilitate access to financial opportunities. EAX's goal is to facilitate trade across all five East African Community member states.[55]

Also, the establishment of the East African Cross-Border Payment System (EAPS) in late 2013 represents yet another concrete move towards the integration of money and capital markets.[56] The EAPS is an on-the-spot payment system that links the Real Time Gross Settlement System (RTGS) in the three central banks – Kenya, Uganda and Tanzania – and allows for the movement of cash between different banks and branches in the region in place of cheques. Rwanda and Burundi are expected to join over time. The EAPS is a multi-currency system in which payments are effected using any of the currencies of the EAC partner states vastly reducing costs of transactions in the form of commissions. It is worthy and important to note that beneficiaries are diverse and include large investors but also SMEs and citizens who are typically on the periphery and excluded in the design of large cross-border systems. Citizens who have been using informal methods – with high transaction costs – are now able to make payments, including school and medical fees for relatives, across national borders using the EAPS. It can, therefore, be said that integration is being driven at a level that impacts on communities in a manner that is relevant to its people.

Integration efforts by the Coalition of the Willing

Members of the Coalition of the Willing are driving infrastructure projects, accelerating movement of peoples and reducing costs of ICT. Regarding infrastructure, the three countries (Kenya, Rwanda and Uganda) signed a tripartite agreement for the development and operation of standard gauge railway (SGR) that is to run from Mombasa through Nairobi to Kampala and

Kigali, and construction commenced in October 2014. The standard gauge signifies progress towards common specification in cross-border infrastructure. Non-alignment in terms of standards and specifications is a typical non-tariff barrier on the continent. Regarding labour mobility, Rwanda abolished work permit fees for all EAC citizens with Kenya following suit and Uganda abolishing work permit fees for Kenyans and Rwandans.[57] For multinationals – whether foreign of African – with offices in the three countries, this development is a welcome relief. In terms of movement of people, citizens of Kenya, Rwanda and Uganda, as of February 2014, have been able to travel anywhere in the three countries using only their national identity cards instead of passports. Moreover, the three countries launched an East Africa six-month visa in June 2014 allowing foreign residents and expatriates residing in the three countries to travel freely within the three countries. Finally, the establishment of a single tourist visa for the three countries set a clear and positive tone for movement within the region. Finally, in terms of connectivity, the Coalition of the Willing established a single area mobile network that was launched in October 2014. This eliminates roaming charges on cross-border calls for mobile phone users in Kenya, Uganda and Rwanda.[58] The net impact is expected to be greater connectivity and a reduction in the cost of doing business.

Individual country efforts that have benefitted EAC

Evidence shows that 'economies that have efficient business registration also tend to have a higher entry rate by new firms and greater business density'. In terms of the continual improvement of the business environment, the EAC performs well. However, it is important to note here that the EAC has been the beneficiary of progressive individual country efforts rather than a concerted effort at the EAC level. To start a business in the EAC requires only 8 procedures and 20 days on average. The EAC's average ranking on the ease of starting a business is 84, higher than that of other regional blocs in Africa – 104 for the SADC, 110 for the COMESA and 127 for the ECOWAS. Of the 74 institutional or regulatory reforms implemented by EAC economies in the past 8 years, the largest numbers were in the areas of starting a business, registering property and dealing with construction permits. These efforts have led to clear results. In 2005, starting a business in the EAC took 29 days on average; today it takes 20. But the time needed to register property had the biggest reduction, dropping from an average of 140 days in 2005 to 56 days as of today. As average figures, they mask the accomplishment of high performers such as Rwanda. For example, Uganda ranked 120, Kenya 121, Tanzania 134 and Burundi, 159 while Rwanda, ranked 52 globally among 181 countries in 2013, was named a top reformer by the World Bank and second best reformer globally. It earned the distinction by enacting sound business policies and removing bottlenecks to establish small to medium-sized firms. In terms of doing business, Rwanda has reduced the number of procedures from 8 to 2, and the length of time it takes to register a business from 14 days to 24 hours. It could be said that Rwanda has compensated for its small market size by making itself attractive as a destination to do business in with leadership compensating the lack of inherent comparative advantages.

The EAC economies have leveraged technology to underpin business reforms. Rwanda has an integrated system for company registration while Kenya offers online procedures for tax and value added tax (VAT) registration. Kenya also introduced online name search, reducing the time and cost to start a business. Uganda has an online system allowing entrepreneurs to apply for corporate tax and value added tax identification numbers at the same time. Tanzania has consolidated and digitised registered company names, allowing the company name search to be done online and speeding up name clearances.

The MeTL Group: an industrial conglomerate operating in the EAC

Mohammed Enterprises Tanzania (MeTL Group) employs 24,000 people and is Tanzania's largest private sector employer. Its revenues are US$1.3 billion, contributing 3.5 per cent to Tanzania's GDP, with a 5-year plan to grow to US$5 billion. MeTL is diversified and is into a diverse range of activities, including grain-milling, rice, the refining of edible oils, sisal farms, tea estates, cashew fields, logistics and warehousing, financial services, distribution, real estate, transport and logistics, energy and petroleum. From an initial capacity of 60 tons, which then grew to 600 tons, MeTL now refines 2,250 tons of edible oils per year following an acquisition that expanded its capacity in 2013. Regarding textiles, MeTL is Sub-Saharan Africa's largest entity operating along the entire value chain from ginning to spinning, weaving, knitting, processing and printing. Of the 24,000 jobs created by the group, 8,000 are in textiles. The group also exports 50 of its brands taking advantage of the fact that Tanzania borders with eight countries, thus leveraging the country's 'land-linked' position.[59] MeTL is now present in 11 African countries and is, arguably, the largest private company in East and Central Africa.

While the group – as a diversified conglomerate – appears to be involved in seemingly disparate activities, there is a common thread. Speaking to Mr Mohammed Dewji, the CEO of MeTL Group, it is clear that the common thread across the businesses is the enabling EAC policy frameworks and specifically:

- harmonisation of external tariffs across EAC countries;
- harmonisation of internal tariff systems within EAC country states, themselves; and
- rules of origin.

The EAC trading bloc, under the Common External Tariff system, is designed to keep out foreign competition whilst at the same time promoting trade within the EAC countries. To put it otherwise, it is protectionist vis-à-vis outsiders but protective of insiders within the community. This has helped ensure that the countries gain their competitive strength and are strong as the building blocks of the EAC. According to Mohammed Dewji, at a time when Africa is particularly vulnerable to cheap imports from China, certain industries in East Africa are cushioned given the tariff regime. He confidently asserts, 'They (the Chinese) cannot compete with me in my market'. He explains it thus: in a bid to promote local value-addition and beneficiation, the Tanzanian government has recognised the job creation potential of the textiles sector and has accorded the industry a tax relief status for local producers whilst imposing 25 per cent import tariffs on finished goods and 18 per cent VAT for those importing into the country. Moreover, Tanzania grows cotton and is the third largest grower on the continent whereas China has cotton but insufficient to meet demand and has to import to address the supply gap. Textiles accounts for 5 per cent of Tanzania manufacturing value-add (MVP) with it being a significant exporter of textiles to other EAC countries.[60]

The MeTL Group has leveraged the rules of origin to its advantage – a regional integration policy instrument that is normally fraught with complications. Shoprite, the South African retailer that is now Africa's largest retailer, prefers not to exercise its rules of origin entitlement within the SADC region opting to pay full tariffs because it deems the process of administering rules of origin documentation to be too cumbersome.[61]

The determination of the eligibility of products to EAC origin and the granting of Community Tariffs to goods originating in the Partner States are important processes in the implementation of the EAC trade regime.[62] The MeTL Group has a different experience of rules of origin and the business model has been structured to leverage the benefits of rules of origin. Thus, MeTL imports wheat, not flour, and crude palm oil is imported from Malaysia and Indonesia which is then processed in Tanzania. But to then export the refined oil to Uganda, for example, would mean Uganda would have to pay tariffs. However, for sunflower oil which is grown in Tanzania, the group can process and export it to Uganda at 0 per cent tariff. Over the years, the EAC member states have aligned their tariffs in accordance with and support of the rules of origin regime. Tanzania, for example, migrated towards it over a period of five years, going from 20 per cent to 15 per cent to 10 per cent, 5 per cent and then 0 per cent. Mohammed Dewji explains that different countries have different comparative advantages and this allows the different EAC countries to beneficiate locally while benefitting the EAC intra-trading of goods in a complementary manner. The EAC's approach is consistent with a key tenet of regional integration: that 'a continental customs union requires that all Africa countries have a single commercial

Table 3.5 Progress towards elimination of tariffs and equivalent measures by EAC partner states (Based on 2008–2013 Data; all values in per cent)

	Per cent	Rwanda	Burundi	Kenya	Uganda	Tanzania
Compliance with tariff schedule	20	20	20	20	20	20
Adoption of rules of origin requirements	20	20	20	20	20	20
Use of charges of equivalent effect to tariffs	30	30	27	24	21	18
Recognition of certificates of origin	16	14.4	16	14.4	11.2	8
Compliance with EAC Council Recommendation about issuance of certificate of origin by customs authorities	7	7	7	7	0	0
Compliance with Custom Union Protocol Annex III about false documentation for certificates of origin	7	0	0	0	0	0
	100	91.4	90	85.4	72.2	66

Source: K'Ombudo, A.O., East Africa Common Market Scorecard 2014: Tracking EAC Compliance in the Movement of Capital, Services and Goods. The World Bank, International Finance Corporation and East African Secretariat.

(tariff) policy vis-à-vis the rest of the world while trade within Africa is totally free, respecting the continental rules of origin'. The EAC has made formidable progress on this, at least, relative to other African RECs with regards to the implementation of a customs union.

Airbus: a case of practical regional integration

Moyo[63] is a proponent of a different 'architecture' for economic integration – a more pragmatic approach to regional integration.[64] Airbus's dispersed and integrative manufacturing of aircrafts is illustrative of this approach. In the mid-1960s, tentative negotiations commenced regarding a European collaborative approach in response to European manufacturers' dwindling market share and competitiveness in the aircraft sector on the global stage. France, Germany and the United Kingdom entered into an agreement covering both component production and aircraft assembly. Spain is part of this agreement and in the specific context of the production of the Airbus 380. Under this partnership, the UK specialises in wing manufacturing; Spain focuses on tail, fin and pitch elevator; France and Germany share fuselage construction while final assembly takes place in Toulouse, France. This multi-territory production template distributes the benefits across various countries and eventually leads to the emergence of captive markets.

There are important lessons to be extracted from the Airbus example for African regional integration. Firstly, '[African] countries with more capacity need to be prepared to lead from behind and to lead by giving away certain benefits in order to create the cohesion that is necessary. Thus, there is a 'disproportionate responsibility on large economies such as Nigeria and South Africa to drive integration'.[65] Secondly, the Airbus's distributed-benefits model is seen as the outcome of a political, rather than an economic, decision-making process. By accepting this political dimension, it is also easier to build in the 'self-interest' that is necessary for politicians and civil servants to embrace integration by stating 'right up-front, how the benefits flowing from such cooperation are going to be distributed and how they could justify such participation to the electorate'. The Airbus architecture tends to understand that each country would need to account to its citizens in terms of why it should be part of the club. Finally, to operationalise such a model, political will, on its own, is not sufficient. There is also a need for a secure environment and the harmonisation of business legislation and regulations. The question of visas to facilitate skills movement must be resolved in a pragmatic manner, in both the short and long terms and should be issued online as a matter of course.[66]

To summarise, the key lessons from the Airbus case study of relevance for African regional integration are as follows:[67]

- It is easier to commit to economic integration if the dividends to each participant are clear right up front.
- Even with global products, take a commanding position on the expanded domestic front first.
- Create mutual vulnerability and win-win in which the success of one is the success of all in the club.
- Go global on the back of technical and strategic partners' networks.
- Be clear about the 'political economy' nature of integration.
- The 'bigger' participants must be prepared to be champions to the cause.

Conclusions and recommendations

Based on the aforementioned strategic context and state of play of regional integration on the African continent, a number of conclusions are drawn and recommendations framed.

Conclusions

- In the context of globalisation, Africa's rising and the competitiveness of countries such as China, there is greater urgency to expedite the regional integration agenda. These dynamics render the issue of integration inherently more complex and Africa finds itself in a somewhat disconcerting and unique position where it, at once, needs to raise intra-REC trade whilst simultaneously confronting external competition that is cost competitive.

- In light of evidence suggesting slow progress towards the attainment of the African Economic Community, it would appear there is a lack of urgency or political will on the part of regional bodies in addressing regional trade issues. This was similarly observed by Peters-Berries,[68] who noted that 'the political will for regional integration has not been adequately translated into action'. Despite all the pronouncements, there still appears to be a lack of appreciation of how regional trade can truly lead to the economic transformation of African countries. Consequently, effective integration needs to be repositioned as a win-win for both the private sector and governments, themselves, in helping the latter deliver on their mandates to their people.

- The African private sector is conspicuous by its absence in the regional integration discourse. In attempting to raise intra-REC trade levels, regional bodies need to work with the private sector in understanding their concerns and in co-crafting the solutions. According to the African Development Bank,[69] 'government and the national/regional Chambers of Commerce and Business Councils are already interacting in the region, but the contact has to extend beyond information sharing to involvement in policy making and program implementation process' and infrastructure building via public-private-partnership arrangements (PPPs). The East African Exchange (EAX), a private sector initiative, is a fitting example of how the private sector can play a lead and pivotal role in driving the aspirations of a common market, in a manner that is mutually beneficial to the private and public sectors.

Recommendations

- Removal of trade and non-trade barriers is a necessary but not sufficient condition for effective regional integration. A broader integration paradigm that addresses supply-side constraints is needed. To that end, RECs need to identify the infrastructure gaps that hinder effective trade across borders and attract investors, *as regional bodies*, to fill those gaps.

- Soft issues need to be actively managed alongside policy issues. Citizenry awareness and education are vital to ensure buy-in into the regional trade vision and to minimise the tensions between ceding sovereignty and raising the greater regional common good.

• There needs to be a mainstreaming of regional trade mandates into national policies. The supra-national and national realms and agendas will have to be managed jointly and in parallel and should be mutually reinforcing. While regional communities can provide the framework for reform, responsibility for implementation lies with each member country.

• Leadership, leadership, leadership! Leadership compensates for natural disadvantages, be they locational or a lack of resources. Rwanda has defied its relatively small market size within the EAC by making itself attractive as a destination to do business in. It is the largest attractor of intra-EAC investments having positioned itself proactively to seize the regional trading opportunity.

• The adage 'what cannot be measured, cannot be managed' is particularly apt in the context of the EAC. The EAC case highlighted the importance of assessing progress, as illustrated by two initiatives. The first is the EAC Time-Bound Programme for Elimination of Identified Non-Tariff Barriers (NTBs), where the heads of delegation of each country report detected NTBs either in its own country or imposed by another member state to the EAC Secretariat, and then all five EAC member states agree on characterising such measures as NTBs. The programme was formally adopted in 2009 and since then has been regularly implemented on a yearly and quarterly basis since August 2011.[70] The second initiative is the East Africa Scorecard launched in 2014 to define a baseline regarding the status of integration vis-à-vis capital goods and services and to measure progress, going forward. Paradoxically, while the EAC is lauded as a model REC, vis-à-vis other African RECs, an assessment of the EAC's progress against its own ambitions found the it wanting in a number of respects. But the identification of these gaps is entirely in keeping with the spirit in which the Scorecard was established. According to Dr. Sezibera, the EAC Secretary-General, the EAC plans to use the scorecard to provide benchmarks to guide faster implementation of the common market and to 'foster peer learning and facilitate the adoption of best practices in the region. This will strengthen the regional market, grow the private sector and deliver benefits to consumers'.[71] Stemming out of this, a key recommendation to African RECs is the need for measurement of progress towards integration and even more importantly, the responsiveness to the outcomes of the measurement system.

• Both the EAC and Airbus experiences have highlighted that the 'bigger' participants'[72] must be prepared to be champions to the cause. 'Those 54 countries are not going to be in phase with each other every step of the way – it's not possible. So those countries that "get it" need to be prepared to move on ahead of the laggards, while creating a framework that says: "When you are ready, you can join. But we are not going to wait for you"'.[73] The EAC's Coalition of the Willing has demonstrated this by demonstrating urgency and setting the cadence and tone for economic integration but perhaps – controversially – at the expense of the broader political alignment of the EAC.

Notes

1. World Bank, 'Harnessing Regional Integration for Trade and Growth in Southern Africa' (2011), http://siteresources.worldbank.org/INTAFRREGTOPTRADE/Resources/Harnessing_Regional_Integration_Trade_Growth_SouthernAfrica.pdf, p. xvi.
2. J. Chimhanzi, 'Mitigating Business Risk through Regional Integration', *Deloitte on Africa Series* (2012a).
3. L. Lapadre and F. Luchetti, Trade Regionalisation and Openness in Africa. European Report on Development. EUI Working Paper RSCAS 2010/54. European University Institute, Florence (2010).
4. 'The World's Fastest-Growing Continent: Aspiring Africa', *The Economist* (2 March 2013).
5. Chimhanzi, 'Mitigating Business Risk through Regional Integration'.
6. D. A. Mohammed, 'Size and Competitiveness: An Examination of the CARICOM Single Market and Economy (CSME)', *The Round Table* (Vol. 97, No. 395, 2008), pp. 287–303.
7. R. Kaplinsky and M. Morris, 'Do the Asian Drivers Undermine Export-Oriented Industrialization in SSA?' *World Development* (Vol. 36, No. 2, 2008), pp. 254–273. K. Ighobor, 'China in the Heart of Africa: Opportunities and Pitfalls in a Rapidly Expanding Relationship', *Africa Renewal* (Vol. 26, No. 3, 2013), pp. 6–8.
8. UNCTAD and UNIDO, Economic Development in Africa Report 2011. Fostering Industrial Development in Africa in the New Global Environment. United Nations Publication. Sales No. E.11.II.D.14. New York and Geneva (2011).
9. UNCTAD, 'Economic Development in Africa Report 2013 – Intra African Trade: Unlocking Private Sector Dynamism' (July 2013), http://unctad.org/en/PublicationsLibrary/aldcafrica2013_en.pdf (retrieved 21 January 2014).
10. 'A More Hopeful Continent: The Lion Kings', *The Economist* (6 January 2011). 'The Hopeless Continent', *The Economist* (11 May 2000).
11. 'The Hopeful Continent: Africa Rising', *The Economist* (3 December 2011).
12. Chimhanzi, 'Mitigating Business Risk through Regional Integration'.
13. Jessica Pugliese, 'Will There Be an African Economic Community?' *Brookings Institute* (9 January 2014).
14. M. Ndulo, 'Harmonisation of Trade Laws in the African Economic Community', *International and Comparative Law Quarterly* (Vol. 42, 1993), pp. 101–118.
15. V. Ihekweazu, 'A Proposed Framework for an Effective Africa Free Trade Area', Unpublished thesis, University of Pretoria, The Gordan Institute of Business (2014).
16. EAC Secretariat, *Manual on the Application of East Africa Community Rules of Origin*, Directorate of Customs and Trade, Arusha, Tanzania (2006).
17. B. Omilola, 'To What Extent Are Regional Trade Arrangements in Africa Fulfilling the Conditions for Successful RTAs?', *Journal of African Studies and Development* (Vol. 3, No. 6, 2011), pp. 105–113.

18. Ihekweazu, 'A Proposed Framework for an Effective Africa Free Trade Area'.
19. African Union Commission, 'Boosting Intra-Africa Trade: Issues Affecting Intra-African Trade, Proposed Action Plan for Boosting Intra-African Trade and Framework for the Fast Tracking of a Continental Free Trade Area' (2012).
20. African Union Conference of Ministers of Trade, 6th Ordinary Session, 29 October–November 2010.
21. UNECA, 'Assessing Regional Integration in Africa (ARIA V): Towards an African Continental Free Trade Area' (2012a).
22. H. Ben Barka, 'Border Posts, Checkpoints, and Intra-African Trade: Challenges and Solutions', The African Development Bank (2012).
23. TradeMark Southern Africa, EAC Customs Union – Uniform Laws to Enhance both Regional and External Trade (2012).
24. World Bank, 'Harnessing Regional Integration for Trade and Growth in Southern Africa' (2011), http://siteresources.worldbank.org/INTAFRREGTOPTRADE/Resources/Harnessing_Regional_Integration_Trade_Growth_SouthernAfrica.pdf.
25. P. Brenton and I. Gözde, 'Linking African Markets: Removing Barriers to Intra-Africa Trade' in Brenton, P and Gözde, I (eds.), *De-Fragmenting Africa: Deepening Regional Trade Integration in Goods and Services, World Bank Report*, (Washington, DC, 2012).
26. World Bank, 'Harnessing Regional Integration for Trade and Growth in Southern Africa'.
27. UNCTAD, 'Economic Development in Africa Report 2013 – Intra African Trade: Unlocking Private Sector Dynamism' (July 2013), http://unctad.org/en/PublicationsLibrary/aldcafrica2013_en.pdf (retrieved 21 January 2014).
28. World Bank and IFC, 'Doing Business in the East African Community 2013. Smarter Regulations for Small and Medium-Size Enterprises' (2013).
29. E.M. Medalla and J. Balboa, 'ASEAN Rules of Origin: Lessons and Recommendations for Best Practice', Philippine Institute for Development Studies (PIDS), Philippines (2009).
30. African Union Conference of Ministers of Trade, 6th Ordinary Session, 29 October–November 2010.
31. UNCTAD, 'Economic Development in Africa Report 2013 – Intra African Trade: Unlocking Private Sector Dynamism'.
32. TradeMark Southern Africa, EAC Customs Union – Uniform Laws to Enhance both Regional and External Trade; Ihekweazu, 'A Proposed Framework for an Effective Africa Free Trade Area'.
33. B. Rippel, 'Why Trade Facilitation is Important for Africa', in World Bank 2012: 'De-Fragmenting Africa: Deepening Regional Trade Integration in Goods and Services.
34. UNCTAD, 'Economic Development in Africa Report 2013 – Intra African Trade: Unlocking Private Sector Dynamism'.
35. Rippel, 'Why Trade Facilitation is Important for Africa'.
36. Ibid.
37. UNCTAD, 'Economic Development in Africa Report 2013 – Intra African Trade: Unlocking Private Sector Dynamism'.
38. Ibid.
39. Ibid.
40. UNECA, Study Report on Mainstreaming Regional Integration into National Development Strategies and Plans. Economic Commission for Africa, Addis Ababa (2012b).

41. M. Stampini, R. Leung, S.M. Diarra and L. Pla, How Large Is the Private Sector in Africa? Evidence from National Accounts and Labour Markets, Institute for the Study of Labour, IZA Discussion Paper No. 6267 (2011).
42. UNCTAD, 'Economic Development in Africa Report 2013 – Intra African trade: unlocking private sector dynamism'.
43. A.O. K'Ombudo, East Africa Common Market Scorecard 2014: Tracking EAC Compliance in the Movement of Capital, Services and Goods. The World Bank, International Finance Corporation and East African Secretariat.
44. E. Iruobe, 'EAC Trade Climbed To $5.5bn In Last Decade' Ventures Africa magazine (2014).
45. UNCTAD, 'Trade Liberalisation, Investment and Economic Integration in African Regional Economic Communities towards the Africa Common Market' (2012).
46. Africa Practice, 'East Africa Integration: State of Play', Africa Practice InDepth (August 2014).
47. C.G. Ntim, 'Why African Stock Markets Should Formally Harmonise and Integrate Their Operations', *African Review of Economics and Finance* (Vol. 4, No. 1, December 2012).
48. Ntim, 'Why African Stock Markets Should Formally Harmonise and Integrate Their Operations'.
49. Ibid.
50. Ibid.
51. Ibid.
52. Ibid.
53. Ibid.
54. 'East Africa Exchange Launched in Kigali', *The New Times* (4 July 2014).
55. *Ibid.*
56. M.L. Oketch, 'Boos to Trade as Cross-Border Payment System Comes Live', *The East African* (7, December 2013).
57. Africa Practice, 'East Africa Integration: State of Play', Africa Practice InDepth, August 2014.
58. Africa Practice, 'East Africa Integration'.
59. M. Campioni and P. Noack, eds., *Rwanda Fast Forward: Social, Economic, Military and Reconciliation Prospects* (Palgrave Macmillan, 2012).
60. UNIDO, Tanzanian Industrial Competitiveness Report (2012).
61. World Bank Report, 'De-Fragmenting Africa: Deepening Regional Trade Integration in Goods and Services' (2012).
62. EAC Secretariat, 2006.
63. N. Moyo and A. Leke, 'Lessons Learned from the Airbus Success Story: A Template for Regional Integration', Unpublished (2014).
64. T. Creamer, 'Could Airbus Revive Africa's Stalled Economic Integration?' *Engineering News* (August 2014).
65. Moyo and Leke, 'Lessons Learned from the Airbus Success Story'.
66. African Development Bank, 'Regional Integration: The Importance of the Economy and Political Will', May 2014, AfDB Annual Meetings, Kigali, Rwanda.
67. Moyo and Leke, 'Lessons Learned from the Airbus Success Story'.
68. C. Peters-Berries, 'Regional Integration in Southern Africa – A Guidebook', Capacity Building, Germany (2010).
69. African Development Bank, Eastern African, Regional Integration Strategy Paper, 2011–2015 (September 2011).
70. K'Ombudo, East Africa Common Market Scorecard 2014.

71. Ibid.
72. Moyo and Leke, 'Lessons Learned from the Airbus Success Story'.
73. Creamer, 'Could Airbus Revive Africa's Stalled Economic Integration?.

Other Works Consulted

Chimhanzi, J. (2012). 'Whither Africa?' *Development*, Vol. 55, No. 4, pp. 503–508. Palgrave Macmillan.

Curtis, B. (2009). 'The Chirundu Border Post, Detailed Monitoring of Transit Times'. Sub-Saharan Africa Transport Policy Program (SSATP) Discussion Paper No. 10, World Bank.

ECA, AUC and AfDB (2010). Assessing Regional Integration in Africa IV. Enhancing Intra-African Trade. United Nations publication. Sales No. E.10.II.K.2. Addis Ababa.

Ihucha, A. (2 November 2013). 'Intra-EAC trade Rises 22pc, Defies Barriers and Politics'. *The East African.*

Ligami, C. (7 December 2013). 'Cost of Doing Business in EA Could Come Down as Non-Tariff Barriers Reduce'. *The East African.*

Oluoch-Ojiwah, F. (8 February 2013). Rwanda's Full Participation in EAC Provides Limitless Opportunities to its Economy, Trademark East Africa, http://www.hope-mag.com/news.php?option=lnews&ca=6&a=1227. Accessed 24 July 2014.

Rankin, N., Söderbom M. and Teal, F. (2006). 'Exporting from Manufacturing Firms in Sub-Saharan Africa.' *Journal of African Economies*, 15(4), 671–687.

Schwab, K. (ed.) (2014). The Global Competitiveness Report 2014–2015, World Economic Forum, Geneva.

TradeMark Southern Africa. (2011). 'Improving Service Delivery and Reducing Clearing Times at Chirundu Border Post'. TMSA Case Study Series, Pretoria.

——. (September 2013) General Equilibrium Analysis of the COMESA-EAC-SADC Tripartite FTA. Retrieved 25 November 2013 from http://trademarksa.org/sites/default/files/publications/2013-11-06 per cent20TFTA per cent20CGE per cent20-Impact per cent20Analysis per cent20IDS per cent20Final per cent20Report.pdf.

World Economic Forum. (2013). African Development Bank and The World Bank, The Africa Competitiveness Report 2013, World Economic Forum, Geneva.

WTO and OECD – AID-for-Trade Case Story. (2011). 'Improving Service Delivery and Reducing Clearing Times at Chirundu Border Post'.

4
Transport Infrastructure
Mark Pearson

Much has been written about Africa's lack of transport infrastructure and the detrimental effect poor transport infrastructure has on economic development. The Programme for Infrastructure Development in Africa (PIDA) Study Synthesis[1] shows that infrastructure plays a key role in economic growth and poverty reduction and that, conversely, the lack of infrastructure adversely affects productivity and raises production and transaction costs. This, in turn, hinders growth by reducing the competitiveness of businesses and the ability of governments to pursue economic and social development policies. According to the PIDA Study Synthesis, 'Deficient infrastructure in today's Africa has been found to sap growth by as much as 2 per cent a year (Calderón 2008)'.

The Africa Infrastructure Country Diagnostic (AICD)[2] estimated in 2009 that it would cost US$93 billion a year to raise Africa's infrastructure endowment to a reasonable level over the following decade, with the split in expenditure being two to one between investment and maintenance. The AICD report calculated that African countries already spend US$45 billion a year on infrastructure and that efficiency gains could raise an additional US$17 billion from within the existing envelope, leaving an annual funding gap of US$31 billion.

These headline figures highlight the daunting task African countries face if they are to take infrastructure to levels that will allow African-based firms and businesses to become competitive both within Africa and globally. In a lecture[3] in September 2014 at the London School of Economics, Donald Kaberuka, the President of the African Development Bank, said that African countries are now able to spend only about 5 per cent of their GDP on infrastructure, a figure which must rise to nearer 15 per cent. Even this figure of 15 per cent will not be enough for some countries. For example, the AICD report estimates that the so-called Fragile States would need to spend the equivalent of about 70 per cent of their GDP on infrastructure to close the perceived infrastructure gap and, without external support, this is obviously not a feasible proposition.

African countries do receive a considerable amount of external support in terms of infrastructure development so the continent is not facing this challenge totally alone. In 2010 total external commitments for African infrastructure were US$50.7 billion, but this represented a significant increase from the previous year of US$38.4 billion.[4] Investments in African infrastructure slowed down during the economic crisis of 2008, especially investments from the private sector, but since 2008 investments from the Infrastructure Consortium for Africa countries and from China have increased significantly.[5]

In addition, in recent years, a number of emerging economies have begun to play a more prominent role in the finance of infrastructure in Sub-Saharan Africa. Their combined resource flows are now comparable in scale to traditional official development assistance (ODA) from OECD countries or to capital from private investors. These non-OECD financiers include China, India and the Gulf states, with China being by far the largest player.

The AICD report also estimated, in 2009, that Africa's transport infrastructure required an average capital expenditure of US$10.7 billion per year for the following 10 years, which, at that time, was equivalent to 1.7 per cent of continental GDP, and an average of US$9.6 billion per year for the next 10 years in operating costs.

African countries are among the least competitive in the world, and infrastructure, combined with poor logistics and poorly implemented trade facilitation tools, is one of the main reasons for this lack of competitiveness. Short-term fixes can be made in other sectors where Africa faces economic and social challenges, such as importing skills and expertise, where these are lacking, and until African countries can build up their own skills bases, but the infrastructure deficit can only be addressed in the long term. Of equal importance in the infrastructure sector is the absolute need for infrastructural upgrading to be accompanied by a set of policy reforms and implementation modalities that will allow a more efficient service delivery using the improved infrastructure.

Efforts made to address Africa's infrastructure deficit

The shift in focus by the Organisation of African Unity (OAU) from political liberation to economic development in the last quarter of the twentieth century led to the design of a number of pan-African development approaches, such as the Lagos Plan of Action (1980), the Abuja Treaty (1991), and, of particular relevance to transport infrastructure, the adoption of the Trans-African Highway (TAH) concept by the OAU, with the TAH first proposed by the United Nations Economic Commission for Africa (UNECA) in 1971.

The TAH consists of nine main road corridors with a total length 59,100 km. As originally formulated, the proposal was to construct a network of all-weather roads of good quality connecting Africa's capital cities as directly as possible. This was to contribute to the political, economic and social integration and cohesion of Africa and to ensure road transport facilities between important areas of production and consumption.[6]

The nine highways[7] that made up the TAH programme were: Cairo-Dakar, Algiers-Lagos, Tripoli-Windhoek-Cape Town, Cairo-Gaborone-Cape Town, Dakar-Ndjamena, Ndjamena-Djibouti, Dakar-Lagos, Lagos-Mombasa, and Beira-Lobito.

Implementation of the Trans-African Highway project has not gone to plan. According to UNECA's most recent assessment in 2011,[8] 21 per cent of the TAH is still unconstructed, and in Central Africa only 3,891 km of a planned 11,246 km of roads have been paved, meaning that, after more than four decades, 65 per cent of the planned roads remain unconstructed in that region. Only one of the nine original roads, a 4,400-km stretch across the Sahel, connecting Dakar in Senegal to Ndjamena in Chad, is completed. All eight of the other routes are missing significant links.

The African Development Bank's (AfDB) 'Review of the Implementation Status of the Trans-African Highways and the Missing Links: Volume 1: Main Report,' published in 2003, reported that the completion and development of the TAH concept would depend on the following factors, amongst other things:

- determination of a minimum standard for TAH and the gradual harmonising of the axle load and total weight regulations;
- the very high cost of completing the TAH network makes the application of a least cost approach and a careful priority setting (through feasibility studies) a must in the planning for the improvement of existing links in the system, including the completion of missing links; and
- the role of the private sector in the funding of the TAH network needs to be given more attention.

All three of these recommendations are key to the successful development of the road transport sector in Africa. However, none of them have actually been implemented. Standards for construction are not harmonised, meaning that road quality, even at construction, varies widely. As axle loads and vehicle dimensions have also not been harmonised, it means that cross-border traffic is disrupted and causes time delays, which pushes up transport costs. For example, most countries in Eastern and Southern Africa have a gross vehicle mass (GVM) limit of 56 tonnes[9] applied to trucks using the road networks, which allows the use of truck and semi-trailer seven-axle combinations (referred to as interlinks in some parts of Africa) with an overall length of 22 metres. The tare weight of an interlink is 24 tonnes so the allowed cargo weight, before a vehicle is considered to be carrying an abnormal load, is 32 tonnes. If an interlink crosses a border into a country with a different set of vehicle specifications (such as a GVM of 48 tonnes or a vehicle length restriction of less than 22 metres or a maximum allowable number of six axles on a vehicle before an abnormal load license is required), then the logistics of the whole journey are affected. If one country or one bridge, or river crossing by pontoon, has a GVM of 48 tonnes on a transport corridor that is otherwise regulated with a GVM of 56 tonnes, then the entire journey would need to be completed with a load and vehicle with a GVM of 48 tonnes and a payload of 24 tonnes instead of 32 tonnes. This represents a payload reduction of 25 per cent which obviously means higher transport costs per kilometre for the importer or exporter, which may make the import or export sub-economic.

The TAH has at least been a major push to develop Africa's continental roads. There have not been similar initiatives in other modes of transport in Africa. The railway sector, in particular, has seen a catastrophic decline in quality of service delivery. Railway infrastructure and public-sector owned and managed railway companies were allowed to deteriorate almost, in some instances, to a point of no return. The reliability of most of Africa's national railway networks, with the exception of South Africa, is now extremely poor; accident and failure rates are high, operating costs are also high, and, in general, the volumes of goods transported by rail are so low as to be uneconomical and most, if not all, national railways are financially loss-making. However, recently, some countries have started to make concerted efforts to improve their national railway systems. This return to recognising the potential of railways in an African context owes much to the fact that the road sector can no longer cope with the volumes of cargo that are being transported. Putting so much cargo onto Africa's roads has resulted in high wear and tear on the road network, associated high costs of road rehabilitation and maintenance and congestion at border crossings. All of these factors contribute to delays in freight movement and escalating costs of imports and exports. In addition, there are environmental, safety and economic benefits to moving certain goods, such as fuel, acid, coal, minerals, cement and grain, in bulk by rail rather than by road.

In revitalising their railway systems, some African countries are laying new standard-gauge rail track, sometimes as dual track and electrified, and procuring new rolling stock and locomotives. However, if railways are to become viable once again, much more than revamping infrastructure needs to happen. The reasons for the decline of Africa's railways are many and include a lack of investment in the railways and poor management, coupled with the rise in importance of the road sector which has received high levels of public sector investment and subsidies.[10] Of equal importance has been the deregulation of the road sector compared to the rail sector, and this, coupled with advances in technology, has allowed trucks to carry higher payloads at lower costs. Therefore, if railways are to be a major component in an improved transport and logistics system for Africa, then improved infrastructure will need to be accompanied with policy reforms, revised regulations, and, most importantly, improved management. It is not enough to construct a standard-gauge, electrified, high-speed rail track and not put in regulations and processes to allow service providers to make efficient and effective use of this state-of-the-art infrastructure.

African ports and harbours have been modernised, developed and deepened and capacities have been expanded by national governments and through concessioning, but this has not been done in any continentally sequenced or coordinated manner, and these infrastructure upgrades have not been integrated with other modes of surface transport or by taking into account the continent's other ports and their capabilities. In addition, the introduction of larger and larger cargo vessels have transformed the economics of maritime transport. The Maersk Triple-E class of container ship are 400 m long and 59 m wide and have a draft of 14.5 m, making them too large to use the Panama Canal but not too large for the Suez Canal. More important, however, is the fuel efficiency of this class of ship, which is the lowest per TEU of any ship.[11] The ship is powered by two 32 MW (43,000 hp), ultra-long, two-stroke, diesel engines driving two propellers at a design speed of 19 knots (35 km/h; 22 mph) for 'slow-steaming' which lowers fuel consumption by about 37 per cent and carbon dioxide emissions per TEU by about 50 per cent.[12] The Maersk Triple-E class of ships, when fully introduced, will predominantly be used to service routes between Asia and Europe. Owing to the size and draft of the Triple-E class of ships (and because of the size, special ship-to-shore cranes are required for loading and off-loading), the number of ports capable of being able to accept fully laden Triple-E class ships, carrying 18,000 TEUs, is very limited. There are, currently, no African ports that can accommodate a fully laden Triple-E class of ship, with the largest ports in Africa, these being in South Africa, Morocco and Egypt, being limited to handling, at most, post-Panamax ships that have a capacity of between 5,000 and 10,000 TEUs.[13] If, in future, African traders are to benefit from the efficiencies of a Triple-E class ship, then cargo from and to Europe and Asia will need to be landed at a port that can accommodate a Triple-E class ship that is on, or close to, the main Europe-Asia shipping lanes. This means that the continent's policy makers should agree on one or two 'hub' ports for Africa that could be developed to take the largest container vessels (or agree to use a port outside of Africa) and a system of feeder ports that will deliver containers to the hub port(s) so that cargo can be loaded onto larger ships for delivery to Asia and Europe and the reverse for imports.

Airports on the continent have been developed at a fast pace and many of Africa's international airports have improved their facilities so that they are able to take the world's largest passenger aeroplanes, such as the Airbus A380. However, the fact remains that air transport would have been considerably more efficient and competitive if these improvements in infrastructure had been accompanied with the full implementation of the 1999 Yamoussoukro Declaration by all African governments. The Yamoussoukro

Declaration, concerning the liberalisation of access to air transport markets in Africa, remains the single most important African air transport reform policy initiative.

Enter the New Partnership for Africa's Development (NEPAD), a coming together of two initiatives, South Africa's Thabo Mbeki's Millennium Africa Recovery Plan (MAP) and Senegal's Abdoulaye Wade's Omega Plan, which were merged to create the New African Initiative (NAI). The need for further compromises saw the morphing of the NAI into NEPAD in 2001.

Since its ratification by the African Union in 2002, NEPAD has been promoted widely both within Africa and by Africa's Cooperating Partners and is seen as the mechanism by which support to Africa's development efforts can be best delivered. Thus, the NEPAD process has come to be accepted as the way forward and as the framework for their development efforts not only by African countries and Regional Economic Communities (RECs) but also by Africa's Development Partners.

The component of NEPAD that addresses infrastructure is the Programme for Infrastructure Development in Africa, a continent-wide programme to develop a vision and strategic framework for the development of regional and continental infrastructure. The PIDA initiative is being led by the African Union Commission (AUC), the NEPAD Secretariat and the African Development Bank. One of the strengths of PIDA is that it builds on the past efforts of the Organisation of African Union and the African Union to promote the development of Africa's infrastructure. PIDA is not, therefore, a re-invention of the wheel and merges various existing continental infrastructure initiatives, such as the NEPAD Short Term Action Plan, the NEPAD Medium to Long Term Strategic Framework (MLTSF), and the AU Infrastructure Master Plans initiatives, into one coherent programme for the entire continent. It aims to put in place an adequate, cost-effective and sustainable regional infrastructure base to promote Africa's socio-economic development and integration into the global economy, and this is instantly recognisable as being consistent with the overall aims and objectives of the African Union.

The sectoral focus of PIDA is Energy, Transport, Information and Communication Technologies (ICT) and Trans-boundary Water Resources. Simplistically put, PIDA is a collection of infrastructure projects the AU member states and the regional organisations consider to be priority infra-structure projects and vital for the development of Africa with an investment cost of US$68 billion up to the year 2020. It provides the strategic framework for African stakeholders to build the infrastructure necessary for more inte-grated networks to boost trade, promote economic growth and create jobs through deeper regional integration and linkages into the global economy. Successful implementation of PIDA is, therefore, intended to enhance Africa's competitiveness within itself and in the global economy, while acting as a catalyst to Africa's economic transformation.

A sub-set of the full list of PIDA projects is the Priority Action Programme (PAP) list of projects which, as the name suggests, are the projects in the PIDA full list that should be developed and implemented as a priority and before the other projects in PIDA.

A database (AID – African Infrastructure Database) for PIDA is being developed to assist in the coordination and implementation of the programme. The Virtual PIDA Information Centre (VPIC) is the central technology mechanism to support monitoring and reporting of regional projects in all RECs. Stakeholders will access the project data and related reports through the front-end interface of VPIC, which then becomes the central information management system for all information related to PIDA projects. With VPIC, the NEPAD Planning and Coordination Agency (NPCA) is able to facilitate sharing of PIDA-PAP information, promote participation in PIDA implementation, enable tracking of progress in PIDA implementation, and promote investment opportunities in PIDA-PAP projects.

VPIC can be accessed via www.au-pida.org. The VIPC software enables the AID database to be interfaced with the COMESA-EAC-SADC regional infrastructure database developed by TradeMark Southern Africa.[14] The VPIC also allows users to browse through, search, filter and view the decomposed projects of the PIDA Priority Action Programme in so-called project fiches, thus giving the users the needed information on each project and its implementation status. VPIC allows the RECs to collect information on PIDA-PAP projects at national and regional levels and to populate AID accordingly, thus making up-to-date PIDA project information accessible in VPIC. At the time of writing, project information in the African Infrastructure database is far from complete but there are a number of programmes supporting the AU member states, the RECs and NEPAD to collect information on priority infrastructure projects so that these projects can be prepared and hence moved towards a stage where they can be financed and implemented.

In 2013–2014, the 51 original PIDA priority infrastructure programmes were decomposed into 433 discrete projects. Detailed project fiches were generated for 83 of these projects and documented in reports. In parallel, the COMESA-EAC-SADC Tripartite has entered just over 600 priority projects into the Tripartite Regional Infrastructure Projects Database (TRIPDA; see www.tripartitegis.org). Since TRIPDA offered a consolidated dataset for four (including IGAD) of the eight RECs, with a combined membership of 26 countries, but not yet including South Sudan or Somalia, it made sense to build AID on the back of TRIPDA.

Recently, efforts have been made to review the pipeline of the 433 projects and the list of 83 for which project fiches were generated. These have been rationalised and cleaned up and the process of mapping the PIDA and TRIPDA projects has started and is well under way.

Not only have there been great strides made in the technical aspects of the Programme for Infrastructure Development for Africa, but there remains significant political support as well. At their 22nd Ordinary Session of the Assembly of the Union on 31 January 2014, the Heads of State and Government of the African Union agreed on a Common African Position on the post-2015 Development Agenda and, in terms of infrastructure development, also that accelerating Africa's infrastructural development is pivotal to connect African people, countries and economies as well as to help drive social, cultural and economic development. In this regard, the AUC Heads of State and Government stated that they were determined to:

1. develop and maintain reliable, sustainable, environmentally friendly and affordable infrastructure in both rural and urban areas with a focus on land, water and air transport and storage facilities, clean water and sanitation, energy, waste management and information and communication technologies (ICTs);
2. implement infrastructure projects that facilitate intra-African trade and regional and continental integration including, with the assistance of the international community, enhancing research and technological development and the provision of adequate financial resources; and
3. promote the delivery of infrastructure programmes to generate local jobs, strengthen domestic skills and enterprise development, as well as enhance technological capability.

Challenges faced in developing Africa's Infrastructure

From the previous section, it becomes clear that Africa is on the right track in terms of developing the infrastructure it requires for its social and economic development, with the continued global support of NEPAD and PIDA. However, the challenges still faced by Africa in its quest to develop its infrastructure should not be under-estimated. Going back to the aforementioned lecture by Donald Kaberuka given at the London School of Economics,[15] the President of the African Development Bank highlighted three major challenges to be overcome in Africa to ensure sustainability, these being integration, institutions and infrastructure – what he termed as 'the three I's'. As regards infrastructure, President Kaberuka outlined the main ways to close Africa's infrastructure financing gap as being: de-risking (such as broadening and deepening risk mitigation instruments); building a pipeline of bankable projects; developing template standard contracts; and addressing the present apprehensions of non-African Sovereign Wealth Funds, Pension Funds, and so on in investing in Africa's infrastructure.

Financing of infrastructure projects involves considerable risks, which diminish as the project moves from concept stage, to pre-feasibility, to feasibility, to design and finally to implementation stages. The most risk faced by financiers in funding a project is in the early stages of the project. If an infrastructure project has access to even a small amount of grant funds, or a soft loan, then these funds could be most usefully applied to reduce risk, such as using these grant funds or soft loan to reduce debt repayments or as an equity investment that would give comfort to other investors who are either providing loans or who are also equity investors. De-risking a project in this way can make all the difference as to whether or not the project is 'bankable' or not.

Building a pipeline of bankable projects is currently being addressed through PIDA. However, in a paper entitled 'Unlocking Private Finance for African Infrastructure,'[16] Paul Collier and Colin Meyer make the point that 'the combination of political complexity and the lack of African public sector specialist teams able to prepare projects mean that there is no pipeline of projects ready for funding'. The authors suggest a range of strategic uses of public money in infrastructure financing and conclude that to generate a pipeline of bankable projects there is a need for catalytic finance for specialist teams equipped not just with technicians but with political entrepreneurs who can overcome veto players. There have been attempts to establish these specialist teams as suggested by Collier and Meyer, such as the COMESA-EAC-SADC Tripartite Task Force's Project Preparation and Implementation Unit (PPIU), but these attempts have been half-hearted at best and lack strong political support from the RECs and the REC member countries themselves.

The development banks have been developing templates for standard contracts so, in addressing president Kaberuka's list of ways to close Africa's infrastructure financing gap, this leaves the issue of the present apprehensions of non-African Sovereign Wealth Funds, Pension Funds, and so on to investing in Africa's infrastructure. There are a number of recent initiatives involving the use of public funds to encourage private financiers to invest in African infrastructure projects such as the Africa50 initiative and the Private Infrastructure Development Group (PIDG), a multi-donor organisation led by DFID, the aim of which is to encourage private infrastructure investment in developing countries using a range of facilities and investment vehicles which provide varying types of financial, practical and strategic support in order to realise this objective. Support for infrastructure under the European Union's Eleventh European Development Fund will also use blending and leveraging mechanisms and instruments which should reduce risk and act as a facility which should encourage inclusion of investments from Sovereign Wealth Funds, pension funds and other private sector investment funds into Africa's infrastructure. However, as Collier and Mayer also note, the inability of Africa to finance its infrastructure requirements is not a capacity constraint but an institutional and organisational one and, as such, needs an imaginative approach which goes beyond what has been attempted to date.

There are also other practical constraints that need to be addressed if Africa is to develop its transport infrastructure to the levels required to support sustainable economic development. One major issue is how African policy makers prioritise infrastructure projects, and here it is suggested that a para digm shift in thinking about how projects are designed and prioritised is required.

There are a number of ways in which infrastructure projects can be prioritised, including using political, geographical, financial, economic and social criteria. The reality is that infrastructure projects, at least in Africa, are selected on the basis of some or all of these criteria in combination but, if the project is to stand any chance of being financed (meaning that it has to be considered by financiers to be bankable[17]), then it must at least be seen to be economically, if not financially, viable. The main concerns about the systems used in prioritising infrastructure projects in Africa are that they are backward-looking (as opposed to forward-looking) and the projects themselves are usually evaluated in isolation to other projects and other factors that will affect the projects viability. For example, it is possible to evaluate the feasibility of a bridge across a river independently from the railway the bridge is a part of or the port the railway services, but this evaluation of a project out of context will lead to an unrealistic prioritisation of regional projects. In the transport sector it is probably sensible to prioritise transport/transit corridors and then the individual projects on the corridors that are needed to get the corridor to an efficient corridor which, if managed efficiently, will reduce transport costs and make African producers more competitive. But this is not how transport infrastructure in Africa is prioritised.

The PIDA-Priority Action Programme was compiled through a consultative process where NEPAD asked the RECs to obtain priority projects from their member states that were considered to be at least economically (if not financially) viable and which could be considered to be regional[18] (rather than purely national) in nature. There are a number of constraints in using this project selection methodology.

The first constraint is derived from the fact that transport infrastructure project planning is done on the basis of what was economically relevant in the past and not planning transport infrastructure for the future.

According to various World Bank and African Development Bank publications, and as quoted in the Agence Française de Développement (AFD) and World Bank joint publication entitled 'Youth Employment in Sub-Saharan Africa,' published in January 2014, Sub-Saharan Africa has just experienced a decade of unprecedented economic growth, with the GDP growing at a rate of 4.5 per cent a year on average between 2000 and 2012, compared to around 2 per cent for the previous 20 years. In 2012, the region's GDP growth was estimated at 4.7 per cent and at 5.8 per cent if South Africa was excluded. About one-quarter of countries in the region grew at 7 per cent or more, and several African countries are among the fastest growing in the world and medium-term growth prospects remain strong. In just over a decade, Africa has graduated from being the *Economist* magazine's 'Hopeless Continent' (May 2000) to a continent with a bright future ('Africa Rising'; December 2011). These impressive economic growth figures are based on a strongly performing global economy but a global economy in which Africa is largely not participating. Economic growth which is reliant on a demand for commodities is neither sustainable nor inclusive. It is not sustainable as it is dependent on demand and relatively high prices in markets that are not controlled by the supplier, and it is not inclusive because exports of largely unprocessed commodities are not job-creating and so a small elite (which is not necessarily based in the African country that is the supplier) benefits.

Already, Africa is the second-largest and second most populous continent on earth with an estimated population in 2013 of 1.1 billion people. The Population Reference Bureau (www.prb.org) estimates that Africa's population doubled between 1982 and 2009 and is expected to almost double again to a total of about 2.4 billion people by 2050 and to quadruple in 90 years, by the turn of the twenty-first century. The boom in Africa's population will be in Sub-Sahara. Nigeria, a country the size of Texas, is projected to have a population of about 1 billion by the turn of the century and, as China's population shrinks and India's population plateaus, Nigeria is projected to be the most populous country on earth. Tanzania, 13 years ago, had a population of 34 million, which has now grown to 45 million but is projected to reach 276 million by 2100, which is close to the current population of the United States.

The implication of combining increases in wealth with population increases is that Africa will have a sizable middle class, with significant amounts of disposable income, by 2050. This constitutes a sizable African production base and consumer market. Yet, although 2050 is only 35 years away, there appears to be little effort being made to plan what infrastructure will be required to service the demands and expectations of this African production and consumer base. Instead, policy makers are using the rear-view mirror as their main planning tool and are still assuming that Africa needs large and efficient transport corridors to African sea ports to export largely raw materials and import consumer and manufactured items. More realistically, the actual case could be that Africa needs to start to construct transport networks to join up African centres that will become production and consumption centres where greater value addition of Africa's raw materials and food crops is done within Africa and consumed within Africa and with less export of raw materials and basic commodities.

A further constraint could be that many of the projects listed in PIDA may not be economically or financially viable. There are a number of projects in PIDA, which are, by definition, classified as priority projects necessary for Africa's economic development and which have been priority regional projects for decades but which have not been implemented. For example, the first detailed survey of a railway route between Zambia and Zimbabwe across the Zambezi rift valley, crossing the Zambezi River at or near Chirundu, was done in 1916. The purpose was to reduce the haul distance of copper from the Copperbelt as the existing railway line followed the watershed through present-day Zambia and crossed into present-day Zimbabwe at Victoria Falls. A line from the railhead at Kafue to the railhead at Lions Den would cut hundreds of kilometres off the journey and hence save money in transport. Another survey of the 'short-cut' route was done in 1932 to shorten the proposed 1916 route even more, and yet another survey was done in 1953 (because construction of the Kariba Dam necessitated another 'short-cut' track realignment) and more studies and surveys have been done since then.

This infrastructure project was first proposed almost a century ago and yet construction has not started. The inclusion of this project into PIDA is presumably on the assumption that there have never been sufficient funds to construct this railway line, ignoring the fact that this line may no longer be financially or economically viable or that this proposed route may no longer be important for DR Congo or Zambia as alternative routes to regional coastal ports that now exist. The Kafue–Loins Den railway project may, on the other hand, be financially or economically viable, but there is insufficient information for this to be determined. This is the case for many PIDA projects, and if there is insufficient information to do an economic or financial evaluation it is difficult to prioritise a project. If the project is justified purely on political or social criteria, then it is unlikely to be bankable; and if it is not bankable, it is unlikely to be implemented.

Most projects in PIDA are at the concept stage; hence, until there is a feasibility study done, there is no way of determining whether these projects are viable. Despite the finances that are being made available for infrastructure projects, it remains the case that it is difficult to get funding to do pre-feasibility and feasibility studies. Thus, and to avoid a situation where NEPAD would have to carry out a multitude of feasibility studies, NEPAD adopted the PIDA-PAP, which is a sub-set of all PIDA projects that have been developed beyond the concept stage. Using the parlance of PIDA, PIDA-PAP projects should be classified as being at the S2 or S3 project preparation stage (where S1 = early concept proposal; S2 = feasibility/needs assessment; S3 = programme/project structuring and promotion to obtain financing; S3/S4 = financing and roll out; and S4 = implementation and operation). If a project is classified as being in the S1 stage, it is unlikely that it will be ready for implementation within the next five–seven years, and if a project is in the S4 stage, it will, most likely, already have secured financing. Therefore, by definition, projects in the PIDA-PAP have had a feasibility study done and so have been a priority project possibly for quite some time. However, given the rapid changes taking place in Africa, and advances being made in engineering techniques, unless the feasibility study has been done in the recent past, it may no longer be valid and may need to be redone.

Project feasibility also needs to be appropriately interpreted. For example, in engineering terms, it may be feasible to build a bridge across a river. But, unless the bridge is evaluated as part of a transport or trade corridor, the project, in isolation, will not be viable. The purpose of building trade and transport infrastructure is, primarily, to reduce the cost of doing business and, for a regional project, to reduce the cost of cross-border business. It is, therefore, important that an infrastructure project be synchronised with other infrastructure and with the existing regulatory and administrative environment. Transport infrastructure projects need to be synchronised with other infrastructure projects along a transport corridor so that each infrastructure project re-enforces the impact of the next project and the cumulative result is a more efficient transport and logistics system. The same is the case for synchronising infrastructure with regulatory, legal and administrative regimes – such as ensuring a road rehabilitation project is done together with an axle-load control regime and a periodic and regular maintenance regime so that the investment in the road is sustainable and meets value-for-money criteria.

An example of measuring the viability of an infrastructure project as part of a transport corridor can be found on the North-South Corridor (NSC) road network. In this case, the University of Birmingham,[19] England, did a road-condition analysis, using a regional HDM-4 approach to assess the condition of the entire NSC road network of about 8,000 km. HDM-4 is a software package and tool used by all Roads Departments/Agencies in countries the North-South Corridor traverses to analyse, plan, manage and appraise road maintenance, improvements and investment decisions. From the NSC regional (total corridor) HDM-4 analysis, roads were categorised into those that were in good condition, fair condition and poor condition, based on the International Roughness Index (IRI). A maintenance schedule, which was costed, was devised; this, when implemented, would bring the entire road corridor to a fair-to-good condition. The benefit of bringing the entire road corridor to a fair-to-good condition, combined with a saving of time at border crossings (50 per cent saving of time on average), was then calculated as a net present value (NPV). In this way individual sections of the corridor, be these roads, border posts, or bridges, could be prioritised in terms of the impact the upgrading of that particular piece of infrastructure would have on the service delivery performance of the transport corridor as a totality.

This holistic approach to project selection and prioritisation is missing in PIDA, at least in the transport sector, meaning that scarce resources may not be allocated, primarily, to projects and programmes where there is the highest return on investment in terms of improved service delivery and logistics efficiencies. In addition, PIDA projects are derived from a 'backward-looking' (rear-view mirror) approach to planning. The PIDA project planning process does not start from where Africa wants to be in 2050 and work back from there – instead it starts from where Africa was in the last century and assumes that the economic growth trajectory will be the same as it was in the past century in terms of infrastructure. This scenario, where Africa will need 'more of the same' going into the twenty-first century, is highly unlikely owing to Africa's rapid population and economic growth contributing to a rising middle class with disposable income, constituting a market for consumer goods, combined with exponential technological advances, especially in communications.

Conclusion

In conclusion, steady progress is being made in addressing Africa's perceived infrastructure deficit by African governments, international cooperating partners, private sector investors and development banks, and within the framework of a continental plan, this being the Programme for Infrastructure Development in Africa. Considerable effort, and good progress, has also been made in addressing Africa's infrastructure financing gap. This has been done by bringing new financial instruments to the market, such as the African Development Bank's Africa50 facility, by African countries benefitting from flexible financing mainly from China, through more effective and efficient use of public-private partnerships, and through the blending and leveraging of grants and soft loans to mitigate against risk, especially in the early stages of project development.

However, despite these very promising and positive developments, it is not certain that the transport infrastructure being planned and developed under PIDA will meet the needs of Africa in the future. The Africa of the future will be considerably more populous and affluent than it is today and will need a transport network that will link production centres in Africa with markets in Africa. Currently, there is no mechanism in Africa's infrastructure planning methods, including PIDA, to ensure that the infrastructure to be built is going to link these new internal markets with new internal industrial centres and agricultural production. Infrastructure planning in Africa is not referenced to the future economic development strategies of the African continent. The Trans-African Highway network conceived in the early 1970s, and reflecting a political regional integration ambition of joining up Africa's major capital cities, is still a PIDA priority; standard-gauge railways are being planned mainly on a national, and not regional, basis and where there are regional railway plans, such as in EAC, the projects are not financially viable and need to be financed from treasury; there is no continental 'hub and spoke' plan for maritime transport to take account of the global reality of using bigger and bigger ships for inter-continental maritime transport; and airports are planned primarily to serve national interests, with greater air transport freedoms given to non-African carriers than African carriers, reflecting poor implementation of the Yamoussoukro Declaration concerning the liberalisation of access to air transport markets in Africa.

In essence, Africa's infrastructure development plans are still heavily biased towards political, rather than economic, continental and regional integration considerations. This is clearly seen in the list of PIDA projects that reflect a geo-political balancing act rather than the outcome of a hard-nosed financial and economic analysis. Given that the primary goal of most decision-makers in the world of high-finance is to make as much money as possible in as short a time as possible and with the least amount of risk possible, it is not surprising that finance for most of Africa's priority transport infrastructure projects is hard to secure.

If Africa's infrastructure gap is to be closed and done so in a way that reflects Africa's future infrastructure needs, a more balanced approach to infrastructure planning will be required, with less emphasis placed on political factors and more on economic and financial factors. In essence, the continental infrastructure plan will need to start with where Africa wants to be in, say 2050, and what production systems should be prioritised. This could best be done using a value-chain analysis where, for instance, a region would prioritise value addition in certain sectors where there is a perceived comparative or competitive advantage, such as in agro-processing and mineral beneficiation (upstream and downstream). The transport infrastructure that is required to achieve this value addition can then be planned and, once planned, checked for feasibility and bankability, although this also assumes the availability of funds to carry out feasibility and pre-feasibility which, for large infrastructure projects, run into the millions of dollars in costs. The end result would be a greatly strengthened and more credible PIDA and a plan for transport infrastructure that stands a chance of meeting Africa's future needs.

Notes

1. Study on Programme for Infrastructure Development in Africa (PIDA) Phase III PIDA Study Synthesis. Prepared in September 2011 for the African Development Bank, NEPAD, and the African Union Commission by a consortium headed by SOFRECO.
2. Vivien Foster and Cecilia Briceño-Garmendia, Africa Infrastructure Country Diagnostic Report. World Bank.
3. http://www.lse.ac.uk/publicEvents/pdf/2014-MT/20140923-Kaberuka-Transcript. pdf.
4. R. Schiere and A. Rugamba, 'Chinese Infrastructure Investments and African Integration', AfDB Working Paper 127, May 2011.
5. For a detailed analysis of the trends in external support to the African infrastructure sector, see ibid.
6. Review of the Implementation Status of the Trans-African Highways and the Missing Links: Volume 1: Main Report. Africa Development Bank (SWECO INTERNATIONAL/NCG/UNICONSULT/BNEDT), 2003.
7. For a map of the proposed Trans-African Highways, see: http://mapsof.net/map/ map-of-trans-african-highways.

8. Quoted in an article entitled 'Trans-African Highway Remains a Road to Nowhere', http://www.howwemadeitinafrica.com/trans-african-highway-remains-a-road-to-nowhere/39863/.

9. According to the Truck Drivers' Guide for Ghana, http://www.borderlesswa.com/ sites/default/files/ resources/aug10/Drivers%20Guide%20to%20Ghana%20small. pdf, UMEOA and ECOWAS implemented a new GVM regime in January 2011, but it should be mentioned that ECOWAS has made several attempts over the years to achieve intra-regional harmonisation of axle loads as specified in the ECOWAS Land Transport Programme but, as yet, regional harmonisation has not been achieved.

10. In most Sub-Saharan African countries roads are regarded as a public good and the construction, maintenance, and rehabilitation of roads have been covered using public funds from donors and the government budget. Although recently there have been moves to introduce taxes, such as fuel tax, to finance the upkeep of the road network, and the introduction of road tolls, it is still the case that road users are subsidised from public funds. Conversely, railways operate on a user-pays-all basis with no, or very small, public sector subsidies.

11. The name 'Triple-E' is, apparently, derived from the class's three design principles: 'Economy of scale, Energy efficient and Environmentally improved'.

12. http://en.wikipedia.org/wiki/Maersk_Triple_E_class.

13. Ports in Djibouti, Sudan, Nigeria, and Namibia can now accommodate vessels with a capacity of around 4,000 TEUs.

14. TradeMark Southern Africa (www.trademarksa.org) was a DFID-funded programme that supported COMESA, EAC, and SADC in trade policy, including the design and negotiations of the COMESA-EAC-SADC Tripartite Free Trade Agreement, trade facilitation, and infrastructure planning and development but which closed in March 2014.

15. http://www.lse.ac.uk/publicEvents/pdf/2014-MT/20140923-Kaberuka-Transcript.pdf.

16. http://novafrica.org/papers%20financial%20conference/Paul%20Collier.pdf.

17. There are some situations where a project may not be proved to be economically or financially viable by an independent source, but the project still goes ahead. This is particularly the case where a country requests financing (usually on the basis of a turn-key project where the financer, in effect, selects the constructor) and repayments are made by the national treasury rather than from user fees from the project itself. This is the model commonly used by the Chinese where funding for an infrastructure project comes from, usually, China Exim Bank, and the contractor is a Chinese company which is paid directly by, in this case, China Exim Bank.

18. For a project to be regional in nature, it is either located in two or more countries (such as a dam on a river bordering two countries or a road, railway, or power transmission line that traverses two or more countries) or it is located in one country but the infrastructure services more than one country (such as a port or a section of a regional transport corridor – road or rail or power transmission line – located in one country).

19. The University of Birmingham is part of HDMGlobal, an international consortium of academic and consultancy companies that have formed a partnership for the future management of HDM-4.

5
The Growth of Continental African Brands

Nicholas J.W. Kühne

To gain a better understanding of the drivers behind the recent growth of consumer brands across Africa, two very important demographic groups need to be highlighted.

The first is the 'basic needs consumer' a distinct group of around 220 million people. This group is the bread and butter for packaged food companies such as Tiger Brands, Dangote, Golden Penny, Wilmar and similar commodity suppliers across the continent. The second, and more interesting, group is the African 'middle class' believed to represent around 340 million individuals.

Africa's middle class has tripled over the past 30 years, with one in three people now considered to be living above the poverty line. The current trajectory suggests the African middle class will grow to 1.1 billion (42 per cent) in 2060.[1]

Although this is a massive number of people, the African middle class is in no way similar to the North American or European understanding of the term 'middle class'. The African Development Bank defines the African middle class as individuals who spend between $2 and $20 a day.

The Chinese middle class (which is currently of comparable size) is defined as individuals spending between $25 and $94 a day. A much better prospect for business! Nevertheless, there is an increasing interest in doing business in Africa by companies from countries as diverse as Brazil and Thailand.

Branded consumer goods play an important role particularly in the basic needs consumer set. If a consumer spends $2 a day, he or she cannot (and will not) continue to buy a product that doesn't meet his or her (albeit modest) expectations. Essentially, a brand's message is a promise of quality; the producers of the item guarantee a certain level of quality and the consumer has recourse if the product doesn't fulfil its promises.

This is one set of reasons why *international* brands are generally regarded as more trustworthy than local brands. It is well known, for instance, that the detergent branded OMO is not going to burn the users' hands or destroy clothing, and therefore the manufacturer is able to charge a premium and the consumer doesn't pay grudgingly. But this attitude is slowly changing, and increasingly, local brands are now beginning to offer a similar degree of confidence to consumers, thereby creating a genuine threat to established multi-national brands.

Wunderbrand, a company dealing with branding in Africa, refers to 1950s American style advertising campaigns when considering up and coming consumers. A major insight discerned by Wunderbrand is the phenomenon of 'firsts' in many African countries with emerging economies – the first trip to a cinema, first microwave oven, first credit card or first restaurant experience; many of the middle class and basic needs consumers are beginning to experience activities, products and services for the very first time.

Because new consumers require educating, education is the first and most important element when marketing a product. A brand which understands this clearly is Nando's. Many years ago, Nando's subtly promoted their offering as a 'first restaurant experience' for the new up and coming middle class in South Africa – migrating up from takeaway chicken meals like KFC (international brand) and Chicken Licken (local).

Continental African brands making their mark

The impact of international brands in Africa during the past hundred years or so is clear. Unilever, Nestlé and others have cornered the lion's share in many consumer markets in Africa and continue to grow their footprint as they seek new markets.

However, there are many local brands with strong positions in local markets and more of them are beginning to expand in their local territories while also branching out into neighbouring countries. This is resulting in a tougher time for multi-nationals, as strong indigenous brands begin to make their mark.

There are many positive spin-offs from this growth in African brands.

African brands that have made a mark – legacy brands

Throughout Africa there are legacy brands that form part of the day-to-day purchases by local consumers. These include the obvious international brands such as Coca-Cola, PZ Cussons and Unilever. In the past few decades, local fast moving consumer goods (FMCG) brands have been actively competing with international brands. The monopolies colonial and other foreign interests were able to establish in the continent for most of the previous century meant that most if not all branded products were imported or set up by British, American, French or Portuguese companies. An example is Lever Brothers (now Unilever) who started operations in Nigeria in 1923 and now owns large swathes of market share in all of the sectors it operates in.

Similarly, PZ Cussons was founded in 1879 as a trading post in Sierra Leone and now has a big footprint across West Africa. Probably the sole early and best-known African luxury brand was a dessert wine from Groot Constantia in South Africa. The wine became unavailable for decades until 2003 when the estate began production of a dessert wine, called Grand Constance, for the first time since the 1880s. In the nineteenth century, the wine was acknowledged as Napoleon's, Sir Walter Scott's and the French king Louis Philippe's favourite tipple.

African brands that are starting to make a mark – new entrants (b-brands)

Sanctions, liberalisation, indigenisation, nationalism, industrialisation, population growth and a variety of other factors have powered the growth of home grown brands, typically in protected industries such as cement (Dangote) and sugar and flour, but also in areas where getting a product to market is based on local understanding and empathy. A product such as the Gala sausage roll produced by UAC foods/Tiger Brands is synonymous with rush hour traffic in Lagos.

'Globacom' is one of the largest indigenous mobile networks in West Africa, which unfortunately has come under pressure due to the nature of its ownership structure and lack of growth outside its primary Nigerian market. It is nevertheless well placed to make a mark in the region, but will need to compete in a category that is fast becoming commoditised.

'Kasapreko', an alcoholic beverage company started in 1989 in Ghana, has been progressively building its brand presence across the continent. Its flagship brand Alomo Bitters, an aromatic herb-based liquor, is enjoyed in bars and taverns from Accra to Cape Town. They are also attempting to expand further afield in order to take advantage of the growing demand for alcoholic beverages on the continent.

A prolific advertiser at airports, GT Bank prides itself as being 'the African bank'. Although not nearly the size of its South African counterparts, the bank has made large strides in creating a respected Nigerian bank brand that can be found in neighbouring Ghana and also in Kenya. Access Bank is another Nigerian bank that has been taking advantage of the continued growth in the banking sector, with over six million customers and branches in eight countries.

UAC, mostly unknown outside Nigeria, has come into prominence and will probably be swallowed up completely by future deals – such as selling off a portion of its fast food business (Mr Bigg's) to South Africa's Famous Brands restaurant chain. Famous Brands is the largest African fast food company, and by including Mr Bigg's in its already enormous South African portfolio of brands, it is more than likely to signal the start of their expansion into

Nigeria. Zimbabwe also features INNSCOR, represented by fast food holding company, which owns around 210 stores in six countries. INNSCOR also has a variety of other regionally respected brands in its portfolio.

African brands have also been part of driving technological advancement in Africa. MTN, for example, leapfrogged local and international telecoms companies by taking the huge gamble to start operations in Nigeria when all the signals probably pointed to disaster. They managed to do this through seeing the opportunity, giving the market what it desperately wanted (access to communications) and quality service.

What have been the main constraints in building 'African' brands?

Because of such a long history of international brands owning the market, the respect for local brands has tended to be limited. It also means that growth in local brands typically has been in the commodity space such as water, beer, snacks and energy. Brands that rely on prestige and exclusivity have only recently been making an entrance on the local front (Yswara) as Africans are quietly developing a stronger sense of confidence in their own style. This is often helped by African brands doing well or being picked up in the international market, Oswald Boateng, the Ghanaian fashion star, being an example.

What impact have these brands had on the local economies?

Fashion brands are one example of an industry creating jobs by penetrating the formal market for low-skilled workers, women in particular. The growth in popularity of African fashion week, fashion tourism and interest from the US and Europe are examples that show that this sector is steadily increasing in size. The Ethiopian shoe brand SoleRebels, owed by Bethlehem Tilahun Alemu, has expanded internationally. As mentioned previously, respect for African brands is still low, so the majority of SoleRebels's sales and press coverage has been in international markets. What is exciting about this industry is that it is a creative industry versus one that is easily replicated. The best way to create strong brands is through creative leadership – something that is hard to replicate.

The size of the growing banking sector in most African countries has also resulted in the growth in the number of African graduates being head hunted for a limited number of positions. Coupled with the training and business exposure many young, educated individuals receive, many of them are leaving the banking sector to work on start-ups in the burgeoning mobile and digital finance sector.

What impact have these brands had on the perception of Africa internationally and locally?

An exciting aspect of this is that 'Made in Africa' has very limited connotations. Unlike the Chinese experience of changing the perception of 'Made in China' to 'Created in China', Africa is in the enviable position of being able to create its own story around its products.

However, it should not be forgotten that Africa is not a homogenous continent. Kenya is known for producing splendid teas, and Ethiopia as the originator of coffee; for gold and diamonds, think South Africa, and for exotic spices and textiles, Morocco.

What are the most entrepreneurial and marketing savvy countries?

This often is based on geographic location and government assistance, or the lack of it. Mauritius, for example, has made tourism and finance its two major focus areas. Rwanda is trying its level best to become the technology hub for Africa. When there is a vision from the government and business leadership in a country, one finds that there is a growth in the supported sectors as they try to build a competitive advantage.

Countries and what are they doing? (prolific brand creating regions)

The 2013 Brand Africa 100 Most Admired and Valuable Brands in Africa report delivered some interesting results showing that African brands are making headway at 34 per cent of all the brands nominated in the survey, with international brands steady at 66 per cent. A further breakdown of the African results indicate that South African brands represent 24 per cent of the share, Nigerian brands represent 9 per cent with Kenyan brands representing the remaining 1 per cent.

Conclusion

The continent is in an enviable position of being courted by companies from all around the world. However, in order for Africa to grow strong local industry and weather economic storms, it needs to build strong local brands to compete with the many other international competitors vying for emerging consumers. African continental brands are emerging, meaning that smaller African brands are being overtaken not only by multi-nationals, but by other African brands. Brands focusing on only single markets could find that they are going to struggle in the near future as economic blocs start to open up borders and ease trade restrictions. There are many advantages of being a home-grown brand, but it does not guarantee success. There is only a short window for smaller African companies to make the move from being products to becoming brands. International companies who are desperate for new markets and revenue have the skills and drive to overtake local brands, so before this happens, a BRAND new Africa is needed.

Note

1. Deloitte, March 2013, http://www.deloitte.com/assets/Dcom-India/Local%20 Assets/Documents/Africa/Deloitte_on_Africa-(1)_rise_and_rise.pdf.

6
Is It Time for Open Borders in Southern Africa? The Case for Free Labour Movement in SADC

Adrian Kitimbo

Southern Africa is facing significant skills shortages. This is evident in countries such as South Africa, where the scarcity of particularly high-skilled workers in sectors including engineering, medicine and senior management has the potential to limit the country's long-term economic growth.[1] A recent report[2] by Adcorp, a labour market specialist, estimates that there are 470,000 vacancies in South Africa's private sector which are currently not filled because of unavailable skills. These shortages are attributed to 'brain drain' from South Africa, immigration restrictions on high-skilled foreigners and failings in the education system.[3] South Africa is not alone – regional neighbours such as Namibia also report that their economic growth targets are stymied by shortages of workers in industries that are critical to their economies.[4]

Migration experts largely agree that one way to address skills shortages is through increased labour mobility among countries.[5] It is argued that mismatches in the labour market occur when companies' demand for workers are not met with people that have the right skills and competencies. These gaps, as is the case in a number of Southern African countries, hurt workers who cannot find employment suited to their skills. They also decrease the productivity of companies, which in turn damages the economic growth of countries. Yet the benefits of labour mobility go beyond providing workers to sectors where there are shortages. The movement of labour also has the potential to enhance trade and spur entrepreneurship. Evidence[6] from the European Union (EU), home to the most progressive migration system in the world, attests to these benefits.

Despite clear gains that emanate from labour movement, Southern African Development Community (SADC) members are reluctant to embrace the idea of free movement of persons, including labour. Even as other African Regional Economic Communities (RECs), including the East African Community (EAC) and the Economic Community of West African States (ECOWAS), have made significant progress toward opening up borders for their labour migrants, SADC seems a long way off in achieving this goal.

The debate over free movement in SADC is often hijacked by populist senti-ments. Inter-regional labour movement tends to evoke security concerns, as well as the fear of a 'flood' of migrants to major receiving countries such as Botswana. The eruption of xenophobic attacks against Zimbabweans and other foreign African nationals in South Africa in 2008 highlights the diffi-culties in promoting a balanced discussion on free labour movement.

Against this backdrop, this Discussion Paper draws from interviews with migration experts to explore some of the potential economic benefits of free labour mobility for both sending and receiving countries in SADC. Mindful of the possible drawbacks of increased labour movement such as brain drain and the dampening of wages for particularly low-skilled workers, migra-tion experts such as Lorenzo Fioramonti[7] nevertheless argue that a 'regional governance framework' that allows for a multilateral approach to develop-ment can limit some of these problems. The paper also draws on the EU experience as well as the migration policies of two other African RECs – ECOWAS and the EAC – in an effort to draw lessons for SADC.

A snapshot of global and regional migration trends

According to the United Nations (UN), the number of international migrants has increased by 53 million in the global North and 24 million in the global South since the 1990s.[8] As of 2013, there were 232 million international migrants.[9] There is also significant intra-African migration. In 2010, close to 30 million migrants were African and most of them moved within African borders.[10] In Southern Africa, a region which is the focus of this paper, there were 1.4 million migrants in 1990, and by 2010 that number had increased to 2.2 million.[11]

Botswana and South Africa stand out as the most sought after destina-tions for migrants from within SADC. In 1990, for example, South Africa and Botswana hosted 510,000 and 10,000 migrants, respectively, but by 2010 those numbers had risen to 1.2 million and 76,000 respectively.[12] Most migrants to major host states, including South Africa, are from Zimbabwe. Largely driven by economic circumstances, many Zimbabweans clandes-tinely cross into South Africa and Botswana for a chance at a 'better life'. While the media in South Africa often exaggerates the number of 'undocu-mented' Zimbabweans living in the country, the volume has undoubtedly increased in the past ten years. The rise in numbers explains, in part, why some SADC members are hesitant to embrace free movement of labour, as they fear that they will see the number of migrants who enter their territo-ries increase to unprecedented levels.

The reality, however, that migration numbers continue to rise, even within Southern Africa, underscores the need to deal with migration at a broader level (a regional level in this case). Present national approaches to migration, combined with bilateral agreements and informality within SADC, are not just unsustainable in the face of growing numbers, but also hinder economic opportunities that are associated with free movement of persons, including labour.

Labour movement is not new to Southern Africa

Labour mobility in Southern Africa stretches back to the pre-colonial era, when people traversed the region to work in various employment sectors. In the late 1800s, Mozambicans, for example, worked in the Western Cape as seasonal farmers.[13] Pedi and Sotho males also often moved across the Cape Colony to work on public works and farms as a way to earn wages to buy weapons such as guns, as well as purchase agricultural products and pay for a bride.[14] Like the Pedi and Sotho, the Tsonga travelled across modern-day South Africa for work, mainly engaging in seasonal labour on farms in the Western Cape.[15]

A major form of migration that dominated Southern Africa in the twentieth century was the movement of contract labourers throughout region.[16] In countries such as South Africa, contract labourers largely worked in the mining sector, an industry which attracted workers from countries including Botswana, Mozambique and Lesotho to work on gold mines on the Witwatersrand and on diamond fields in Kimberly. Mining companies hired foreigners partly because they were cheap, but also because many locals at the time did not want to engage in this kind of manual labour.[17] Other countries, including what is now Zimbabwe and Namibia, also received thousands of unskilled migrants to work on their mines. In Zimbabwe, coal and asbestos mines were a big pull for workers from Zambia and Malawi in the early 1900s. It is estimated that in 1935, up to 150,000 migrants left Malawi to work in mines in Zimbabwe, South Africa and Zambia.[18] Another important sector that attracted labour migrants in Southern Africa was commercial farming. Thousands of workers (mostly women) were hired to work on farms in several countries, including Zimbabwe and Mozambique.[19] Yet mining and commercial farms were not the only sectors that attracted labour migrants; to a smaller extent, particularly in South Africa, factories and domestic services also hired foreigners.[20]

The history of labour migration in Southern Africa illustrates that migration for work does not only have a long past in the region, but also, notwithstanding the serious social issues that attended it, formed an economic backbone for especially host countries, such as South Africa, that relied on low-skilled foreign workers for many decades. Furthermore, this history shows that systems of migration in Southern Africa are deeply rooted even though governments have tried to do away with them in recent years. The unintended consequence of restrictions on free movement of labour between countries has been an increase in problems such as irregular migration, a phenomenon which has created enormous social, political and economic problems for SADC members. The regional SADC economy would be better served by a coherent and implemented regional policy on labour migration than it is with the current practice of trying to continually limit it.

Management of labour movement within SADC

Only recently, SADC members adopted a Regional Labour Migration Policy Framework that 'seeks to promote sound management of intra-regional labour migration for the benefit of both the sending and receiving countries as well as the migrant workers'.[21] But it is yet to be seen if the objectives in the Framework, including the 'harmonisation and standardisation of national labour migration policies', will be implemented by member countries. According to Joe Rispoli of the International Organization for Migration (IOM), labour mobility is currently dominated by policies at national level and by bilateral agreements between countries.[22] This is despite the Declaration and Treaty establishing SADC whose stated goal, among others, is to 'gradually eliminate obstacles to movement throughout the region'.[23] National interests, as opposed to those of the region, seem to be at the forefront of migration management within SADC. In regions such as the EU, integration has moved forward to such an extent that member states have given up some of their sovereignty to supranational institutions. Indeed EU law is superimposed and sometimes replaces national laws. As a result, EU members find it easier to domesticate EU law. Also, there is more pressure and urgency in domesticating EU laws, as enforceable penalties do kick in for those countries that do not implement them. In SADC, however, domestic laws determine migration policies of respective states.

In order to work within SADC, most foreigners, including those from within the region, are required to obtain work permits or visas before they can engage in employment. In the Republic of South Africa, for example, there are various permits that have to be obtained before foreigners can commence work. These include general work permits, intra-company visas, critical skills visas and business permits.[24] These permits and visas are obtained through the Ministry of Home Affairs. But in South Africa and other SADC countries, acquiring authorisation to work is not always easy. In fact, South Africa's recently adopted immigration law has been sharply criticised by business leaders, non-profit organisations and migration experts within the country and the region. It is argued that the new stringent rules that affect labour migrants threaten South Africa's long-term economic growth, as they could turn away tourists, potential investors and skilled migrants.

Bilateral agreements are also a centrepiece of current labour migration governance in Southern Africa. Of all SADC states, South Africa is perhaps the country with most bilateral agreements with countries in the region.[25] South Africa's dominance when it comes to these agreements is much attributed to its old labour migrant system, which recruited foreign workers from neighbouring countries to work on mines, farms and factories.[26] Some of the countries with which South Africa has previously signed bilateral agreements include Malawi, Swaziland, Lesotho and Mozambique.[27]

SADC needs to re-think its management of labour mobility. Current national and bilateral policies, which largely favour restriction on movement, have had debatable outcomes. For example, Zaheera Jinnah, a migration expert at University of Witwatersrand,[28] points out that these agreements, which are meant to help tackle skills shortages, have not been able to achieve their goal, as a number of high-skilled sectors in SADC member states continue to struggle to fill positions. But more importantly, the present lack of free labour movement, for particularly high-skilled workers, is a big hindrance to potential economic benefits that could result from such mobility.

Evaluating some of the potential economic benefits and costs of free labour movement in SADC

Economic arguments alone do not influence migration policies. Other considerations, including those that are social and political, also play a role. However, the cost benefit analysis of increased mobility can have an even stronger influence in shaping policies that impact labour migrants. There is an array of literature and migration models on the economic impact of free labour movement. Classical and neo-classical theories of migration have long emphasised its benefits.[29]

The EU, which has the most progressive policies on free movement in the world, provides the best 'experiment' on open borders. Even as the recent economic crises in some member states have aroused fierce, inward-looking migration debates, labour mobility remains integral to the EU project. European labour migration dates back to post–World War II Europe, a period that was characterised by colonial immigration regimes and temporary guest worker policies.[30] During the former period, European countries took advantage of the large supply of unskilled workers in their colonies to meet their labour needs. The guest worker system was largely used during the economic recovery of countries such as Germany who looked South to Turkey and North Africa to meet their demand for workers.[31] The signing of the Treaty of Rome in 1957 made the free movement of labour among one of its central goals. The Maastricht Treaty of 1991, establishing a single market, reinforced the free movement of persons among EU member states.[32] The idea of European citizenship also emanated from the Maastricht Treaty and further strengthened the notion of free movement of persons, which resulted in giving EU citizens the right to move freely and live in other member countries.

Inter-regional labour mobility in the EU has enabled economic gains to both receiving and sending countries. One of such positive effects has been to help fix mismatches in the labour market. This is most evident in countries with high-skilled workers but lacking enough labour in the low-skilled sectors. Even more, societies with an ageing workforce have been able to expand their shrinking labour force by drawing from a larger labour market. A recent study of inter-regional migrants in EU cities shows how places such as Turin, Italy, have capitalised on Romanian immigrants to fill gaps in sectors that some locals consider undesirable. These include agriculture, construction and domestic work.[33] Similar trends are seen in Hamburg, Germany, where foreigners are increasingly taking up jobs in sectors including the port industry.[34] Yet the supply of labour across the EU also extends to skilled sectors such as engineering and medicine. Germany, for example, has in recent years hired thousands to Spaniards and Portuguese to make up its shortfall of engineers and other professionals.[35] As the examples illustrate, because of free labour movement in the EU, countries experience less economically stinging skills shortages. Increased intra-regional mobility in SADC for specifically high-skilled workers can have similar resultant effects. Companies in countries such as South Africa would struggle less to fill available vacancies as there would be a larger pool of candidates with the right skills to select from.

Beyond tackling skills shortages, free labour movement has the potential to boost trade. In regions such as SADC, where intra-SADC trade as a percentage of the community's total trade has stagnated at around 15 per cent over the past decade,[36] an increase in mobile labour could enhance trade. Migration studies suggest two ways by which the movement of persons can improve trade. It is argued that migrants can reduce bilateral business costs between the host and sending countries. This is achieved through personal business connections with people from home countries.[37] Secondly, the specific knowledge that migrants bring about foreign markets can also lessen the cost of trade between countries. In cases where the political and social institutions of a foreign state are very different from that of the host state, the knowledge that migrants bring can prove especially useful.[38] Indeed, if a country possesses a significant number of ethnicities, the information on markets provided by these communities can spur trade between countries.

Another issue that is worth mentioning as part of the potential economic gains is the ability of increased labour mobility to reduce irregular migrants. Irregular migrants are people who enter host countries through illegal channels and without proper documentation. Presently, host countries spend enormous amounts of money on tightening border controls and in the deportation of undocumented migrants. South Africa and Botswana are perhaps two countries with the highest influx of these migrants. Other regional countries such as Namibia and Mozambique have also experienced a rise in undocumented workers. It is also important to highlight that the majority of irregular migrants in SADC are from within the region. In both Botswana and South Africa, most undocumented migrants who enter their territories have their origins in Zimbabwe, a country where harsh economic realities have forced millions to look for work in other countries within the region and beyond.[39] It is estimated that since 1990, South Africa has deported over one and a half million people, most of them back to Zimbabwe and Mozambique.[40] Yet deportations and border controls do not seem to have the desired effect of preventing and deterring irregular migrants, as many desperate people often find clandestine channels to re-enter destination countries. According to Lorenzo Fioramonti,[41] the lack of free labour movement has facilitated the growth of irregular entry channels to host states, which are often managed by traffickers.[42] Recent reports reveal that traffickers financially exploit those who use their services, as well as physically abuse them.[43] In addition, because irregular labour migrants cannot work in formal sectors, they often take up employment in conditions where labour standards are not observed and are paid very low wages. Additionally, skilled labour migrants who could be of benefit in high-skilled sectors within host countries end up in jobs way below their skill levels. A managed regional labour migration regime that allows for the free movement of particularly high-skilled workers can help reduce the number of irregular migrants in the region and the problems that come with it. Furthermore, tackling irregular migration through an increase in the mobility of workers could also reduce 'brain waste' by enabling un-regularised skilled migrants to move into industries where they can best employ their skills.

But the benefits of free labour movement are not just limited to host states. An outflow of workers can reduce unemployment rates in sending countries, and remittances sent back home can be a source of foreign exchange as well as economically improve the lives of those left behind. In Zimbabwe, for example, remittances from abroad are credited with staving off a complete economic collapse in recent years. In addition, in case of return, the skills migrants gain abroad can prove useful in the sender's labour market.

From this, it may seem like free labour movement is a win-win situation for all parties involved. Overall, its benefits do clearly outweigh the costs. However, it also important to highlight some of the drawbacks from an increase in inter-regional labour mobility, as it helps in understanding why some countries are reluctant to embrace it. The threat of immigrants competing for jobs with locals is a real fear in host states. Joe Rispoli[44] stresses that in regions such as Southern Africa, where unemployment rates especially among low-skilled workers are high, an increase in labour movement arouses serious concerns over jobs. Moreover, if foreigners work for lower pay, this may dampen the wages for local workers, creating tensions between the two groups as a result. And while remittances are of significant benefit to countries of origin, brain drain and the possibility of losing people of the working age could have negative economic repercussions for sending countries. It is also possible that large outflows of labour from the least developed to the more developed countries in SADC may create labour shortages in countries of origin, stunting their economic growth as result. Some of these problems are well evidenced in the Zimbabwe case. The millions of Zimbabweans escaping their country's economic turmoil for 'greener pastures' elsewhere has robbed the country of both its skilled and unskilled workers who could play a role in rebuilding the country. This brain drain is sure to further hinder Zimbabwe's path toward economic recovery. Furthermore, this mass exodus has also raised serious concerns over security and job losses for locals in countries such as Botswana. As a consequence, hundreds of thousands of Zimbabweans have been deported from Botswana.

However, an increase in labour movement does not have to necessarily trigger these drawbacks. A clearly well-developed and managed regional labour migration regime can limit these problems. Experts[45] argue that a multilateral framework like the recently developed 'SADC Labour Migration Policy Framework' can ensure that SADC benefits from free labour movement without many of the resultant problems of increased labour mobility.

Efforts to establish free movement in SADC

The first Draft Protocol on free movement in SADC was proposed in 1995. It was an ambitious Protocol that sought to gradually eliminate obstacles to free movement among member states within a period of ten years.[46] It was crafted in alignment with the African Union's objective of eventually building an 'African Regional Economic Community' where there would be free movement throughout the continent.[47] More specifically, the 1995 Protocol set out, in relation to every citizen of a member state, to 'confer, promote, and protect onto SADC citizens (i) the right to freely enter another Member State for a short visit without needing a visa (ii) the right to reside in the territory of another Member State (iii) the right to establish oneself and work in the territory of a Member State'.[48]

However, this rather ambitious Protocol was never adopted, as SADC countries, including South Africa, Namibia and Botswana, rejected it. The idea that there would be free movement of persons in a region that was then seen as having enormous economic disparities did not bode well with some members.[49] Also, concerns over the potential for free movement to usurp national policies, as well as socially and economically burden receiving countries, were a big influence on the decision by a number of members to reject the Draft Protocol.[50]After successfully thwarting the 1995 Draft Protocol, South Africa crafted a new version and titled it the 'Facilitation of Movement Protocol'. The new Protocol, among other things, sought to assert national interests over those of the Region, prevent countries from committing to an implementation time-table, as well as delay harmonisation of policies.[51] However, this version was seen as a significant step backwards by some SADC members and was hence not adopted. Following the rejection of the Facilitation Protocol presented by South Africa, the secretariat redrafted the original Protocol, taking into account the concerns of member states, but kept the name proposed by South Africa – 'Facilitation of Movement'.

The Facilitation of Movement Protocol seeks to progressively eliminate obstacles to movement among and within SADC member states and facilitate entry of citizens into a second country visa-free for a maximum period of three months.[52] The SADC Charter of Fundamental Social Rights supports the Protocol with regard to the free movement of labour. Article 2 of the Charter seeks to 'promote policies, practices and measures, which facilitate labour mobility, remove distortions in labour markets and enhance industrial harmony and increase productivity, in SADC Member States'.[53] After being shelved for many years, the Facilitation of Movement Protocol was finally tabled in 2005 at the SADC Summit. Presently, thirteen SADC member states have signed and adopted it. But only six members (South Africa, Zambia, Lesotho, Mozambique, Botswana and Swaziland) have ratified it. For the Protocol to come into force, it has to be signed and ratified by at least two-thirds of SADC members.

Factors limiting the ratification of the Protocol include lack of funding and technical expertise required to put it into force.[54] Implementation requires funding administrative practices and making policy changes. For some SADC members, the Protocol is seen as both an extra burden and not really a priority. This is especially the case in countries such as the DRC who are struggling with internal conflicts among other social and economic challenges. Harmonisation of laws, which requires modifications in domestic laws as well as subordinating national political interests to long-term regional goals, is also not regarded as much of a priority by some SADC states. In addition, present bilateral agreements also contribute to a reluctance to ratify the Protocol.[55] Because some countries already have strong bilateral ties which allow their citizens to move freely, the Protocol is not seen as contributing much. The failure of SADC to implement the 'Protocol on Facilitation of Movement' is also attributed to a lack of commitment and political will to embrace policies on labour movement.[56] Other African RECs, as the figures demonstrate, have taken much faster steps toward opening up borders for member citizens.

ECOWAS' Protocol on free movement of persons

Founded in 1975, ECOWAS is a regional body comprising fifteen countries, these being: Sierra Leone, Cote d'Ivoire, Togo, Niger, Mali, Nigeria, Ghana, Guinea-Bissau, Guinea, Cape Verde, Liberia, Benin, Burkina Faso, Gambia and Senegal. The ECOWAS Protocol on free movement of persons is perhaps the most ambitious and advanced on the continent (Figure 6.1).[57]

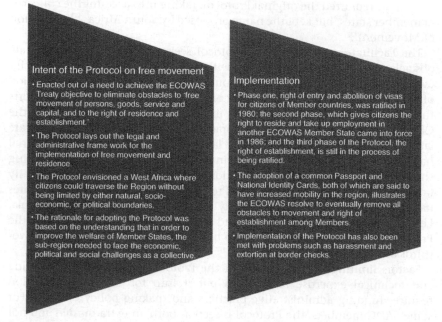

Figure 6.1   Intent and implementation of the protocol on free movement

Sources: Adapted by the author from the Treaty of ECOWAS; A Region without Borders? Policy Frameworks for Regional Labour Migrations towards South Africa', MiWORC Report, 2013.

The EAC Common Market Protocol

The EAC is a Regional Economic Community comprising Uganda, Kenya, Tanzania, Burundi and Rwanda. The Treaty establishing the existing EAC was signed in 1999 by the original three founders (Kenya, Uganda and Tanzania) and came into force in 2000. Rwanda and Burundi joined the Community after acceding to the EAC Treaty in 2007.

How can SADC catch up with EAC and ECOWAS?

SADC can begin with harmonising labour movement policies among member states. The EAC, for example, already had relatively uniform labour movement policies between partner states. In SADC, current policies vary from one country to another. One example of this is the procedures for granting work permits which are different in every country. This lack of uniformity makes the process of applying for work permits confusing and extremely cumbersome for those who wish to work in another member state. The recently adopted Regional Labour Migration Policy Framework is a step in

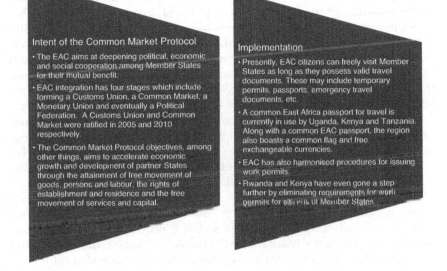

Intent of the Common Market Protocol

• The EAC aims at deepening political, economic and social cooperation among Member States for their mutual benefit.

• EAC integration has four stages which include forming a Customs Union, a Common Market, a Monetary Union and eventually a Political Federation. A Customs Union and Common Market were ratified in 2005 and 2010 respectively.

• The Common Market Protocol objectives, among other things, aims to accelerate economic growth and development of partner States through the attainment of free movement of goods, persons and labour, the rights of establishment and residence and the free movement of services and capital.

Implementation

• Presently, EAC citizens can freely visit Member States as long as they possess valid travel documents. These may include temporary permits, passports, emergency travel documents, etc.

• A common East Africa passport for travel is currently in use by Uganda, Kenya and Tanzania. Along with a common EAC passport, the region also boasts a common flag and free exchangeable currencies.

• EAC has also harmonised procedures for issuing work permits.

• Rwanda and Kenya have even gone a step further by eliminating requirements for work permits for citizens of Member States.

Figure 6.2   Intent and implementation of common market protocol

Sources: Adapted by the author from the Treaty Establishing the East African Community; A Region without Borders? Policy Frameworks for Regional Labour Migrations towards South Africa', MiWORC Report, 2013.

the right direction. If all member countries do indeed implement its objectives, the Framework will ensure that national labour migration policies are harmonised throughout the entire region.

SADC should also strive to gain the full support of its members to finally bring the 'Facilitation of Movement Protocol' into force. One way of enabling this is to pool technical expertise and resources to help those countries that have not ratified the Protocol because they lack the know-how and resources to domesticate its provisions.

More communication between the Ministries of Labour and Home Affairs is also needed if the Protocol is to garner full support. Joni Musabayana, the Deputy Director of the International Labour Organization (ILO) in South Africa, spoke about the tension that often exists between the security concerns of Home Affairs and the labour needs of Labour Ministries.[58] These competing interests have played a role in stifling progress toward free labour movement in the region. Dialogue between these Ministries is significant to ensure that the security concerns of SADC countries are addressed, while at the same time allowing for the free movement of labour that is economically beneficial to member states.

Furthermore, unlike the EAC and the ECOWAS, SADC seems to lack the same sense of urgency and political will to enable free labour movement in the region. Commitment to free movement in ECOWAS is, for example, reflected in the Common Approach, a Policy Paper meant to speed up the implementation of the free movement protocol. The Paper also re-emphasises the significance of free movement to regional integration and the link between migration and development. Realising the benefits of free movement, Rwanda and Kenya have also moved faster than other EAC countries by abolishing work permit requirements for citizens of member countries. If SADC is to fulfil its Treaty objective of free movement among members, leaders in the region have to take free movement of labour more seriously.

Another important way forward is for major host states (South Africa and Botswana) to do a better job of highlighting the benefits of labour migration to their citizens. Since migration in the region often invokes negative sentiments, it is imperative that governments spell out to their citizens the potential economic gains of this kind of movement.

The private sector, which has a large stake in migration, particularly labour mobility, can help push the region toward a larger labour market. Labour mobility is significant for the private sector, especially because companies and businesses are not accountable to the public but to their shareholders and they understand that migrants and increased mobility generate profit. Also, private sector companies are among the most affected if the labour market lacks workers with the right competencies to fill vacancies. Intra-company transfers, which are critical to human resource strategies, also depend on the ease of workers to move from one country to another. Unfortunately, however, there is very little interaction between governments and private sector on migration policies. Loane Sharp, the Labour Market Specialist for Adcorp, pointed out that the South African government, for example, rarely consults the private sector when drafting migration laws.[59] Migration laws are often passed in response to political and social concerns but with little economic considerations. But it is also fair to say that the private sector throughout Southern Africa could take a more active role in lobbying governments to act more quickly in enabling free labour mobility for the much needed high-skilled workers. This lack of engagement or limited communication between the public and private sectors is a problem, as governments tend to pass laws which are not in tandem with private sector labour needs.

Private sector companies and businesses are major drivers of economies in Southern Africa. A united voice from them can provide the impetus to quickly implement the Labour Migration Framework as well as the ratification of the free movement protocol by those countries that are still on the fence.

Conclusion

This chapter illustrates that there are several potential economic benefits from increased labour mobility within SADC. Free labour movement has the potential to address skills shortages, reduce the number of undocumented migrants and also enhance trade within the region. While the drawbacks from such labour mobility including brain drain and the dampening of local wages cannot be overlooked, these problems can be addressed through a managed regional labour migration system that, for example, initially allows for the free movement of workers with particular skills (e.g., high-skilled workers).

Conditions do exist to finally establish free labour movement in SADC. A Regional Labour Migration Framework that would allow for the harmonisation of labour migration policies across the region is already in place. It is incumbent on member states to implement what is set out in the Framework. A protocol to facilitate free movement, including labour, also already exists. More political will as well as the pooling together of technical expertise and resources are required to finally bring the Facilitation of Movement Protocol into force. And, as stated earlier, successful implementation of the protocol (when it finally comes into force) requires a closer working relationship between the Ministries of Labour and Ministries of Home Affairs in individual SADC countries to ensure that the concerns and needs of both Ministries are met. Furthermore, a united voice from the private sector and a stronger working relationship with the public sector could also go a long way in enabling free labour movement in the region.

If SADC wishes to strengthen its integration, as well as collectively address the economic imbalances in the region, the migration-development nexus cannot be forever avoided. Other African RECs, including ECOWAS and EAC, show that even among regions where there are significant economic disparities among neighbours, free labour movement is possible and can be beneficial. While SADC does have a few strong economies such as South Africa and Botswana, most of its members have weak economies and markets. These economies cannot grow in isolation. More regional integration, through increased labour mobility, can generate the impetus needed to solve the socioeconomic problems this region faces.

Notes

1. See http://www.adcorp.co.za/NEws/Pages/SA%E2%80%99seconomydesperatelyneedshigh- skilledworkers.aspx.
2. See http://businesstech.co.za/news/general/52918/south-africas-critical-skills-shortage/.
3. See Ibid.
4. At http://sun.com.na/content/national-news/skills-shortage-biggest-obstacle-growth.
5. Bertelsmann Stiftung, 'The Case for Harnessing European Labour Mobility: Scenario Analysis and Policy Recommendations' (2014), http://www.labourmobility.com/wp- content/uploads/2014/04/HELM.pdf.
6. European Commission, 'Evaluation of the Impact of the Free Movement of EU Citizens at Local Level' (2014), http://ec.europa.eu/justice/citizen/files/dg_just_eva_free_mov_final_report_27.01.14.pdf.

7. Lorenzo Fioramonti, 'Is It Time to Take Free Movement of People in Southern Africa Seriously?' *Africa Development Bank*, June 2013.

8. OECD, World Migration Figures, http://www.oecd.org/els/mig/World-Migration-in-Figures.pdf.

9. Ibid.

10. Christopher Nshimbi and Lorenzo Fioramonti, 'A Region without Borders? Policy Frameworks for Regional Labour Migrations towards South Africa', MiWORC Report, 2013.

11. Nshimbi and Fioramonti, 'A Region without Borders?'

12. Ibid.

13. Marie Wentzel, 'Historical and Contemporary Dimensions of Migration between South Africa and its Neighbouring Countries', HSRC Migration Workshop, 2003.

14. Marie Wentzel, 'Historical and Contemporary Dimensions of Migration'.

15. Ibid.

16. Jonathan Crush and Vincent Williams, 'Labour Migration Trends and Policies in Southern Africa', SAMP Policy Brief, March 2010.

17. Crush and Williams, 'Labour Migration Trends and Policies in Southern Africa'.

18. Jonathan Crush, Vincent Williams and Sally Peberdy, 'Migration in Southern Africa', Global Commission on International Migration, September 2005.

19. Crush and Williams, 'Labour Migration Trends and Policies in Southern Africa'.

20. Crush et al., 'Migration in Southern Africa'.

21. SADC Labour Migration Policy Framework, 2013.

22. Interview with Joe Rispoli, International Organization for Migration (IOM), 21 May 2014.

23. SADC Treaty (1992), http://www.sadc.int/files/8613/5292/8378/Declaration__Treaty_of_SADC.pdf.

24. Department of Home Affairs, Republic of South Africa, http://www.dha.gov.za/index.php/immigration-services/types-of-temporary-permits.

25. SADC Migration Policy, International Labour Organization (ILO) (December 2013), http://www.ilo.org/wcmsp5/groups/public/ − -africa/ − -ro-addis_ababa/ − -ilo-pretoria/documents/meetingdocument/wcms_239821.pdf.

26. Nshimbi and Fioramonti, 'A Region without Borders?'

27. Crush and Williams, 'Labour Migration Trends and Policies in Southern Africa'.

28. Informal Interview with Zaheera Jinnah, migration expert at University of Witwatersrand, 23 May 2014.

29. Costs and Benefits of Migration, World Migration (2005).

30. Kristina Touzenis, 'Free Movement of Persons in the European Union and Economic Community of West African States: A Comparison of Law and Practice', UNESCO Migration Studies (2012).

31. Nshimbi and Fioramonti, 'A Region without Borders?'

32. Ibid.

33. European Commission, 'Evaluation of the Impact of the Free Movement of EU Citizens at Local Level' (2014), http://ec.europa.eu/justice/citizen/files/dg_just_eva_free_mov_final_report_27.01.14.pdf.

34. European Commission, 'Evaluation of the Impact of the Free Movement of EU Citizens at Local Level'.

35. See http://www.nytimes.com/2013/05/28/world/europe/28iht-letter28.html.

36. At http://allafrica.com/stories/201307051072.html.

37. Reiner Munz, Erste Bank, Thomas Straubhaar, Florin Vadean and Nadia Vadean, 'What Are the Migrants' Contributions to Employment and Growth? A European Approach', Hamburgisches Weltwirtschafts Institute, 2007.

38. Munz et al., 'What Are the Migrants' Contributions to Employment and Growth?'
39. Crush and Williams, 'Labour Migration Trends and Policies in Southern Africa'.
40. Ibid.
41. Fioramonti, 'Is It Time to Take Free Movement of People in Southern Africa Seriously?'
42. Ibid.
43. International Organization for Migration (IOM), http://www.iom.int/cms/en/sites/iom/home/where-we-work/africa-and-the-middle-east/southern-africa.html.
44. Interview with Joe Rispoli, International Organization for Migration (IOM), 21 May 2014.
45. See http://www.opendemocracy.net/chris-nshimbi/state-of-denial.
46. Hussein Solomon, 'Toward the Free Movement of People in Southern Africa?', Institute for Security Studies (1997), http://www.issafrica.org/uploads/paper_18.pdf.
47. Solomon 'Toward the Free Movement of People in Southern Africa?' (1997).
48. Draft Protocol on the Free Movement of Persons in SADC, http://www.unisa.ac.za/contents/faculties/law/docs/FACILITATION_OF_MOVEMENT_OF_PERSONS_SADC_1996.pdf.
49. V. Williams and L. Carr, 'The Draft Protocol on the Facilitation of Movement of Persons in SADC: Implications for State Parties', Migration Policy Brief No. 18, 2006.
50. Williams and Carr, 'The Draft Protocol on the Facilitation of Movement of Persons in SADC'.
51. Nshimbi and Fioramonti, 'A Region without Borders?'
52. Protocol on the Facilitation of Movement in SADC, http://www.sadc.int/files/9513/5292/8363/Protocol_on_Facilitation_of_Movement_of_Persons2005.pdf.
53. Charter of Fundamental and Social Rights, http://www.sadc.int/files/6613/5292/8383/Charter_of_the_Fundamental_Social_Rights_in_SADC2003.pdf.
54. Interview with Joni Musabayana, Deputy Director, International Labour Organization (ILO), South Africa, 25 July 2014.
55. Informal Interview with Zaheera Jinnah, migration expert at University of Witwatersrand, 23 May 2014.
56. Nshimbi and Fioramonti, 'A Region without Borders?'
57. Ibid.
58. Interview with Joni Musabayana, Deputy Director, International Labour Organization, South Africa, 25 July 2014.
59. Interview with Loane Sharp, Labour Market Specialist at Adcorp, 23 July 2014.

Part II
Sectors with African Champions

7
Banking and the Financial Sector

Lite J. Nartey

Investment in Africa's financial sector has the ability to transform the lives of individual Africans by greatly enhancing access to financial resources and opportunities and increasing economic development across the continent. Indeed, 'banking is not one sector in a vibrant economy: it is the foundation upon which most other sectors are built'.[1] However, as the global financial industry moves towards convergence in terms of regulations and practices facilitating investment across countries, across the African continent the ease of investment is less realised. Only 12 per cent of total trade and investment on the African continent is between African countries.[2]

Several factors such as poor infrastructure, inadequate skills in the work force, corruption, economic instability, weak currencies, and diverse laws and legal backgrounds have been carefully explored and discussed as key variables limiting intra-African investment. In this chapter on the banking sector in the *Africans Investing in Africa* project, the focus is on less explored factors hindering intra-African investment: social, cultural and geopolitical variables including culture, stereotypes and language that are often not considered variables of traditional importance to financial firms. These less explored factors are critical to the ability of African banks to successfully invest in other African countries and are often underlying drivers of the more well-known factors. This chapter explores the issues surrounding intra-African investment through the insights and lessons of three leading African banks: Standard Bank, the United Bank for Africa (UBA) and Ecobank Transnational Inc. (Ecobank).[3]

Standard Bank

A Sustainable Strategy[4] (Vision & Mission): To build the leading African financial services organization using all our competitive advantages to the full. We will focus on delivering superior sustainable shareholder value by serving the needs of our customers through first class, on-the-

United Bank for Africa

Vision:[11] To be the undisputed leading and dominant financial services institution in Africa.

Mission: To be a role model for African businesses by creating superior value for all our stakeholders, abiding by the most professional and ethical standards, and by building an enduring institution.

The legacy of United Bank for Africa (UBA) began in 1949 as the British and French Bank United (BFB), and it was established as a limited liability company in 1961. Headquartered in Nigeria, UBA was first listed on the Nigerian Stock Exchange in 1970 and merged with Standard Trust Bank through one of the largest mergers in Nigeria in August 2005. Standard Trust Bank's initial investment outside Nigeria was in Ghana in 2004, making Ghana the first African country in UBA's portfolio at the time of the merger. In 2007, UBA initiated its aggressive growth strategy and over the period of three-and-one-half years quickly expanded its African presence to include investments in 18 African countries, beginning with Cameroon. In 2008, UBA invested in Côte d'Ivoire, Liberia, Sierra Leone, Uganda, Burkina Faso and Benin Republic. In 2009, the bank entered Kenya, Chad and Senegal, and in 2010 added Zambia, Tanzania, Gabon and Guinea to its African portfolio. UBA's most recent African investments include Mozambique, the Democratic Republic of Congo and Congo Brazzaville in 2011. It has operations outside of the African continent also, including the USA (business office opened on 1 May 1984 and it remains the only Sub-Saharan African bank outside of South Africa with an office in the USA), the United Kingdom (business office opened 1 May 1984) and France (business office opened 13 March 2009).[12] Important to note is the establishment of the USA and UK offices as the bank's first offices outside of Nigeria.

UBA serves over 7.2 million customers using the infrastructure of 603 branches and retail outlets, 1,500 ATMs and 5,303 point-of-sale machines operated by a staff of 11,529 members[13] and holds total assets of 2.27 trillion Naira (equivalent to roughly US$14 billion). UBA has become recognised as a leading financial institution as demonstrated by its international awards including: Best Bank of the Year 2012 Africa, Bank of the Year 2013 in Cameroon for the third consecutive year, and Best Bank of the Year 2013 in Senegal for the second consecutive year, all by *Financial Times Bankers Magazine*; Best Bank In Short-Term Financing in Ghana from the *Bank of Ghana*; and, it is listed among the top 25 Companies by *Forbes Africa*.

The motivation for rapid internationalisation of UBA is based on the vision of the bank to be the leading bank in Africa. In order to achieve the status of leading bank, 'of course a significant geographical spread across the continent is necessary'. The selection of countries in which to enter in the early stages of its internationalisation strategy in 2007 was to gain 'quick wins' by entering countries where UBA's ability to obtain a banking license was facilitated by the use of its existing network. This internationalisation strategy did not necessarily follow macroeconomic variables or factors which would have precluded its entry into countries such as Liberia or Sierra Leone. Alternatively, UBA viewed these countries as development opportunities and important strategic locations where the bank 'could make an impact'. This development-based view is significantly different from the more limited (traditional finance) view of simply avoiding high-risk post-war environments. Since the completion of the bank's early internationalisation strategy, UBA's more recent investments have been driven by economic prospects, including an entry into Kenya where banking is relatively more common and the competition more fierce. Therefore, UBA's intra-Africa investment strategy has been based on a mixture of both development-based and financial incentives; however, the overarching driver is the vision of the bank.

Given the rapid expansion from 2007 through 2011, the period from 2011 was one of consolidation for UBA. In 2012, the bank's assets outside of Nigeria reached a significant milestone contributing 10 per cent of group profits for the first time with a total of 5.4 billion Naira in profits. The bank's assets outside of Nigeria also generated 41.5 billion Naira in revenue contributing to total group revenues of 220.1 billion Naira.[14] UBA's experience of successfully implementing its broad intra-African investment and its nationality as a Nigerian bank affords lessons and insights for other African financial institutions seeking to invest in Africa.

Ecobank

Our vision[15] is to build a world-class pan-African bank and to contribute to the economic and financial integration and development of Africa.

Our mission is to provide all of our customers with convenient and reliable banking products and services. We believe we have a responsibility to be socially relevant to the communities that we serve. We are also strongly committed to sustainable development of the region and are a signatory of the Equator Principles, the UNEP Finance Initiative and the UN Global Compact.

Ecobank Transnational Inc. (Ecobank) is a leading independent pan-African banking group. By geographic reach, it is the largest African bank operating in 36 African countries (more countries on the African continent than any other bank), it is one of the fastest growing banks and is considered one of the most innovative.[16] At the end of 2012, Ecobank served 9.6 million customers with a staff of 18,564 across 1,226 branches and offices, operated 1,681 ATMs, and held total assets of US$20 billion and total equity of US$2.2 billion.[17] In 2013, Ecobank's net revenue grew 16 per cent to over US$2 billion, signifying the strong growth of the bank despite the 'tough operating environment'.[18] By the end of 2013, Ecobank's customer base swelled to 10.4 million, served by 19,546 employees through 1,284 branches and offices, operated 2,314 ATMs, and held total equity of US$ 2.1 billion and total assets of US$ 22.5 billion.[19]

Ecobank Transnational Inc. was incorporated in 1985 as a collaboration between the Francophone and Anglophone Chambers of Commerce of West Africa and was one of the earliest commercial banks in West Africa owned and managed by the private sector. At its incorporation, the largest shareholder was the development financing arm of ECOWAS – the ECOWAS Fund for Cooperation, Compensation and Development (ECOWAS Fund). Ecobank is headquartered in Lome, Togo, under a headquarters agreement with the government of Togo, signed at its incorporation, which granted Ecobank the status of a nonresident financial institution. Since 2006, Ecobank has been listed on the Nigerian and Ghanaian Stock Exchanges as well as on the Bourse Regionale des Valeurs Mobilieres (BRVM).

Founded with shareholders from ten African countries, from its inception Ecobank has enjoyed the status of an international financial institution. Focusing on the movement and needs of its customers, Ecobank's intra-Africa investment strategy was based solely on 'following the trade routes of its customers'. The bank began its initial intra-African investment and internationalisation phase in 1988 with five countries in Africa, including Benin, Côte d'Ivoire, Ghana, Nigeria and Togo. Its second internationalisation phase, from 1998 through 2001, added seven more countries in Africa, including Burkina Faso, Cameroon, Guinea, Liberia, Mali, Niger and Senegal. From 2006 to 2009, Ecobank expanded into another 18 more countries to create a portfolio totaling 30 countries on the African continent. During this period, Ecobank added to its portfolio Burundi, Cape Verde, Central African Republic, Chad, Congo, the Democratic Republic of Congo, Gabon, Gambia, Guinea-Bissau, Kenya, Malawi, Rwanda, Sao Tome, Sierra Leone, South Africa, Tanzania, Uganda and Zambia. Between 2009 and 2011, Ecobank added Angola and Zimbabwe, on the African continent, and broadened its global focus to include a subsidiary in Paris, France, and representational offices in Dubai, UAE, and London, UK, per the trade routes of the bank's customers. Since 2011, the bank has added another five countries, including Equatorial Guinea, Mozambique, South Sudan, Ethiopia, and its first presence in the United States. In December 2012, the bank opened a representative office in Beijing, China; in January 2013, Ecobank opened a subsidiary in Equatorial Guinea;[20] and in May 2014, Ecobank expanded into Mozambique through the acquisition of a 96 per cent stake in Banco ProCredit Mozambique.

An important structure and regulatory consideration of this large pan-African bank is that Ecobank Transnational Inc., the parent company, is supervised by the Commission Bancaire de l'UMOA; however, each subsidiary is supervised by the respective host country regulators. The bank is structured 'as a network of locally incorporated, regulated banking entities'[21] and the 36 countries in Ecobank's portfolio are arranged according to shared common currencies, similarities across the central banks and leverages existing Regional Economic Communities.[22] Ecobank's geographical clustering comprises seven groups: six African clusters and the International cluster formed by the non-African countries in its portfolio. The six Regional Economic Communities within the Ecobank structure include (1) Francophone West Africa (UEMOA), (2) Nigeria (considered as an individual regional economic community due to its size), (3) Rest of West Africa (West African Monetary Zone [WAMZ]), (4) Central Africa (Communauté Economique et Monétaire de l'Afrique Centrale [CEMAC]), (5) East Africa (East African Community [EAC]) and (6) Southern Africa (Southern African Development Community [SADC]).[23]

With the creation of eProcess International S.A., the technology and telecom subsidiary of the Ecobank Group, Ecobank has become a leader in the technology arena of banking on the African continent. eProcess International was set up to provide technology services to all Ecobank Group affiliates. Initially set up in Lome, Togo, in 2002, a second branch of eProcess International was opened in Ghana in 2006 to address the need to build capacity for its technology platform due to the rapid growth of the group portfolio. Since 2010, Ecobank has focused on upgrading the capacity of the eProcess data centres in Accra and Lome and plans the establishment of new data centres in Europe, specifically, in London and Paris.

Ecobank has been widely recognised as a best-practice financial institution. *Global Finance* in 2013 named Ecobank Best Frontier Markets Bank, and also Best Bank in Africa for the second consecutive year. Ecobank Ghana was named the Bank of the Year 2013 by the Ghanaian banking community, and for the third consecutive year, Ecobank Research won the *African Investor's* award for the Best Africa Research Team for 2013. In 2012, *Global Finance* named Ecobank Best Regional Bank in Africa, and Best Emerging Markets Bank in Burkina Faso, Cameroon, Côte d'Ivoire, Guinea, Senegal and Togo. In addition, at the Africa CEO Forum in Geneva, Ecobank was named African Company of the Year 2012.

Being the only regionally-developed pan-African bank, Ecobank has unique insights and lessons gained through its intra-African investment in the financial sector.

Benefits

Knowledge sharing for financial sector development

An important benefit of intra-Africa investment by African banks is the impact upon the financial and banking sector in the host country in terms of knowledge sharing for financial sector development. Undoubtedly, it is banks from larger, stronger and more developed financial markets that dare to venture abroad, especially in highly underdeveloped emerging markets. According to insights from the traditional international business literature, a business will internationalise to leverage its home country developed comparative advantages (e.g., unique products, skills, capabilities or services) that afford it a competitive advantage abroad.[24] The three banks under study are unquestionably leading banks on the African continent. In the 2013 ranking of the Top 200 African banks according to *The Africa Report*,[25] Standard Bank Group and Standard Bank of South Africa take first and second places, respectively; Ecobank Transnational Inc. is ranked number 14, and is the highest ranked non-South African bank from Sub-Saharan Africa; UBA Group is ranked number 19 and UBA Nigeria is ranked at 27. *Africa Business* in October 2013 ranked Standard Bank Group at number 1, Ecobank at number 12 (with Ecobank Nigeria at number 22) and UBA at number 19. In both rankings, financial institutions from South Africa, Northern Africa and Nigeria dominate the financial sector on the African continent. The resources, skills and knowledge of financial sector regulations and practices of these larger banks hailing from economies with more developed financial sectors cannot be understated. With their entry into less developed economies, these banks have a significant opportunity to help shape the regulatory environment of these underdeveloped financial markets.

Coming from the strong regulatory environment of South Africa, Standard Bank has a clear regulatory advantage. The prestige and general respect given to the South African Reserve Bank across the African continent affords Standard Bank, and other South African banks, *de facto* influence over banks from the rest of the continent who are investing in less developed economies. While Standard Bank considers it a 'duty to help local regulatory authorities', of course any such involvement is a marriage of self-interest of the bank and the broader public good, both at home in South Africa and in their new host country environment.

A classic case of the sharing of knowledge to develop the host country's financial sector is UBA's operations in Ghana. In October 2013, the governor of the Bank of Ghana 'praised UBA Ghana for instituting a robust risk management system which has led to zero infractions on regulatory provisions on the part of UBA Ghana'.[26] In addition, the governor 'called on UBA to organise seminars and workshops on risk management for indigenous financial institutions in the country to help build a strong risk management culture in Ghanaian financial institutions'.[27] This clear call by the Ghanaian government for a leading bank to help develop the financial sector by sharing its knowledge demonstrates the often welcome role leading African banks have in developing the financial sectors of less developed economies.

However, the ability of established banks to share their knowledge, and the impact of such knowledge sharing, is contingent upon the willingness of the host country's central bank to accept and implement the initiatives shared with them. Unfortunately, not all African governments and central banks welcome knowledge sharing. In an example given by UBA regarding a recent acquisition, UBA executives have sent two proposals to the governor of the central bank of the new host country with ideas and initiatives on how to better develop the financial sector, including insights on strengthening measures such as building interbank placements, establishing bank treasuries and establishing standard regulatory requirements. Over one year later, UBA is yet to receive a response.

Novel products for broad economic development

African banks are able to introduce products into certain markets that better meet the needs of the local people or products that larger foreign banks are less-interested in or unwilling to implement. As stated by Diana Layfield, Standard Chartered's chief executive for Africa, 'What you have seen, particularly in some of the newer local regional banks, is an ability to serve emerging mass market consumers where other financial institutions haven't necessarily been able to cover effectively'.[28]

An example is the 2012 launch of Ecobank's large-scale mobile money platform which enables lower income individuals access to financial services Within six months of its launch, 320,000 customers were using its product.[79] Through a joint venture with the Indian firm Bharti Airtel,[30] Ecobank provides access to mobile banking services in 14 countries in its portfolio. In 2013, Ecobank won the Innovation in Banking award from the *African Banker* in recognition for 'its significant contribution to improving financial inclusion across Africa, leveraging technology and its pan-African footprint'.[31]

In March 2013, Stanbic Bank launched 'Heartland Banking', a novel product that enables African Diaspora residents living in the UK to bank and accumulate wealth in their country of origin. The product specifically targets citizens of Nigeria, Ghana and Kenya residing in the UK – approximately 1.3 million people who in 2010 alone collectively remitted over US $3.2 billion.[32] The Heartland Banking initiative was implemented in two phases: the first, targeting Africans living on the African continent but not in their home countries; and the second, targeting Africans in the UK who remit money to their families back home. In early 2014, Stanbic launched a complementary product for Africans living on the continent called the Travel Wallet, a prepaid Mastercard that enables African travelers access to foreign currency, including Euros, US dollars, Pound Sterling and Australian dollars, when traveling outside the continent.

UBA's entry into Ghana has introduced new products into the Ghanaian financial sector. At its entry, Ghana had a minimum account balance requirement of USD $1,000 in local currency to open a savings account. UBA introduced the Freedom Savings Account where customers can open a bank account for as little as 50 Ghanaian cedis. This new product 'created significant pressure' for other banks in the country to also institute similar products with lower initial balances. Through the institution of this novel product, UBA 'introduced a spirit of competitiveness' among banks within the Ghanaian financial sector with unquestionable benefits for customers.

In May 2013, UBA introduced its UBA Africard, 'a visa-enabled re-loadable card' which is 'a better alternative to a bank account as it is not tied to any bank account but can be used on over 1.9 million ATMs and at 30 million Point of Sales (POS) terminals in over 179 countries across the world'.[33] The Africard, like the remittances and the mobile money initiatives, enables formerly unbanked customers access to financial systems. These products are not within the purview of the large traditional foreign banks who have historically dominated the financial and banking sectors of many African countries.

The ability to modify products from developed western economies for adoption in African markets is an important benefit of intra-African investment. Leveraging its international status as a dominant player within the African continent, Ecobank has partnered with MasterCard in one of the 'largest multi-country licensing projects completed by MasterCard in Africa' to license 28 Ecobank subsidiaries. These Ecobank subsidiaries now accept MasterCard debit, credit and prepaid cards at Ecobank ATMs. Plans to license subsidiaries across the continent are under way.[34]

The broad economic development opportunities created by the investment of large African banks into smaller African economies is critical for millions of consumers in these economies, for whom access to banking and saving is a means to escape poverty. Of course, the investment of African banks in other African countries introduces competitiveness across products thereby improving services and options for consumers. However, key factors facilitating these investments are the visions and legacies of these African banks which 'have an affinity for' and 'bear a sense of responsibility toward' African economic and social development.

Development of national champions

The development of national banking champions (large national or local financial institutions) is another economic benefit of intra-African investment. Many African countries have no national banking champions, but the financial sectors within these countries may be relatively developed through a long history of banking by large foreign banks such as Barclays Bank and Standard Chartered Bank, whose origins hail from the colonial era.[35] While the presence of these larger foreign banks guarantees some level of financial sector development within the country, the very presence of these foreign banks may stymie the development of local and national banking systems within these countries. It is interesting to note that the dominant banks on the African continent are South African, North African or West African; that is, from countries and regions which have historically suffered periods of relative political and/or economic isolation. Intra-African investment spurs local financial sector growth. For example, although Ghana has a long history of banking by the international banks, Ghana's own local banking sector has been spurred by the entry of foreign African banks, particularly the Nigerian banks largely because Nigeria is the only other Anglophone West African country with a similar colonial history.[36]

Obstacles

Culture and stereotype-induced risk

A critical and less explored obstacle to intra-African investment within the financial sector is the importance of culture and the associated factors of stereotypes and languages; all factors stressed by executives from all three banks in this study. In a recent article exploring 'An African banking model',[37] the Executive Director of I&M Bank states that '[a feature] that distinguishes African banks [from Western banks] is the perception of them by local customers. African banks indeed inspire more trust in their customers'. However, this assumption does not take into account that African banks from different countries face cultural distance and not cultural proximities, which can adversely impact intra-African investment. As shared by a UBA Executive, 'some cultural differences are merely perceptions whereas some cultural differences are very real', and both perceived and real cultural differences have significant adverse impacts upon the ability of a bank or firm to invest within Africa.

For Standard Bank, while it is 'natural' to invest in Africa, the issue of culture has raised significant roadblocks. In its investments, Standard Bank executives have had cultural clashes with local executives as well as with local customers in other countries. In a bid to mitigate these clashes, the bank has adopted a strategic model which carefully considers cultural differences, especially as Standard Bank's primary investment model is through acquisitions. Across the continent, South Africans are associated with a 'reputation for arrogance and imperialist behavior', and being culturally aware of this stereotype, Standard Bank has sought to ensure that each of its acquired banks is 'locally run and autonomous'. The Standard Bank approach to foreign acquisitions is that these banks remain 'local' (i.e., must be perceived by local employees and customers as fundamentally unchanged and still 'their' local bank) and the Head Office in South Africa 'avoids any form of micromanaging'. The fine balance however, is that these local banks must also adhere to general Standard Bank Group standards.

Nigerian banks and Nigerian businesses more broadly face a different perspective and cultural problem when seeking to invest in other countries – a perceived 'liability of being Nigerian'. In negotiations with central banks of the African countries in which UBA sought to invest early in its African internationalisation, the very idea that UBA was coming from Nigeria proved to be a significant problem. *The very fact that UBA is a Nigerian bank in-and-of-itself created a perception of risk* largely due to existing stereotypes of Nigerian people and organisations being associated with illegal financial practices, financial scams and money laundering activities, commonly known in West Africa as '419' activities. Openly hostile executives of host country central banks apparently complained that UBA and the other Nigerian banks were coming to 'pollute' the existing banking system. The hostility of these central banking executives and their hesitancy to issue the requisite licenses to UBA due to cultural stereotypes rather than the firm's strong financial metrics was an important insight into investing in other African countries for UBA. Interestingly, UBA has found it easier to invest in Western countries (UK, USA and France) than to invest in some African countries.

Learning quickly from these adverse examples, UBA began each new investment discussion with the host country central bank by speaking at length about why a Nigerian bank should be considered as a good investment in the financial sector of that country. With each new internationalisation, UBA 'acted as Nigeria's ambassador' not only speaking for itself and the benefits that an investment by UBA would bring to the country, but also about the broader, more general value that a Nigerian firm would bring. Over time, with the spread of UBA's investment footprint across the continent and overseas, this adverse stereotype has reduced in significance, although it has not been completely eradicated. With UBA's growth, the bank's impressive portfolio of investment activity across the continent serves as the basis upon which it can now argue its strong financial position and the benefits of its operations to subsequent host country central banks; however, the cultural bias is likely to remain.

In addition to resistance from host country central banks to the entry or takeover of a local bank by UBA, significant resistance also arises from the general public who are unhappy about the idea of a Nigerian bank coming to 'take over their national assets'. Some of this public resistance is triggered and perpetuated by employees who, again, holding adverse stereotypes about the way Nigerian banks operate, generate significant adverse media coverage on the takeover.

UBA has also faced resistance from local shareholders resulting in sometimes turbulent shareholder meetings and general ill-will where regulatory minutiae have been leveraged against the bank. In a recent example, an extraordinary general meeting had to be completely rescheduled because of a (believed to be deliberate) one-day miscalculation by the banking executives of the local bank being acquired. Having understood how this stereotype of being Nigerian adversely impacts its ability to operate within certain countries and in a bid to better manage the resistance from local shareholders, UBA seeks majority ownership (over 50 per cent share) in all its investments, especially as in the past, shareholder decisions have been pushed to a vote. With the exception of Ghana (91 per cent), Burkina Faso (64 per cent) and Benin (76 per cent), all UBA assets on the African continent are 100 per cent owned by UBA.

Additional issues include significant problems due to differences in work ethic and accepted work conduct in other African countries. For example, the work-life balance in Ghana is very different from that in Nigeria. In Ghana, employees are less likely to work on Saturdays and more likely to demand that work done over the weekend be compensated by the appropriate level of allowance. Based on the fact that both Nigeria and Ghana hail from the same British colonial legacy, cultural similarity tends to be an underlying assumption, an assumption that is often detrimental to the investing bank or firm. An example of different professional conduct from the Francophone countries is the two-hour lunch break which is considered an anomaly in Nigeria. Adapting to these culturally accepted, but widely understated, obstacles to doing business across various African countries is critical to enhancing intra-African investment.

Issues with staff benefits such as staff loans vary across different countries. Within Nigeria, 13 per cent of an employee's salary can be provided as a loan from the bank. This percentage is higher in other countries such as in Burkina Faso where the bank can offer loans up to 55 per cent of an employee's salary. This loan program in Burkina Faso is nationally legislated whereas the 13 per cent loan in Nigeria is simply a policy stipulation and therefore voluntary. Understanding some of these differences is critical to fostering employee morale and generating a level of employee trust.

Language is unquestionably a significant issue. On entering Francophone countries, the need for an interpreter greatly diminishes the effectiveness of communication among executives. To address this issue, UBA has instituted a recent policy where, going forward, all CEOs must be bilingual. A less discussed stereotype which has significant adverse impact upon communication between executives is sometimes the nationalistic pride associated with the French language by nationals from Francophone African countries. In some places, even when people do understand English, they may sometimes pretend not to and insist on the use of an interpreter to translate. This Francophone-Anglophone territorial separation with regards to intra-African investment has been carefully upheld in the past, particularly by banks from strong Anglophone countries. However, in February 2014, moving from its preference to expand within Anglophone countries with the same language and more similar legal systems, Standard Bank became the first South African bank to venture into Francophone territory with the opening of a representative office in Côte d'Ivoire.[38] This step was a strategic move to 'follow its clients' and enter the West African Economic and Monetary Union comprising Benin, Burkina Faso, Cote d'Ivoire, Guinea-Bissau, Mali, Niger, Senegal and Togo.

Another interesting cultural difference and stereotype is the local power structure within different countries. Africa has widely been discussed by anthropologists as a clash of cultures, tribes and languages. Therefore it is not surprising that long-standing informal power structures and traditional approaches to meetings and gatherings are upheld by the various individuals

cultural biases faced when investing across the African continent is that Ecobank's leadership team comprises executives from many other African countries, and these national and cultural differences are highlighted in the Ecobank Annual Reports. This is in contrast to the UBA leadership team which comprises primarily Nigerian executives, and Standard Bank which is led by primarily South African executives.

Unfortunately, local business schools within the African continent seem to also follow the Western training programs which summarily ignore the importance of African cultural diversity in business. In the short-term view, executive programs should explore and highlight the diversity derived from the cultures, languages and colonial histories of the over 50 countries that comprise the African continent. Internal bank and consultant-led training programs within banks and other firms should also focus on understanding and managing cultural diversity. In the longer term, this issue of a lack of knowledge about other African countries and cultures is fundamentally one of educational policy in each country.

Cultural training that overcomes stereotypes is critical to overcoming negative stereotypes facing executives seeking to drive intra-African investment, particularly in the financial sector. Executive management training initiatives, such as the African Management Initiative (AMI)[44] which seeks to build and develop management talent for the African continent as a means to increasing economic and social development are key. However, even within these initiatives, what is clearly missing is an understanding of the cultural differences among African countries.

Ecobank has attempted to address the cultural information void it faces across its subsidiaries by leveraging its technology platform to ensure that every week all country managers of subsidiaries around the world take part in a common conference call to synchronise and explore issues and questions arising in their various countries. In addition, a constant cycle of travel visits is initiated by executives in a bid to build camaraderie and trust, and gain a better understanding of the other African cultures in the bank's portfolio, which will inevitably enable these executives to better jointly lead Ecobank.

Outlook

African value versus Western value

The concept of intra-African investment is an important one; however, the fundamental value of the concept can only be determined when compared to the value of foreign investment. In the case of the banking sector, the question remains: What is the economic and social value of investment in African economies by African banks versus the economic and social value of investment in these economies by foreign banks such as Standard Chartered and Barclays?

As stated by the executives of all three banks interviewed, African banks often consider themselves to be African and have a 'deeper commitment to the long-term development of the continent'. While the 'soft' value of an African identity and commitment can be important to the investment country (as exemplified by the types of products and services offered), the 'hard' value and possibly true benefit of intra-African investment is 'where the profits end up'. The true benefits of investment in African economies are only realised when the bulk of the profits gained by these financial institutions remains within the local host country. For example, the fact that Standard Bank is headquartered in South Africa means that this is: where 'tax is paid, making a substantial contribution to the South African Treasury and hence to public spending'; where 'the large majority of the bank's back-office functions are conducted, hence sustaining employment in South Africa'; and where '53.8 per cent of the bank's dividends' are paid out. Clearly, because Standard Bank is South African, the financial benefit of investment to South Africa is greater than the investment benefit afforded by foreign British banks whose funds are repatriated to the UK. UBA has the same positive impact upon Nigeria. In the case of Ecobank, the pan-African bank with no single national country identity, the financial beneficiaries are the bank's shareholders including: the Public Investment Corporation–Government Employees Pension Fund (PIC-GEPF) of South Africa, 18.2 per cent; Asset Management Corporation (AMCON) of Nigeria, 9.7 per cent; IFC Managed Funds, 7.3 per cent; IFC Direct, 6.9 per cent (total direct and indirect ownership of IFC is 9.4 per cent); Social Security and National Insurance Trust (SSNIT) of Ghana, 5.2 per cent.[45]

For the African host countries into which these African banks are investing, the hard financial benefit is considerably less as the value created in-country is still repatriated, albeit to another African country. Arguably, for these host countries, the difference between an African investing bank and a Western investing bank is less realised, especially given the deep cultural differences discussed earlier. The key is to ensure that these African investing banks have large local minority shareholders. For example, with Standard Bank's subsidiaries, although much of the value created is repatriated to South Africa, 'most of the Stanbics' have 'large local minority shareholders, so dividends stay in the host country as well as on the continent'. However, with 53.8 per cent of dividends being paid in South Africa alone and the largest shareholder with over 20 per cent share being Chinese (i.e., ICBC), there is relatively little value left over for the other 19 countries in which Standard Bank invests across the continent. In the eyes of some of the African host countries, Standard Bank is primarily a South African bank which invests, as its niche opportunity, within the African continent and is no different from a foreign bank such as Barclays or Standard Chartered. The same applies to UBA and the other African banks investing across the continent.

This view of an African investment bank as being similar to the Western banks in impact within the host country is a hindrance to intra-African investment, especially as it entrenches the zero-sum 'us versus them' perspective within African countries. In addition, in many parts of the African continent, the Western product is valued over the African product – a concept aptly described by a banking executive as 'the governor general mentality,' which is essentially a lingering colonial perspective surprisingly found even in the millennial generation. Due to this mentality, Western investors are readily given preferential access as compared to African investors. For the true benefit of intra-African investment to be realised across the continent, African investing banks must aim to provide more direct value to the host countries in which their subsidiaries are located. For example, more can be done by these African investing banks to increase the numbers and ownership by local minority shareholders to ensure much more of the profits stay within the host country.

An additional factor where African investing banks can and possibly should provide greater value within the investing African host country than Western banks is through the 'central bank evaluations of other country risk ratings'. In theory, an African bank should be able to better assess the nature of the environment and the degree of risk in another African country, and therefore should be able to provide better rates and services. In practice however, the central banks of the African investing banks assess the African host countries 'just as an OECD bank would'; that is, 'from the outside in', with no application of locally-relevant or context-specific metrics. Therefore, in this area, there is no difference between African investment and Western investment.

Defining a common economic language

As discussed by an executive interviewed, the value of intra-African investment versus Western investment can only be realised when African countries create a 'common economic language'; that is, create practices and systems that provide universal guidance on the salient aspects of business specifically in the African context. For example, in developed economies the registration of companies, licensing, labour regulation, tax laws and other business practices are 'different but recognizable'. A Norwegian, for example, does not need to learn a different language in terms of business practices to invest in the UK and in the USA. These countries have some uniformity or common business language. For the Frenchman, the Swede, the English or the American, 'business is like music, they all do the same thing'. But in Africa, it is not so; across the continent, registering a company is different, even across cities within the same country. The basic investment institutions are underdeveloped, and because a uniform set of practices is nonexistent, the businessman 'has to go through patronage'. This patronage, is essentially that the businessman has to get someone who knows the ropes and has expeditious ties to relevant actors who can influence the outcome of the business transaction. This, of course, leads to corruption within the financial sector. Further, this patronage is exacerbated by the different cultures, stereotypes and national languages, as discussed earlier.

Critically, while Africans often decry the differences in cultures and traditions and often lay these differences at the doors of colonialisation, an important fact is that 'even though the colonial powers have different languages and different legal systems, all of these former colonial powers interact *and interact well*. But, African countries themselves, have allowed colonial lines to splinter and divide them, even many decades after independence'. While the colonial powers forge ahead together, Africans are nowhere near moving towards an economic understanding across the continent. For example 'an Ivorian from Côte d'Ivoire is unlikely to think that they're going to invest in Ghana, nor a Ghanaian to think they are going to invest in Senegal or even in Angola'. For intra-African investment to flourish, African countries must move towards a common language of business practices.

The question, of course, is how to build this common economic language of business practices? Intra-African investment in the financial sector can, and indeed already does, play a significant role in this creation. However, an important means of alignment is to establish four solid regional economic blocks, where: South Africa anchors the southern region, Kenya anchors the Eastern region, Nigeria anchors the Western region and the northern countries form the fourth regional economic block. Driven by the financial power houses in each of these regional blocks, a common regional economic language can be developed and over time, these practices will merge into a single African economic block. Only with the creation of a common economic language of business practices tailored specifically for the unique and complex African business context, can African banks (and African businesses in general) forge ahead to realise the benefits of intra-African investment.[46]

Developing a new Africa-specific investment model

As financial sectors in the various African countries grow and strengthen, an increase in intra-African investment by banks from small economies is very likely. To guide the investment of these firms, an Africa-specific investment model is required. The effectiveness of this model is contingent on melding the lessons of the Western world with context-specific lessons from each of the over 50 African countries on the continent. Important to further development of an understanding of the costs and benefits of intra-African investment is large-scale and in-depth qualitative and empirical research that explores managerial, historical, political, social, cultural and economic factors and dynamics across the financial sectors on the continent. In addition, such scholarship should also explore and seek to understand the impact of Western banks with long histories of operating in the African continent, such as Barclays Bank and Standard Chartered Bank, as these banks historically shaped the fundamentals that underlie existing financial structures within and across the many different African countries today. Although intra-African investment in the financial sector can and does have an impact on shaping existing regulatory structures, greater insight will be obtained from longitudinal empirical studies.

Additional key insights that could significantly enhance our understanding of an intra-African investment model is an empirical exploration of the underlying mechanisms that may have created the dominant capabilities of the South African, North African and Nigerian banks. Clear identification of the specific capabilities and a better understanding of how these capabilities were developed is critical to enhancing effective intra-African investment by smaller financial institutions. Engagement of local academics from a wide range of fields, including sociology, anthropology and business, to explore these issues more deeply is essential.

Notes

1. Neil Ford, 'Banks Stand Still in the Midst of Economic Growth', *African Business* (October 2013).
2. Ecobank Research and World Bank, Ecobank Group Abridged Annual Report (2012).
3. The author gratefully acknowledges and thanks the executives from Standard Bank, UBA and Ecobank for sharing their insights and knowledge for this case study.
4. Standard Bank Annual Integrated Report (2012).
5. Richard Steyn and Francis Antonie, 'Hoisting the Standard: 150 Years of Standard Bank', *Standard Bank Group* (2012).
6. fDi Markets – Global Investment Database, fDiMarkets.com.
7. Standard Bank Annual Integrated Report (2013).
8. Standard Bank Annual Integrated Report (2012).
9. Standard Bank Annual Integrated Report (2012).
10. Standard Bank Annual Integrated Report (2012).
11. UBA Annual Report (2012).
12. UBA website, www.ubagroup.com/countries; www.ubagroup.com/group/ourachieve.
13. UBA Annual Report (2012).
14. UBA Annual Report (2012).
15. Ecobank Group Abridged Annual Report (2012).
16. KPMG: Financial Services in Africa. Full Sector Report (2013), www.kpmgafrica.com.
17. Ecobank Group Annual Report (2012).
18. Ecobank Group Abridged Annual Report (2013).
19. Ecobank Group Abridged Annual Report (2013).
20. GlobalData, Ecobank Transnational Incorporated Financial Analysis Review (November 2013), www.globalcompanyintelligence.com.
21. Ecobank Group Abridged Annual Report (2012).
22. Ecobank Press Release (30 April 2014), Ecobank Reports Full Year 2013 Audited Results: Pre-tax profit of $222 million on Revenue of $2.0 billion.
23. Ecobank Press Release (30 April 2014), Ecobank Reports Full Year 2013 Audited Results: Pre-tax profit of $222 million on Revenue of $2.0 billion.
24. J. Dunning, *Multinational Enterprises and the Global Economy* (Addison-Wesley Publishing Company, 1993). C. Bartlett and S. Ghoshal, *Managing across Borders: The Transnational Solution* (Boston: Harvard Business School Press, 1989).
25. The Africa Report, Finance Special (September 2013).
26. Business News of Sunday, 'Bank of Ghana Lauds UBA Ghana', *Graphic Business* (13 October 2013), http://www.ghanaweb.com/GhanaHomePage/business/artikel.php?ID=288779.

27. Business News of Sunday, 'Bank of Ghana Lauds UBA Ghana', *Graphic Business* (13 October 2013), http://www.ghanaweb.com/GhanaHomePage/business/artikel. php?ID=288779.

28. Neil Ford, 'Banks Stand Still in the midst of economic growth', *African Business* (19 September 2013), <http://africanbusinessmagazine.com/special-reports/banks-stand-still-in-the-midst-of-economic-growth/>.

29. Ecobank Group Abridged Annual Report (2012).

30. Ecobank Group Abridged Annual Report (2012).

31. Ecobank Group Abridged Annual Report (2013).

32. Diasporian News of Friday, 'Stanbic Bank Revolutionises Diasporan Banking', *Stanbic Bank*, (15 March 2013), http://www.ghanaweb.com/GhanaHomePage/ diaspora/artikel.php?ID=267761.33.

33. Business News of Sunday, 'UBA Introduces New Product', *Graphic Online* (26 May 2013), http://www.ghanaweb.com/GhanaHomePage/business/artikel. php?ID=275072.

34. Ecobank and MasterCard, 'MasterCard and Ecobank Group Partner to Accelerate Electronic Payments Adoption in 28 Sub-Saharan African Countries' (15 January 2014), http://www.ecobank.com/upload/20140116090736496377q4BVxE3bYA. pdf.

35. *Handbook on the History of European Banks*. Edited by Manfred Pohl and Sabine Freitag for the European Association for Banking History e.V. (Aldershot: Edward Elgar, 1994), pp. xiv, 1,303.

36. Liberia is the third Anglophone West African country, however, unlike Nigeria and Ghana, it has suffered years of civil war.

37. Sarit Raja Shah, Executive Director, I&M Bank, 'An African Banking Model', Private Sector & Development, www.proparco.fr.

38. Phakamisa Ndzamela, 'Standard Bank Leads the Way in to Africa for South Africa's Banks', *Business Day Live* (20 November 2013), http://www.bdlive.co.za/business/ financial/2013/11/20/standard-bank-leads-the-way-into-africa-for-south-africas-banks.

39. KPMG, 'Financial Services in Africa. Full Sector Report' (2013), Kpmgafrica.com.

40. Laura Secorun Palet, 'The Nigerian Buck Stops Here', *Provocateurs* (11 February 2014), http://www.ozy.com/rising-stars-and-provocateurs/nigerias-ngozi-okonjo-iweala/6423.article.

41. Geert Hofstede, 'The Business of International Business Is Culture', *International Business Review* (Vol. 3, No. 1, March 1994), pp. 1–14, http://www.sciencedirect. com/science/article/pii/0969593194900116.

42. USC currently holds the number one ranking in international business for both graduate MBA programs (2014) and the undergraduate programs (16 consecutive years including 2014).

43. The lack of knowledge about the African continent is often reflected in erroneous claims that Africa is a country.

44. http://www.africanmanagers.org/.

45. *Ecobank Group Investor Presentation*, November 2013. http://www.ecobank.com/up load/20131205035850833747ZZJKgsFdAc.pdf.

46. The idea of the common economic language and the solution being the development of four economic financial blocks is attributed to one of the banking executives interviewed for this case study.

8
The Case of Cement

Lyal White

Cement is an integral part of economic growth and development. As economies grow, so too does the demand for these commodities. This direct correlation extends to productivity and overall economic performance, where the per capita consumption of cement is highest in some of the larger, more developed economies.

Development of basic infrastructure from roads, rails and ports to hospitals, schools, shops and housing all require cement as a primary input, making it a key indicator of performance and the trajectory of an economy – especially those coming off a low base. Given the growth story in Africa and the requirements around infrastructure development and construction, cement is clearly a key strategic sector on the continent, with significant players and, increasingly, African companies investing and exporting to other African markets.

Africa's average cement consumption is 92 kg per person. The global average, including China's, is 513 kg per person.[1] With African economic growth rates well above the global average over the past decade, and as the economy and population in Africa continues to grow and urbanise, cement consumption is expected to surge in the next few years. The World Bank estimates that Africa needs US$93 billion of investment in infrastructure each year over the next decade to make up the shortfall and meet the basic infrastructural requirements of the growing market and its population.[2] Demand for cement in Africa will thus follow a similar trend to that of previous rapidly industrialising regions like Southeast Asia. Expected demand in Africa through the urbanisation of transport, business and housing is likely to outstrip local supply, even with large lime deposits spread across the continent and as cement plants are being rolled out at a pace never seen before.

Despite the current shortages, there is a long history of cement production in Africa. This has attracted foreign investment from some of the biggest global players for many years and continues to do so today. Most local cement manufacturers in East, West and Southern Africa were acquired by global leaders like Lafarge from France,[3] Holcim from Switzerland or

Heidelberg Cement from Germany between 1960 and the early 2000s. Some of these have sold back their majority shareholding to local family businesses in over the years – mostly in East Africa – but by-and-large the African cement market is dominated by a handful of players, with the global majors carrying a majority shareholding in key plants in some of the more established African markets, alongside two heavy weight African players: Pretoria Portland Cement (PPC) of South Africa and Dangote of Nigeria. What could be described as the African minnows competitively service localised markets – with the occasional regional extension – but are far from having an Africa-wide footprint, due to capacity constraints, and their preference for acute competitiveness in localised areas over a much broader – and perhaps less competitive – footprint.

Even with abundant deposits of lime across the continent, Africa has a history of cement imports from cheaper producers in Asia (Figure 8.1) and, in the case of Sub-Saharan Africa, North African manufacturers.

High levels of imports are largely due to the high prices of cement across the continent. Despite the increase in supply of local manufacturers, cement prices in Africa are still the highest in the world, averaging around 200 per cent higher than in any other region.[4] Underdeveloped financial markets and inconsistent government policy are largely to blame. Building financial markets that will provide the means to purchase cement and harness

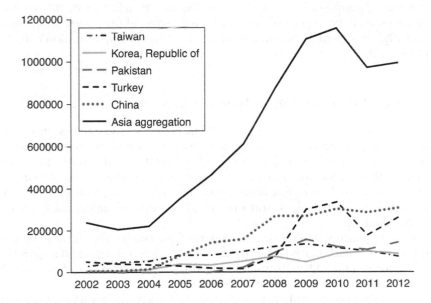

Figure 8.1   Africa's imports of cement from Asia, 2002–2012 (US$ 000)
Source: Trade Map, 2014.

lower cost local supplies along with progressive policies aligned to develop the competitive production of cement on the African continent will have a direct and immediate impact on reducing the price of cement, which will in turn serve as an economic multiplier through infrastructure development and construction towards Africa's urban future.

Some of the key markets in Africa are doing this. Nigeria is the best example of how certain protective measures and investment incentives have moved it from a primary cement importer, grossly under-supplied, to a self-sufficient market and ultimately an exporter of cement to other African markets over a relatively short time frame of 10–15 years. South Africa had similar policies in place and is now a key cement exporter to surrounding countries like Mozambique, Namibia and Angola. While there is much debate around the levels of protection and the nature of government intervention, this certainly has contributed directly toward the rise of Africa's two largest home-grown cement manufacturers, Dangote and PPC. This has in turn facilitated their expansion into new African markets. Dangote, for example, has used the favourable environment to increase capacity back home in Nigeria, which has helped finance an aggressive investment drive into 13 new African markets.[5]

Africa's growth story is now a reality that is intrinsically related to cement. This is an exciting prospect, with high costs and a range of inter-related factors that contribute to the high risk of cement supply in Africa. There is a real opportunity for Africans to be the true benefactors of this crucial commodity. But competition in a region with some of the lowest input costs and highest potential demand is fierce. If African companies don't do it, others will.

The benefits of the cement business in Africa

Africa is the last great cement frontier.[6] The collective story across the continent is remarkable with forecasts and figures of astronomical proportions. But the discrepancies in numbers and expectations are quite dramatic, making the current situation – not to mention the future – difficult to interpret from a solid empirical foundation. For this reason, it is best to look at each sub-regional block and individual country separately for a deeper understanding.

Each region does share similar benefits and challenges, but contextual differences in each market – not to mention leading countries and important role players – do add slight nuances to the supply and demand of cement from Southern Africa to East and West Africa.

The biggest opportunity across all three regions is the low level of cement consumption per capita, which is expected to rise dramatically off low base levels on the back of infrastructure mega-projects and rapid urbanisation.

The per capita consumption of cement in Southern Africa is currently 82 kg per annum, with South Africa leading this demand at around 280 kg per person. East Africa's per capita consumption is comparatively low at 60 kg per person, led by Kenya's 85.7 kg per person. West Africa meanwhile averages 115 kg of cement per person with Nigeria averaging 108 kg per capita consumption per annum. Two of the biggest markets in terms of population size, the Democratic Republic of Congo and Ethiopia, have a cement consumption of 24 kg and 35 kg per capita per annum, which, alongside anticipated high growth rates in those economies, offer the biggest untapped potential on the continent. Until manufacturing plants with the required capacity are established in those markets, the DRC will be serviced by Southern and East African suppliers, while Ethiopia is a great prospective market for East African cement producers.[7]

While poor infrastructure and various tariff and non-tariff barriers continue to hinder trade and investment across the continent (which will be elaborated on in the following section), cement manufacturers in regional markets have benefited from regional trade agreements. In East Africa, manufacturers based in the East African Community (EAC) comprising Kenya, Tanzania, Rwanda, Burundi and Uganda, benefit from tariff free access to other members' markets. In addition to this, the EAC has a common external tariff ranging from 10 per cent for cement clinkers and Portland cement, 25 per cent for white cement, aluminous cement and other hydraulic cements, to 55 per cent for other white cement, common external tariff, which helps protect local producers of cement.

This has helped encourage PPC's recent acquisition of a 51 per cent stake in a plant in Southern Rwanda valued at $69 million,[8] with plans to increase capacity in the next few years, as well as Dangote's much-anticipated $400 million investment in Kenya.[9] Dangote has already invested in Tanzania,[10] along with AfriSam, which has a 62.5 per cent share of Tanga Cement[11] – the largest supplier in Tanzania – all with an eye on the East

Table 8.1 Estimated average per capita consumption of cement

Region	2011 (kg)
West Africa	115
Southern Africa	82
East Africa	60
Sub-Saharan Africa	*84*

Source: Adapter by the author from Standard Investment Bank, PPC, ICS, Cardinal Stone Equity Research, Dangote, ICR, Imara and ZKG International.

Table 8.2 Per capita consumption of cement

Country	2011 (kg)
Nigeria	108
Ghana	123
South Africa	300
Mozambique	45
Angola	95
Zambia	75
DRC	16
Kenya	86
Tanzania	51
Uganda	40
Rwanda	25
Burundi	7
Malawi	19
Zimbabwe	50
Ethiopia	35

Source: Adapted by the author from PPC, ICS, Cardinal Stone Equity Research, Dangote, ICR and Bloomberg.

African Community. Ethiopia's possible inclusion into the EAC has sparked a substantial interest among various investors, including cement manufacturers, which have recently assisted existing operations to increase capacities and improve efficiencies – in the case of PPC – as well as in developing greenfield operations, which Dangote is currently exploring.

Both Southern Sudan and the DRC offer enormous untapped potential for cement suppliers. Exports from operations in East Africa (from Rwanda in the case of PPC) and Southern Africa to the DRC are currently under way, facing staunch competition from both Chinese and Pakistani suppliers. But there are also initial investment plans under way by both PPC and Dangote, which are looking to develop new plants in the DRC. The Pakistani company Lucky Cement is already building a $240 million cement plant in the DRC in partnership with the DRC Rawji group, which is expected to be operational by 2015, with a capacity to produce 1.2 million tonnes of cement per year – double the current annual capacity of the country. Based on various interviews with cement producers around the continent, the demand for cement reports the need for infrastructure and construction, the DRC's potential for growth in cement is enormous.

The Economic Community of West African States (ECOWAS) is also operating as a free trade area with duty-free access for originating goods to member markets. No duties are applied on locally produced cement between members of the community, and ECOWAS has a common external tariff of

35 per cent, due to come into force in January 2015. Individual countries also have certain protective constraints.

Nigeria, in particular, is phasing out imports, with no further licenses having been granted since the start of 2012, and those with existing licenses to import can only do so with a planned mandate to develop their domestic manufacturing. This, despite calls by the Cement Producers Association of Nigeria (CPAN) to lift the suspension on cement import licences, which is still in place. This was how Dangote started, first as a cement importer, which supplemented local manufacturing shortages until capacities were increased. Cement imports have been slowly phased out in Nigeria as the country becomes self-sufficient in cement with new local production facilities coming online. In 2013, 1.1 million tonnes of cement was imported into Nigeria by just one remaining import company, Ibeto.

Nigeria is both the principal supplier and consumer of cement in West Africa. With domestic production capacity in the region of roughly 20 million tonnes per annum – dominated by Dangote, which has around 70 per cent of the local market   demand hovers around 18 million tonnes, allowing for a small surplus for exports to regional markets. This currently goes mainly to Ghana. In fact, Dangote's recently completed Ibese plant, which has a 6 million tonne per annum capacity, has targeted Ghana as its primary market. With little in terms of lime deposits in between Nigeria and Senegal, Nigeria is described as a cement industry 'sweet-spot', poised to continue to dominate West Africa's supply and to become a leading global supplier in the not-too-distant future.

South Africa has dominated the supply and demand of cement in Southern Africa for decades. This is changing as demand for cement in South Africa declines and economic growth rates fall well behind neighbouring countries that are growing and developing at a fast pace, albeit off a much lower base, and demanding increasing volumes of cement each year. In this respect, PPC, which has about 43 per cent of the local market in South Africa, has seen export volumes rise by 30 per cent over 2012/2013, even as new cement manufacturers are entering the Southern African market. PPC expects over 40 per cent of its revenues to come from outside of South Africa by 2017.

The Southern African Customs Union (SACU) allows for the free movement of cement between member countries (Botswana, Lesotho, Namibia, South Africa and Swaziland), while the Southern African Development Community (SADC) allows for duty free trade of cement that originates within SADC. This means that cement that is classified as originating from countries such as South Africa, Zambia, Zimbabwe and Namibia can enter member markets such as Mozambique and Angola free of duty. Better infrastructure – road, rail, ports and power – in South Africa has facilitated production and allows higher trade efficiencies.

Across all three regions, knowledge of the market, the development of supplier and buyer networks and complications around poor infrastructure have kept some competitors out while benefitting local suppliers. They have managed to find innovative ways of minimising their costs, establishing their export markets and building their competitiveness around the institutional gaps and complexities that are strongly associated with these markets. These complexities – often referred to as 'institutional voids' in strategy literature – have helped protect African cement suppliers that have developed ways and means to overcome the difficulties and even prosper in the process.[12] This knowledge of complex markets has also informed the expansion strategies of African suppliers. PPC, for example, has targeted countries that not only have large potential markets for cement, but are also difficult to access or penetrate by competitive imports. The rationale is to be an early mover that services a market that is under-supplied with minimal competition. The initial capital outlay is high. But the medium-to-long term returns are also very high, coupled with the healthy relationship that develops between the first mover investor and host government (and community), who see them as an early development partner.

Obstacles to expanding in Africa

Despite the important role of cement in economic development, productivity and job creation, not to mention its enormous potential and obvious returns in emerging Africa, cement producers face enormous obstacles to trade and investment across the continent. While constraints to trade and investment do vary slightly from region-to-region and country-to-country, there is a common list of problems, which manufacturers of cement highlight as major obstacles and which add to the cost of business and trade and undermine the competitiveness of the sector vis-à-vis external suppliers.[13] These include:

1. Availability and proximity to lime deposits.
2. Poor infrastructure: roads, rail and ports
3. Inadequate power and water supply
4. Inconsistencies in policy and regulation
5. Competition from cheap and inferior imports

Limestone deposits

The physical composition of cement is integral to its strategic relevance, geography and players involved. Cement is manufactured through a closely controlled chemical combination of calcium, silicon, aluminium, iron and other ingredients. Key materials used to manufacture cement include limestone, shells and chalk or marl combined with shale, clay, slate, blast furnace slag, silica sand and iron ore. These ingredients, when heated at high temperatures form a rock-like substance that is ground into the fine powder that we commonly think of as cement.[14]

Limestone is thus the essential base product for cement. It typically comprises 85 per cent of the raw material input of the product. Investors will, first and foremost, seek out countries and locations with these deposits and assess proximity, access and ease of extraction for a manufacturing plant. The plant will preferably be as close to the lime deposit as possible. But the process of mixing, heating and cooling calcareous minerals to form a clinker product, which is then ground into cement used for construction, commonly known as Portland cement, requires access to large amounts of power and water. Africa is fortunate to have large deposits of lime stretching across the continent. But accessibility is the challenge, which brings into play the balance between these deposits, electrical power and water supply and transport of either clinker, bulk or bagged cement to local and regional markets or ports for export. Most often plants are built on top of or nearby deposits that are large enough to supply the plant for its full 30-year life span. The size of the deposit is thus also an important factor.

Infrastructure

The infrastructure deficit in Africa is seen as one of the biggest impediments to trade. In fact, one Kenyan producer noted this as their biggest constraint in East Africa, undermining the free movement of products between EAC members, which has been negotiated but, due to infrastructure constraints, not fully practiced. This is amplified in the case of cement given the nature of the commodity and location of lime deposits vis-à-vis the market. Roads are poor and rail is largely absent across the continent, which creates enormous delays and, in turn, adds significantly to higher costs.

Power and water

Electrical power is in short supply across Africa. Cement production requires large amounts of regular electricity supply. Electricity is astronomically expensive in both East and West Africa, while in Southern Africa, where this cost has traditionally been relatively low compared to other regions, price-hikes have increased input costs over night and are now almost on a par with their counterparts in East and West Africa. This undermines the competitiveness of the sector at the crucial production phase of the operation, since electricity costs – traditionally a competitive advantage in Southern Africa – is no longer lesser than that in other sub-regions.

In Kenya, which one manufacturer claims has the highest industry electricity costs in the world, the manufacturing sector consumes 60 per cent of the country's electrical power but pays 75 per cent of the country's electrical costs.[15] Construction – of which cement is a key component – foots the majority of this bill. This adds directly to the cost of manufacturing cement, which is borne by the consumer who pays 200 per cent more for cement in Sub-Saharan Africa than anywhere else in the world.[16]

Policies and regulation

Cement manufacturers maintain that policies in their countries don't necessarily help or encourage them to produce and export cement. Nigeria is an exception. Favourable tax breaks are awarded to encourage investment in the cement manufacturing sector and import licenses have been discontinued to encourage local production. The Nigerian government has also started supporting cement exports through subsidies. However, cement suppliers across the continent (including Nigeria) complain about the inconsistencies in policy and regulation. Certain policies or regulations may be in place, but these are also often poorly exercised, resulting in inconsistencies in the operating and trading environment.

One example mentioned was the poorly executed and corrupted policy or even lack of regulation around weigh-bridges and truck loads in the EAC. This allows overloaded trucks to transport cement from established local producers in Uganda to Rwanda, thus undermining start-up local production in Rwanda on a sub-regional level by manipulating rules and regulations that are poorly implemented on a case-by-case basis.

In Nigeria, Ibeto, the last remaining importer of cement into the country, maintains they have not been granted the same preferences as Dangote. The company has accused Dangote of bullying the federal government to continue the ban on imports of clinker cement or drastically increase the duties and taxes on clinker imports.[17] This puts smaller producers and cement bagging companies at a significant disadvantage as they try and grow to become self-sufficient manufacturers.

Ibeto Cement Company also claimed that the Dangote Group, by its statement, wanted the federal government to ban the importation of clinker or in the alternative drastically increase the duties and taxes on clinker imports so as to destabilise cement manufacturers in the south and maintain a monopolistic domination of the cement market in Nigeria.

Other manufacturers in both East and West Africa complain about changes overnight whereby permits can be cancelled or the terms of trade altered. The best example of this is around the mega-projects in East Africa, like the trans-railway system or bypass highways, which are currently under way in Kenya. Local cement producers were surprised by bilateral agreements between the Kenyan government and China that allowed for duty-free imports of inputs like cement in the construction of roads and railways. The so-called bilateral agreement with Chinese contractors exempted cement imports from the standard 25 per cent tariff and effectively cut local cement producers out of some of the biggest infrastructure projects in the region. This has apparently been rectified for future megaprojects. But local suppliers are reminded that nothing is certain, and this too could change yet again to allow for cheaper imports as a result of inconsistent tax and policy regimes.

Cheap imports

African markets are still flooded by cheap and inferior alternatives mostly from China and Pakistan.[18] While these cement products do face hefty tariffs of between 25 and 35 per cent – depending which sub-region of Africa they are entering – with the high costs of production in Africa and the alleged subsidising of these products by their governments back home, they are still able to sell for around 25 per cent lower than locally produced cement products. This is perpetuated yet further through the special 'bilateral agreements' various African governments have signed with Asian contractors – particularly the Chinese.

These agreements help ensure far lower costs and shortened timeframes for the completion of important projects, but they exclude local providers and products, which undermines local manufacturing, job creation and other multipliers that are supposedly linked with these megaprojects. In short, cheaper imports undermine local manufacturing through unrealistically (and often subsidised) prices and inject inferior products into new infrastructure and buildings across the continent.

Leading African cement champions: PPC versus Dangote

The two largest African-owned and Africa-based cement companies on the continent are PPC of South Africa and Dangote of Nigeria. Both dominate their respective home markets and both are expanding across the African continent, investing in manufacturing plants and developing export markets in neighbouring African countries.

But their Africa expansion strategies are different. While PPC, a much older company with a well-established name in the cement industry in Southern Africa, has pursued a slow and very cautious approach to markets beyond South Africa – and focusing specifically on one or two key strategic markets to start with, Dangote has expanded at breakneck pace, aggressively entering around 13 new markets in the past few years with a number of others lined up for entry before 2016. Dangote's entry strategies have made use of political diplomacy, accompanying state visits and promising large capital outlays in new greenfield operations. PPC, by contrast, has made little use of high-level political relations and has partnered with development banks (and local financiers) in purchasing existing plants with a view to rebuild on the site or upgrade and increase capacities over a stipulated period of time.

PPC and Dangote epitomise the notion of 'Africans investing in Africa' in the cement sector. Interestingly, they also seem to represent the changing geopolitical dynamics in Africa and the shift in economic power with the rise of Nigeria as the largest economy on the continent, overtaking South Africa, which has been Africa's largest economy for generations. The companies illustrate the style and approach of their respective home countries in their engagement with other African countries. While PPC and Dangote have operated exclusively in their home markets and a few selected nearby markets, they are now investing in common markets and will soon be producing and exporting to the same markets. This introduces a new scenario in the African cement industry where markets will be dramatically and positively disrupted in terms of economic alternatives, through the influence of two of Africa's most competitive players.

PPC and its future in Africa

PPC was, for a long time, the largest home-grown cement producer on the continent. It is also the oldest cement company in Africa, started in 1892, and has been listed on the Johannesburg Stock Exchange since 1910. Described as a large-scale domestic player in the South African cement industry, PPC accounts for around 43 per cent of South Africa's market share, traditionally focused on manufacturing and supply to the South African market with a moderate amount of exports to surrounding countries. It is also the only cement producer with a complete national footprint of integrated plants.[19]

The high demand for cement in South Africa has always encouraged PPC to concentrate its efforts on the local market, with little interest beyond the borders where low levels of efficiency and high costs were not necessarily met with market demand. This was especially the case between 2004 and 2010 when large-scale infrastructure projects were being rolled out in South Africa along with a spike in construction around the FIFA World Cup Football Finals. This was a period of substantial growth in nearby African markets, when most observers would have expected PPC to expand outward. However, capacity constraints due to the company structure as a subsidiary of Barlow kept the company at home, apart from moderate exports to neighbouring countries, a few exploration projects in the Southern Africa region and one or two investments in neighbouring Zimbabwe and Botswana. PPC acquired Portland Holdings Limited in Zimbabwe in 2001 and PPC-Botswana, originally CEMPACK, was a partnership PPC entered into with the Botswana government in 1994.

In 2007, with the unbundling of PPC from Barlow, PPC were able to launch their Africa-wide strategy with the help of a large capex injection into the share market from Barlow's 70 per cent holding over the company. PPC also focused its offering on becoming more vertically integrated in their customer's business model, adding value through efficient capacity and strong customer relations. This, inadvertently, started drawing them further into new African markets, as local demand for cement commodities began to taper off. With an eye on expanding into the rest of Africa, PPC adopted the strategy of growing beyond the South African market but as head of PPC for Africa Pepe Meijer described, 'Keeping the home fires burning'.

In 2013, the South African cement industry ran at roughly a 75 per cent capacity utilisation, while PPC's utilisation was in the region of 70–75 per cent, which indicates some leeway for growth. But sales have continued to slow down domestically. PPC's export volumes from 2012 to 2013 have grown around 30 per cent – mostly to Mozambique and Angola.

With current manufacturing capacity of 8 million tonnes per annum in South Africa and sales and revenue below par in the African context, PPC have now prioritised their African expansion. Sub-Saharan Africa is expected to have a 40 million tonne capacity shortage over the next few years, and PPC is positioning itself to capture 10–15 per cent of that. The company's current revenues outside of South Africa make up around 24 per cent of total revenues. This is expected to increase to 40 per cent of PPC's revenues by 2017.[20] By the end of September 2013, rising sales of cement in their Zimbabwe and South African operations drove PPC's revenue to R8.3 billion.[21] This was further buoyed by the consolidation of Rwandan operations and the Rand depreciation which boosted sales volumes.[22]

PPC's expansion plans targeting high potential infrastructure markets, where there is currently low per-capita cement consumption and gross shortages of cement, have led the company to markets in East and Central Africa, with a few expansionary plans in surrounding Southern African markets. The company has also consciously avoided coastal locations, ironically favouring landlocked countries that are difficult to access by importers, citing the flood of cheap imports from Asia as a major deterrent to the development of local cement production.

Proximity to lime deposits is important, but PPC is willing to put in the necessary infrastructure absent in these areas that will allow the plant to operate effectively for the full 30-year life cycle. If there is a growing market and access to the required resources, their capital outlay in infrastructure can be factored into the long-term investment arrangement with the host country – given the economic multiplying effect of cement manufacturing in that market, and a win-win for development and returns that has been exercised in some of their more recent projects.

In 2012, PPC invested $69.4 million in a 51 per cent acquisition stake in Cimerwa in southwestern Rwanda, where it plans to increase the capacity from 100,000 tonnes per annum to 600,000. In the same year, along with the South African Industrial Development Corporation (IDC), PPC invested in the greenfield Ethiopian Habesha plant. The combined PPC/IDC share amounted to 47 per cent of the company, with PPC contributing 27 per cent or around $16 million.[23] The remaining shares reside with 16,000 local shareholders.

In addition to these investments, PPC has pledged $260 million to a greenfield operation in western DRC to produce 1 million tonnes of cement per annum. With the price of cement around $400 per tonne (or $20 per bag) in the DRC, and severely undersupplied, PPC – like other suppliers – sees the DRC as potentially the largest untapped opportunity in Africa. PPC are also investing a further $200 million in the construction of a new plant in Zimbabwe, with a capacity of 1 million tonnes per annum, to improve supply to the rapidly growing central and northern regions of Mozambique. Construction of these new facilities in both the DRC and Zimbabwe are expected to begin in early 2014.

Dangote's rise to the leading cement manufacturer in Africa

Dangote has emerged, in a very short period of time, as the largest cement producer in Africa. This was built off a platform of the largest cement provider in Nigeria, where the company has over 65 per cent of the market share, which is still rising each year.[24] Founded in 1981, the Dangote Group is a conglomerate covering a range of sectors from sugar and salt to confectionary and oil refinery. But cement, which started off with the importation of cement until manufacturing capacity was established, is the foundation of the Dangote business empire, accounting for the lion's share of employees, operations and profits.

Dangote currently has a capacity to produce just over 20 million tonnes of cement per annum. Its profit in 2012 was $1.1 billion on sales of $1.9 billion. With a market capitalisation of $24.5 billion, Dangote is the largest company on the Nigerian Stock Exchange, accounting for 29 per cent of the total value of the exchange. It is little surprise that Dangote's

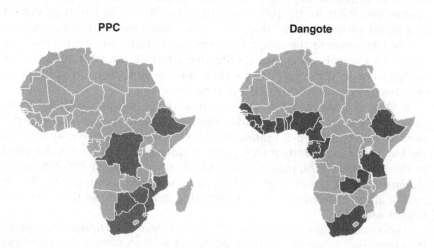

Figure 8.2   African presence: PPC vs Dangote
Source: GIBS Centre for Dynamic Markets, 2014.

stellar performance in 2013 was the primary reason for Nigeria's Exchange recording the best performance in Africa for 2013.[25]

Dangote's market capitalisation also catapults it into the major league of global cement players. At $24.5 billion, Dangote is the second largest cement company in the world by market capitalisation, behind Holcim at $25 billion and ahead of Lafarge ($22 billion), Heidelberg ($14.6 billion) and Cemex ($14 billion). While the capacities of the 'big four' far outstrip that of Dangote, with both Holcim and Lafarge boasting well over 200 million tonnes per annum, Dangote's return on equity and comparatively low levels of debt at $558 million versus the likes of Lafarge at around $10 billion places it in a uniquely favourable position for expansion, especially in Africa, which is still perceived by international investors as a relatively high risk environment, making the spread between equity and debt in new investments relevant to healthy investment decisions.

Most remarkable of all is the pace of Dangote's ascendency. What took global players – including PPC – over 100 years to achieve in terms of size and geographical presence has taken Dangote a fraction of the time. This can be attributed to the growth rate and insatiable appetite for cement and concrete in Nigeria, along with the relative absence of feasible alternatives and competitors, and – as those in Dangote cement insist – the visionary drive of Aliko Dangote himself, who identified the opportunity at precisely the right time.

But Dangote's growth and geographical presence is still in its infancy. As Carl Franklin, head of investor relations, insists while explaining Dangote's African expansion, 'We are *IN* the process of expanding, not *HAVE* expanded'. He is referring to the $4.7 billion expansion planned from 2012 to 2016, with $1.6 billion dedicated to increasing Nigeria's capacity and $3.1 billion for the rest of Africa.

This spread of investment across Africa makes sense when considering the potential and costs of manufacturing in various markets. Nigeria's growth and impressive investment returns in recent years have helped fuel this expansion and provided necessary capital to invest in new African markets, without plunging Dangote deep into debt. The funding plan for Dangote's Africa expansion is 60 per cent equity and 40 per cent debt, a very different scenario to other cement majors, which have gone deeper into debt in their efforts to expand and compete in the long term.[26]

With attractive cement prices, relatively cheaper input costs given abundant supplies of lime and the availability of low-cost natural gas to power manufacturing plants, a strong domestic demand with per capita consumption of cement at 108 kg per annum – well below the global average, along with an ideal location to access other fast growing ECOWAS markets duty free – not to mention government support through incentives like a five-year tax break for new factories and export credits, Nigeria remains Dangote's principal market and largest recipient of new investment. Producers in Nigeria are already reaching peak capacity, clearly indicating that demand is outstripping supply. Analysts believe that Nigeria needs a new 2.5 million tonne per annum cement plant per year to keep up with the growth and demand in the market.[27]

Dangote has begun its expansion, with different types of operations, into 13 other African markets beyond Nigeria. This is expected to increase production capacity from current levels of around 20 million tonnes per annum to over 60 million tonnes per annum by 2017.

The rest of West Africa is still predominantly an export market for Nigerian cement, which means Dangote's investments will focus on export terminals in Nigeria along with import terminals and grinding plants in selected countries like Ghana, Ivory Coast, Cameroon, Liberia and Sierra Leon. These will facilitate bulk exports of clinker from Nigeria and future Dangote plants planned in the Republic of Congo and Senegal.

Investments in Eastern and Southern Africa are mostly large-scale capital-intensive integrated plants. Those in Ethiopia, Kenya, South Sudan and Tanzania range from between $300 million to $470 million for each plant. East and Southern Africa has thus attracted roughly $1.8 billion of Dangote

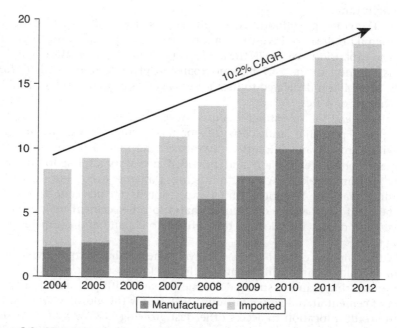

Figure 8.3   Nigerian cement sales, 2004–2012 (mt)
Source: Dangote Cement, 2014.

investment, increasing cement capacity by 8.5 million tonnes per annum by the end of 2016.

Investments in South Africa and Zambia amount to $326 million and $300 million, respectively. The South African operation is expected to generate 3.3 million tonnes of cement per annum, while the Zambian plant will have a capacity of 1.5 million tonnes. With other potential prospects under consideration in Zimbabwe and the DRC, Dangote could soon become the second largest cement supplier in Southern Africa, close behind PPC.

The cement showdown in Africa

Dangote and PPC are now expanding across Africa and increasingly towards each other, in markets of common interest. They already share some of the same markets and have identified certain key growth markets as their priority investments. Ethiopia in particular and perhaps the DRC in time are two markets that come to mind. This has led some observers to suggest a cement industry showdown in Africa, with geopolitical relevance around Dangote representing Nigeria and PPC representing South Africa.

This does invite interesting speculation around the transfer of economic power and influence in Africa, especially given the strategic importance of cement. But in the context of the cement business for both Dangote and PPC, the story is much more about strategic expansion for new opportunities, scale,

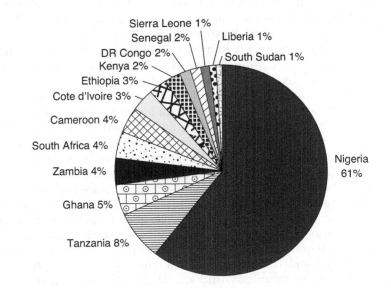

Figure 8.4 Dangote's estimated share of EBITDA per country in 2016
Source: Dangote Cement, January 2014.

building efficiencies and, most importantly, retaining and increasing returns on investment. In short, it is more about business than higher politics.

It is true that Dangote has used political leverage and diplomacy to accelerate the company's expansion in Africa. But this is merely a reality of how business is conducted in African markets. Despite on-going objections and the criticism of the West, business in Africa continues to be closely aligned to politics. Engagement with, and even working with, government and policy makers is part of the practice of business in Africa. Both Dangote and PPC understand this in the strategic context of cement and exercise their engagement, albeit at varying degrees. PPC likewise prides itself in building long-running and healthy relations with partner governments in the countries in which it has invested.

But the approach to new African markets and overall expansion strategies adopted by Dangote and PPC are fundamentally different and may well originate in the cultural orientation of their home markets which have informed their style of business practice and nature of expansion. Dangote has undertaken a rapid expansion rollout, fuelled by large amounts of capital and raw energy that is driven directly by the top leadership and Aliko Dangote himself. His hands-on approach and engagement with role players in new markets has gone a long way in opening up opportunities and in implementing operations quickly.

PPC, on the other hand, has cautiously entered into new markets with key strategic partners like the IDC and local partners. While PPC are seen to add value, experience and know-how, partners like the IDC contribute toward the capital expenditure of the project and add political weight, thus taking on some of the perceived risks of expansion into Africa. They have also opted to purchase existing plants and, in most cases, rebuild them to their requirements, to improve efficiencies and increase capacities significantly. This supports the strong argument for new technologies and new facilities. Many plants in East Africa are still using equipment that was installed over 50 years ago, and many of the plants in South Africa are 30 years old, which results in relatively high production costs. New facilities and new technology will ultimately reduce the costs of operation. But the risk of the initial capital outlay needs to be managed effectively to ensure these operations come online smoothly to allow new technology to be implemented.

Dangote, the company, is widely admired for its scale and use of technology to advance the cement sector through new plants and new practices. It is building a string of plants and related operations from scratch across the continent. But the company is also staunchly criticised for its lack of corporate professionalism and highly centralised approach around decision-making and communication, despite its size and spread. The company has grown so quickly into an Africa-wide operation and global brand but is yet to corporatise, which poses a number of challenges in maintaining growth rates, levels of efficiency and image. Executives at Dangote are the first to admit, despite the technology and scale they have brought to the African market, they are yet to prove themselves among the global heavyweights.[28]

Both Dangote and PPC are aware of the contribution they are able to make to Africa through the supply of cement and by fundamentally altering the cement market across the continent. Dangote has described itself as an unashamed market disruptor, where it sees its role – over and above supplying cement – in creating jobs and reducing prices from their current astronomical levels.

Both companies are perceived as contributors toward development through the jobs they create and inputs into the reconstruction of the economies in which they are investing. Cement is after all one of the great economic multipliers, which creates growth and opportunities across the entire economic spectrum. It is for this reason they are by-and large welcomed into new African markets. Unlike other industries, their contribution is tangible and there are increasingly obvious benefits they bring despite cheaper alternatives from Asia.

While there does seem to be some sentimental preference toward an African supplier of cement, apart from a few tax breaks in Nigeria, this has not brought PPC or Dangote preferential access into new markets. There is no record of preferences granted to either company or any African-based cement manufacturer for that matter. They are not favoured for their African origins or through preferences due to trade or investment agreements signed by their home and host countries. Rather, they are liked for their size, track record, and – in the case of Dangote – they are well-funded. Personal touches do make a difference. Host countries and partners in those countries do seem to prefer negotiating directly with Aliko Dangote, who regularly and happily meets with policy makers, heads of state and business partners throughout Africa.

Proposed solutions to improve intra-African trade and investment: the outlook for African cement

Cement is a crucial part of Africa's development and growth trajectory. The sector is a key indicator of the state of economic development on the continent. Leading cement companies like Dangote and PPC are often described as bellwethers of their home-based economies and, more broadly, the African growth story. The rise of Dangote is a direct result of growth and large-scale development in Nigeria. Meanwhile PPC's solid foundation is based on decades of development in a relatively advanced South African economy, but where demand is now on the decline while new opportunities in the rest of Africa are emerging. While Dangote is seen to bring scale and well-financed projects to other African countries, PPC is recognised more for the skills, expertise and knowhow it brings, having developed these over the past 120 years. Both will disrupt the current status quo through increased competition, serving as agents of development, job creation and productivity in the countries in which they enter.

The African cement industry is one of the greatest untapped opportunities in the world today. Returns on investment and the rate of growth of companies like Dangote confirm this status. But trade and investment by African cement companies across the continent is still hampered by a number of obstacles. The high cost of energy and transport undermines their competitiveness against cheaper (and often inferior) products from Asia, which are less vulnerable to increasing costs since they don't produce in country and most often distribute their cement in close proximity to the ports where they land their product. These cement exporters are often able to land in coastal regions across the continent at below the input costs of countries from South Africa to Kenya and Tanzania, and even Nigeria, suggesting these have been subsidised in their home governments. Imported products are also able to enter countries like Kenya and Tanzania through preferential access – below regular tariff rates – by way of a separate bilateral agreement linked to the large infrastructure projects serviced by contractors in China or elsewhere in Asia.[29] These special arrangements (and subsidised products) must be stopped, and greater consistency around policies and licenses related to long-term investments and manufacturing need to be practiced if intra-African trade and investment in the cement industry is to be encouraged and made more competitive.

Apart from improving infrastructure in roads, rails and ports to encourage the movement of cement between neighbouring countries – not to mention easier movements across borders – African governments can implement greater tax breaks for *new* cement manufacturers to encourage investment in local production by helping to counter the high costs of production and transport in their countries – especially as margins decrease with the changing market and potential inflows of imported cement on the back of higher demands from industrial growth.

While the returns on investment in the African cement industry are potentially very high, the initial capital costs of building or upgrading manufacturing and grinding facilities are excessive and – in some cases – prohibitive, given the myriad of operating constraints that prevail in the African business context In short, despite Africa's potential returns, the cost of doing business and the risks remain high. These need to be countered sooner rather than later through policy interventions and long-term arrangements. This is an important role for governments to play in encouraging investment and enabling the business environment.

The story of Dangote is one that is closely linked to government support and progressive policies that have helped develop the company (and the industry) in Nigeria. The Nigerian government is now supporting Dangote as a primary exporter and investor across the continent. This may be criticised by those favouring traditional approaches to business and economic incentives, but in Africa, where the state-business interplay is an important and growing reality of on-going business – especially where local content and production is sought – the case of Dangote in Nigeria may be instructive (at least in part) for others.

The cement industry outlook is optimistic for Africa. Market dynamics and demographics around consumer needs, housing, construction and infrastructure suggest on-going increases in demand for many years to come. Apart from direct policy responses to support the cement industry, the improvement of financial markets and the development of financial instruments and sources of finance will have a significant impact on the industry. Sustained supply and demand of cement requires finance. This is another area where governments and government agencies – including development banks – have an important role to play. The provision of finance will open the market, lower the entry costs with security and guarantees, to allow for greater inclusiveness through the entry of new players, stimulate greater demand and encourage competitiveness. This will also encourage greater integration and backward integration into other industries related to cement.

Finally, and looking ahead at long-term development and construction, the largest builder of cement plants in Africa is Sinoma, the Chinese contractor. While they are currently performing an excellent and much-needed service at a competitive cost, perhaps through deeper financial development not only will intra-African trade and investment in the cement industry improve, but perhaps this will also help facilitate the development of manufacturing and grinding facilitates by African contractors in the near future.

Notes

1. See the Global Cement Report (2013).
2. The World Bank, 'Africa's Infrastructure: A Time for Transformation' (2009), http://siteresources.worldbank.org/INTAFRICA/Resources/aicd_overview_english_no-embargo.pdf.
3. Bamburi Cement, *Bamburi Official Website* (2014), http://www.lafarge.co.ke/wps/portal/ke/1-About_us.
4. This is according to the report, 'Imara African Cement Report: Africa, the Last Cement Frontier', Imara Investing in Africa (February 2011), www.imara.co.
5. Business Monitor International, 'Industry Forecast – Company News Alert – Dangote Cements Its Position as African Giant', *Business Monitor International Ltd.*
6. Imara Securities, 'Imara African Cement Report: Africa, the Last Cement Frontier' (2011), www.imara.co.

7. This is apart from cheap imports from Asia.
8. World Cement, 'Pretoria Portland Cement Seizes Opportunity in Rwanda' (2012), http://www.worldcement.com/news/cement/articles/Cement_PPC_Cimerwa_Rwana_expansion_789.aspx#.UuEP9LS6LIV.
9. K.Guenioui, 'Dangote Cement Plans US$400 Million Investment in Kenya' (2014), http://www.worldcement.com/news/cement/articles/Dangote_Cement_expands_into_Africa_159.aspx#.UuEJPLS6LIU.
10. World Cement, 'Dangote Cement Lays Foundation Stone for New Tanzanian Plant' (2013), http://www.worldcement.com/news/cement/articles/Dangote_Cement_inaugurates_Tanzanian_plant_996.aspx#.UuEQO7S6LIV.
11. MarketLine, 'Company Profile: Tanga Cement Company Limited', *MarketLine Ltd* (2013).
12. Institutional Voids is a concept developed by Harvard Business school professor Tarun Khana. See T. Khana and K. Palepu, *Winning in Emerging Markets: A Road Map for Strategy and Execution* (Boston, MA: Harvard Business Press, 2010).
13. This is based on interviews with leading cement companies in Nigeria, Kenya and South Africa as well as members of the manufacturing associations in those countries and analysts tracking the industry.
14. See http://www.cement.org/cement-concrete-basics/how-cement-is-made.
15. This figure was provided during interviews with cement producers and the Kenyan Association of Manufacturers (KAM) in November 2013 and January 2014.
16. Imara African Cement Report (2011), http://imara.co/uploads/stockbroking/africa-securities/Imara_African_Cement_Report_-_Feb_2011.pdf.
17. PM News Nigeria, http://www.pmnewsnigeria.com/2012/12/21/cement-palaver-dangote-ibeto-at-war/.
18. It was noted in various interviews that Chinese and Pakistani products are landed at below the local production costs. These, it is alleged, are subsidised back home. This would suggest dumping, but the interviewees declined to give details. In addition to this, related to quality, the cement does not match the strength and safety standards of locally produced products but does meet basic regulatory standards which allows for cheap alternatives in some cases.
19. The full history and background is available on the PPC website, www.ppc.co.za.
20. In an interview with Pepe Meijer, Head of Africa for PPC, in January 2014, it was confirmed that PPC was on track to reaching this figure.
21. http://ppc.co.za/investors/financials/2013%2011%2019%20Investor%20Presentation.pdf.
22. See http://www.bdlive.co.za/business/industrials/2013/11/19/ppc-earnings-up-on-revenue-from-rest-of-africa.
23. MarketLine, 'Pretoria Portland Cement and Industrial Development Corporation Acquire 47% Stake in Habesha Cement', *MarketLine Ltd* (2012).
24. K. Guenioui, 'Dangote Cement Scores Big Increases in Profits' (2013), http://www.worldcement.com/news/cement/articles/Dangote_Cement_issues_3Q13_interim_statement_368.aspx#.UuEQQLS6LIV.
25. I. Nwachukwu, 'Nigeria's 47% Stock Market Returns, Best in Africa 2013', *BusinessDay* (9 January 2014), http://www.businessdayonline.com/2014/01/nigerias-47-stick-market-returns-best-in-africa-in-2013/.
26. PPC shares the same ration of equity to debt in its Africa expansion plans.
27. This is based on the presentation generated by Dangote, "Dangote Cement: An Emerging Cement Major Building Shareholder Value and Prosperity in Africa" (January 2014).

28. This was a point re-iterated in various interviews at Dangote in Lagos and with the Dangote investment relations team in London in January 2014.
29. World Cement, 'Tanzanian Government Stands Firm on Common External Tariff for Cement' (2012), http://www.worldcement.com/news/cement/articles/Tanzania_cement_producers_common_externa_tarriff_imports_780.aspx#.UuENo7S6LIU.

Other Works Cited

ARM. (2014). *Athi Rivier Mining Official Website: Financial Records 2012*. [online] Available at http://www.armafrica.com/?page=financial-reports.

Business Monitor International. (2012). *Industry Trend Analysis: Building Materials – Output Boom but Familiar Hurdles Ahead*. Business Monitor International Ltd.

——. (2013). *Business Environment Alerts— Dangote Cement Plans New Plant*. Business Monitor International Ltd.

——. (2013). *Industry Forecast – Infrastructure & Construction – Q1 2014*. Business Monitor International Ltd.

——. (2013). *Industry Trend Analysis – Cement Boom Not Necessarily Renofitting Domestic Producers*. Business Monitor International Ltd.

——. (2013). *Project News – Dangote's Advance Continues with New Cement Plant*. Business Monitor International Ltd.

Dangote Cement. (2014). *Dangote Official Website*. [online] Available at: http://dangcement.com/new/index.php?page=129.

Cardinal Stone Partners. (2013). *Nigeria Cement Sector Report*. [online] Available at: http://www.proshareng.com/reports/6294/CSPR – Cement-Sector-Report – Emerging-Prominence-from-a-Deficit-Past.

Fordham, L. (2013). *Habesha Cement's CEO says Construction of New Plant Will Start This Year*. [online] Available at: http://www.worldcement.com/news/cement/articles/Habesha_Cement_new_plant_construction_scheduled_345.aspx#. UuEJQ7S6LIU.

Guenioui, K. (2013). *Lafarge Revenues Increase in Zambia*. [online] Available at: http://www.worldcement.com/news/cement/articles/Lafarge_Cement_Zambia_revenues_increase_143.aspx#.UuEQT7S6LIV.

——. (2013). *Tanzanian Cement Companies Seek Greater Protection against Cheap Imports*. [online] Available at: http://www.worldcement.com/news/cement/articles/Tanzania_calls_for_return_of_2005_cement_levies_149.aspx#.UuENprS6LIU.

Financial Times. (2014). *fDi Markets Tool*. [online] Available at: http://www.fdiintelligence.com/fDi-Tools/fDi-Markets.

International Trade Centre. (2014). *Market Access Map*. [online] Available at: http://www.macmap.org/.

——. (2014). *Trade Map – Trade Statistics for International Business Development*. [online] Available at: http://www.trademap.org/.

MarketLine. (2003). MarketLine Industry Profile: Global Cement.

——. (2013). *Company Profile: The East African Portland Cement Company Ltd*. MarketLine Ltd.

Pretoria Portland Cement. (2013). *PPC Annual Report 2013* [online] Available at: http://ppc.investoreports.com/ppc_ar_2013/2013-performance-review/operations-review/.

——. (2014). *2012 Investor Presentation*. [online] Available at: http://www.ppc.co.za/investors/presentations/financials.aspx.

Slabbert, A. (2009). *Shake Up in Cement Industry*. [online] Available at: http://www.fin24.com/Companies/Shake-up-in-cement-industry-20091115.

Standard Investment Bank. (2012). *East Africa Cement Sector*. [online] Available at: http://www.sib.co.ke/analysis.php.

TotallyConcrete. (2014). *Shaping the Future of Concrete and Cement in Africa – South African Cement Industry 'Shaping Up'*. [online] Available at: http://www.totally-concrete.co.za/news-and-media/media-centre/news/item/south-african-cement-industry-shaping-up.

World Cement. (2013). *New Cement Projects Planned for Angola*. [online] Available at: http://www.worldcement.com/news/cement/articles/Cement_plant_storage_distribution_projects_Angola_966.aspx#.UuEP77S6LIV.

———. (2013). *Nigeria's Cement Production Surpasses South Africa*. [online] Available at: http://www.worldcement.com/news/cement/articles/Nigerias_cement_production_surpasses_South_Africa_461.aspx#.UuEQRrS6LIV.

9

The Fast-Moving Consumer Goods and Retail Sectors

Dianna Games

The new battleground in Africa is that for the soul – and the disposable income – of the African consumer. Multinationals from across the globe are ramping up their investments in the continent and local industries are growing, flexing muscle in highly competitive markets with some of the most rapidly growing populations in the world. Rising incomes, changing tastes and shopping profiles, and urbanisation have sparked a vibrancy in African markets that is driving opportunity across the board, but particularly in the consumer goods and retail sectors

McKinsey & Company predicts that by 2015, there will be 221 million basic-needs consumers in Africa.[1] While the biggest growth is at the base of the pyramid – a market targeted by Western multinationals, local producers and Asian traders – formal retail is starting to develop as a growing middle class exercises its economic muscle and demands better quality goods and services. The mobile phone revolution in Africa has been a strong indicator of consumer growth and demand across income groups.

This trend does represent a paradox – the growth of consumer markets is normally an outcome of development; in Africa, it is happening in spite of the relative underdevelopment of many markets.

Urbanisation is playing a critical role in this consumer explosion. In 1980, just 28 per cent of Africans lived in cities; by 2011, it had risen to 40 per cent of the continent's one billion people – a population roughly the size of China's – and higher than India's. It is estimated that by 2030, the number will have risen to 50 per cent in Africa.[2] According to Standard Bank's projections, by 2050, more than 60 per cent of Africans – with an expected population of more than two billion people by then – will be living in cities. This suggests that about eight hundred million Africans will either migrate to, or be born in, urban areas over the next four decades.[3]

Africa has another feature that is attracting investors in consumer facing industries – the fastest growing youth population in the world, a demographic that is increasingly concentrated in urban areas. In many cases, they have access to better education as a result of their families' improving fortunes. They have energetically joined the digital age and are aspirational, brand conscious and not bound by the traditions of their forebears. This, in short, makes them like consumers anywhere in the world.

The fast-moving consumer goods (FMCG) sector has traditionally been dominated by foreign players with deep roots in the continent – Unilever, Nestle, Heineken, Diageo and others. But increasingly, African-owned and managed companies are muscling their way into the business spotlight, tapping into consumer tastes and market gaps in local markets as a platform for regional expansion.

South African consumer brands have also made their way across the continent, and in the retail sector, companies from the southern economic powerhouse dominate the landscape north of the border. It is a natural leader in this regard, given the country's own long history of formal retail and the growth of large diversified retail multi-nationals. While Africa's biggest market, Nigeria, has formal retail penetration of about 5 per cent, South Africa's is more than 70 per cent, with Western-style shopping malls spread across the country.[4] South Africa's well-developed, and still expanding, domestic retail market has attracted international retailers such as Zara, Paul Smith and Top Shop and luxury brands such as Louis Vuitton and Cartier.

The retail sector in the rest of Africa is dominated by informal shopping – entrepreneurs in lock-up garage-type outlets, large informal markets and street traders. Imported goods, mostly from Asia, line the streets – electrical appliances, kitchen utensils, computer and car parts, cigarettes, drinks and cosmetics as well as cheap, either second hand or end-of-the line clothing brought in bulk from Asia and Europe – alongside local fresh produce and bolts of traditional cloth. In many cities, locally made furniture and other household goods are sold on roadsides, undercutting formal retail where it exists.

But slowly, shopping malls are appearing in African cities, a development driven not only by the ready availability of capital for commercial property development and the expansion by retailers out of South Africa but also to meet the changing lifestyle needs of a new generation with rising incomes, changing aspirations fed by increased global linkages and the growth of a returning diaspora.

The size of the middle class, noted as a key driver of FMCG and retail, is vague although some have attempted to capture the figures. For example, the African Development Bank in 2010 estimated this segment to be 34 per cent of Africa's population or nearly 350 million people, up from about 220 million in 2000 and 126 million in 1980.[5] However, it defined this consumer group as being people earning US$2 and US$20 a day even though the World Bank uses US$2 a day as a threshold for measuring poverty. The definition was criticised for being unrealistic, given that most people falling into this definition would be in danger of falling back into poverty.

In 2014, Standard Bank released a report, 'Understanding Africa's Middle Class', which showed the results of a study covering 11 African countries (including Nigeria, Ethiopia and Kenya but excluding South Africa) defining the middle class by a Living Standards Measure rather than income bands. It found that although the number of middle-class households in these 11 top countries had risen from 4.6 million in 2000 to 15 million in 2014 – an increase of 230 per cent – most were in the low-income bracket. However, the report predicted that this number would triple to 22 million by 2030.

This represents a major opportunity for retailers and FMCG producers going forward, which is driving increased investment in these sectors in Africa, despite the many challenges they face in doing business on the continent.

A new driver of both the consumer growth story and the emerging middle class trend is the development of the African private sector, which is itself growing on the back of these changing demographics.

The trend in African companies expanding in Africa and challenging foreign multinationals has been most notable out of South Africa since 1994, which, after the end of apartheid, opened up to the global economy – and to Africa. Its large companies had pent up demand, sophisticated supply chains, world-class goods and services and war chests built up over a long period of political and economic isolation.

South African retailers have not faced much competition in their north-ward expansion from local players with a few exceptions such as Zimbabwe and Kenya where relatively strong local competition existed. Potential international competitors such as France's Carrefour, Britain's Tesco and the United States' Wal-Mart had, until more recently, avoided Sub-Saharan Africa, preferring to invest in South America and Asia where the short-term gains seemed easier. However, this is starting to change as Carrefour has started expanding its Sub-Saharan footprint, eyeing Nigeria in particular, and Wal-Mart plans to drive its African expansion through the acquisition of South Africa's Massmart group.[6]

In terms of FMCG, South African home-made brands are found in retail outlets across the continent and in the supermarkets of other retailers. Fruit juice, milk, tea, beer, pharmaceutical goods, snack foods, wine, cosmetics and many other goods made both by South African manufacturers and multi-nationals based in the country have made their way into homes across the continent and large consumer brand companies have set up shop in markets such as Kenya and Nigeria.

On the regional front, competition is also starting to grow. As other economies benefit from economic reform and improving political openness and stability, African-owned FMCG and retail companies are building scale, footprint and capacity in their regions. These companies, along with others in the services industry such as banks and mobile phone operators, have become benchmarks for the 'Africa rising' narrative that is much espoused by analysts, fund managers, economists and others flagging the new continental growth story. The projections are certainly attracting investor attention, given the potential.

But it is not all good news. Growth is relatively slow compared to the potential these sectors could contribute to Africa's economic upliftment. This is highlighted by the low levels of intra-African trade – estimated to be just 12 per cent of Africa's total trade compared to other regions – 25 per cent in Latin America, and almost 50 per cent in Asia, for example.[7] This highlights the challenges companies face in pursuing pan-African strategies.

There are many reasons offered for this situation. One is weak infrastructure. According to the African Union's Programme for Infrastructure Development in Africa, transport costs in landlocked African countries account for as much as 70 per cent of the value of exports because of infrastructure deficits.[8] It estimates that savings of up to $172 billion could be achieved through a properly implemented African regional transport network.

Others are poor policy support, a shifting landscape of non-tariff barriers and ineffective regional economic communities. While manufactured exports account for 70 per cent of the continent's total annual exports in Asia, in Africa the figure is closer to 20 per cent.[9] Most African economies are unable to produce the types of goods its rising consumer base and growing sectors such as ICT, mining and agriculture demand. In 2011, just 8 per cent of Africa's machinery requirements, electrical and electronic equipment, vehicles and ships/boats were produced on the continent.[10]

South Africa is a key driver of intra-African trade and accounts for half of Africa's total manufactured exports. In 2011, a quarter of the continent's trade was accounted for by South African exports to the continent. In the same year, almost 75 per cent of the continent's total exports consisted of four categories of hard commodities. Only 6 per cent of these were absorbed regionally.[11]

A weakness in the statistics is that they fail to capture the extent of informal cross-border trade. The UN Economic Commission for Africa (UNECA) suggests that although it is difficult to get an accurate overview of the extent of informal cross-border trade in Sub-Saharan Africa, it is undoubtedly significant.[12]

The benefits of urbanisation may also be undermined by under-investment in African cities, coupled with poor planning and official neglect. This is a growing concern globally but the scale of the problem in Africa is huge. Although the growth of megacities is widely seen as a consumer opportunity, and there is no doubt that it is, it also presents risks.

Large swathes of Africa's cities are either informal settlements or slums with large areas of squalor barely touched by municipal services and decent infrastructure. Unable to impose order on untrammelled development and congestion, some governments are building new cities on the outskirts of the old in places such as Port Harcourt, Lagos and Nairobi. There is limited trickle down of new wealth and opportunity beyond these 'city states' unless it is in towns close to resources. This means assessment of opportunity – and risk – is not necessarily a country story but a much more disaggregated picture.

Retail sector

The South Africans

South Africa has played a key role in Africa's new growth story, particularly in the retail sector. It is the largest and strongest economy in Africa, accounting for nearly 37 per cent of Sub-Saharan Africa's gross domestic product (GDP) and almost 70 per cent of the GDP of Southern Africa. The strength and diversity of the country's economy makes it a natural investor in a continent comprising mostly small, weak economies with low manufacturing capability.

The expansion of South African trade and investment into the rest of Africa has been manifested in the retail and property sectors with shopping malls and similar developments dominated by their retailers, funders and developers. This has been a driver of related business in areas such as franchising, property management, construction and supplier services and also a catalyst for development of local skills, services and goods at home and in the markets in which they operate.

The growth of most of the country's retail giants has taken place over decades, mostly through a combination of organic growth and acquisition strategies. They trade under different brands catering to various market segments. The retailers that have expanded into other African countries include:

- Supermarket chain, Shoprite. The JSE-listed Shoprite Group of Companies was formed in 1979 with the purchase of eight supermarkets for a nominal fee. Today, it is a R82 billion listed company with nearly 1,300 stores in South Africa and several hundred corporate and franchise stores in 15 countries across Africa with plans for more than 1,000 in the next few years. Like other retailers in South Africa that have expanded into the region, Shoprite has not curtailed its local expansion and in 2014 announced it would build more than 100 new stores in South Africa to push up its market share.[13]
- Massmart, now controlled by Wal-Mart, owns multiple brands and has taken several into the continent. By 2014, it had stores in 14 African countries and had branched into food retailing, putting it in competition with Shoprite in Nigeria, for example. However, its expansion programme has slowed down since the acquisition by Wal-Mart.
- Pick 'n Pay, launched in 1967, had nearly 800 stores in South Africa by 2014 and almost 100 in eight other African countries, including 50 stores

in Zimbabwe as part of its 49 per cent investment in local retailer TM Supermarkets.

- Pep Stores, a subsidiary of the giant investment group Pepkor, started with one store in the 1960s and today has 3,400 stores and trades in a dozen African countries.
- Clothing, household goods and food retailer Woolworths, established in 1931, has operations in 11 other African countries, which were once mostly franchises but are now corporate stores. Its food offering, a key attraction in South Africa, is limited north of the border.
- Truworths, which effectively began trading in South Africa in 1917, had nearly 600 stores in South Africa by 2014, 40 corporate stores in eight other African countries and 5 franchise stores in Kenya.
- The Foschini Group, which started trading in 1924, had nearly 120 stores outside South Africa, mostly in Southern Africa, by 2014 with nearly 2,000 outlets in South Africa by 2014 under different brands. Its aim is to have 300 stores outside South Africa by 2016.
- Mr Price's roots date back to 1885 although it has only traded under the Mr Price brand since 1987. Listed on the JSE since 1952, it had nearly 1,000 stores in South Africa, several dozen franchised stores in nine other African countries and a handful of corporate stores in Nigeria and Ghana by 2014.

The geographical expansion of South African companies started before the end of apartheid in neighbouring states that were, with South Africa, members of the Southern African Customs Union (SACU) – Botswana, Lesotho, Swaziland and Namibia. Zimbabwe was not part of SACU but by then already had long trading ties with its southern neighbour. Zambia, a market Shoprite entered in 1997, provided a second phase of expansion along with Mozambique, Tanzania and Uganda as well as Ghana in West Africa.

Angola became another large market for South African companies, despite the difficulty of operating in this opaque market with poor transport links and high operating costs. Relative proximity along with rapid economic growth, rising incomes and urbanisation has attracted everyone from manufacturers of biscuits to beer.

Despite cultural similarities in business culture and language, gaining access to the East African market has been challenging for the South Africans. While a number of multinationals have a strong footprint in Uganda, Kenya has been difficult to penetrate, partly because of local competition but also because of a protectionist attitude by their own companies, which has kept the expansionist South Africans reined in on their business turf in these sectors.

Tanzania has defeated the South African supermarket chains. Score Supermarkets, a subsidiary of Pick 'n Pay, opened three supermarkets in the country in 2000 but losses and a difficult trading environment led it to sell off to Shoprite two years later. For years, Shoprite was the biggest retailer in Tanzania, dominating local players such as Shreejis Supermarkets. However, in 2013, after a long period of weak trading, the indefatigable Shoprite sold the stores to Kenyan retailer Nakumatt. Rwanda has become a market dominated by Kenyan chains and the local Simba group. While Nakumatt and Uchumi from Kenya are also in Uganda, the South Africans have a strong foothold there.

South African investment in West Africa, specifically Nigeria and Ghana, is now sizeable. In addition to significant investments in telecoms, hospitality and other sectors, the South Africans are funding and building shopping malls and drawing their retail chains into these developments. The competition in these relatively underdeveloped markets is mostly from other South African companies expanding into the region in this sector – although they also face competition from informal traders and small shops, growing local companies and less obvious competitors such as smugglers.

The main drivers of retail expansion have been:

- early mover advantage into lucrative but underserviced markets;
- limited competition in almost all Sub-Saharan markets;
- stiff competition at home;
- the search for a new revenue stream. In 2012, turnover growth in Shoprite's non-South African supermarkets has been consistently almost double that of its South African stores, contributing about 11 per cent of the total.[14] CEO Whitey Basson says he wants to bring it to 50 per cent of total turnover over time;
- the prospective size of these new markets and rising incomes on the back of steady continental growth;
- demand from a rising middle class and returning diaspora for new goods, services and lifestyle choices;
- the growing number of formal retail malls in the rest of Africa;
- ready availability of technical and management skills at home to support expansion;
- a hedge against risk in South Africa; and
- a long-term vision for Africa, given the continent's relatively long track record of consistent growth.

Doug McMillon, President and Chief Executive of Wal-Mart International, noted in 2012: 'Going to South Africa right now at this moment, with the current consumer demand for retail, might not be a great idea. But when you look forward at the region, the growth and what's going to happen there, we have created headroom. We can create short-term profits, we can add a good business to the company with some strong and talented leaders, but we also create an opportunity 5, 10, 20 and 30 years out to continue to grow'.[15]

Rest of Africa

The number and size of companies in the retail sector in the rest of Africa is not on a par with those in South Africa, but this is starting to change. There are a number of key drivers, some of which mirror the drivers of South Africa's commercial expansion across the continent: a search for new markets as a result of pent-up capacity, increasing competition in local markets and natural ties with the region. New regional infrastructure projects and improving trade facilitation are also helping to push growth.

This growth is most notable in East Africa, where it is estimated that about 30 per cent of the retail sector is formalised, compared to only 5 per cent in Nigeria,[16] for example. Retailers such as Nakumatt have replicated modern retail trends such as loyalty schemes and 24-hour shopping, not just for Kenya but also for regional operations.

The larger economies in East Africa enjoy deeper levels of trade integration with the rest of Africa than most other regions. In 2011, almost 45 per cent of East African countries' total exports were among each other and the rest of Africa, compared to 14 per cent among Southern African Development Community (SADC) members and 15 per cent among the countries in the Economic Community of West African States (ECOWAS).[17] The EAC includes about 300 million people across five countries – Kenya, Uganda, Rwanda, Tanzania and Burundi. Nearby is Ethiopia, Africa's second largest country by population size after Nigeria, with more than 80 million people, while an emerging South Sudan provides yet more scope for consumer goods and services.

Growing companies in the sector include:

- Kenyan supermarket group Nakumatt, now the largest retail chain in East Africa with nearly 60 outlets across four countries. The company is majority owned by a Kenyan family.
- Uchumi in Kenya, a listed company with 33 stores across the EAC and a store under development in South Sudan. The government has a 13.4 per cent stake in the company.
- Naivas Supermarkets, a family owned chain in Kenya, which has about 30 stores in the country. In 2013, Wal-Mart started talks with the owners to take a controlling stake in the company, but this did not come to fruition.
- Botswana retailer Choppies Enterprises, which is rapidly expanding into South Africa. By March 2014, it had more than 100 stores – nearly 70 in Botswana, 24 in South Africa's highly competitive market and another dozen in Zimbabwe where it bought a retailer in Bulawayo;
- Innscor in Zimbabwe, a diversified conglomerate with Spar franchises in Zimbabwe and in Zambia where it is in a joint venture in the Spar supermarkets with Platinum Gold Zambia Ltd. Its food franchises include

Creamy Inn, Chicken Inn and Pizza Inn which operate in key markets across Sub-Saharan Africa;

- The Artee Group in Nigeria, owners of the Park 'n Shop supermarket chain who have the Spar franchise in Nigeria;
- Deacons in Kenya, which has, for some years, been the master franchisor for South African retail chains in East Africa such as Woolworths and Mr Price. In 2013, Woolworths abandoned the franchise model and is now a majority stakeholder in a joint venture with Deacons. Mr Price is looking at the same model. The company also represents international brands in Kenya and in 2013, it brought the Spanish retailer Zara to Kenya;
- The diversified Melcom Group of Companies, which is Ghana's biggest retail chain and a distributor for many international brands including Yamaha, Hitachi and Samsung. It also manufactures plastic household goods and assembles household appliances;[18]
- TM Supermarkets in Zimbabwe, part-owned by Meikles, Zimbabwe's oldest conglomerate, with South Africa's Pick 'n Pay supermarket group a 49 per cent shareholder.

International retail

A survey of international brands by property services company Broll in 2012 showed that out of 326 companies interviewed, only a handful were looking at African markets. Those that were seeking opportunities on the continent had South Africa and North African markets in their sights, not the high-growth markets that the South Africans are targeting such as Kenya, Nigeria, Zambia and Mozambique. The survey said international brands were hesitant about going into markets where there was little or no market research and where market dynamics were so different from other regions.[19]

It is true that international retailers have been scarce in Sub-Saharan Africa with a few exceptions such as France's Casino and Carrefour chains which have a presence in North Africa and a few Francophone countries in Sub-Saharan Africa, and brands such as Adidas, are now favouring shopping malls in Africa. Although international brands are to be found in big cities in Africa, they are franchised, with the companies reluctant to commit to a corporate presence on the continent just yet.

Carrefour, however, is now looking to expand its presence in Africa from North Africa into Sub-Saharan Africa with its store planned for Cote d'Ivoire in 2015. The expansion into Francophone countries as well as Ghana and Nigeria, will be carried out in a joint venture with CFAO, which distributes vehicles and pharmaceuticals in 32 African countries. CFAO is majority owned by Toyota Tsusho, the Toyota Group's trading arm.[20]

South Africa has attracted top brands such as Zara, Cotton On, GAP and Top Shop which are looking for new markets but need a soft landing in

Africa while they assess the opportunities elsewhere on the continent. Analysts predict that other brands such as Swedish fashion retailer H&M and possibly other UK fashion retailers such as Next, Marks & Spencer and Debenhams may look at the South African market in the search for new franchise growth.

Fast-moving consumer goods

The fast-moving consumer goods (FMCG) sector in Africa is one of the most attractive to investors, given growing populations, rising incomes, aspirations for quality goods and expansion of formal retail outlets, which are providing a ready market for locally manufactured and imported goods from all over the world. Foodstuffs, wine, cosmetics and household goods from Asia, South Africa, Latin America and Europe line supermarket shelves and even market stalls. Increasingly, they sit alongside a growing number of locally manufactured goods that have brand recognition and loyalty from consumers and often, but not always, cheaper prices.

Manufacturing in African countries tends to be a high-cost business, given power shortages that necessitate the use of expensive, fuel-guzzling generators to run factories, expensive bank funding, regulatory barriers, transport costs to market and many other factors. South Africa is becoming a high-cost producer despite its economies of scale at home that once made its goods very competitive in other African countries. A long and difficult supply chain also pushes up landed costs. In Zambia, for example, the destination for a large number of South African products, transport costs to the landlocked country can push up costs by as much as 40 per cent.

Dominant players in FMCG remain foreign companies, many of which have been on the continent for decades, including Unilever, Nestle, Diageo, Heineken, Colgate Palmolive and Proctor & Gamble. For the African consumer, many of the products of global multinationals are regarded as being local, a testament to their success in creating a sense of local buy-in to brands that are foreign-owned but locally consumed and often produced in Africa. Their deep pockets, global experience and supply chains have kept Africans at bay for a long time. Even in South Africa, home to many large local FMCG manufacturers, Unilever claims to be the market leader in seven out of its nine product categories including laundry, skincare, ice cream, tea and deodorants.[21]

The multinationals are ramping up investment as the competition increases. Nestle Nigeria, for example, has invested $446 million in that country alone since 2003 and plans to invest a further $635 million over the next decade to triple sales to $2.2 billion by 2023. In 2013, Unilever announced a $90 million expansion in South Africa and its intention to build a manufacturing plant in Ethiopia during 2014. Cosmetics companies such as L'Oreal are also expanding.

There is significant expansion in the brewing industry with Diageo and Heineken both increasing their African footprint on the back of good profits. Africa now accounts for 13 per cent of Diageo's total sales, up from 9 per cent in 2006. In Nigeria, one of its biggest markets, it sells more Guinness than it does in Ireland. Coca Cola has committed to investing $12 billion in African markets in the decade up to 2020 – more than double its investment over the previous decade.[22]

Pernod Ricard, the world's second-largest spirits group, has increased investment in Africa over the past two years, creating five affiliates in Sub-Saharan Africa in the past year in Nigeria, Ghana, Angola, Kenya and Namibia.[23] A taste for luxury brands in the rising middle class is pushing demand for high-end drinks such as wine, spirits and champagne.

'The last two decades were about the Brics (Brazil, Russia, India, China and South Africa) – now it's about Africa', Andy Fennell, Diageo's chief operating officer for Africa, told investors in a 2013 briefing, citing the 65-million extra drinking-age consumers expected to enter the market over the next decade.[24]

Global brewing giant SABMiller is still regarded as an African company given its South African roots although it moved its primary listing to London in 1999. It has been successful in Africa despite strong competition from Diageo and Heineken as well as local brewers – although it has bought up most of the potential local competition. The group has doubled its capital investment in the continent from $200 million a year in 2010 to $400 million a year since then. In 2013, it invested $100 million in its first greenfield brewery in Nigeria, a market where stiff competition from its foreign competitors meant a long delayed entry. In 2014, it said it would invest a further $110 million to expand capacity in Africa's biggest market.[25] It is also doubling capacity in Ghana and bringing on new capacity in other countries. It enhanced its Africa footprint through an Africa-wide deal with French drinks group Castel in 2001. The strategic alliance, formed in 2001, meant SABMiller took a 20 per cent stake in Castel's beer and soft drinks operations in Africa and Castel acquired a 38 per cent stake of SABMiller's African subsidiary.[26]

More recently, it has moved into brewing traditional beer with cassava and sorghum to tap into low income markets. Analysts estimate that home brews or cheap spirits account for three-quarters of alcohol consumed in Africa and the brewers want to occupy that market and transform these consumers to higher end brands over time.

Mark Bowman, managing director of Africa at SABMiller, told the "Drinks groups scent opportunities brewing in Africa", 1 November 2013, S Daneshkhu, *Financial Times* in 2013: 'In the last two years, there has been a significant increase in competition, both in marketing spend and competition for assets, such as breweries. Africa is currently one of the most highly prized regions for the global brewers'.

In some cases, there has been a crossover of multinationals and local companies. For example, Bidco Oil Refineries acquired Unilever's cooking oil plant and UAC in Nigeria was formerly part owned by Unilever before the multi-national divested its stake in 1994. There are many cases of African companies becoming success stories further afield. South African franchise chain Nando's has become a big hit in the UK and the US, for example. Nigeria Bottling Company, owned by the Leventis Group based in Lagos, has expanded into a multi-national company operating in 28 countries from its home base in West Africa. The region provided it with a platform for expansion into Europe and a later tie up with Coca Cola brought the company into the global Coca Cola Hellenic group.[27]

Conversely, there has also been some pull back of African retailers, with Shoprite exiting India in the mid-1990s and Pick 'n Pay closing up shop in Australia in 2010 and selling off the chain stores it had acquired as part of its entry strategy.

Many FMCG products found across Africa come out of South Africa, produced by the multinationals mentioned earlier but also by large local companies. The supermarket groups, such as Woolworths, Shoprite and Pick 'n Pay, have built up a large portfolio of in-house store-branded consumer goods, and many of the other brands carried on their shelves in South Africa and elsewhere are owned by South Africa's giant brand companies.

There are a large number of African-owned FMCG companies in Africa, ranging from family-owned enterprises to large multinationals. They have tapped successfully into the consumer base in their own areas, towns or countries with some expanding across borders.

The larger players in this sector include:

- JSE-listed Rainbow Chicken and Country Bird – the two dominate the poultry business in South Africa
- Premier Foods, a major South African food manufacturer focused on maize and wheat products;
- Pioneer Foods, one of the largest producers and distributors in South Africa of a range of food, beverages and related products. It has a strategic tie ups with international companies including HJ Heinz Company in the US to market Heinz products. Its Bokomo cereals and Ceres fruit juice brands are widely distributed around the continent;
- Illovo Sugar, one of Africa's biggest agri-businesses, with operations across Southern Africa in both upstream and downstream processing in the sugar industry;
- Tiger Brands, a South Africa-based brand company, which owns many locally entrenched brands that are found across the continent. In addition to distributing its products across Africa, the company has made acquisitions in Nigeria, Kenya, Zimbabwe, Ethiopia and Cameroon;

- AVI, another large South African brand company, owns a range of household brand names found in many other African countries from tea and biscuits to cosmetics and clothing;
- South Africa-based Promisador, which built its business on the back of milk powder and has diversified into other products. It sells directly into 15 African countries;
- Zimbabwe's Innscor, which has stakes in several other FMCG companies in Zimbabwe, including Colcom and National Foods and integrated poultry producer Irvine's;
- Nigeria's diversified Dangote Group, which has several FMCG subsidiaries including Dansa Foods, which produces fruit juices, dairy products and bottled water;
- Beloxxi Biscuits in Nigeria, which has started exporting to the region;
- Leventis Foods, a subsidiary of the Nigerian conglomerate A.G. Leventis (Nigeria) Ltd, one of the largest bakeries and snack producers in Nigeria;
- Delta Corporation in Zimbabwe, a brewing and bottling company with a significant stake held by SABMiller;
- Bidco in Kenya, a soap and edible oils manufacturing company with operations in three other East African countries;
- National Foods in Zimbabwe, founded in 1920, which is the largest manufacturer and marketer of local brands;
- Kenya's KenAfrica Industries, which manufactures foodstuffs and confectionary and exports to 10 African countries.
- Zimbabwe's Dairibord, one of the country's largest food and beverages manufacturing and distribution companies, which produces dairy products. It also has operations in Malawi;
- UAC Foods in Nigeria, founded in the 1800s. In addition to its food and franchising divisions, the company has businesses in real estate, logistics and paint; and
- Zambeef, a vertically integrated food and agriculture company, which is a market leader in Zambia and by expanding with Shoprite, now has successful operations in Nigeria, Ghana and Uganda.

Mobile phone companies have been another major success story in the FMCG sector, and operators in the sector count themselves as being among the most successful in Africa. They have played a key role in economic growth across Africa because of the strong linkages they have to broad economic activity and efficiency improvements. A number of African countries have recently rebased their economies, partly to take into account the sector's growing contribution to GDP. A key example in this regard is Nigeria which, in 2014, valued its telecoms sector at $19 billion with its contribution to GDP growing from 0.8 per cent in 1990 to 8.6 per cent in 2014.[28]

South Africa's MTN has mobile licences in 22 countries in Africa and the Middle East and ISP businesses in 13 countries, making it the biggest African player by far. By April 2014, it had 210 million subscribers with Nigeria overtaking South Africa as its biggest market. Its main rival at home, Vodacom, has a much smaller African footprint with operations in Mozambique, Tanzania, Lesotho and the Democratic Republic of Congo with 56 million subscribers by February 2014. Other significant players in the industry are Nigeria's Glo, which also operates in Ghana, and Kenya's Safaricom, which, although regarded as local, has a majority shareholding by the UK's Vodafone. International competitors in Africa include Airtel, Orange and Etisalat.

As the diversity and quality of products improves in African markets, packaging is becoming more important, reflecting both market realities with smaller packaging sizes for low income consumers and growth in canned food and drink as well as higher food safety standards, being driven by a rising middle class. The changing market is also a response to challenges. For example, cans are becoming more popular than glass for beer and other drinks because they are cheaper to produce and require less power to manufacture.

Nampak, a key South Africa player in this industry, is following clients such as SABMiller into the rest of Africa. It has developed huge capacity at home and is following a strategy of greenfield start-ups as well as acquisitions to expand. The company says its margins in Africa outside its home base are 18 per cent compared to 8 per cent in its UK operation, for example. Its risk is reduced by focusing on the business of multinationals. Nigeria and Angola are driving Nampak's growth, and by 2015 it aims to have 50 per cent of its profits from the continent outside South Africa. Other large players in South Africa are Mpact and Consol Glass.

The packaging sectors in the bigger countries are fragmented, with more than 100 small companies operating in the sector in Nigeria, for example, but just a handful that service large local and multinational clients. However, a combination of increasing opportunity, private equity funding, expansion and merger and acquisition activities are building more players of size in local markets.

Improved packaging is also playing a role in making African brands more competitive, both in terms of exports and in attracting local consumers to products. As a result, many local brands, once marked by low-quality packaging, are now becoming indistinguishable from international brands on supermarket shelves.

The growth of smaller local brands, known as B-brands, is an emerging trend in Africa. Mostly these brands are developed and fine-tuned in the provinces by family-owned companies before becoming distributed nationally, or they are products of local conglomerates. Tanzania's Azam Cola, for example, entered the market in 2011, produced by Bakhresa, a family-owned company that has grown into a diversified conglomerate. About 18 months after Azam's launch, it had already gained 30 per cent market share, taking on giants such as Coca Cola. The latter changed its bottle size from 330 ml to 500 ml and from glass to plastic in order to compete.[29]

Homefoods in Ghana has a large share of the edible oil market at home and exports foodstuffs such as oils, spices and jams to the UK and other overseas markets as well as to several African countries.[30] It doubled its production in 2011 and 2012 to meet rapidly rising demand.

The progression of B-brands is summed up in an article in *Africa Report* magazine.

These companies are already well woven into the fabric of African economies, but their founders receive little of the attention garnered by players such as Nigerian cement magnate Aliko Dangote. Their coming of age marks a significant new chapter in the history of African business. Most of these local brands are family-owned businesses that have been steadily growing their consumer goods brands for more than a decade without much fanfare. Now the children of their founders are professionalising their marketing and distribution strategies, and investing in regional expansion to boost their brand recognition and scaleability.[31]

Acquisitions are becoming a popular way for investors to get a stake into new markets. For example, UAC has proved to be popular with the South Africans in this regard.[32] In 2010, South African branding giant Tiger Brands bought a significant stake in UAC's food and dairy operations; in 2013, food franchise company Famous Brands bought 49 per cent of UAC Restaurants Ltd, including Nigeria's largest local franchise, Mr Bigg's; while logistics multi-national Imperial bought UAC's logistics business, MDS. UAC also used to manage South African chicken franchise Nando's before the latter closed its Nigeria operation.

The acquisition trail is proving to be a win-win situation for companies. According to Kevin Hedderwick, CEO of Famous Brands, UAC brings to the table 'a formidable brand, local expertise and existing franchisees as well as a nation-wide distribution network and manufacturing infrastructure. In exchange, Famous Brands will add value to the business through our expertise in managing intellectual property, growing brands and optimising supply chain operations and efficiencies'.[33] Complementary value addition, rather than simply management control, is increasingly a consideration in M&A in Africa.

An advantage African and other emerging market companies have is the flexibility of their corporate structure. This is less evident in South Africa because of its more structured economy and longer corporate history, but in other countries, companies tend to retain a distinctly entrepreneurial structure. Says Bidco CEO Shah, 'We love competing with the multinationals because they're the easiest to compete with. We don't make decisions in Paris, in Dubai, or in London or Atlanta. Decisions are made here within minutes'.[34]

Food franchises

Franchising is become popular as a business model across the continent, particularly in food. Until recently, this was a feature confined mostly to the advanced economies such as South Africa and Egypt. South Africa's franchise sector is valued at about $30 billion and employs nearly half a million people directly.[35] As they have grown at home, so they have also started targeting opportunities in other African countries.

Famous Brands, for example, is one of South Africa's biggest franchising operations with brands such as Wimpy and Mugg & Bean as well as fast food outlets Steers and Debonairs Pizza. By February 2013, its African network outside South Africa comprised 172 restaurants in 15 countries. The acquisition of the Mr Bigg's food franchise chain in Nigeria almost doubled the number of franchised restaurants in the Famous Brands group.

Its main South African rival, Spur Corporation, has taken its restaurant and food brands across Southern Africa and into Kenya and Nigeria. By mid-2013, the company had 25 restaurants in Africa outside South Africa, including nine in Mauritius. The group plans to open up to 30 restaurants in the rest of Africa between 2015 and 2017.[36] Taste Holdings, with several pizza brands, has 16 outlets outside South Africa and more than 600 in South Africa across five diversified brands. The seafood restaurant Ocean Basket is expanding into other African countries as well as into Cyprus and Dubai while Barcelos, a chicken brand based in South Africa, has opened outlets in 10 African countries as well as in Canada, the UK, Middle East and Singapore. Nando's chicken business has been more successful in developed markets, notably the UK and US, than in Africa.

Nigeria has become a significant market for food franchises. Mr Bigg's is the largest and joins more recent entrants such as Tastee Fried Chicken, Tantalizers, Sweet Sensation, Munchies and Kilimanjaro. Food Concepts, owner of the Chicken Republic brand, has 65 outlets across Nigeria and Ghana and is looking at opening 50 franchises in Kenya. The company is generally regarded as the main Nigerian competitor to the fast-growing KFC restaurant chain.

Zimbabwe is another success story, with the food franchise business dominated by Innscor, which has 320 quick service restaurants across East, West and Southern Africa. The franchises are creating employment, improving supply chains and providing a market for local agricultural produce.

Growth of shopping malls

Changing taste and lifestyle profiles of an emerging middle class are driving the development of shopping malls in African capitals. South Africa is the clear leader, with 1,500 malls by 2014, up from just 240 in 2000. Retailers, banks, private equity firms, developers and construction companies have fanned out across the continent to take advantage of limited competition and higher margins than they can get at home, seeking early mover advantage in the development of modern retail centres.

Although government have been slow to wake up to the opportunities presented by formal retail, it is a catalyst for multiple areas of economic activity. For example, hundreds of farmers across many African countries have been contracted to produce specifically for supermarket chains. Freshmark, the fresh produce arm of supermarket group Shoprite, has negotiated production contracts with 500 large- and small-scale farmers in South Africa and more than 350 in other African countries.[37] Nakumatt has 100 contract farmers in Kenya alone.

Formal retail also provides a ready market for locally manufactured goods. Nakumatt says 55 per cent of its products in stores are locally made. Only about a quarter of Shoprite's goods in Nigeria are imported directly. The remainder is made up of local goods and also those imported into the country by local companies and sold on. Formal retail has also been a catalyst for an improvement in the quality of local goods, particularly with regard to packaging as they have to compete with imports on supermarket shelves.

But the scale of challenges in many markets has tempered the dream. Although the potential for more formal retail outlets in Lagos, with a popu lation of anything up to 20 million, is enormous, cost factors, a shortage of sites, land claims and logistical challenges means there are just a handful. In Accra, up to 3 million people are served by one Western-style mall. Johannesburg alone has 70.

Online retail is a relatively new trend outside South Africa, but it is quickly taking off. Markets are starting to notice companies such as Jumia in Kenya and Konga in Nigeria which have looked for innovative models to address issues such as low credit card penetration, logistics and, most of all, trust.

Luxury goods sales are also starting to show promise outside South Africa, which is already home to Cartier, Louis Vuitton, Burberry and Gucci, among other international brands. Some luxury brand companies are putting a toe in the water in markets such as Nigeria and Angola with a view to capturing those wealthy consumers who typically fly to Western capitals to indulge their desire for status symbols such as expensive cars, jewellery and high-end clothing. Although brands such as Gap, Nike, Boss and Mango are available in many African countries, they are sold under licence to franchisees with these international companies still reluctant to venture outside South Africa as corporate stores.

Challenges

The benefits of intra-African trade to the FMCG and retail sectors are obvious. The greater the mobility of products, the more exposure they have to consumers across a broad geographical range. African consumers are rapidly getting connected. More than 720 million Africans have mobile phones, about 167 million already use the Internet and 52 million are on Facebook. Millions of Africans can now tap into consumer trends, marketing campaigns and advertising, meaning increasing brand awareness. But creating demand is one thing. Moving goods to market in regions with weak infrastructure, trade blockages and long supply chains is another issue. Getting goods to market in landlocked countries at the right price is an even bigger challenge.

Weak infrastructure is one of the problems. Many railway systems from the colonial and post-independence era are hardly functioning and freight has had to move onto the roads, which have taken a beating. As road freight is more expensive, this also has had a significant knock-on effect on the landed cost of consumer goods. This is particularly a concern for landlocked countries, which make up the majority of African countries.

According to the World Bank, road freight charges in Sub-Saharan Africa are much more expensive than anywhere else in the world and even in the continent's most developed market, South Africa, they are significantly higher. There is limited competition along trade corridors, feeder infrastructure is weak and road density is low.[38]

South Africa may be a main contributor to intra-African trade across the continent but moving goods across the continent has been a steep learning curve. Retailers, manufacturers and logistics companies have succeeded largely because of their world-class and technology-driven supply chains. An inherent understanding of the terrain has also been a factor and the regional interconnectedness of road and rail networks with South Africa's own infrastructure network.

The port of Durban, on South Africa's east coast, is the busiest in Africa. It is a hub not just for goods coming into South Africa but for those in transit to other countries.

Despite strong investment in trade facilitation measures and the emergence of free trade areas within the SADC, the Common Market for Eastern and Southern Africa (COMESA) and the ECOWAS, Africa still accounts for just 3 per cent of global trade and a mere 11–12 per cent of trade among its own countries. The reasons intra-African trade is so low are barely changed from a decade ago. They include cumbersome import and export procedures, tariff and non-tariff barriers, a lack of harmonisation of operating requirements across borders and unsupportive policy frameworks for exports.

It still takes a truck up to five days to clear one border post in Southern Africa – pricey, given the average cost of $400 a day for a stationary truck. Beitbridge, one of Africa's busiest crossings and South Africa's gateway to the region, remains a blockage to trade, with truckers plagued by long queues, touts, inefficient systems, corruption and unpredictable service.

According to the World Bank's Africa Action Plan,[39] businesses in Africa face more business obstacles in Sub-Saharan Africa than in any other region. It cites the combination of high regulatory costs, unsecured land property rights, inadequate and high-cost infrastructure, unfair competition from well-connected companies, ineffective legal systems, policy uncertainty and corruption, which combine to make the cost of doing business in Africa 20–40 per cent more than in other developing regions. Companies, particularly small and medium-sized companies, also complain of high financing costs, or little or no access to credit. But opportunity in Africa's fast-growing countries and large numbers of virtually untapped consumers drive companies to find ways to counter these challenges to gain market advantage and good profits.

A challenge for companies operating in Africa's consumer sector is that they are heterogeneous and highly segmented despite some common operational challenges. Not only are there different cultural, geographical and language differences, consumer behaviour, preferences and spending power vary widely. Understanding these nuances is not always easy, and the challenge is the same for African companies going to new regions - from east to west, for example - as it is for foreign firms.

In West Africa, foreign goods are perceived to be more valuable and attractive. The consumer mind-set is not particularly well disposed to locally made goods as they are perceived to be - and have been for a long time - inferior and of low quality. In Nigeria and Ghana, wealthy consumers fly to Western markets and to South Africa to find the brands they prefer. In Kenya, the picture is slightly different. If you want to sell to Kenyans, it is better to flag goods as 'Kenyan made' to tap into a strong sense of patriotism about local goods that is highlighted by brands such as the payment system M-Pesa, a product devised by the mobile phone company Safaricom.[40]

The M-Pesa story highlights an interesting fact about the interplay of foreign and local brands in Africa. Although M-Pesa is held up as a symbol of Kenyan pride, Safaricom, majority owned by the UK's Vodafone, is technically a foreign company. This is just one of many popular brands in Africa that, although perceived to be local, are actually owned by foreigners.

Food, grooming products, drinks and other products that have become household names in African countries are now viewed as being local brands despite being manufactured by foreign multi-nationals such as Unilever, Nestlé and GlaxoSmithKline. Similarly, favoured beer brands perceived as local, such as Tusker, are owned by British brewer Diageo. But in Nigeria, beer seems to buck the trend of favouring imported goods where the best-selling brands, Star and Guinness, are regarded as local brands although they are produced by Heineken and Diageo.

Some South African brands have been adopted as local in countries where they are popular. A favoured tea brand, for example, is seen as a Botswana product in Gaborone and a Zambian product in Lusaka.

Everyday consumer products are thus not African or foreign in the minds of many consumers, which has implications for marketers potentially but not necessarily for the degree of difficulty they may experience in operating in Africa.

The problems experienced in intra-African trade are not specifically targeted at foreign or African companies but are part of the fabric of doing business in Africa for all players. Large multinationals, however, do tend to have greater capacity to deal with the issues with deep pockets, ready availability of supply chain teams in house and international logistics companies on hand to assist with their supply chain needs. Large retail companies such as Shoprite and Wal-Mart also have built sophisticated IT infrastructure to run their operations efficiently.

But this is not a silver bullet. For example, Unilever in Kenya has complained about the need to route goods produced in Nairobi through Djibouti to Ethiopia, a journey that can take up to three months, because of the lack of a decent road connecting Addis Ababa and Nairobi. Local companies may have a greater appetite for the arduous road journey on bad roads and thus gain an advantage in terms of the length of the supply chain but their goods may be stolen along the way or be damaged in transit.

An international company such as Nestle, choosing the much longer, but safer, route through Djibouti has other problems. For example, the lengthy journey means that some goods reach – or pass – their expiry dates by the time they arrive at their destination and the authorities can refuse to let them in. This is costly for companies.

Shoprite has had similar experiences in its African markets. For example, in Nigeria, where goods can often be stuck in the port for weeks, it has been criticised for having expired goods on the shelves from time to time.

The degree of operational difficulty is the same for international and local companies and depends on how sophisticated, and innovative, their supply chain is and also what risks they are prepared to take to reach their target market.

The number of large, African-owned conglomerates outside South Africa is growing, with their fortunes boosted by rising incomes and the rising tide effect of high growth rates as well as improved operating environments. They also have, in many cases, some influence with policy makers.

But it is easy to regard the new wave of growing African multinationals as being representative of the whole, which would be misleading. The greater number of companies in FMCG and retail, as in other sectors, tend to be small and medium enterprises have their own particular challenges. Most are family-owned companies that have only limited access to credit, professional and technical skills and capability to reach across borders or even expand nationally.

The fact of Africa being 55 countries, most of them small markets, is a constraint for both local and foreign companies that have to deal with lengthy and often inefficient and costly procedures at multiple border posts. Kenyan business magnate Manu Chandaria says that if there were no trade barriers in Africa, the size of the continent's private sector could be at least double what it is now. He said that in 55 years he had opened up 17 operations across Africa. In a fraction of that time, he had opened more than half that number in China. It is one country, he pointed out. 'I can move faster because I do not have to deal with 54 different countries with different borders and regulations'.[41]

The large number of landlocked countries and limited transport routes means trade can also be held hostage to political instability or criminal activity along the supply chain. For example, the post-election violence in Kenya in 2007 and associated transport blockages led to the loss of millions of dollars' worth of trade across East Africa because of the dependence on Mombasa port for logistics and Nairobi as a source of goods and services. For example, 80 per cent of Uganda's imports come through the port of Mombasa.

Ad hoc road blockades, theft of cargo and burning of rail tracks resulted in congestion that took about three months to clear and some transport companies in the region collapsed, according to the Kenya Shippers Council.[42]

During several months of election turmoil, fuel costs in Uganda, eastern DRC and Burundi rose by up to 50 per cent while those in Rwanda more than doubled. The shortages caused by supply chain disruptions prompted the government in Rwanda to introduce fuel rationing for a period.[43]

South African companies across sectors have cited the time it takes to set up shop in other African countries as a major obstacle to expanding their African footprint outside their home base. Shoprite took five years to set up its first shop in Nigeria; Nampak reports that it took several years to get its now highly lucrative operation in Angola up and running. Although executives are reluctant to spell out exactly what the problems experienced were, it is generally seen as issues related to over-zealous bureaucracy and associated corruption, getting past regulatory barriers and finding solutions to issues such as cost-effective premises, port challenges, energy and other infrastructure shortages as well as negotiating different business cultures.

Spur Corporation Chief Executive Van Tonder says, 'African expansion is made out to sound like it's a pot of gold. But whatever you think is going to take 12 months there actually takes you 24 months. You need to be a facilitator in developing Africa, you need to be flexible, and you cannot take your corporate governance baggage out of South Africa and expect to develop in the rest of Africa'.[44]

Even though shopping mall development is helping to grow formal economies, create skills and provide lifestyle improvements, developers are not finding it easy, particularly in Nigeria, a key target for African expansion plans. As one says: 'It's not twice as difficult to develop a shopping mall in countries such as Nigeria as it is in South Africa; it is three to four times more difficult'.[45]

Problem-free land title is one of the challenges. Litigation from multiple claimants remains an ever-present threat. Says Louis Deppe, South Africa-based Real Estate Director of UK private equity company Actis, 'In Ghana, we had a land claim on opening the Accra Mall. Literally as we graded the site, we had a chief claiming that we had destroyed his land and demanding a large sum of money as compensation'. Some governments, eager to find ways to appease investors, have set up fast-track courts to deal with problems. In the case of Actis, the matter was settled quickly through just such a court, increasing confidence in the ability of the country to deal with problems affecting investment. 'We only invest in markets where we have complete confidence in the ability of the legal system to deal with potential problems concerning property rights and contracts', says Deppe, echoing the sentiments of most investors, particularly those putting down long-term money.

The limited availability of long-term debt and a relatively low level of interest from international institutions in African property funds are other challenges. Imported professional skills and inputs, power shortages and a range of other factors in the supply chain ramp up costs, so high rentals are necessary in order to yield a decent return. This, in turn, means fewer local tenants to fill these mushrooming developments. The growth of local brands able to pay top dollar for rentals is still small. Even South Africa's Pep Stores has mostly avoided taking space in shopping malls in Nigeria because of the high rentals, taking its low-cost model to the streets of Lagos. It has been successful but admits that being close to a supermarket anchor is undoubtedly a good model for a retailer.

As in other sectors, laws and regulations can be changed without consultation or notice, which affects long-term projects negatively and can have major cost implications, further increasing costs and, down the line, tenant rentals. The lack of land registries in many countries mean land claims are common and can bring expensive developments to a standstill.

Construction costs form a high proportion of overall costs. Price of materials is high and likely to increase and most materials need to be imported because of issues with the quality of local goods for internationally funded developments. Delays at the port can push up the price. In one instance, a shipment of $5,000 worth of tiles was stolen in the supply chain. It cost $40,000 to fly in new tiles in order to complete the construction of the mall on time. Lack of power is another major cost factor, with expensive, diesel-guzzling generators being a vital business accessory.

Developers also have to be mini municipalities providing sewerage, water, power and other services offered in more developed countries by local government. Players in real estate need to grapple with legislation and regulations across different tiers of government, each of which usually have different building regulations, tax requirements and other regulatory measures. Failure to be on top of this information could result in delays and other problems along the lifespan of the project.

Ad hoc government policy is an issue that companies cannot plan for as mostly changes in policy tend to be without consultation with the private sector. For example, in 2003, Nigeria imposed an import prohibition[46] on a wide range of goods without warning, which included finished clothing. The removal of clothing from the list some years later was the catalyst for building shopping malls, which relied on foreign clothing chains to make them viable.

Nigeria's import prohibition regulation was not accompanied by supply side measures to develop local industry, beyond the act of banning goods that the government believed local companies should produce. The onerous operating environment made it difficult for small, underfunded local companies to step into these market gaps.

Large local conglomerates such as the Dangote group were the original beneficiaries of the ban on importing items such as pasta, fruit juice and bagged cement. Over time, the number of items on the list has been reduced and smaller companies have been able to benefit, partly because they have had time to build capacity to produce these goods but also from being contracted to foreign investors to produce for them.

International investors have mostly been slow to put down manufacturing roots within the country as a result of the ban but those who did also benefited. For example, South African packaging giant Nampak set up a plant to manufacture cartons, which were banned, for cigarette multinational British American Tobacco. With a foot in the door and guaranteed business from a large client, the company has built a large diversified packaging business in Nigeria.

The use of excise duties on 'luxury' goods such as alcohol is a risk factor for companies. For example, in 2008, the Botswana government introduced an alcohol levy of 30 per cent. It has been adjusted upwards over the past few years and by 2014 was 45 per cent and it has shortened trading hours. This is an attempt to curb the spread of AIDS through reckless behaviour. SABMiller says Botswana overnight went from one of its low-risk markets to a high-risk one.

Botswana is not alone. Other countries have done the same in an attempt to curb drinking but also to raise revenue. However, the government needs to balance this against the benefits of downstream industry of properly priced alcoholic beverages, for example, tourism, packaging, restaurants, distributors and many other companies, many of them local firms, whose survival is partly dependent on thriving industries such as beer.

The cost and administrative burden of import licensing in the region is also significant. According to a study done by the South African Institute of International Affairs, Shoprite spends an average of R136,000 a week on import permits for meat, milk and plant-based products for its exports to Zambia alone. It has to apply for about 100 permits (single entry) each week and up to 1,600 documents can accompany each truck in order to cross a border in SADC. Shoprite produces up to 8,000 SADC certificates of origin per month, all done manually, with up to 150 certificates of origin required per load.[47]

Getting permission to trade new products can be a long process. The study said one company had taken three years to get permission to export processed beef and pork from South Africa to Zambia.[48] The same study says Shoprite spends about R40 million to secure R93 million worth of SADC tariff reductions with regard to rules of origin and import documentation. If a single concession allowing grouping of Harmonized System codes were granted, this could potentially reduce Shoprite's workload in administering tariff preferences by 40 per cent – an estimated cost saving of more than R1 million a year for the company while the move to electronic data transfer and authorised economic operator states would cut costs by a further ZAR30 million.[49]

With regard to FMCG, there are many obstacles to producing goods competitively. With foodstuffs it begins at the production process where low yields and inefficient farming methods compromise production. Inadequate infrastructure to transport goods to market, storage and warehousing deficiencies and other issues affect the cost of the product. Where there is value addition, high costs of power, taxes, inputs and tariffs all combine to make goods expensive. Often it is the case that goods produced locally are more expensive than imports, which has had the overall effect of deindustrialisation and import dependency in most countries.

Even where producers have a competitive cost structure when leaving the farm or factory gate, comparable to those of countries producing like goods, issues such as transport, storage and handling, and finally customs procedures on reaching the border raise the costs of exporting a product.[50]

Currency depreciation is another challenge, particularly for multinationals but also because of high import costs. South African companies suffer from being held hostage by one of the most volatile emerging market currencies in the world – the rand. Although most companies are reinvesting profits as they put down deep roots in the rest of Africa, the swinging currency can have a dramatic impact on the bottom line. Ghana is another country whose currency has hit troubles in recent times. Unilever, for example, saw revenue in Ghana grow but net income decreased by 44 per cent as a result of high input costs and local currency depreciation.[51]

The currency affects local and foreign investors differently in many instances. Local investors tend to raise capital in local currencies and plough back profits into their national operations, thereby avoiding the worst risk. However, manufacturers and traders are affected by the cost of imported goods and inputs, which can compromise the competitiveness of their goods.

Competition law, which is gradually being adopted by countries outside South Africa, may be cause for concern for new investors on the continent.

It certainly adds another layer of compliance for investors, particularly as it is not just being applied nationally but also regionally, with COMESA, for example, introducing its own supranational competition policy in January 2013.[52] The concerns are not so much about the existence of laws guaranteeing anti-competitive behaviour, but rather their application and the additional legal and bureaucratic issues. But such laws are generally well received because of the protection they offer to consumers and businesses against cartels and the abuse of opaque private interests, which can undermine competition.

Also an issue for investors are labour issues. Strikes are an issue of concern particularly in South Africa with its very strong trade unions. In other African countries, the threat is more about the ability to get rid of employees and the cost of doing so. Governments in many countries require large payouts for retrenching or firing employees, in some cases tantamount to several years' salary. The state tends to support workers rather than employers, particularly if the employer is a foreign multinational. For example, in 2013, Shoprite fired 3,000 workers in Zambia who were striking for higher wages and who ignored a second ultimatum to return to work. Shoprite's argument that it was paying in line with the government's own minimum wage legislation was dismissed by the state. It contended that this legislation did not apply to foreign companies, which should be paying wages much higher than the minimum wage. The government further threatened to revoke Shoprite's trading licence if it did not back down.[53]

This highlights the tendency for foreign investors to be singled out for their labour practices, pricing issues, local content and other issues that are not similarly applied to indigenous companies. However, they also benefit from incentives that are in many case denied to their local competitors.

The close relationship governments in Africa have had with China has been a particular issue, particularly with regard to the FMCG space. They have turned a blind eye to the tsunami of cheap Asian goods flooding into Africa, often accompanied by Chinese traders setting themselves up in China-specific malls. This, despite the fact that the development has undermined the ability of many Africans to make a livelihood by importing and selling Chinese goods or manufacturing goods in competition with cheap Chinese imports. Foreign companies are, in some instances, also facing competition from cheap Chinese goods, for example, Massmart, whose stock comprises the kind of white goods the Chinese are also selling at much lower prices.

Governments pay a lot of lip service to fostering private sector enterprise but tend to stifle it with the tendency to over-regulate. For example, protecting consumers from harmful imported foodstuffs and medicines has led to the establishment of strict – but inefficient and often corrupt – regulatory agencies who are a real brake on trade. There has been little attempt at regional certification of goods and each country has its own agencies, creating major headaches for companies exporting to multiple African countries.

Countries' own policies are a big part of the problem. Governments in many countries in Africa tend to make regulations based on one part of the value chain without considering the entire process. For example, in Kenya, the government in 2011 passed the Price Control (Essential Goods) Bill which sets prices for goods deemed to be essential. These include sugar, maize, rice, wheat, sugar, cooking oil, petrol, diesel and paraffin. This is intended to stop rising prices of basic goods but fails to tackle the structural problems in the production process that push up costs in the first place.

Governments should work towards streamlining regulatory services, and in making policy, consider the entire chain of production and unintended consequences of their actions instead of looking at products and policies in silos.

Recently, pockets of export success – cut flowers from Kenya, vegetables from Senegal, clothing from Lesotho – have highlighted the fact that African producers can succeed in the global economy. But to multiply the stories of business success, African governments and their international partners will have to move in two directions: first, they must make the regulatory and legal climate for enterprise less costly and more transparent; equally important, they must increase their investment in infrastructure, particularly roads and power supply.

Policy makers should be more cognisant of new growth sectors in African economies. For formal shopping to grow and the property sector to reach its potential, governments must come to the party. They need to see malls not as a luxury item but as a creator of jobs, skills training and infrastructure. In the construction pipeline, there are thousands of people employed. Shoprite employs 250 people directly per store on average. Multiplied by 100, that is 25,000 people directly just in Shoprite stores over 100 malls. There are other areas where governments could make a difference. Reviewing other legislation and regulation that hampers the growth of commercial property, including loosening the strings on pension funds and removing obstacles to local manufacturing, which will encourage foreign manufacturers to partner with local companies to produce building inputs, are other measures.

Conclusion

Governments do need to balance many issues in making policy – the protection of consumers, the need to raise revenue, the necessity of building local industry and supply chains and many others that often imply conflicting interests with investors. Companies, too, typically motivate for their own interests rather than those for business at large. Multinationals and local companies have many intersecting interests but also specific needs that do not necessarily cohere.

But the question is whether local and foreign companies have different experiences of doing business in Africa in the retail and FMCG sectors. At one point in Africa's history, foreign companies were generally regarded as being multinationals from outside the continent. Over the past few decades, particularly after the expansion of South African companies across the continent after 1994, the view of what is foreign has changed. African companies themselves are now foreign in markets in which they operate on the continent outside their home base.

This makes the question of whether foreign companies have different experiences of doing business in Africa from local companies more problematic.

Although the picture is inevitably nuanced, it is fair to say that in many instances, companies experience the same challenges in doing business, particularly where trade is across borders and where they are required to intersect with government agencies. There are many differentiating factors that could also apply to both local and foreign companies.

For example, a large foreign investor may have its path smoothed by governments because of the size of their investments, its resonance with relevant government officials and the type of incentives they may be offered to set up shop. Local companies may also have access to people of influence within government because of historical ties, local business networks and offers of political party funding, for example, or even the offer of directorships or other incentives to policy makers. These factors could tip the balance in their favour in terms of policy, regulation and contracts that foreign investors don't.

Levels of corporate flexibility, shareholder obligations and corporate governance principles are other issues that may affect the experiences of local and foreign companies. Many foreign investors are either listed companies at home that are bound by listing and shareholder requirements in terms of corporate behaviour or international companies that are bound by conventions, such as anti-corruption protocols, in their countries of origin that may preclude them from doing business a particular way.

Local companies, too, may have some corporate governance constraints in home markets but many large African conglomerates competing in markets with foreign multinationals are not listed and are therefore more flexible in terms of their corporate structure and obligations or their companies are structured to more efficiently deal with issues relating to local business culture and challenges.

Size, capacity and access to funding are key sources of differentiation. International multinationals have deep pockets and are able to spend money on external service providers such as global logistics companies and expensive lawyers, to solve many of their business challenges. Infrastructure and basic service gaps can also be solved by having deep pockets. They also have access to the best brains in the business in terms of marketing and branding in the highly competitive world of FMCG and retail – although local companies may also have the edge in some areas because of their peculiar local knowledge.

Local companies typically do not have ready access to well-priced bank funding, venture capital or other sources of money. Bank lending rates in most countries are high and act as a brake on the ability of local companies to grow and to themselves become foreign companies elsewhere on the continent.

Foreign companies tend to have more scrutiny in terms of their labour practices and other operational areas both from governments and from the local media, which reflects an inherent mistrust of foreign investors that harks back to the days when many African countries were under socialist rule. The same scrutiny is generally not applied to local competitors who can adhere to the same practices without fear of public criticism.

Local companies have benefits that foreigners may not have which is not policy related but simply about having a different understanding of the business culture of a country, having the local business networks and often having local support for their goods and services. As highlighted earlier, the issue of what is foreign and what is local is highly nuanced but as African companies in the FMCG and retail sectors become more sophisticated, consumers may well factor in local pride into their buying choices.

Notes

1. McKinsey & Company, 'Picking Products for Africa's Growing Consumer Markets', Insights & Publications (June 2010).
2. A. Leke, S. Lund, X. Roxburgh and A. van Wamelen, 'What's Driving Africa's Growth?', Insights & Publications, McKinsey & Company (June 2010).
3. S. Freemantle, 'The 5 Trends Powering Africa's Enduring Allure', Africa Macro Insight & Strategy, Standard Bank (21 September 2011).
4. S. Thomas, 'Shoprite's African Expansion', *Financial Mail* (27 December 2012).
5. M. Mubila and M.S. Ben Aissa, 'The Middle of the Pyramid: Dynamics of the Middle Class in Africa', African Development Bank (20 April 2011).
6. Euromonitor International, 'Retailers Strategies in Sub-Saharan Africa' (30 March 2012), Euromonitor International website, http://blog.euromonitor.com/2012/03/retailers-strategies-in-sub-saharan-africa.html.
7. S. Freemantle, 'Intra-African Trade: Challenging and Critical', Standard Bank Insight and Strategy report (19 April 2013).
8. N. Smith, 'Africa Could Save $172 Billion by Developing Transport Infrastructure', *Business Day* (8 August 2012).
9. T. Hawkins, 'Manufacturing Share of GDP Falling', *Africa Investor* magazine (9 March 2011).
10. Freemantle, 'Intra-African Trade'.
11. Ibid.
12. UN Economic Commission for Africa, 'Informal Trade in Africa', African Trade Policy Centre Briefing No 7, UNECA, Addis Ababa (September 2010).
13. Z. Moorad, 'Shoprite to Open 101 Stores in SA in an Aggressive Bid to Gain Market Share', *Business Day* (26 February 2014).
14. Thomas, 'Shoprite's African Expansion'.

15. C. Bra, 'Retailers' Strategies in Sub-Saharan Africa', *Euromonitor International* (30 March 2012).
16. K. Manson, 'Queues Form for East African Retailers but No One Is Selling', *Financial Times* (30 October 2013).
17. Freemantle, 'Intra-African Trade'.
18. R. D'Souza, 'The Melkom Group Dominates Retail in Ghana', African Business Review Company Reports, no date given, http://www.africanbusinessreview. co.za/reports/the-melcom-group.
19. D. Games, 'Myriad Challenges Slowing the Growth of Malls in Africa', *Business Day* (10 September 2012).
20. J. Kew, E. Dontoh and A. Robert, 'Carrefour CEO Follows Stock Surge with African Expansion', *Bloomberg* (12 August 2013).
21. Accessed on Unilever website, http://www.unilever.co.za/aboutus/introduction tounilever/.
22. IGD, 'Coca Cola: A Long-Term Partner in Africa', Initiative for Global Development website (26 June 2013).
23. IGD, 'Coca Cola'.
24. S. Daneshku and A. Thomson, 'Drinks Giant Diageo Taps into Growth in Africa', *Financial Times* (23 October 2013).
25. N. Hedley, 'SABMiller to Invest $110m in Nigeria', *Business Day* (24 January 2014).
26. D. Jones and L. Laurent, 'Castel Rules Out SABMiller African Beer Deal', *Reuters* (7 October 2010).
27. T. Salako, 'Secrets of Leventis Group's Success in Nigeria', *The Nation* (29 October 2011).
28. S. Mzekandaba, 'Telecoms Boom Helps Nigeria become Africa's Biggest Economy', *IT Web* (7 April 2014).
29. G. Ware, 'The Rise of Africa's B-Brands', *The Africa Report* (16 May 2013).
30. Homefoods website, http://www.homefoodsghana.com/about.html.
31. Ibid.
32. S. Planting, 'Famous Brands-AUC Deal No Happy Coincidençe', *Moneyweb* (17 September 2014).
33. Famous Brands website, http://www.famousbrands.co.za/#0.
34. Ware, 'The Rise of Africa's B-Brands'.
35. 'Franchises Target Africa with Fashion, Food and Fitness', *Reuters* (8 September 2012).
36. Z. Moorat, 'Spur Corporation Ventures out of South Africa', *Business Day* (14 October 2013).
37. Freshmark website, http://www.shopriteholdings.co.za/RetailingServices/Pages/ Freshmark.aspx .
38. ITS South Africa website, http://www.itssa.org/blog/2010/02/27/sub-saharan-road-freight-costs-200-more-expensive/.
39. World Bank, 'Accelerating Action Outcomes in Africa: Progress and Change in the Africa Action Plan', World Bank (6 April 2007).
40. D. Games, 'Consumer Preferences in Africa a Stew of Nuance and Complexity', *Business Day* (20 January 2014).
41. M. Chandaria, Speech at Africa Governance Leadership and Management Convention, Mombasa, Kenya (4 September 2013).
42. Kenya Shippers Council, Supply Chain Security during Election Period', Kenya Shippers Council Policy Paper (2012).

43. Ibid.
44. Bizcommunity.com, 'Spur Plans to "Spur" African Growth', Franchising news, http://www.bizcommunity.com/Article/196/173/82452.html.
45. Interview with private equity company, 2013.
46. See https://www.customs.gov.ng/ProhibitionList/import.php for the current list
47. N. Charalambides, 'What Shoprite and Woolworths Can Tell Us about Non-tariff Barriers', South African Institute of International Affairs Economic Diplomacy Programme, Occasional Paper No. 148 (October 2013).
48. Charalambides, 'What Shoprite and Woolworths Can Tell Us about Non-tariff Barriers'.
49. Ibid.
50. AU Commission and Economic Commission for Africa, 'Boosting Intra-African Trade', AU and ECA Conference Background note (January 2012).
51. Ware, 'The Rise of Africa's B-Brands'.
52. F. Martineau, 'Recent Competition Law Developments in Africa', polity.org.za, http://www.polity.org.za/article/recent-competition-law-developments-in-africa-2013-08-13.
53. 'Shoprite Reinstates Zambian Workers', *Business Report* (South Africa) (18 October 2013).

Other Works Cited

Standard Bank Research. (2014). *"Understanding Africa's Middle Class"*, Insight & Strategy, July 2014.

10
Information and Communications Technologies

Bitange Ndemo and Muriuki Mureithi

A new dawn for Africa

Africa is transforming from a continent that has been riddled with poverty for the past 50 years to one with an emerging middle-class income status, with its economy growing spectacularly at an average GDP growth rate of approximately 7 per cent per annum. Assisting this growth is a decrease in armed conflict that has placed most African countries at peace, increasing foreign direct investments and improvements in life expectancy. Additionally, the Information and Communications Technology (ICT) sector is increasingly becoming a major driver in enabling greater efficiencies in the continent by allowing Africans to communicate more with each other – the basis of greater intra-Africa trade and investment.

Box 10.1 Africa leads the world in Mobile Money

Africa leads the world in mobile money. As of the end of 2013, there were 219 mobile money services globally (233 as of April 2014) and SSA is home to 52 per cent of them. At the top of mobile money providers in SSA is Kenya, which has the highest mobile payments penetration levels with approximately 74 per cent of adults (23 million) being registered mobile money users. Kenya's leading mobile money platform is M-Pesa, which has a network of 45,000 agents and in 2013 facilitated transactions equivalent to 25 per cent of Kenya's GNP.

Source: IPC Data shots as cited by Balancing Act Issue 704.

The success story of ICT in Africa is facing a number of challenges including liberalization and its impact on pricing and quality of service and limited geographic coverage due to underinvestment and corruption. Other issues include regional differences and general influences and legacy policies of the colonial powers. It is therefore important and urgent that both the achievements and the failures that characterize the African telecommunications sector today are evaluated, with the focus on how to encourage greater intra-Africa investments. To this end, this chapter shall strive to answer the following questions:

1. To what extent are Africans investing within the African ICT sector?
2. To what extent have Africa's old problems in ICTs been eradicated?
3. What in Africa remains to be done in the ICT sector to spur intra-Africa investments?
4. Are there new problems that Africa must address to increase investments in ICT within the continent?

To answer these questions, three ICT firms were selected for this study in 2014 on the basis of their extensive branch network across Africa. Two of the organizations, Cellulant Limited[1] and Seven Seas Technology Group,[2] are medium-sized enterprises started in Kenya. The third organization is a large multinational enterprise, MTN,[3] that was started in South Africa. Detailed face-to-face qualitative interviews were conducted with the founders of the two medium enterprises and with the top leadership at MTN.

Considering Africa's progress in the past 50 years of independence, the achievements in several countries are large indeed especially considering that some countries lacked the technical capacity to drive the sector. African nations emerged from colonial rule not as nation states but as a collection of different tribal groupings that almost immediately after independence led to several armed conflicts throughout the continent. Ironically, the general colonial influences and policies are increasingly becoming the unifying factor of Africa that has helped build the current stability. Colonial languages such as English and French are the dominant languages of business in Africa. Some investments in the continent are done along the lines of colonial influences, and the ICT sector to some extent follows that pattern.

Box 10.2   Africa sets its sights on digital future

Today, following a decade of economic expansion, Africa is going digital. Approximately 16 per cent of the continent's one billion people are online, but that share is rising rapidly as mobile networks are built out and the cost of Internet-capable devices continues to fall. More than 720 million Africans have mobile phones, some 167 million already use the Internet, and 52 million are on Facebook.

Source: 'Lions Go Digital: The Internet's Transformative Potential in Africa', McKinsey Global Institute.

Achievement and optimism for growth in Africa's ICT sector

There is a consensus that certain African countries are moving towards a market-led economic system, paving the way for inward investment opportunities and economic growth. Research from McKinsey & Company,[4] Boston Consulting Group, and the Center for Global Development all confirm Africa's emergence into the global economic landscape.

The Economist[5] indicated that six of the world's ten fastest-growing economies over the past decade were in Sub-Saharan Africa. This emergence can be attributed to sharp increases in global commodity prices, unprecedented global demand for a range of natural resources and primary commodities – particularly from China – resurging general international investor interest in emerging markets, unprecedented investment opportunities in Africa specifically and the explosion of mobile penetration in the continent.

The awakening of the African economy provides an opportunity for African entrepreneurs and enterprises to leverage on their 'Africaness' (knowledge of the business landscape, cultural diversity, understanding the problems and possible local solutions) to service the close to one billion customers in the continent.

The McKinsey Report[6] (2010) estimate that by 2020, Africa's GDP will hit $3 trillion. As Africa's population becomes increasingly educated and affluent, there is a real market for a wide range of goods and services that were unreachable to many just a few years ago. The emergence of e-commerce and mobile commerce is increasingly breaking the geographical boundaries expanding the market possibilities for businesses.

Mobile phone services account for more than 6 per cent of the Sub-Saharan African GDP, which is higher than any other region, and it is forecasted that this figure may increase to over 8 per cent by 2020 according to the mobile operators' body GSM Association (GSMA) in its latest report 'Sub-Saharan Africa Mobile Economy 2013'. In monetary terms, the mobile ecosystem contributed $60 billion to the region's GDP in 2012; the report projected that it will reach $119 billion in terms of GDP contributions by 2020. Overall, McKinsey estimates that the Internet will contribute $300 billion to the GDP by 2025.

There appears to be a 'new optimism for future economic prospects for Africa' – and hence fresh interest in the technology sector highlighted by the entry of large multinational corporations in the continent. At the August 2014 Africa Summit in Washington, DC, the US government pledged $14 billion in direct investments to Africa, most of which will go into technology solutions. Local technology companies have also joined the party, either by developing their own solutions, re-selling solutions from multinational corporations or blending both local and international technologies to deliver solutions to their customers.

Africa has seen a significant increase in investment in technology infrastructure in the past five years. The continent is now well covered by undersea fibre optic cable providing strong intra-Africa connectivity in most regions. The continent is beginning to see major changes in virtually all sectors of the economy as it begins appreciating the power of broadband. In the next few years, it will be difficult to recognize some of the industries seen today due to broadband. Broadband is the basis for technologies such as cloud computing that are completely revolutionizing the way data is computed and stored. Additionally, by extension, it is providing an opportunity for businesses to innovate and create solutions for different sectors of the economy.

McKinsey's report[7] shows that telecommunications has been an important driver of Africa's economic growth in the past five years with the market becoming increasingly competitive, and world-class local enterprises emerging in voice and data services. Telecom revenues have increased at a compound annual growth rate (CAGR) of 40 per cent, and the number of subscribers rapidly exceeded 400 million.

About 50 per cent of the growth in voice will come from rural areas. Data services are the other large growth pocket of about US\$5 billion, and experience in other countries suggests that a 10 per cent increase in broadband penetration translates into additional GDP growth of some 0.5–1.5 per cent.

Unfinished business

In the past 10 years, most African countries have liberalized the telecommunications sector allowing greater competition. It started with privatization of the incumbent state-owned operators. Most were split into three different enterprises including an independent regulator, a postal services company and a telecommunications operator. The regulator's role was to license new players and manage a new competitive environment. This process is still unfinished in some African countries. In Ethiopia, for example, the Ethiopian Telecommunications Corporation (ETC) is still a virtual monopoly.

Even in some of the countries that have liberalized the sector, there is still need to open up to more competition especially to encourage the creation of Mobile Virtual Operators to provide effective competition.

Another area of concern in many countries is the licensing of the international gateway operators. It is often not clear to ordinary citizens how their international calls, especially voice over internet protocol (VOIP), can be made more affordable.

Box 10.3 Hostile political dynamics and...high cost of access

Cameroon sits on multiple submarine fibre in Douala – unfortunately Cameroon is not on 3G purely due to political reasons and literary has no Internet. I could not download mail attachments in Yaoundé. I could however buy Internet per hour at a 5 star hotel at only US$6 per hour. This is just as useless due to low speeds. There are many illegal vsat based suppliers of Internet due to the cost and quality.

Source: A colleague in this study who travelled to Cameroon in March 2014.

Every company aspires to become a giant monopoly and reap the benefits of high pricing, but this is where most of the telecommunications problems begin. Oftentimes, the quality of service is poor in countries that have dominant players. Mobile as well as internet penetration is only possible if the pricing is affordable to the majority of people. The regulator should introduce certain measures to lower the interconnection rates to enable affordability but even with such a simple solution, there is often war especially from those firms that can exert political influence. In such a situation, it makes the business environment very difficult for new entrants.

Investment and coverage

ICT investments are capital intensive due to the nature of the sector where technologies change from time to time. To this end, most telecommunications investors concentrate their efforts on large cities and rarely invest in remote villages. Some regulators are known to have given incentives for investments in remote parts. Some incentives come from the distribution of the Universal Service Fund to assist in coverage of the networks to far-flung areas. It is also imperative that operators be forced to share infrastructure to minimize the cost of capital expenditure and enable greater coverage. It is also possible to require local roaming such that consumers are connected even in areas where their provider does not have network. This is how the investment costs can be minimized to enable Africans to afford investments in the ICT sector.

Corruption

As countries liberalized their telecommunications sectors, little attention was paid to the emerging sector policies. Some of these policies, either by design or inadvertently, encouraged corruption. In Kenya, for example, the policy framework required up to 70 per cent local share ownership (later revised down to 30 per cent and eventually to 20 per cent). The industry at the time required such heavy capital investments that there was no local person with significant financial muscle to raise 70 per cent of the capital investment. As such, this policy requirement forced the new investors to pay for the locals who could not raise the money. This indeed led to a creation of fraudulent companies purporting to have invested as a local partners. In reality, such companies were fronted for suspected government officials who traded their rights to the license leading to scandals such as the infamous Mobitelea scandal that has not been resolved to date.

Box 10.4   Challenges of local partnerships in services development

Kenya ICT policy capped foreign investments at 30 per cent. Locals often failed to raise the balance. As a result, the policy was revised downwards to 20 per cent local ownership and opened up greater foreign direct investment in the sector. At the time, even 20 per cent was proving difficult for the locals to raise. When Kenya tendered for the second mobile operator license, it could not get an investor since local partners could not provide sufficient guarantee to cover their part of the bargain. Most local investors would ask for a deferral of their capital contribution, which they hoped would come from dividends that they did not invest in the first place. Realizing this would delay investments in the sector, Kenya changed the policy to allow 100 per cent foreign ownership within the first three years before finding a local partner or floating an equivalent of 20 per cent share on the stock market.

Source: The author.

Corruption related to licensing especially with mobile communication licenses is widely practiced in Africa and it is a well-acknowledged cancer that must be dealt with. MTN is still embroiled in the Iran licensing scandal in which Turkcell has accused it of corruption.

Multi-national telecommunications equipment suppliers have also been accused of bribery allegations in big projects around Africa. Many other non-traditional ICT vendors have taken advantage of lack of capacity in human resource to fleece the continent off billions in phony works.

Corruption hinders growth by escalating costs that are passed on to the consumer making ICT services unaffordable to a large population in the continent. When bribery is rampant, it obscures the essence of competition which leads to poor services. Studies have shown that a high level of corruption leads to low level foreign direct investment. Intra-Africa investments will therefore be a mirage if corruption persists.

Box 10.5   The ugly face of corruption

Corrupt officials in the government of Kenya signed up with a briefcase enterprise out of Britain, Anglo-Leasing, to provide telecommunications services. It cost the country $1 million per 1MB for broadband. In 2006, as new office bearers, the government terminated the services on grounds that they were fraudulent.

Ethiopian inquiry revealed illegal imports worth $13 million and corruption on the part of Huawei Technologies. Zambia terminated a $210 million ZTE contract over corruption allegations.

Source: The author.

Colonial influences and regional differences

The pattern of ICT investments in Africa highly correlates with countries that were the previous colonial powers. For example, British ICT companies are disproportionately represented in Anglophone countries in Africa while French companies are common investors in the ICT sector in Francophone countries. This unnecessary divide makes it difficult to build business across the continent and needs a conscious fight through African Union by strengthening regional languages like Swahili that unites both Francophone and Anglophone countries. Additionally, development of cross-border infrastructure will lead to more trade and intra-Africa integration to close the communication gap between French- and English-speaking countries. The closer ties in East African countries that were separated by foreign languages has largely occurred because of the Swahili language and the infrastructure across the countries that can be extended to DRC Congo and create a new Africa to enable cross-border enterprises throughout Africa.

Are Africans investing in Africa?

Until recently, Africa's largest trading partners have been the ex-colonial countries. For example, Kenya's volume of trade with Britain is greater than that with its East African neighbours. This is also the case with Francophone countries. Africa's infrastructure was developed in such a way that it was much easier to travel to Europe than moving, for example, from Zambia to Nigeria. A similar plight can be observed in the telecommunications sector where Europe provided the exchange points, and to call Rwanda, one had to be switched through Europe, making the cost of calling extremely expensive and prohibitive and making communication among Africans impossible. This is changing as more exchange points are developed throughout Africa and the call cost is dropping significantly.

Box 10.6 The Internet Exchange imparative – keeping local traffic local

In a study on intra-regional Internet traffic exchange, the situational analysis is shocking – a packet, for example, leaves Kigali through Kampala, Nairobi, on to London where it is switched to Kampala through Nairobi. The reason being lack of awareness and poor business strategy by operators and ICT regulators who do not know what to do. In the meantime, big operators make a killing on small operators while the region loses. Due to latency, some programmes cannot run across the countries. EAIXP is now under implementation to resolve this problem.

How new infrastructure is designed will determine the levels of intra-Africa trade. Although still expensive, in the past few years the transport sector has managed to create greater African interactions than in the past 50 years. Challenges still exist, such as air travel from Harare, Zimbabwe, to Ouagadougou, Burkina Faso, is still easier via France than with direct flights. Similarly, some of the barriers in creating seamless communications in Africa have not been removed. In East Africa, the East African Communications Organization – a leading inter- governmental organization established by ICT regulators and operators from the East African Community, is helping to create exchange points (enabling intra-regional communication without having to go through Europe as has been the case) that will not only bring investors from each country closer to one another but also reduce communication costs tremendously.

The Communication Regulators' Association of Southern Africa (CRASA) in the Southern Africa Development Community (SADC) has as its main objective to create an enabling infrastructure. Article 3.1.2 of the CRASA constitution stipulates their objective as promoting the establishment and operation of efficient, adequate and cost-effective communications networks and services in the Southern Africa region in order to meet the diverse needs of customers while being economically sustainable. If this is replicated to other regional economic blocks like the Economic Commission of West Africa States (ECOWAS), and the East African

Communications Organization (EACO), an Africa-wide network that will bring its people closer to one another and improve the environment for local investments within the continent will have been created.

To understand the intra-Africa trade dynamics, we looked at three companies, two from Kenya (Cellulant Ltd and Seven Seas Group) and one from South Africa (MTN). The three companies do not just cover different segments of the technology spectrum but have very distinct DNA illustrating the diversity in vision by the founders. The objective of the study was to get detailed information in the form of narratives or stories, and experiences of African firms that have invested in Africa and have a presence in different African countries. The focus is on how they identified the opportunity, on how they dealt with any challenges, and on sharing knowledge on conducting business in Africa.

The three ICT firms were selected on the basis of their extensive branch networks spread across Africa. Detailed face-to-face qualitative interviews were conducted focusing on the founders of the two medium-sized enterprises and senior executives at MTN. The interviews were validated with extensive literature reviews on all three firms. The information gathered was mapped into a model that assisted in comparing experiences from different firms and established common themes. Although only three firms were covered, the findings are generally representative across board.

Cellulant Ltd

Ken Njoroge (Kenyan) and Bolaji Akinboro (Nigerian) founded Cellulant in 2004 with the initial business concept of distributing digital content, including music, through mobile phones. The company has since grown in leaps and bounds and is now one of the biggest players in mobile banking and mobile commerce in Africa. Cellulant has a presence in eight countries, serving twelve banks and thirty-four merchants and benefitted over four million customers.

The vision of Cellulant's founders is to create a Fortune 500 company in Africa, out of Africa and by Africans. Njoroge currently serves as the group's Chief Executive while Akinboro is a partner and director. The company has 130 staff seated in their Kenya operation and smaller operations in Nigeria and Zambia.

Seven Seas Technology Group

Seven Seas Technology Group (SSTG) was founded in 2003 by Mike Macharia with the aim of delivering technology infrastructure solutions.

An opportunity arose in Rwanda for such services and that informed the decision to start operations in Kigali. The company has since moved its base to Nairobi and has grown its business into different technology segments including consulting and training. SSTG now has five board members with Wanjuki Muchemi as the Board Chairman and Macharia as the CEO. The company has operations in nine countries including Portugal and is targeting other tier one markets such as those in North and South Africa.

SSTG is a beneficiary of liberalization of the telecommunications landscape in Africa.

Figure 10.1 shows the African footprint of Cellulant and Seven Seas.

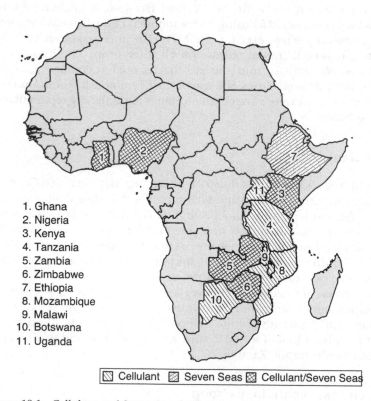

1. Ghana
2. Nigeria
3. Kenya
4. Tanzania
5. Zambia
6. Zimbabwe
7. Ethiopia
8. Mozambique
9. Malawi
10. Botswana
11. Uganda

Cellulant Seven Seas Cellulant/Seven Seas

Figure 10.1   Cellulant and Seven Seas footprint

Source: Adapted by the author from Cellulant Corporation http://www.cellulant.com/.

MTN

MTN was founded in 1993 as a Black Economic Empowerment enterprise; one of the development strategies by the new democratic government of South Africa that was specifically meant to open up the telecom sector and provide cellular telephony. Two licences were issued with MTN getting one license and Vodacom getting the other. Although the MTN licence was issued in 1993, the lobbying started three years earlier by a consortium led by media company Naspers.

MTN was formed as a response to the frustration of the then Postmaster General Judge de Viliers. He disapproved of the way the post and telecommunication authority was developing the cellular motor phone. The only available car phone then was the Siemens C-450 service, which was expensive and not in standard use with the rest of the world. The new government saw access to communication as one of the tools for empowerment.

MTN has since established itself as a leading emerging markets mobile operator with more than 204 million subscribers in 22 countries across Africa and the Middle East. It has a 27,000 staff with most of them outside of South Africa. More than 70 per cent of MTN's $15 billion in revenue came from operations outside of South Africa. MTN has $22 billion in assets with most of its business coming from the rest of Africa and some key international markets. Figure 10.2 below displays MTN's global presence.

MTN has established foundations in each operating country for their Social Corporate Responsibility (CSR). The CSR activities mainly focus on Health, Education and Economic Empowerment. The Foundation is set up as a separate legal entity with its own independent Board of Directors and Patrons who oversee the operations of the Foundation.

'Africaness' of the businesses

There are several factors that have been used to gauge the 'Africaness' of the study companies. These include the ownership, operation base and market. All the three companies are to a larger extent owned by African nationals but they all have foreign investment, which means they have an international board. The CEOs and Chairmen of the boards of all the study companies are of African descent and domiciled in Africa.

Of the three companies we studied, MTN has the most complicated ownership history which involves mergers, acquisitions and share swaps

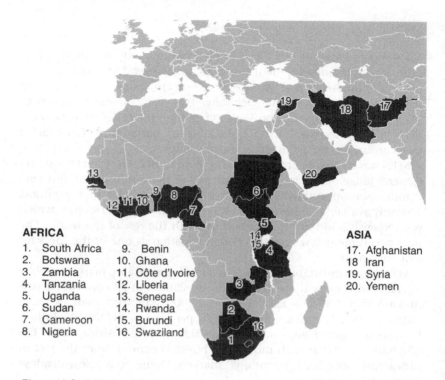

AFRICA

1.	South Africa	
2.	Botswana	
3.	Zambia	
4.	Tanzania	
5.	Uganda	
6.	Sudan	
7.	Cameroon	
8.	Nigeria	

9.	Benin
10.	Ghana
11.	Côte d'Ivoire
12.	Liberia
13.	Senegal
14.	Rwanda
15.	Burundi
16.	Swaziland

ASIA

17. Afghanistan
18 Iran
19. Syria
20. Yemen

Figure 10.2　MTN's global presence

Source: Adapted by the author from MTN: Major African Mobile Markets: Future Growth Prospects, http://www.africantelecomsnews.com/resources/AfricaOpp_MTN.shtml.

by different players including Multichoice, M-Cell, Cable and Wireless and Johnnic. By 2011, MTN comprised three wholly owned companies which included the MTN Group; MTN Service Solutions; and MTN International which consisted of the non-South African operations and MTN Mauritius, an investment holding company based in Port Louis.

With African roots and controlled by Africans, both MTN and SSTG have operations outside the African continent. MTN, for instance, considers itself a connectivity provider for the emerging markets, which include South East Asia and South America. Currently, the company has operations in Afghanistan, Cyprus, Iran, Syria and Yemen. Reports also indicate that the company is moving its headquarters from Johannesburg to Dubai while SSTG has an operation in Portugal. Cellulant, on the other hand, though solidly African, has a large multinational bank, with its headquarters in the United Kingdom, as one of their largest clients.

Therefore, although these companies are founded, owned and to a large extent serve the African markets, they are inherently built as global players offering global solutions to global clients. This means they attract some of the best brains both within and outside the continent and are globally competitive.

Benefits for intra-African trade

Intra-African trade presents opportunities for sustained growth and development in Africa. It has the potential to reduce vulnerability to global shocks, contribute to economic diversification, greater economies of scale and create employment. Governments in Africa have made several attempts to exploit this potential of regional trade for development, including the decision in January 2012 by African leaders at the Summit of the African Union to boost intra-African trade and fast-track the establishment of a continental free trade area. Against this background, the Economic Development in Africa Report 2013, subtitled "Intra-African Trade: Unlocking Private Sector Dynamism', focuses on how to strengthen the private sector to boost intra-African trade.[8]

Save for MTN who designed and developed an expansion strategy into other countries after they solidified their base in South Africa, both Cellulant and SSTG started as regional players by default – Cellulant as a result of its shareholders, and SSTG as a result of an opportunity that had presented itself in a different African country other than the founder's country. All the companies indicated that by moving to other countries, they opened up new markets for their products and services. Out of the 204 million MTN subscribers (as of September 2013) only 25.2 million are from South Africa. There are more than 56 million MTN customers in Nigeria alone. With an expanded market, the companies had an opportunity to increase their revenues based on the number of client's services or subscribers acquired. MTN, for instance, reported in its 2013 financial interim report that 70 per cent of its revenue is generated from operations outside South Africa.

Both Cellulant and SSTG work with partners in the different geographical regions they operate in. The increased partnership base has contributed not only to the company's customer base but also increased their sphere of influence and skills base. SSTG, for instance, believes that local companies in the markets they operate understand the markets better than they do and have wider relationships and therefore partners with local complementing firms when implementing solutions for their customers. In another example, SSTG wanted to enter the Zimbabwean market and identified a company in Zimbabwe that was keen to enter the Kenyan market. They got into an agreement where they swapped shares in the different countries, used each other's capabilities and competencies at a local level and co-shared each other's offices so the cost of entry in each market was very low, as was the cost of marketing and labour.

Due to the diversity in needs and requirements in different markets, the study companies benefited from extending functionality and usability of existing products by customizing them to the new markets they went to. This is more visible with MTN who have designed 'local' products to capture local markets but these are mostly innovations on their existing products. The benefit of this is that the companies have a shorter product development cycle and therefore go to the market with 'new' products quickly.

Obstacles to intra-African trade

There are many obstacles in intra-Africa trade and investment. All the study companies identified different challenges at different stages of the business life cycle while trying to get to different markets. These range from just registration of a business in a different country to work permits and foreign exchange restrictions in countries like South Africa. Cellulant identified capital as one of the challenges they faced when operating in different markets. This is mainly because it takes time to develop a profitable business in a new market that sometimes could take months if not years. Out of the eight markets that they are in, for instance, only three – Kenya, Nigeria and Zambia – are profitable. To sustain these operations they needed financing, which was not easy to come by.

All the three study companies identified difficulty in getting the right staff in some markets. The companies started employing expatriates and moving them between countries and building capacity in those countries. MTN, for instance, introduced psychometric testing and did detailed assessments of staff in South Africa to see whether they had personalities that could cope with the different environment outside South Africa. SSTG and Cellulant also used staff from Kenya and Nigeria as they built capacity in the countries they have operations in.

Several countries have unhealthy capital, and current, account restrictions, which are a huge hindrance to intra-African trade and investment. Controls on repatriation of profits and dividends as well as direct controls on foreign investment are cited as major barriers to intra-Africa trade. Though most countries have reduced control on capital and current accounts, there are a few countries that are yet to relax these restrictions.

Some countries still have protectionist laws that deter competing companies from setting up bases in those countries. South Africa has been identified as one such country. Laws such as the Black Economic Empowerment (BEE) skew the market and hand an unfair advantage to local companies and at the same time provide a good opportunity to the local companies to launch their business in other countries. Similar laws can also be found in North African markets making it very difficult to penetrate markets such as Tunisia, Morocco and Egypt.

The three firms concur that the procedures involved in obtaining various business licences make cross-border business registration difficult, cumbersome and expensive. In most countries multiple licences are needed for a business to operate but these licencing requirements are never clear and put businesses at unnecessary risk.

Unlike countries in other regions, most countries in Africa apart from South Africa lack support structures for assisting their private sector companies to expand into other countries. This is an obstacle especially when the target countries either subsidise or protect local companies from competition. Countries like China have support mechanisms that assist their private sector players to venture into other countries and continents by providing both financing and quality guarantees. Mike Macharia emphasized the need for African governments to assist companies investing within and outside of Africa.

Language continues to be one of the big barriers to intra-Africa trade and investment. Most companies, especially the smaller ones, are boxed in one linguistic block and find it difficult to move to other regions. While English is the agreed-upon language across most countries, French and Portuguese are used in others for the purposes of administration, public trade facilitation and private transactions.

Stereotyping and suspicion particularly in neighbouring states also face African entrepreneurs. Newspapers, notably the *Observer* of 19 September 2013, have often referred to Tanzania as a shy East African Community (EAC) partner due to the country's calculated approach to EAC matters. Businessmen from partner countries complain that they go through more stringent regulations while trying to set up in neighbouring countries because of suspicion. Since the collapse of the first East African Community in 1977, trade relations between Tanzania and its neighbours have been blowing hot and cold with Kenyan businesses citing harassment and sometimes expulsion from the country. In 2005, Nation Media Scribes were expelled (The Monitor 2005). Stereotyping and suspicion is also rampant against Nigerian businesses trading with the rest of the continent because of the 419 scams.[9]

What roles do and should governments play?

African governments are aware of the low levels of intra-Africa trade and investment in the region and have been the subject of discussion within the Economic Commission for Africa (ECA). There have been several attempts to create interventions to reverse the situation. Notably, the ECA and the New Partnership for Africa Development (NEPAD) have made efforts to create Africa-wide fibre optic network linking all the countries. Effective regional communications networks in Africa would not only enhance trade within Africa but would also attract investment in different sectors of the economy. The Abuja Treaty defines the framework for attaining Africa's regional integration by gradually consolidating all African countries' economies into a single regional market, which is expected to come to fruition by the year 2028. But this cannot be achieved without effective communications infrastructure. Experience in other regions has demonstrated that opening up markets where there is free flow of labour, goods and services can be a major source of job creation and economic growth.

Governments need to create partnerships with the private sector and assist the private sector in their expansion programmes. Through this partnership, governments can promote their leading companies and offer guarantees that the private sector may need when entering a new market. This will reduce the risk factor for the procuring entities and therefore encourage adoption. Governments within the East African region partnered with private sector to develop the East African Submarine Cable System (EASSY).

African governments need to learn to buy local technological solutions. In any market the government is mostly the largest consumer. By government buying local solutions, several things happen. First, the local companies get ready market for the products and services and therefore become sustainable and able to expand to other markets. Second, this becomes a vote of confidence to the products developed by the local companies providing the needed trust for other consumers to buy local.

Solutions to increase services trade in Africa

Among the companies surveyed and particularly the Kenyan companies, certain pertinent issues arise which form a basis to help promote intra-African trade and investment.

Firstly, the *raison d'être* for investing across borders is driven by the need to: stay competitive, take advantage of opportunities in other countries, grow the company, take advantage of skilled personnel in other counties and take advantage of technology. One of the companies, Cellulant, was inspired by virtue of directorships from across borders to grow its market beyond Kenya; Seven Seas on the other hand because the first opportunity was across the border that helped the company become more competitive; and finally because the domestic market appeared challenging but opportunities lay across the border inspired MTN to become more competitive and grow the company while taking advantage of technology. Governmental structures or incentives did not play any role in encouraging business across the borders. This intrinsic need among entrepreneurs continues to drive businesses across borders that have now entered multiple markets.

In addition to the intra-governmental structures of regional economic blocs, governments have embassies in certain countries in the region. Unfortunately, embassies were not the first point of support for market entry. Where the businesses approached the embassies, it became obvious that the embassies were not fully equipped to help businesses. It appears that the strategic intent of establishing embassies is political rather than economic promotion of businesses wishing to venture in cross-border trade and investment.

All the governmental effort on economic development is premised around tangible goods and very little attention is given to the services sector. Although UNCTAD 2013[10] says that data on services is not available and therefore difficult to track as a basis for developing policies around services trade and investment, Regional Economic Communities lay more emphasis on goods. Policies developed by the regional economic blocs therefore focus on trade on goods across borders. It is only recently that regional efforts are including services. AU is developing a framework for cyber security for the region and some of the regional economic blocs have developed regional-wide telecommunication policies that seek to harmonise services and development.

In establishing the regional economic blocs, the focus, at least for most of the Regional Economic Communities, has been on integration, cross-border infrastructure and tariff and non-tariff barriers to trade. Unfortunately, these developments have not moved in tandem with enabling policies for private sector to boost production and to become more competitive to export services or invest across borders. There will, therefore, continue to be a limitation to the gains from removing trade barriers until there are mechanisms to empower the private sector operators. UNCTAD (2013) proposes a paradigm shift of developmental regionalism which envisages developing common policies to support growth right from company level and an integrated policy framework to address constraints to trade and to foster trade.

Other challenges noted that are specific to the size of our economies are small countries, small national economies and a multiplicity of borders and jurisdictions. EAC, for example, is perhaps the most integrated of the regional economic commissions, but it still is struggling to have a single telecommunications policy to harmonise standards. In 2010, 24 of the 53 countries in Africa had a population of less than 10 million; of these, 17 countries had a population of less than 5 million and additionally 29 countries had a GDP below $10 billion, with 18 of these below $5 billion. With small economies and multiplicity of legal jurisdictions, the private sector lacks an opportunity to build economies of scale to compete across borders. In 2012, 266 companies in the Fortune 500 had revenues of over $10 billion.[11] It is therefore important to look at the big picture as African governments develop strategies for the increased cross-border trade. As Njoroge of Cellulant said, 'Although Rwanda had the best business environment, we were more interested in Ethiopia simply because of the size in population'.

In a publication 'The Middle of the Pyramid: Dynamics of the Middle Class in Africa' by the African Development Bank, the bank argues a strong case for the region to target policies to grow the middle class to jumpstart growth through increased consumption and higher advocacy for growth policies.[12] The middle class also provide the requisite skills for cross-border investment operations.

The insights from the field research and literature review provide a framework to propose solutions for increased cross-border trade and investment in services. To improve services trade in Africa, a multi-stakeholder approach is needed to engage multiple actors with various roles as discussed here.

Government, policy makers and regional economic blocs

Governments continue to lead in the development of intra-African agencies to promote trade. This is a mandate governments have and will continue to enjoy. Data cited by UNCTAD (2013) indicate that intra-African trade over the past decade has only marginally grown. The challenge is that the private sector, which is the primary actor in business, is rarely incorporated in decision-making on matters of trade. It is time for a paradigm shift to mainstream the private sector to not only inform government policies and strategies but also help drive these policies.

Governments are however positioned to help harmonise national policies that will elicit economies of scale and elimination of barriers across the borders. Most importantly, it is necessary for governments to put in place strategies to nurture and strengthen private sector capacity at the national level to venture across borders.

Private sector

With globalisation, we are moving closer to a borderless world, especially with the telecommunications sector. The private sector therefore has to build strategies to compete with the rest of the world. The African private sector should seek to exploit competitive advantage that includes geography, cultural affinity and deeper understanding of the home market. The African private sector needs to develop linkages with other operators to create alliances to leverage on their strength and experience. Seven Seas demonstrated this by their partnership with a Zimbabwean company. Seven Seas could access the specialised skills of the company and in return gave the company easier market entry into Kenya by using Seven Seas infrastructure. While competition is good in the long term, it is necessary for African companies to seek to build such alliances for growth and expansion. These alliances could and should nurture regional and eventually global value chains.

Thought processes motivating businesses to invest and trade within Africa

Of the three companies investigated in this research, it is clear that there are many considerations motivating the companies to take the risk to invest across borders – from diminishing market opportunity at home to interesting markets across borders. The thinking that promotes growth into other markets was clearly not motivated by nationalist concerns but seeking to exploit market advantage. In this case, MTN having been established on the back of Black Empowerment in South Africa was able to leverage the affinity with African countries and create thriving businesses; and Cellulant was able to ride on the back of cellular innovation in Kenya, notably M-Pesa, to create businesses across Africa.

Formal or informal measures to ensure success in investments across borders and effects of information trade

Our research revealed that while formal processes are important for market entry to conform to the legal framework, the informal processes are equally important to allow businesses not only to gain entry but also get a footing in the market and thrive. Some of the informal strategies include:

- *Connections with people who understand the market* – this is an important factor because it helps the entrepreneur understand the nuances of the market, which is critical in Africa. African markets have a large component of informal trade. According to UNCTAD 2013, African markets have a significant informal cross-border trade that includes such items as mobile handsets, which could be considerably more than the 11 per cent officially recorded intra-African trade. Operating at only the formal level will not inform the entrepreneur of this important market segment.

- *Bringing on board partners from the other country* – this is useful to build rapport in the country so that the business is perceived as local. Other informal measures include building staff capacity within the country as well as very innovative Corporate Social Responsibility (CSR) programmes. This is intended to create an image of a company that is national.
- *Seeking partners that understand the culture and language* – this was notable in the case of Seven Seas' partnership with a company based in Portugal so as to enter Lusophone markets.

Drivers of Africa's telecommunications intergration

History and experience

The historical context of the ONE network can be traced to the innovation by MSI – a cellular operator that had operations in both Democratic Republic of Congo (DRC) and Republic of Congo (Congo Brazzaville). MSI had operations in both capitals namely, Kinshasa, Brazzaville, and both capitals form a conurbation separated by the 7-km-wide river Congo. For a long time, and in line with the ITU tariff structures, calls intended for the neighbouring capital city had to be routed through Europe at great cost. MSI with operations in both capital cities was concerned that the high cost was unnecessary and consequently approached the regulators of both countries for authorisation to construct a microwave link across the river. This was eventually accepted and the direct link was established in 2002. The impact was significant with tariffs falling by 80 per cent and, what was international tariffs between the two capitals became local calls overnight. In 2002, only post-paid traffic was permitted but this was reviewed and the policy reversed to include prepaid calls in 2004.

This arrangement to interconnect all the other border towns was replicated, resulting in significant benefits accruing for consumers in border towns. Mo Ibrahim's Celtel bought MSI in 2004 and with the takeover carried the legacy and experiences demonstrated in the Kinshasa Brazzaville conurbation. This legacy would later inspire Zain with the ONE network in East Africa.

Prior to 1997, the three east African countries Kenya, Uganda and Tanzania were a political community and a number of services operated jointly in the region. One such service was telecommunications, which operated as one network by then known as the East African Posts and Telecommunications Corporation. Being one network, the backbone infrastructure was common. This network legacy is still in existence especially among the incumbent fixed line operators. The close working relations has been enhanced with the revival of the East African Community, under which the telecommunication operators have established a forum to address cross-border issues.

One such decision under East African Postal & Telecom Operators was to encourage operators to provide services across border towns such as Busia, Uganda and Kenya, where calls are local instead of being international. Of course, with the entry of the cellular operators who could radiate the cellular signal across the border, this is no longer an issue. On entry into the East African market through takeover of Celtel, Zain found a closely knit understanding among the telecommunication fraternity that it could ride on to build ONE network, which was a proactive response to travel patterns in the region. Additionally, the national boundaries in the region cut across communities with the same language, imposing international calling rates for communities separated by the borders, which penalised such communities when they called their kin across the national border. This brought about political and regulatory pressure in the region to reduce cross-border tariffs.

Africa outlook

The 2013 McKinsey report 'Lions Go Digital: The Internet's Transformative Potential in Africa' illustrates the picture of Africa in 2025. Internet penetration will exceed 50 per cent of the population; that is, 600 million Internet users, 360 million smartphones, $75 billion in annual e-commerce sales, $300 billion in Internet contribution to GDP and $300 billion in productivity gains.[13] This indeed is a revolution of a kind that we have already started to witness.

The McKinsey report confirms the views of Jonathan Berman in the *Harvard Business Review*. Berman's 'Seven Reasons Why Africa's Time is Now' includes the fact that the continent is: (1) a huge market, (2) incredibly stable, (3) still not trading with Africa and its intra-Africa trade is in its infancy, (4) soon going to have the world's largest workforce, (5) spending 20 per cent of government budget on education, (6) exploding with mobile connectivity and (7) home to most of the world's uncultivated cropland.[14] These are some of the factors that have been driving and will drive the growth of Africa's middle class. Although intra-Africa trade in goods stands at 11 per cent of total trade, it is growing, as is the level of intra-African trade in services. Young enterprises such as Seven Seas and Cellulant are breaking new ground. Trade blocs are expanding with talks of collapsing SADC, EAC and COMESA into the Tripartite. AU in its 2012 summit made ICTs a priority and has been active especially on cyber security. African Telecommunications Union is more active now than ever before. The legacy of looking up to the colonial masters is slowly dissipating. Intra-Africa telecommunications exchange points are being developed. The New Partnership for Africa's development has been incorporated into AU to include building cross-country ICT networks. For example, to call Ethiopia from Kenya a few years ago, one had to go through a London exchange. A new crop of pan-African enterprises such as Cellulant and Seven Seas are emerging and changing the landscape.

Lessons and strategy to position entry in the pan-African market

In the Bible, Mark 6:4, it says, 'Then Jesus told them, "A prophet is honoured everywhere except in his own hometown and among his relatives and his own family"'. Seven Seas started its operations in Rwanda and worked its way into Kenya. Cellulant's partnerships especially with Nigerians gave rise to its success at home. Although MTN owes its success to the policy of Black Economic Empowerment, it never had the home advantage which always was the preserve of Telkom South Africa and perhaps why it moved out to other parts of Africa. It is therefore not an accident that the firms we studied have done relatively better in other African markets than they have done in their home market. Mike Macharia emphasizes this point at every point saying that African countries have less confidence in home solutions often preferring to seek foreign firms to undertake even mundane jobs. Although Seven Seas is a Kenyan company, it started its operations in Rwanda before growing back into Kenya and other African countries.

This mistrust is largely due to perceptions on different aspects of life, including culture, products and governance. Different African countries have different perceptions of other African countries and in some cases Africans have helped create the perceptions considering the fact that European companies leverage on their colonial past to get into the markets. Whilst French-speaking countries are more allied to France, English-speaking countries too are more allied to the United Kingdom.

Sometimes these alliances are stronger than intra-Africa alliances. It is therefore not by accident that France Telkom is more dominant in French-speaking countries of Africa. Similarly Vodafone is more dominant in English-speaking countries.

It may well be that cultural or social perceptions have nothing to do with product perceptions. Position entry into the pan-African market requires detailed analysis of many variables including promotion strategies, cross-country partnerships and regional economic bloc strategies. It must however be noted that some products do fail in other countries when they have succeeded at home. In Kenya, for example, successful South African technology firms failed to make headway yet other South African businesses have been successful in Kenya suggesting that there are other internal variables such as first mover advantage that are critical to Africans doing business with Africa.

In a perception survey amongst all Africans, South Africa will rank high in many aspects including economic and social standing because it is perceived to have closer links to efficient Europe. Complicated medical cases are often referred to South Africa because its healthcare facilities are perceived to be of higher quality and more advanced than in other African countries. According to Indian Times, Africans would prefer Indian healthcare over their own as Africans seek for care from mostly foreign countries including South Africa. Although Africa's narrative is changing in foreign media, past negative perceptions still linger. These perceptions emanated from sustained negative reporting of Africa by the Western media.

Headlines such as 'the dark continent', 'ravages of disease in Africa', 'a continent in crisis' reinforce a negative perception about Africa by Africans. African countries too are at fault for failure to showcase areas of success. In most countries there is no effort to brand. Where there is a big budget for branding such as in South Africa, there is significant improvement of image and this is reflected in the surplus trade balance with most African countries. Kenya which has done significantly better in ICT innovations in the continent, is still perceived as less innovative than South Africa due to failure to build a brand a round its successes.

Remi Adekoya, in his article 'Why Africans Worry about How Africa Is Portrayed in Western Media', has argued that the African continent 'currently has no microphone of its own on the global stage, no loud-speaker with which to tell its stories the way it wants them told. It has to wait in line hoping others lend it theirs from time to time. That won't do'.[15] He concludes that the Arab World created Al Jazeera to tell their story.

A combination of African countries telling their story as well as country and product branding will indeed begin to change the African image not only to the Western world, but will help ensure that Africans begin to have confidence in themselves and their own products. Our three case studies have done well with branding their products, created cross-continent partnerships and truly delivered services with high standards. However, regional or country-specific branding is the next step.

Building local capabilities

Seven Seas is one of the leading firms in the region with a comprehensive capacity building programme often training for the industry and making it easier to deploy their solutions especially when some of their trainees work for the clients. Local African content, especially with Cellulant, has been the major driver of change. Local agricultural content has endeared Cellulant to other African countries after successfully helping Nigeria improve its agricultural productivity.

Some of the East African Community decisions to allow free movement of labour across the region will have a major impact on availability of labour capital in the region. Whereas Western nations embrace immigration of highly skilled labour, Africa has largely discouraged this and yet there is scarcity that needs to be addressed. Free movement of labour is by far the greatest strategy to address Africa's endemic problems that continue to attract bad publicity.

The effect of the broadband revolution in Africa is beginning to be felt. New applications such as M-pesa in the financial sector and M-shamba in the agriculture sector have significantly impacted on productivity in Africa like never before. Research on new applications and software is becoming part of the new scientific society and will impact on the future growth of the continent. For the first time, Africa is at the cutting edge of technology and redefining the future of not just financial transactions but other sectors such as emergency management utilizing innovative applications such as Ushahidi. In agriculture, farmers are no longer at the mercy of middlemen. With the simplest mobile phone handset, they are able to check on commodity prices. They have information and the ability to negotiate with knowledge and confidence.

The convergence of broadcast and Internet brings new opportunities, knowledge and understanding of the continent that has artificially ignored the power of pan-Africanism. Seamless communication networks bring new opportunities for Africans to invest in Africa. The Nigerian film industry is leveraging on IT infrastructure to deliver content to several other African countries. South Africa's DSTV provides across Africa an advertising platform and soon much of the broadcast content will on mobile handsets. This innovation is what will unlock Africa as an investment destination by other Africans.

We are in a jungle and must succeed not only in the global arena but seek to provide better and fast services to citizens and deepen our capacity to be global competitors. To this end Africa must move fast to automate much of its services to create local efficiencies and create back-end jobs, thus empowering its people. This in turn will create seamless integration of African governments. The next generation of governments will largely be on the mobile platform.

These next-generation governments with its next-generation citizens will demand local digital content, which will become a massive source of employment. For example, to improve on agricultural yield a farmer will need to consult the mobile phone, or to renew a driver's license, you will need the mobile anywhere any time, to give evidence in court you will need tele-presence on future mobile phones without stepping in court. These and more are what will characterise the future and create new investment opportunities. These are solutions we want irrespective of which country develops the content. This is what will bring Africa closer to itself and begin to trade with itself. M-pesa (mobile money) has taught us that necessity is the greatest driver of change.

We must strive to satisfy the need for data which the developers need to create solutions. Embracing Open data is the cog that is necessary to developing new applications around the solutions we need to improve on our livelihood. It is the collaborative effort, the people and governments that will drive the future.

Africa is getting stronger and ICT will help it get to where it needs to be.

Notes

1. See http://www.cellulant.com/.
2. See http://www.sevenseastech.com/.
3. See https://www.mtn.com/Pages/Home.aspx.
4. The McKinsey Global Institute. 'Lions on the Move: The Progress and Potential of African Economies' (2010).
5. *The Economist*, 'Africa Rising. After Decades of Slow Growth, Africa Has a Real Chance to Follow in the Footsteps of Asia' (3 December 2011).
6. The McKinsey Global Institute, 'Lions on the Move'.
7. Ibid.
8. UNCTAD. 2103. Economic Development in Africa Report 2013- Intra- African Trade: Unlocking Private Sector Dynamism, United Nations, New York. Emerging Africa: How 17 countries are leading the way.
9. Wikipedia. *491 Scams*.

10. UNCTAD, 'Intra-African Trade'.
11. Ibid.
12. African Development Bank, 'The Middle of the Pyramid: Dynamics of the Middle Class in Africa', Market Brief (20 April 2011).
13. The McKinsey Global Institute, 'Lions Go Digital: The Internet's Transformative Potential in Africa' (2013).
14. Jonathan Berman, 'Seven Reasons Why Africa's Time Is Now', *Harvard Business Review* (2013).
15. R. Adekoya, 'Why Africans Worry about how Africa is Portrayed in Western Media', *The Guardian* (20 November 2013).

Other works cited

Gillwald, A. and Mureithi, M. (2011). 'Regulatory intervention or disruptive competition? Lessons from East Africa on the end of international mobile roaming charges', Info, *Emerald* (Vol. 13, No. 3), pp. 32–46.
GSMA Report 2013.
Hsu, S. (5 May 2014). 'Is Moving Up the Value Chain a Mistake for China? The View That a Nation Must Move Out of Manufacturing as It Ascends the Economic Ladder May Not Be in China's interests'. *The Diplomat.*
IndiaTimes. (30 March 2014). For Africans, India is Healthcare Destination.
MTN Group Limited Reviewed interim results for the six months ended 30 June 2013.
Odhiambo, A. and Mugwe, D. (13 September 2012). 'Tanzania's Kikwete pledges freer flow of goods, labour from Kenya'. *Business Daily*, http://www.business-dailyafrica.com/Corporate-News/Tanzanias-Kikwete-pledges-freer-flow-of-goods-from-Kenya/-/539550/1506750/-/8jlqfaz/-/index.html.
The Daily Nation (April 5, 2012). 12 Expelled Traders Given Travel Papers, http://www.nation.co.ke/news/12-expelled-traders-given-travel-papers-/-/1056/1380994/-/m72l99/-/index.html.
The Economist. (3 December 2011). Africa Rising. After decades of slow growth, Africa has a real chance to follow in the footsteps of Asia.
The Monitor Uganda. (29 June 2005). Tanzania Expels Kenyan Scribes.
The Observer. (19 September 2013). EAC: Tanzania Warns Museveni, Kagame.
United Nations Economic Commision for Africa. 2010. Economic Report on Africa: Promoting High-Level Sustainable Growth to Reduce Unemployment in Africa.

11
Entertainment and Media

Eric Kacou

Africa's media and entertainment: a growing industry with a myriad of stakeholders

The media and entertainment (M&E) industry provides products and services that serve to keep consumers engaged and up to date. It is a key strategic sector with high potential for trade and investment diversification, job creation, creating shared meaning and influencing public discourse.

The United Nations Economic Commission for Africa (UNECA) singled out the arts and entertainment as 'a key service sector that is possible of driving greater diversification'.[1] UNECA's assessment was grounded on the contribution M&E can make to trade in services through differentiation, diversification and intra-industry trade.

UNECA noted that the M&E industry depends on a myriad of stakeholders. It explained that the production of, and subsequent trade in, films, literature, music and broadcast services relies on a multiplicity of inputs and contains linkages to complementary services and physical inputs, including publishing, technical equipment and financial and legal, among others.[2]

PricewaterhouseCoopers (PwC) identifies four key stakeholders that make up the M&E industry value chain (Figure 11.1). These stakeholders include; content creators, programmers, distribution systems and consumer devices.[3] It further segments the industry into twelve industry product segments outlined in Table 11.1.

Global spending on M&E is projected to grow at a 6.1 per cent compounded annual rate over the next five years until 2017 (Table 11.2).[4] Western Europe and North America will have the slowest growth rates, 4.7 per cent and 3.0 per cent, respectively.[5] Middle East/Africa and Latin America will however have the highest increase in overall spending, 11.8 per cent and 10.3 per cent, respectively.

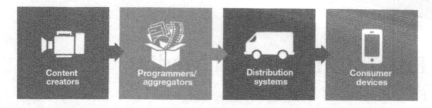

Figure 11.1   Media and entertainment industry value chain[6]

Source: PricewaterhouseCoopers, Game Changer, 'A New Kind of Value Chain for Media and Entertainment Companies', December 2013.

Table 11.1   Media and entertainment industry product segments[7]

Internet	Newspaper publishing
Television	Consumer and educational book publishing
Filmed entertainment	Business-to-business publishing
Radio	Out-of-home advertising
Music	Video games
Consumer magazine publishing	Sports

Source: PricewaterhouseCoopers, 'South African Entertainment and Media Outlook: 2013–2017'.

Overall M&E growth for Africa is forecasted at 5 per cent GDP per annum until 2015.[8] Four countries, Nigeria, Kenya, Ghana and South Africa, are poised to offer the greatest opportunities for content producers and distribution platforms for all modes of entertainment – film, television, digital media and mobile.[9]

South Africa's M&E industry is projected to grow at a compounded annual growth rate (CAGR) of 10.9 per cent until 2017.[10] The industry is expected to generate overall revenues of R175.4 billion (US$16.2 billion) in 2017, having increased from R104.8 billion in 2012. The internet will be the key driver for growth in entertainment and media revenues.[11]

Total M&E expenditure in Nigeria is set to exceed US$9 billion in 2017, representing a 23.7 per cent CAGR between 2013 and 2017. Kenya's expenditure in the M&E sector is expected to exceed US$3 billion in 2017, representing a 16.3 per cent CAGR between 2013 and 2017. Consumer expenditure driven by mobile phones will drive revenue growth for both Nigeria and Kenya.

The M&E industry generates high returns for investors. If US$10,000 was invested in Naspers (a global platform operator with operations in Internet services, pay television and print media[13]) in January of 2000, the value of the shares purchased would now be in excess of US$220,000. While Nation Media Group (a leading multimedia house in East Africa) has not performed as well as Naspers, holding its stock would have still appreciated to over $110,000, a return well in excess of global market rates.[14]

Table 11.2 Total global spending growth by region (per cent)[12]

Region	2008	2009	2010	2011	2012	2007–2012 CAGR	2013	2014	2015	2016	2017	2013–2017 CAGR
North America	-0.1	-4.9	4.2	2.9	4.5	1.2	4.1	5.5	4.2	5.6	4.2	4.7
EMEA												
Western Europe	3.2	-1.6	3.1	3.9	0.9	1.9	2.1	2.7	3.1	3.6	3.6	3.0
Central & Eastern Europe	11.8	-3.8	10.2	13.2	8.5	7.8	9.2	9.3	9.0	8.7	8.1	8.9
Middle East / Africa	15.3	3.8	13.3	26.5	21.3	15.8	12.3	11.0	12.7	11.9	10.8	11.8
EMEA Total	4.5	-1.6	4.2	6.0	3.0	3.2	3.7	4.2	4.7	5.0	4.9	4.5
Asia Pacific	7.5	2.6	8.4	7.5	8.5	6.9	8.5	8.3	8.1	7.4	7.1	7.9
Latin America	14.1	7.8	16.8	13.8	13.3	13.1	11.9	13.4	7.8	10.6	8.1	10.3
Total	*4.2*	*-1.0*	*6.1*	*6.0*	*5.8*	*4.2*	*5.9*	*6.5*	*6.0*	*6.4*	*5.7*	*6.1*

Source: McKinsey & Company, 'Global Media Report 2013: Global Industry Overview'.

Table 11.3 Media and entertainment outlook in South Africa, Nigeria and Kenya

	Industry Value, 2012 (US$ Millions)	CAGR to 2017 (est.)	Contribution to GDP, 2012	Contribution to GDP, 2017 (est.)
South Africa	$11 149	10,85%	2.9%	4.5%
Nigeria	$3 146	23.69%	1.2%	2.3%
Kenya	$1 453	16.31%	3.6%	4.1%

Sources: PwC, IMF.

Investing in the M&E industry is transformative for the society and businesses

Investing in the M&E industry has profound benefits for both society and businesses. This chapter focuses on three key benefits of special importance. They are: gaining first mover advantage in a globalised market; taking advantage of gaps in the value chain which are critical for long-term success; and shaping public discourse.

Benefit 1: competitive positioning

The isolation of African firms from the global business environment is being challenged by rapid globalisation. With large multinationals eyeing the prospects of an untapped African market,[15] historically successful African firms will need to employ a more robust and relevant strategy and more efficient operations into order to remain competitive.

The majority of firms that have been successful have relied on investments in other African markets. Boston Consulting Groups' 2010 focus on the African Challengers identified a group of formidable African businesses with the potential to compete globally. Of these African Challengers' cross-border deals, 65 per cent occur within Africa.[16]

There are three key reasons for the high percentage of continental investment from African firms. Firstly, strong regional market linkages, as a result of shared language, culture, and political affiliations. Secondly, the volume of opportunities available within the African continent. Thirdly, the sense of urgency behind intra-African investment.

Making decisions on foreign investment can be time consuming but each company's sense of urgency depends on its competitive positioning and the importance of early movers' advantage.[17] In a rapidly globalising business environment, it's important to assess relative competitive positions of African firms to the threat of entrants from large multinationals.

McKinsey estimates that brand loyalty, as defined by the sum of consumers loyal to one or few brands, averages 58 per cent in Sub-Saharan Africa (SSA).[18] In addition, their research suggests that only 35 per cent of the same population show a willingness to try new things.[19] For any firm this means that it is important to be first to market and build a customer base. With that in mind, African firms are left with no alternative but to invest in the continent immediately. To strengthen their competitive position against the threat of new entrants, they must be first to market. Conversely, international firms feel less of a sense of urgency and can investigate alternative methods to entering the market.

Benefit 2: taking advantage of gaps in the value chain

In its 2013 report on the M&E value chain, PricewaterhouseCoopers identified the traditional linear process between the four components of the value chain (Figure 11.1). Each component plays an integral role in succeeding in the industry. Yet, not all components are at the same level of development in most industry product segments and countries.

There is an undeniable push toward digitisation of M&E. In Africa, it is estimated that the Internet will generate US$300 billion of GDP by 2025. It is predicted that global growth in consumer spending will be led by broadband (10 per cent CAGR to 2017) and video games (7.1 per cent CAGR to 2017), but for consumer magazines and consumer and educational books to decline.[20]

There are two implications of the push towards digitisation for African M&E firms. Firstly, it's imperative to deliver content to mobile devices and other digital platforms. Secondly, technology firms will lead value creation and those positioned at the distribution and consumption end of the value chain.

Talent, as will be emphasised in the case study on Nollywood, is arguably the most vital input in the M&E value chain. Fortunately, Africa is home to some of the brightest talent in the M&E space – from vibrant musicians of Senegal, to computer programmers of Nairobi's burgeoning technology hub, to business strategists in Johannesburg.

The challenge, however, is that these hubs of talent are dispersed across the continent. The importance of talent is especially true upstream the value chain. Strong content producers are hard to find but critical to the success of an M&E firm. This is one of the main challenges that can be addressed through greater intra-African trade and investment.

Experts argue that success in the entertainment industry (music and film) requires a roster of artists with consistent quality content.[21] However, success rates of such artists are low, and relying on one demographic fails to capitalise on the broad tastes and interests of a globally exposed consumer market.

In considering the geographical spread and rarity of talent, the benefit of intra-African trade and investment in the M&E industry is clear. By establishing linkages to other regional and continental markets, African firms can tap into a strong talent pool to strengthen its value chain.

iROKOtv's success demonstrates that there is untapped opportunity in Africa's M&E value chain. iROKOtv, referred to as the African equivalent of Netflix, purchases the rights to Nigerian films and distributes them online. It not only caters to the Nigerian market that prefers to access content via web-enabled devices, but also to the country's Diaspora across the world.

iROKOtv was born out of the observation that pirated Nollywood films were getting tens of thousands of views online from across the world. iROKOtv was launched in recognition of the significant interest on the demand and supply side for an online platform for Nigerian films. After a successful launch, iROKOtv secured US$8 million from investors to scale the platform.[22]

For African investors in particular, their proximity to markets uniquely positions them to see beyond the traditional components of the value chain to where opportunities exist. In addition, they have the local networks required to practically capitalise on such opportunities. These factors effectively position African investors to benefit from exploiting gaps in the value chain.

Benefit 3: shaping public discourse

Among the many roles M&E plays in society, its impact on public discourse on culture and politics is especially important. Culturally, entertainment industries such as music, film and novels provide a materialisation of the culture of communities. In terms of politics, leadership can be challenged by public dialogue on what is acceptable and what is not.

Oftentimes, the role of an independent media group is underemphasised. Former World Bank President James D. Wolfensohn argued that '[a] free press is at the absolute core of equitable development, if you cannot enfranchise poor people, if they do not have a right to expression … you cannot build the public consensus needed to bring about change'.[23]

M&E play a significant role in society by providing information upon which critical decisions are based. In essence, therefore, the media is a key instrument in decision making, providing information and a platform for articulation and aggregation and formation of public opinion.[24]

The media is also considered a key factor in shaping how society operates by articulating ideas and influencing perceptions and attitudes.[25] It is reckoned that in democratic societies, media and journalism act as vehicles that reflect public opinion. This is effectively done through highlighting public concerns and making people aware of state policies and important events and viewpoints.

The M&E industry oftentimes acts as catalysts for political and social change. In Kenya, various issues such as governance, corruption and violence have come to dominate political discourses mainly because of the 'priming and prioritisation by the media and journalism'.[26]

Influence on the public sphere has inspired the creation of three of Africa's M&E industry giants. In the case of Naspers and Nation Media Group, the influence was both political and social. Nollywood, conversely, is an industry that has emerged as a form of cultural expression. Brief illustrations of these three are captured in the paragraphs that follow.

Naspers's history begins following the Boer War and with South Africa's National Party's rise to power. Following a series of spin-offs and acquisitions, Naspers would take the form of the diversified holding company it is today; however, its roots have not been forgotten as Die Burger continues to be owned and circulated by Naspers.[27]

During the 50th anniversary of Nation Media Group, the Aga Khan reflected on what first drove him to launch Nation Media Group:

> For there is no doubt that relations between governments and the media are central to the future of Africa, challenging and even exasperating as that experience at times may be. In many respects, this has been a new challenge for Africa. Prior to independence there were no national media owners, no national newspapers, television or radio stations, no indigenous corps of trained journalists. Newly independent governments had to work with media, which had no African antecedents, even as both political leaders and journalists wrestled with massive debates about capitalism, communism and non-alignment. It was against this backdrop that I decided to create the first East African media group.[28]

Challenges facing investors in the African M&E industry

Despite the benefits of intra-African trade and investment in M&E, there is clearly a dearth of firms that have been able to capture the opportunities. Although part of the challenge exists in the complacency of firms who have success in their home markets, there are structural obstacles that make such benefits appear unattainable to African firms, especially SMEs.

Three of the most prominent obstacles for African firms seeking to invest and trade within the continent include:

1. Weak intellectual property protection
2. A highly fragmented and disconnected market of content producers
3. Limited reversibility of investments

The first obstacle inhibiting M&E firms from intra-African trade and investment is the pervasiveness of piracy and the challenges in enforcing intellectual property rights. Karaganis identifies that piracy is a pricing problem, which results from '[h]igh prices for media goods, low incomes, and cheap digital technology'.

Although one might argue that the solution to media piracy is stricter laws and more aggressive enforcement, the reality is that this is contentious and hardly practical.[29] As Internet access continues to grow throughout the continent, it will be highly challenging, if not impossible, to hold individual media pirates responsible for theft that occurs from the comfort of their home.

The pricing problem of piracy has implications on not only consumers but also suppliers of media content. Suppliers who often struggle to collect revenues on the vast majority of their content are forced to either raise costs or find alternative business models.[30] Suppliers are forced to target the lower income segments with business models that incorporate their willingness and capability to pay.[31]

The second obstacle facing African investors in the M&E industry is the fragmentation of the market for suppliers (i.e., content producers, technology providers, etc.). This fragmentation is more than just a high number of competitors, each with low market share but an entire industry that suffers from weak linkages that prevent it from forming a competitive cluster.

Arguably the best evidence of the fragility of the M&E industry's linkages comes from Nollywood. Independent content producers are often forced to vertically integrate in order to get products to market. The consequence of doing so is an inability for firms to specialise on one particular aspect of the value chain and learn and adapt.

Closely related to this challenge is the issue of market fragmentation. Figure 11.2 demonstrates one form of fragmentation by highlighting the different languages used across the continent. The African market is one that is divided geographically, culturally and linguistically. In order to be successful across borders, providers must innovatively navigate this fragmentation.

A third and final barrier to intra-African trade and investment for M&E firms is the nature of the investments. In making foreign direct investment decisions, firms are often forced to weigh the marketability of physical assets against the importance of non-recoverable intangible assets in order to determine how reversible their investment is (Figure 11.3).[33]

The M&E industry places a high importance on non-recoverable intangible assets. As alluded to in the discussion on protection of intellectual property, there are significant intangible assets within the content generated. However, even distribution platforms have non-recoverable intangible assets such as distribution rights to content that if pirated can lose value.

With regard to the marketability of physical assets, many M&E firms invest in assets with relatively low lifespans. For example, video equipment has seen a rapid increase in sophistication while each new innovation is obsolete after a few years on the market. Between the lack of knowledge of this technology and the high prices, the ability to recover initial investments is low.

Figure 11.2 Market fragmentation – languages across Africa[32]

Source: http://afrographique.tumblr.com/post/4132889815/a-linguistic-infographic-detailing-the-most; http://www.corfizz.com/images/AfricaLangs2.png.

African investors are best positioned to address the three key challenges addressed earlier. As discussed, African investors' proximity to markets means they have the information and the networks needed to deal with highly fragmented and disconnected market of content producers and to some extent weak intellectual property protection.

African investors face a relatively low challenge of the reversibility of assets. As explained earlier, this is a key challenge for FDIs who are often forced to weigh the marketability of physical assets against the importance of non-recoverable intangible assets. As a result, many FDIs are attracted most to large infrastructure projects, where the importance of intangible assets is low and the marketability of physical assets is high. African investors, however, can more easily invest in specific assets that have relatively long life spans as they are located and domiciled in Africa.

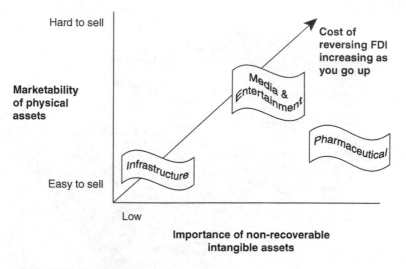

Figure 11.3   FDI reversibility
Source: Moffatt, Ivey Business School.

M&E powerhouses, South Africa, Nigeria and Kenya, offer great case studies

The three key benefits discussed earlier are illustrated by three case studies from Africa's leading M&E Markets: Naspers (South Africa), Nollywood (Nigeria) and Nation Media Group (Kenya). These case studies were also selected because they represent globally relevant M&E industry product segments in the continent.

The Internet will remain the major force behind the growth in M&E revenues in South Africa.[34] Aside from the Internet, the fastest growth will be seen in the video games segment as well as filmed entertainment. The share of advertising in the M&E industry is projected to decrease not due to a fall in advertising revenues but rather due to an expansion of the entire M&E industry.[35]

South Africa's Department of Trade and Industry identified M&E as a strategic sector in the country.[36] This sector is seen as strategic 'not only because it has the potential to contribute directly to economic development in terms of employment, investment and export', but also because of its significant spill-over potential in industries like tourism and retail.[37]

Naspers, a South Africa–based company is a vertically integrated media company, but it is arguably best defined by the platforms it has created for distributing content. As a content distributor, Naspers competes on a global scale where key success factors include scale and innovative technology.

The first Afrikaans-language paper *Die Burger* was launched in 1915. *Die Burger* was owned by the holding company Nasionale Pers and financed with the support of local philanthropists. Following a series of spin-offs and acquisitions, Naspers would take the form of the diversified holding company it is today; however, *Die Burger* continues to be owned and circulated by Naspers.[38]

Total M&E in Nigeria is set to exceed US$9 billion in 2017, representing a 23.7 per cent CAGR between 2013 and 2017.[39] Of this expenditure, consumer expenditure is estimated to account for 82 per cent, while advertising expenditure will be worth just over US$1 billion in 2017.

The fastest growth area in consumer spending will be Internet access (at a CAGR of 49 per cent) and driving this surge will be the power of cellular networks in Nigeria.[40] The Internet will not only be the fastest growth area for expenditure, but it will also be the largest market, worth US$5.6 billion in 2017, ahead of TV (US$1.1 billion) and sports.[41]

The M&E industry in Nigeria has enormous job creation potential. The industry is currently the second-largest employer in the country after agriculture.[42] This industry also has the potential to 'brand' a country and promote shared values. Nigeria has been noted to give 'thought', 'voice' and 'sight' to the society's culture and its shared values through this industry.

'Nollywood', the third largest film industry in the world, originating from Nigeria conversely, consists of a plethora of small teams of artists. These artists are the content producers that succeed by being close to the pulse of the market and developing content that resonates with this market. The emergence of technology based distribution platforms is transforming Nollywood.

Experts credit the birth of Nollywood to Kenneth Nnebue an electrical equipment salesman, who in 1992 produced *Living in Bondage* to unload thousands of what were blank tapes. The film was an instant blockbuster, and it wasn't long before other would-be producers jumped on the bandwagon. Currently, some 300 producers churn out approximately 500–1,000 films a year.[43]

Total M&E expenditure in Kenya will exceed US$3 billion in 2017, representing a 16.3 per cent CAGR between 2013 and 2017.[44] Consumer expenditure which will grow at a 24 per cent GAGR will account for half of the expenditure. The emerging middle class and increased Internet access in the cities of Kenya is also estimated to drive growth in the industry.[45]

The Internet will not only be the fastest growth area for expenditure, it will also be the largest market, worth approximately US$961 million in 2017. TV remains the single most effective channel for advertising in Kenya generating over 50 per cent of advertising revenue in 2017. Radio will generate more than newspapers and out-of home advertising.

Kenya is described as one of Africa's most mature cellular markets. Kenya has an estimated 30 million mobile subscribers, representing population penetration of 70 per cent. Research firms have projected that the number of smartphone connections in Kenya will reach nearly 19 million by the end of 2017.

The Nation Media Group (NMG), a Kenya-based company with branches in Uganda and Rwanda, sits at the intersection of distributors and content producers. Nation Media Group's strategy of being at the center of production and distribution has been key to its success in the M&E industry as it has enabled it to produce reliable sources of news and reach a wide market.

NMG was founded by His Highness the Aga Khan in 1959.[46] It has been quoted on the Nairobi Stock Exchange since the early 1970s. As the leading multi-media house in the East African region, it has print as well as electronic media and the Internet, which is said to attract a regular readership quite unparalleled in the region.

Case study 1: South Africa's Naspers

Naspers is an African enterprise success story. Since its renaming on the Johannesburg Stock Exchange (JSE) in August 1998, it has matured as one of the fastest growing firms in emerging markets. Organic growth and acquisitions have led to a 34 times share price appreciation since 1998. Naspers's capitalisation is now the sixth largest on the JSE at ZAR $434.2 billion (US$39.4 billion).

The essence of Naspers success has emerged from a well-executed and sound strategy. Despite rapid consumer demand change that has led to a print business earnings before interest, taxes, depreciation and amortisation (EBITDA) decline of 20 per cent in its last fiscal year,[47] Naspers has made sizeable and strategic investments in its e-commerce and digital media businesses which are positioning the firm for long-term success. However, these investments are not without risk; e-commerce EBITDA declined at 160 per cent to a loss of almost ZAR $2 billion,[48] and Naspers still must demonstrate a clear path to profitability for these new segments.

Naspers has a diversified product offering spanning ecommerce, other Internet services, pay television and related technologies, as well as print media. The firm has established its footprint in Africa, China, Latin America, Central and Eastern Europe, Russia, India, Southeast Asia and the Middle East.

Naspers's success has been driven by a sound strategy. It focuses on investment and technology, building a digital subscriber base, growing the Internet businesses, maintaining a local approach, providing quality service, and attracting innovative and motivated employees.[49] This success is all focused on creating a ubiquitous digital media platform in Africa and other emerging markets.

In addition, Naspers has an unrivalled workforce of entrepreneurs and engineers, and a diversified product offering that has allowed for constant revenue growth despite a rapidly changing technology industry. This is a formula that Naspers has exported to other markets around the globe.

Naspers's acquisition-based growth strategy has allowed the firm to overcome the challenges that have undermined other South African competitors. Specifically, Naspers's strategy has allowed the firm to overcome infrastructure gaps prevalent across Africa, a weak ecosystem and market fragmentation.

Firstly, Naspers's acquisitions allow the bypass of infrastructure bottlenecks by adding companies with effective distribution models to its portfolio. Rather than learning how to develop and introduce new technology, Naspers integrates such technology into an efficient corporate orchestra. This in turn allows the content to spur trade and investments beyond its traditional markets.

Secondly, Naspers's acquisitions have allowed them to increase their technological capacity while ensuring they had experienced executive teams and engineers. Rather than invest in research and development aimed at producing technology from scratch, Naspers took an incremental approach. Such a talent acquisition strategy is critical to improve competitiveness.

This strategy has been instrumental in Naspers overcoming the weak ecosystems for technology, M&E companies in South Africa and its traditional markets. Naspers has been able to acquire strong businesses but also the talent and experience as a result of their acquisitions' management teams staying aboard.[50]

Thirdly, strategic acquisitions have allowed Naspers to not only acquire technology, but also local market knowledge. For example, acquiring minority stakes in mail.ru and Tencent were strategic technology decisions but also moves to gain access to local market expertise in Eastern Europe and China where many growth opportunities existed.[51]

The primary reason for Naspers's positive outlook is how its acquisitions have created a defense mechanism against continued consolidation in the global industry. Although large, integrated competitors are putting intense pressure on Naspers, it has effectively positioned itself within a market that will grow organically.

Case study 2: Nigeria's Nollywood

The Nigerian film industry, commonly referred to as Nollywood, has seen a boom over the past two decades (Table 11.4). The industry has grown from next to nothing in the early 1990s to a $250 million per year industry that produced one of Nigeria's largest growth clusters and over 500,000 jobs.[52] This industry was singled out as a key contributor in the rebasing of the Nigeria GDP in 2014.

It is estimated that about 30 Nollywood titles go to market weekly. The average film sells 50,000 copies while a hit sells several hundreds of thou-

Table 11.4   Illustration of Nigeria's cinema[53]

Cinema of Nigeria	
Number of screens	100 (estimate, 2011)
• Per capita	0.1 per 100,000 (2011)
Main Distributors	Blue Pictures 50%
	Silverbird 20%
	Ossy Affason 10%
Produced feature films (2009)	
Fictional	987
Number of admissions (2010)	
Total	460 083
National films	117 563 (25,6%)
Gross Box Office	
Total	NGN 374 million
National films	NGN 86,4 million (23,1%)

Source: Adapted by the author from 'Table 8: Cinema Infrastructure – Capacity'. UNESCO Institute for Statistics. Retrieved 5 November 2013; 'Table 6: Share of Top 3 Distributors (Excel)'. UNESCO Institute for Statistics. Retrieved 5 November 2013; 'Table 1: Feature Film Production – Genre/Method of Shooting'. UNESCO Institute for Statistics. Retrieved 5 November 2013; 'Table 11: Exhibition – Admissions & Gross Box Office (GBO)'. UNESCO Institute for Statistics. Retrieved 5 November 2013; 'Movie Producers Beg Banks for Cash as Nollywood Goes Global'. Lagos, Nigeria: Business Day. 13 August 2013. Retrieved 21 February 2014.

sands of copies. Each DVD costs around US$2 making it affordable and very lucrative for producers.

Nollywood's unique business model has yielded low barriers to entry for Nigerian entrepreneurs. McCall[54] notes 'in a country where entrepreneurial imagination is high and economic opportunities are few, the video industry has created the possibility for what might be called a Nigerian Dream – a genuine opportunity for legitimate financial success and even celebrity, open to virtually anyone with talent and imagination'.

Nollywood's secret of success is relevant content. Whether comedy, romance or drama, one key to success is that the content remains relevant and reflective of Nigerian and broader African reality. 'We are telling our own stories in our own way', director Bond Emeruwa says. 'That is the appeal both for the filmmakers and for the audience'.

The reach of Nollywood has extended far beyond Nigeria. With distribution of Nollywood films found in shops and stalls across the continent and access available on satellite TV including M-Net, Nollywood has become a truly pan-African industry that connects the entire African continent and its people. iROKOtv by purchasing the rights to Nigerian films and distributing them online as illustrated earlier has further increased the reach of Nollywood.

The Nollywood case study should inspire all African investors looking to invest in the M&E industry. Indeed, Nollywood is a testimony of how investors even with limited means can still address clearly identified needs innovatively creating a successful industry niche with increasing global competitiveness.

Case study 3: Kenya's Nation Media Group

Right from the onset, the Nation Media Group (NMG) set an ambitious vision for its future. The founder of NMG, His Highness Aga Khan IV, reiterates that they aspired to transform NMG from a loss-making infant enterprise to a profitable blue chip corporation and then from a private venture into a public company.

By 2012, NMG had achieved its vision. With nearly 1,500 employees, the company is today one of the largest media companies listed on the Nairobi Securities Exchange.[55] NMG has posted positive results for shareholders through consistent appreciation and dividend payouts. It has also helped strengthen democracies across East Africa.

Nation Media Group publishes, prints and distributes newspapers and magazines, as well as radio and television broadcasting, while providing electronic media and Internet services. NMG achieves this with state-of-the-art broadcasting facilities.[56] Some of its premier brands include Daily Nation, NTV, NTV on YouTube, Twende Twende, N-Soko jobs, Business Daily, Africa review, Daily monitor.

External support and funding was key to NMG's growth and expansion strategy. With capital from the Aga Khan Development Fund (AKDF), NMG was able to develop international quality media infrastructure. Although the company struggled to achieve profitability in its early years, profitability has consistently improved and peaked at 26 per cent in 2012.[57]

NMG's strategy has proven successful for many reasons, but the importance of AKDF's role cannot be understated. AKDF was more than a capital investor but rather a partner in NMG's growth. This was demonstrated by allowing NMG time to persevere through challenges, and by providing complementary support in areas such as journalism education.

Growing newspaper circulation driven by strong editorial content, marketing promotions and other initiatives has increased NMG's market share.[58] Furthermore, NMG has consistently adopted innovative technology, and recently online content has seen a 32 per cent growth in views to exceed 100 million. In turn, advertising revenues grew by 13 per cent in 2012.

To overcome market fragmentation, NMG focuses on content appealing to a wider African audience. Initiatives such as the Next Big Thing and Top 40 under 40 profiling homegrown innovations and leaders, respectively, attract loyal readership.[59] With offices in its different headquarter offices, content is effectively localised to resonate most with its audiences.

The NMG case study illustrates three key lessons for the African investor. Firstly, it demonstrates the importance of having a big vision that transcends the borders of one country. Secondly, it illustrates the importance of strategic partners for funding and product development. Thirdly, it illustrates the importance of developing relevant content to respond to a fragmented market.

Harvesting the opportunities in Africa M&E

The M&E industry in Africa has the potential to grow and deliver even more benefits and drive economic growth. Three key opportunities that will drive growth in the African M&E industry include the following;

1. Africa's growing middle class
2. Expansion of mobile and subsequently Internet technologies
3. Greater press freedom and liberalisation

Opportunity 1: Africa's growing middle class

The African Development Bank (AfDB) reported that Africa's middle class had risen to 34 per cent of the population by 2010 up from 27 per cent in 2000 (Figure 11.4).[61] Per capita expenditure among Africa's middle class increased almost two-fold in 2005 compared to more marginal increases in other regional economies in the developed countries.[62]

PwC notes that a growth in the middle class has led to an increase advertising revenues, as brands seek to target households with growing disposable incomes.[63] Digital advertising in particular is forecasted to grow by a CAGR of 50.4 per cent as advertisers look to target more affluent households composed mainly of middle class households.[64]

A growing middle class is also associated with increase in magazine spend. Consumer magazine revenues in Kenya are estimated to grow at a CAGR of 9.0 per cent in the next five years. Similarly, the Magazine Publishers Association of South Africa (MPASA) has reported that titles aimed at the emerging middle class have seen more growth than established titles.

A fast-developing middle class is noted to have increased the appetite for access to entertainment and media services in Kenya. In 2012, TV accounted for 35.3 per cent of all advertising spend in Kenya. However, the emergence of a new urban middle class with money to spend on consumer goods this share is projected to increase to 45.8 per cent by 2017, or nearly US$1.5 billion.

Opportunity 2: expansion of mobile and subsequently Internet technologies

The Groupe Speciale Mobile Association asserted in 2011 that 'Africa was the world's second largest mobile market by connections and the fastest growing mobile market in the world' (Sub-Saharan Africa Mobile Observatory 2012).

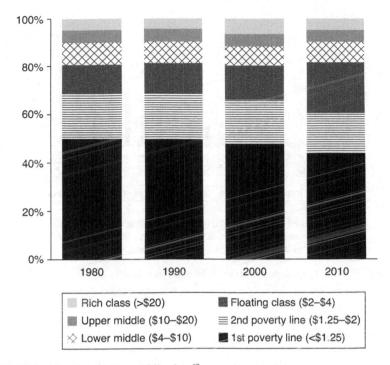

Figure 11.4 Africa's growing middle class[60]

Source: African Development Bank, 'The Middle of the Pyramid; Dynamics of the Middle Class in Africa', Market Brief, April 2011.

Deloitte reports that mobile connections in SSA have grown by 44 per cent compared to 10 per cent for developed regions.

Nigeria, South Africa, Kenya, Tanzania and Ghana in 2012 represented 47 per cent of total connections in the region, and the penetration increased by 81 per cent per year on average between 2000 and 2012. Mobile connections are projected to grow steadily to reach 75 per cent of Sub-Saharan Africa population and 700 million connections in 2016 (Figure 11.5).

PwC reports that the Internet has widened access to M&E products and services and created new opportunities for M&E companies. In addition, smart devices have also changed the way consumers access content and the way advertisers engage with those consumers.

The growth in mobile phone ownership and subsequent mobile Internet access creates numerous opportunities. It creates an opportunity for developing digital content, increased Internet usage, and growth in readership of online content. Nollywood, through the use of iROKOtv, claimed over

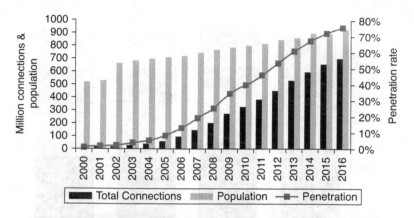

Supported by income growth, it is expected that penetration will continue to grow steadily over the next few years, reaching 75% of the population and 700 million connections in 2016.

Figure 11.5   Mobile growth penetration forecast by 2016[65]

Source: PricewaterhouseCoopers, 'South African Entertainment and Media Outlook: 2013–2017'.

500,000 online subscribers for its library of local 'Nollywood' movies in 2012.[66]

Kenya's growing mobile Internet usage will fuel the growth of digital advertising, which is set to account for 37 per cent of directory advertising in 2017 and 14 per cent of the professional books segment. The market for video games in South Africa on the other hand is forecasted to grow by a CAGR of 9 per cent to reach R3.3 billion in 2017 due to growth in mobile Internet penetration.

Opportunity 3: greater press freedom and liberalisation

As earlier illustrated, media firms first emerged to influence public dialogue and opinion in Africa. African governments were often closely involved with media firms. In many cases, the state exercised direct control over media and placed tight regulations on content. This trend had a stifling effect on the growth of the M&E industry.

In Kenya, for example, the roots of the government's relationship with the media are deeply ingrained in its colonial heritage. During their rule, the British owned the Kenyan press and enacted laws directly targeted at simmering resistance movement.[67] This did not change following independence, as the new government continued to maintain tight control over the media.

The media has often been converted into an 'informal publicity arm of the state' through direct and indirect means both prior and after independence.[68]

Media control was a source of conflict in Kenya, peaking with the ban of nearly 20 publications between 1988 and 1990.[69] Kenya has enjoyed a relatively free press during the twenty-first century leading to a growth in the industry.

The history of media in Kenya is similar to many other African countries. The predominantly authoritarian nature of governance across Africa prior to and directly following independence prevented the emergence of a truly free press. However, since the early 1990s there has been a wave of liberalisation that fundamentally transformed the industry.[70]

UNESCO reports that the seminar on promoting an independent and pluralistic African press, held in Windhoek, Namibia (29 April–3 May 1991), started a process of media liberalisation in the continent.[71] Practitioners have identified five major trends observed on the African media scene since the Windhoek seminar.

Five key trends point to a liberalisation of the African media. These trends include the following; growing awareness about the links between freedom of speech, free press and democracy; reinforcement of independent and pluralistic newspapers; liberalisation of the airwaves; development and reinforcement of regional organisations of media professionals; and training and human resources development for the media in Africa.[72]

New mediums for media are also igniting resurgence in liberalisation, although not necessarily with government consent. A study from the University of Washington[73] analyzed gigabytes of social media data to recognise that social media played a central role in the political discourse around the Arab Spring.

News outlets covered countless stories of social media enabling the mobilisation of people within Arab countries, while providing an outlet to share their stories globally. This has proven not only that social media is playing an increasingly important role as an information source, but that it also has the potential to disrupt regulation and forcibly liberalise the industry.

The liberalisation of the African media provides great opportunities for the growth for the African M&E industry. The African investor now has greater freedom to both produce and distribute content. In addition, the consumers also have greater freedom to engage, contribute and create content creating a vibrant African M&E industry.

Conclusion

The M&E industry is a strong historical, present and future contributor to African growth. Historically, the industry played a critical role in shaping public discourse. Presently, the M&E industry is a key service sector that drives trade diversification, provides jobs and incomes and creates shared meaning while influencing public discourse.

African investors have played a strong role in M&E growth and development in Africa. Indeed, Africa is poised to register the highest compounded annual growth (CAGR) rates in Media & Entertainment spend over the next four years in the whole world. The M&E industry alone will constitute approximately 5 per cent of GDP in key African markets.

Three key challenges however stifle the growth and development of the M&E industry. Weak intellectual property protection, a highly fragmented and disconnected market of content producers and limited reversibility of investments are three of the most prominent obstacles for African firms seeking to invest and trade within the continent.

Despite great challenges, the ensuing Success, Significance and Impact that comes from investing in the M&E industry makes it a worthwhile investment. African investors stand to benefit in three key ways; gaining first mover advantage in a globalised market, taking advantage of gaps in the value chain which are critical for long- term success and for shaping public discourse.

Naspers, Nollywood and Nation Media Group are inspirational success stories for investors at different levels of business growth and strategy. Naspers competes on a global scale where key success factors include scale and innovative technology. Nollywood is the third largest film industry in the world and the second largest employer in Nigeria. NMG is one of the largest companies listed on the Nairobi Securities Exchange.

These success stories can and should motivate and inspire other African investors. Ambitious vision for the future, producing and distributing relevant content for the consumers and access to relevant strategic partners not only for funding but also for product development were key to the illustrated investors.

The future of the M&E industry looks bright for the African investor given the opportunities at play. Africa's growing middle class, as well as the expansion of mobile and subsequently Internet technologies and greater press freedom and liberalisation are key opportunities to be harnessed by the discerning African investor.

Tapping into these opportunities will require interplay of both private and public sector interventions. At the business level, the investor should set out an ambitious vision for the future and configure his business to effectively execute on this vision. The investor should also develop relevant content for their ever sophisticated consumers.

African governments should collaborate with the private investors to effectively harness the opportunities while addressing structural challenges. This partnership should address weak intellectual property regimes as well as provide a network that provides not only funding for capital expansion but also networks that provide ideas for further product development.

Notes

1. United Nations Economic Commission for Africa, 'Export Diversification and Intra-Industry Trade in Africa' (11 October 2012), <http://www.uneca.org/sites/default/files/page_attachments/aec2012-379.pdf>.
2. United Nations Economic Commission for Africa (2012).
3. PricewaterhouseCoopers, Game Changer, 'A New Kind of Value Chain for Media and Entertainment Companies' (December 2013).
4. McKinsey & Company, 'Global Media Report 2013: Global Industry Overview'.
5. McKinsey & Company, Global Media Report 2013.
6. PricewaterhouseCoopers, 'A New Kind of Value Chain'.
7. PricewaterhouseCoopers, 'South African Entertainment and Media Outlook: 2013–2017'.
8. http://www.tradeinvestafrica.com/feature_articles/1132920.htm.
9. Ibid.
10. PricewaterhouseCoopers, 'South African Entertainment and Media Outlook: 2013–2017'.
11. Ibid.
12. Ibid.
13. http://www.naspers.com/page.html?pageID=3; A detailed case study on Naspers is found on page 10, section IV.
14. Calculations derived from Capital IQ.
15. McKinsey African Lions.
16. BCG Challengers.
17. Professor Mike Moffatt, Ivey Business School.
18. McKinsey, http://irokopartners.com.
19. Ibid.
20. McKinsey.
21. IBIS World.
22. http://www.fastcompany.com/3006695/irokos-jason-njoku-is-creating-the-next-netflix-in-nigeria.
23. http://gfmd.info/index.php/tools/quotes_on_importance_of_media_to_development/ (retrieved 31 December 2013).
24. George Nyabuga, 'Mediatising Politics and Democracy: Making Sense of the Role of the Media in Kenya', Media Focus on Africa Foundation, http://www.mediafocusonafrica.org/sites/default/files/result/Mediatising%20Politics%20and%20Democracy%20-%20%20Making%20sense%20of%20the%20role%20of%20the%20media%20in%20Kenya.pdf.
25. Nyabuga, 'Mediating Politics and Democracy'.
26. Ibid.
27. http://www.fundinguniverse.com/company-histories/naspers-ltd-history/.
28. http://www.akdn.org/Content/980/Conference-Marking-the-50th-Anniversary-of-the-Nation-Media-Group-Media-and-the-African-Promise--.
29. http://www.theglobeandmail.com/technology/tech-news/anti-piracy-firm-targeting-canadians-who-download-illegally/article11877622/.
30. Social Science Research Council, 'Media Piracy in Emerging Economies'.
31. Media Piracy in Emerging Economies.
32. http://afrographique.tumblr.com/post/4132889815/a-linguistic-infographic-detailing-the-most; http://www.corfizz.com/images/AfricaLangs2.png.

33. Moffatt, Ivey Business School.
34. Ibid.
35. Ibid.
36. Petrus Jacobus Pieterse, 'A Historical Examination of Disruptive Innovation Management in the Global Media and Entertainment Industry', Master's thesis (March 2012).
37. Pieterse, 'A Historical Examination'.
38. http://www.fundinguniverse.com/company-histories/naspers-ltd-history/.
39. PricewaterhouseCoopers, 'South African Entertainment and Media Outlook: 2013–2017'.
40. Ibid.
41. Ibid.
42. http://parmindervir.com/post/39847536565/the-nigerian-film-industry-now.
43. http://www.thisisnollywood.com/nollywood.htm.
44. PricewaterHouseCoopers, 'South African Entertainment and Media Outlook: 2013–2017'.
45. Ibid.
46. http://www.nationmedia.com/.
47. Naspers Annual Report.
48. Ibid.
49. www.naspers.com.
50. http://www.dailymaverick.co.za/article/2010-07-01-naspers-continues-its-mighty-march#.UsJ2L2QYb-t (retrieved 31 December 2013).
51. http://www.dailymaverick.co.za/article/2010-07-01-naspers-continues-its-mighty-march#.UsJ2L2QYb-t (retrieved 31 December 2013).
52. M. Chowdhury, T. Landesz, M. Santini, L. Tejada and G. Visconti, *Nollywood: The Nigerian Film Industry* (Harvard Kennedy School, 2008).
53. 'Table 8: Cinema Infrastructure – Capacity', UNESCO Institute for Statistics (retrieved 5 November 2013); 'Table 6: Share of Top 3 Distributors (Excel)', UNESCO Institute for Statistics (retrieved 5 November 2013); 'Table 1: Feature Film Production – Genre/ Method of Shooting', UNESCO Institute for Statistics (retrieved 5 November 2013).; 'Table 11: Exhibition – Admissions & Gross Box Office (GBO)', UNESCO Institute for Statistics (retrieved 5 November 2013); 'Movie Producers Beg Banks for Cash as Nollywood Goes Global', Lagos, Nigeria: Business Day, 13 August 2013 (retrieved 21 February 2014).
54. J.C. McCall, 'The Capital Gap: Nollywood and the Limits of Informal Trade'. *Journal of African Cinemas* (Vol. 4, No. 1, 2012), pp. 9–23.
55. NMG Annual Report.
56. Ibid.
57. ISI Emerging Markets.
58. NMG Annual Report.
59. Ibid.
60. African Development Bank, 'The Middle of the Pyramid; Dynamics of the Middle Class in Africa', Market Brief (April 2011).
61. African Development Bank (2011).
62. Ibid.
63. PricewaterhouseCoopers, 'South African Entertainment and Media Outlook: 2013–2017'.
64. Ibid.
65. Ibid.

66. Ibid.
67. P. Mbeke and T. Mshindi, 'Kenya Media Sector Analysis Report', Prepared for CIDA (2008), https://profiles.uonbi.ac.ke/pmbeke/publications/kenya-media-sector-analysis-report-november-2008.
68. G. Ogala, 'The Political Economy of Media in Kenya: From Kenyatta's Nation-Building Press to Kibaki's Local-Language FM Radio', *Africa Today* (Vol. 57, No. 3, 2011), pp. 76–95.
69. G. Ogala, 'The Political Economy of Media in Kenya'.
70. P. Adriantsoa et al., 'Media Proliferation and Democratic Transition in Africa: The Case of Madagascar', *World Development* (Vol. 33, No. 11, 2005), pp. 1939–1957.
71. S.T. Kwame Boafo, 'Trends on the African Media Scene a Decade after the Windhoek Declaration'.
72. Boafo, 'Trends on the African Media Scene'.
73. P.N. Howard et al., 'Opening Closed Regimes: What Was the Role of Social Media during the Arab Spring?', University of Washington, Working Paper 2011.

Part III
Emerging Pan-African Sectors

12
Petroleum, Gas and Mining Sectors in East African Community

Albert Butare

Differences, disparities and community

Contributing to the study 'Africans Investing in Africa', which is aimed at understanding the challenges and latent opportunities existing on the continent for more African involvement, this chapter sheds light on the Petroleum, Gas and Mining Sectors in the East African Community (EAC) countries. The EAC as a block was chosen as a case due to some of its shared similarities, most of which are influenced by the history of the block. For example, Kenya, Uganda and Tanzania fell under the earlier (1970s) East African Community whereby some socio-economic domains, including education, trade (air transport, railways and marine) and so on, were under shared arrangements. On the other hand, Burundi and Rwanda, beyond the fact that they happen to have quite similar geographical and geological features, also happened to fall under a single colony that influenced common trade practices and geopolitical structures. Today, under the current East African Community (with five countries), most of the trade aspects enjoy harmonised trade policies that may characterise attractive investment interests as a block rather than as individual countries.

The region, with two of its member countries, namely, Kenya and Tanzania, enjoying being located on the western coast of the Indian ocean has distinct features and inter-trade relationships that go a long way back during the colonial times. Due to this inter-trade and inter-cultural interactions, today almost all the five countries do speak Kiswahili even if it is only Tanzania, Uganda and Kenya where this is an official national language.

Beyond being endowed with huge valuable natural resources, the region has Africa's three highest mountains, the world's largest permanent desert and alkaline lake, the world's second largest freshwater lake, the world's second deepest lake and one of three lakes worldwide experiencing gas eruptions. Active volcanoes, mountains, deserts, swamps and savanna are all found within the territories of the EAC.

After a long history of regional cooperation, the EAC was reconstituted in 2000 after it had collapsed in the 1970s, and its current member states are: Burundi, Kenya, Rwanda, Tanzania and Uganda. The goal of the EAC is to become fully integrated and thus benefit from the positive effects associated with this integration.

Going through the different steps of social, political and economic integration, the EAC has successfully transformed itself into a customs union and also launched its common market in 2010, allowing goods, labour and capital to move freely within its borders. The community is furthermore envisioning the introduction of a common currency, the East African Shilling. Many policies in different sectors, including the energy and mineral sector, are being aligned.

The member states are very diverse, with the colonial languages including English and French, population sizes varying from 10 to 48 million inhabitants and the GDP (PPP) ranging from US$5.6 to 77.1 billion. This variation allows for a wider range of investment opportunities.

This case study presents the resource status of the member states, attempts to point out differences and similarities and to identify challenges and opportunities for the individual countries, as well as the EAC as a block, available for investments. It also reflects the status of domestic investments attempts in the region by both the local and foreign Africans.

Beyond the resource and investment levels, the study looks on to the institutional and legal framework and procedures for licensing, which helps in understanding the investment environment. The institutional and legal frameworks are considered to be major factors influencing investments although other factors such as governance and capacity are discussed. This situation pertains to both domestic and foreign investments.

The proverbial goldmine: resource potential and availability

Africa is most commonly and superficially described as a continent of great poverty in spite of vast resources. In fact, Africa ranks first or second in terms of the percentage of world reserves of the minerals bauxite, chromite, cobalt, industrial diamonds, manganese, phosphate rock, platinum-group metals, soda ash and zirconium and third after the Middle East and Eurasia in terms of the percentage of world reserves of natural gas, with African reserves estimated at 515.4 trillion cubic feet (TCF). Furthermore, Africa has 8 per cent of the world's proven oil reserves (127.6 billion barrels) and Nigeria is the twelfth biggest oil producer. The fact that much of Africa remains relatively underexplored and recent discoveries of natural gas and oil reserves point to significant potential for improvement of these figures.

Traditionally, the continent's most important energy players are Nigeria, Angola, Libya and Algeria. The Gulf of Guinea and North Africa will thus most likely remain the main hydrocarbon-producing regions on the continent. However, due to recent finds there are great expectations for East Africa. While Tanzania is experiencing huge natural gas discoveries, Uganda has discovered oil and Kenya oil and gas explorations are indicating probable positive prospects.

The member states of the EAC do greatly differ in size, geographical attributes and resources. The two countries which share a border with the Indian Ocean, namely, Tanzania and Kenya, are at the same time the countries with the greatest land masses – 945,087 km² and 580,367 km², respectively. Uganda, with its 236,040 km², is less than half the size of Kenya, while the two countries with the highest population density on mainland Africa, Rwanda and Burundi, each only covers an area of 26,338 km² and 27,834 km², respectively, 3 per cent the size of Tanzania.

Resources in the EAC are vast and its geology is endowed with a wide variety of minerals that provides a big range of investment options and levels for both potential domestic/African (small and medium investments) and foreign (medium and big investments) investors. These include:

Native element minerals, for example, bismuth, copper, diamond, gold, iron, nickel, platinum, silver;
Oxide minerals, for example, coltan (columbite-tantalite), beryl, cassiterite (tin), chromite, columbite, corundum (gemstones sapphire, ruby), lime, tantalite, titanium, uranium (uraninite), vanadium;
Gemstones, for example, alexandrite (chrysoberyl), chiastolite, emerald, garnet, opal, quartz (amethyst, agate, flint), sodalite, tanzanite, topaz and tourmaline;
Industrial minerals, for example, asbestos, bentonite, clay, diatomite, feldspar, fluorspar, granites, graphite, gravel, gypsum, kaolin, kyanite, limestone (incl. travertine), marble, mica, peat, salt, sand, silica, soda ash, talc, vermiculite;
Rocks and Volcanic Ash, for example, amphibolite, quartzite, trachyte and pozollana;
Other minerals include: amblygonite, wolframite, cobaltite, tungstenite, coal and dolomite.

Mining activities in the region started some 80–100 years ago and since then the world's largest diamondiferous kimberlite pipe was discovered in Tanzania. Mineral resources are abundant in the whole of the EAC but remain largely underexploited.

There are thousands of small artisanal formal and informal mining in almost all the countries in East African Countries. Although this subsector provides a lot of employment opportunities, the socio-economic impact remains insignificant due to many factors, including inadequate product, low-quality mostly non-processed product, lack of the necessary skills, lack of exploration and geological information, and overall poor organisation of the miners. Only a handful of local people from the region or other African countries are engaged in serious mining business and mostly in partnership with relatively stronger companies from the developed world. The exploration of hydrocarbons started some 60 years ago in the EAC and since then a number of discoveries have been made. The resources are believed to be large and existing data suggests resource potential especially in areas where successful drilling was conducted, for example, the Tanzanian and Mozambican geological belts, which also extend to Kenya, the Turkana basin in Kenya and the Lake Albert rift basin in Uganda. Rwanda and Burundi are also likely to bear significant resources, for example, in the Lake Tanganyika, Rusizi plain and northwestern Rwanda, all being part of the Albertine rift.

Gas discoveries were first made in 1974 in Tanzania and all discoveries lie along the shoreline. Since 2010 there have been numerous exploration successes and the latest discovery in 2013 suggest a volume of almost 30 TCF. In Uganda, the discovered gas resources are estimated to be 350 billion cubic feet. The recent gas strikes off East Africa's shore have led to predictions that the region could become the third-largest exporter of natural gas in the long-run.

Lake Kivu, which forms the greater part of the border between Rwanda and the Democratic Republic of Congo (DRC), is one of three lakes worldwide containing high levels of gas, and its resource was first discovered in 1937. Besides CO_2 the lake also contains the highest level of methane ever discovered in a water body. The lake is about 1–5 million years old and the methane gas is believed to form from a combination of geological and biological processes. It is thought that methane concentrations have increased by 15 per cent in the past 30 years, which makes methane in Lake Kivu a renewable energy resource. The exploitable portion of methane is estimated at 39 billion cubic meters, which could produce about 700 MW of electricity over 50 years.

In Kenya, Petroleum Exploration began in the 1950s and in 1975 oil and gas were found in the Lamu Basin followed by the discovery of suspected hydrocarbons and microfossils in the Anza Basin in 1976. Recently, in 2012, a first commercial discovery of light oil, currently estimated at 1 billion barrels, was made in the Turkana. In Uganda, another oil discovery is adding to the recent successes in the EAC. The resources in the Lake Albert region, which were discovered in 2010, are estimated at about 3.5 billion barrels, of which 1.2–1.7 billion are commercially recoverable.

Stake and investments in the sectors

As indicated earlier, the EAC has abundant levels of resources. However, exploration and exploitation of these resources to the benefit of the countries and the people is another thing.

In the Mining sector, Tanzania is the strongest player, with 16 companies active, holding a total of 20 licenses. Of these 16 companies, with an exception of few private South African and relatively smaller Tanzania companies engaged in precious gemstones (tanzanite, rubies, sapphire, etc), only the Tanzanian National Development Corporation and the Tanzanian State Mining Corporation (STAMICO) are African. STAMICO is in a public private partnership with a Canadian company, and the National Development Corporation holds 3 licenses. Tanzania is one of the African countries (sixth ranking based on the number of sites and according to the US Geological Survey) where exploration has been focused and furthermore accounted for 9 per cent of African gold production. Tanzania could moreover soon become the third largest producer of coal following recent discoveries in the southern part of the country. An Australian company – Select Exploration – discovered an outcropping coal seam at its newly acquired Ruhuhu Project in southern Tanzania.

Kenya is also doing relatively well, with the mining sector gaining importance in recent years. There are 17 companies holding concessions for mining activities and of these, about a dozen are from Kenya, while one is South African. In the other countries mining remains mainly artisanal and there are few to no industrial mining activities. In Uganda, 363 licenses were active in 2010, and today some 500 small and artisanal mining companies are active in the sector. In Rwanda, a total of about 500 permits are active in the sector. The key players in the industry seem to be small artisanal miners (more than 470) and few external private investors. The 17 external investors include four South African companies, a Thai, an Austrian and an Egyptian company. One of the South African companies and those mentioned here are all in partnership with Rwandan companies. Rwanda is a globally significant producer of various minerals, accounting for about 14 per cent of world tantalum production. Tin was also produced, accounting for 40 per cent of output. There are some foreign companies registered in Rwanda that do purchase minerals from small miners in Rwanda, and from across the border in DRC and Tanzania. These are artisanal miners that find it convenient to just sell directly to foreign companies that export the products abroad. Obviously these companies make good margins, as most of these artisanal miners are not well informed on the actual international prices. Burundi's mining sector is dominated by artisanal mining since there are momentarily no industrial operations. Artisanal miners are grouped into cooperatives and it is estimated that around 300,000 people are employed in the sector. A local Burundian private company is exploiting tin, tantalum and tungsten, while a public Burundian company is exploiting peat. The rest of exploitation is entirely artisanal. Nine international firms are involved in exploration work. Of these, two are from South Africa. There is also one Burundian company involved in exploration works.

The Tanzanian Petroleum Development Corporation, the national state company, constructed 8 wells during the 1970s and 1980s but currently the 17 oil and gas exploring and exploiting companies active in Tanzania are all from outside Africa. The two producing fields are small and provide gas to generate a significant proportion of Tanzania's electricity. Gas is also used by a number of industrial and commercial customers in the Dar es Salaam area. In 2011, Tanzania produced about 30 BCF of natural gas, and today 43 TCF of natural gas has been confirmed according to 'Think Africa Press'. Recent exploration success since 2010 has raised Tanzania's profile as a potential supplier of LNG. Exploration in Kenya started in the 1950s and today 14 companies are operating in Kenya on 29 blocks. Most of the companies are Western in origin, but the Kenyan National Oil company and one Tanzanian company each operate in one block, while a Nigerian company operates in two blocks. This means that out of twenty-nine blocks only four are operated by African companies, while only one is operated by a local Kenyan company. In Uganda, three Western companies are licensed in the oil and gas sector. Since there have been no discoveries in Rwanda and Burundi, there are only companies active in exploration. A Canadian company is carrying out exploration activities on and offshore of Lake Kivu, Rwanda. In Burundi, where first research work on the potential for hydrocarbons began in 1959, four companies have been involved in exploration efforts. An Indian company has carried out exploratory drillings and currently, two of the four concession-blocks are attributed to a British company, while the other two are attributed to a South African and a Nigerian Company.

Regarding the methane gas in Lake Kivu, a number of test plants have been installed over time by different companies: One test plant built in 1963 by a Belgian company, which supplied the local brewery, was recently shut down. A pilot plant of Rwanda Energy Company, designed by a French company, was tested in 2010 and reached 2.4 MW of the envisioned 3.6 MW. Another pilot plant, Kibuye Power Ltd (KP1) of the government of Rwanda, has generated 1.5 MW since 2008, which is far below its envisioned capacity. A US-based company, ContorGlobal, got a 100 MW concession and is currently finalising the first 25 MW through a local registered company the 'KivuWatt'. The project consists of four phases of 25 MW each.

Overall, the hydrocarbon sector of the EAC is mainly attracting foreign non-African investors and only a handful of companies from the EAC, Nigeria or South Africa hold a small share of investments. The mining sector of the EAC has a relatively larger ratio of African involvement. However, it remains evident that the more industrialised the country is, the more foreign players take up an important share. There are however many especially South African and Kenyan firms who are levelling the playing field. The investment levels and number of investors in the different member states seem to vary significantly, which can be partly explained through the different resource availabilities and discovery times, but also through the investment environment and governments' preparedness and readiness to attract investments, which will be presented in the following paragraph.

Framework for investments

The institutional and legal framework

The different member countries have very different institutional structures. The number of ministries, for example, varies between 11 (Rwanda) and 35 (Kenya). In Tanzania, Uganda and Burundi, both mining and hydrocarbons fall under one ministry: The Ministry of Energy and Minerals, The Ministry of Energy and Mineral Development and Ministry of Energy and Mines respectively. In Kenya, these resources are handled by two different ministries, The Ministry of Energy, responsible for petroleum and gas, and the Ministry of Mining. In Rwanda, the Ministry of Natural Resources is responsible for both, the mining and hydrocarbon sector, but as of now all matters relating to the methane gas in Lake Kivu are within the area of authority of the Ministry of Infrastructure. These administrative structures do have influence on decision-making bureaucracy especially when it comes to licensing, policy enforcement and so on. These complicated structures take time to understand and developing a strategic approach on enhancing and encouraging local participation in this industry remains limited as a consequence.

In Tanzania and Kenya, different regulatory bodies for the mining and hydrocarbons sectors exist and both governments have National Oil Companies, which are charged with participation and engagement in the exploration, development, production and distribution of oil, gas and related services, to facilitate a fair trading environment, to safeguard the national supply of petroleum products and to develop quality and safety standards. Uganda started an institutional reform in July 2014 under which a new regulatory body for the petroleum sector and a National Oil Company will be established. In Rwanda, the Natural Resource Authority, within the ministry, is entrusted with the supervision, monitoring and implementation of issues relating to the promotion and protection of natural resources, but the methane from Lake Kivu is a special case. The government of Rwanda has set up a unit for the promotion and exploitation of Lake Kivu Gas, a body under the Energy, Water and Sanitation Authority (EWSA), the utility that falls under the Ministry of Infrastructure, in order to attract investments in this sub-sector, but a bilateral (Rwanda-DRC) regulatory authority has yet to be established. The two governments are working towards harmonising a new version of the Management Prescriptions, a technical document regulating the extraction, as well as establishing a bilateral authority to manage the lake, which was agreed upon in a Memorandum of Understanding in

2007. In Burundi, no regulatory authority exists, but its establishment is a requirement under the new law.

In most countries, policies and legislation are relatively up-to-date and governments are reacting to recent changes/discoveries in the sector calling for stronger legislation and policy (Table 12.1). The Kenyan Mining Act from 1986 was reviewed in 2013 and the Petroleum Exploration and Production Act from 1986 is currently under review. One of the previous law's inadequacies was that the minister played a central figure in the oil activities (e.g., responsibility of setting regulations) but the act did not specify which minister, making three ministries in Kenya eligible: the Ministry of Energy and Petroleum, the Ministry of Environment, Water and Natural Resources and the Ministry of Mining. Under the review, the government says it is seeking stronger legislation on sharing of benefits from the resource and might include the requirement to partner with a local company. Kenya's last Energy Policy was adopted in 2013. Uganda also updated its petroleum legislation in 2010, the same year of the resource discovery and the Petroleum Policy was adopted in 2008. In Burundi, the Mining and Petroleum Code of 1976 was to be updated and a new Mining Code was adopted in 2013. This law was drafted with the intention to introduce international mining best practices, to provide for greater environmental protection, to provide for lesser discretionary powers to the licensing authorities and hence provide for greater security for investors. A Mining Policy as well as a new Petroleum Code are also under review. Tanzania's

Table 12.1   Adoption of laws and policies

	Tanzania	Kenya	Uganda	Rwanda	Burundi
Hydrocarbon legislation	1980	1986/review	1993/2010	*	1976*/review
Mining legislation	1998/2010	1986/2013	2003	1967/2008*	1976*/2013
Hydrocarbon policy		2013	2008		
Mineral policy	2009		2000	2009	In progress

Note: *includes both 2010–2014, 2005–2009, ≥ 2004.

Sources: Adapted by the author from: the Petroleum Exploitation and Production Act, Government of Tanzania, 1980; The Mineral Policy of Tanzania, Government of Tanzania, 2009; The Mining Act, Government of Tanzania, 2010; Petroleum (Exploration and Production) Act, Government of Kenya, 1984, Revised Edition 2012; National Energy Policy, Government of Kenya, 2013; The Mining Bill, Government of Kenya, 2013; Mineral Policy of Uganda, Government of Uganda, 2000; The Mining Act, Government of Uganda, 2003; National Oil and Gas Policy for Uganda, Government of Uganda, 2008; Law on Mining and Quarry Exploitation, Government of Rwanda, 2009; Mining Policy, Government of Rwanda, 2009; Code Minier du Burundi, Government of Burundi, 2013.

Mineral Policy was adopted in 2009 and after Tanzania's shift in economic policy in the 1990s, the privatisation of the mining industry was supplemented by an industry friendly mining code, in 1998 and a new mining act that was passed in 2010. In-line with Tanzania's pioneering role in the mineral sector, its policies and legislations are well developed in this sector. However, the Petroleum Exploitation and Production Act of 1980 has not been reviewed, most likely making it inadequate in light of recent and possible future discoveries. Uganda, which has, as described earlier, made efforts to improve legislation and policy in the petroleum sector passed a Mining Act in 2003 and is relying on an outdated Mineral Policy from 2000, indicating mining not to be a priority sector. The Rwandan Mining Code of 1967 was succeeded by the Law on Mining and Quarry Exploitation in 2008. Under this law, the term 'mines' is defined as including oil and gas and therefore the law also caters to activities related to these resources. A well-designed Mining Policy was adopted in 2009 which includes specific actions and measurable targets.

While some countries are taking a lead in strong policy development, others' institutional and legal weaknesses are strikingly obvious. However, recent reforms across all EAC member states are improving this situation, making a favourable investment environment a possibility.

Licensing procedure and fees

Usually the law defines which steps an investor has to follow to get the permission to be active in the sector, that is, to get licensed. The time, effort and money, which has to be invested and the transparency, fairness and conformity pertaining to licensing will have significant influence on the attractiveness of a sector.

In the hydrocarbon sector, there are different requirements for obtaining a license in the three petroleum and gas bearing countries. In Tanzania, bidding is open for both public and private companies and the bidding process usually takes six months. Bidding instructions and payments are usually well established by the Tanzania Petroleum Development Corporation. Recently, the model production sharing agreement was updated, and it does now include a payment of 7.5 mio. USD (2.5 mio. USD on signing the agreement and 5 mio. USD when production starts), and royalty rates of 12.5 per cent for onshore and 7.5 per cent for offshore production. In Kenya, the Ministry of Energy administers the application process towards the signing of a Production Sharing Contract and theoretically this can be by way of competitive bidding process or through bilateral negotiations. As of now there have been no bidding rounds. In Uganda, licenses can be awarded via direct applications to the minister. The Bill does however not clearly state whether the minister should always seek advice from the commissioners and the Petroleum Authority in case of issuing licenses and there is no provision for competitive bidding in the petroleum law.

Licenses in the mineral sector are issued by the minister, the commissioner for minerals or a zone mines officer in Tanzania, by the Prospecting and Mining Licensing Committee in Kenya, by the Commissioner of the Geology Department in Uganda and through ministerial order in Rwanda and Burundi. In Uganda, Rwanda and Burundi, a written justification has to be provided, in case a license is refused. In Rwanda, this decision has to be made within 30 days, and in Burundi, the application is automatically considered accepted after a period of two months. The licensing systems are different between countries, with Tanzania offering three different types of licenses and Kenya six, and can be, especially in the case of Kenya, very confusing. The costs and royalties to be paid to the government are also different. While the costs for an exploitation or mining license in Rwanda is US$370 (plus an environmental caution fee), the fee for a comparable license is US$600 in Tanzania, US$1,020 in Uganda and between US$1,200 and several tens of thousands of US$ in Kenya. In Tanzania, all fees are higher for foreign investors. In most countries, the fees for licenses are defined by law, but not so in Uganda and Burundi.

Royalties to be paid to the government are defined by law in Tanzania, Uganda, Rwanda and Burundi. The Kenyan law determines an ad valorem royalty to be paid, with rates being determined by the Cabinet Secretary through regulations published in the Gazette. In Tanzania, the royalties are 5 per cent on gross value for uranium, diamond, gemstone, 4 per cent for metallic minerals, 3 per cent for other minerals and 1 per cent for gems. In Uganda, they are 3 per cent of gross value for precious metals, 5 per cent on precious stones, 3 per cent on base metals and ores and royalties for other mining products lie between US$0.2 and US$1.2 per ton. In Rwanda, royalties are 4 per cent of the norm value for base metals and other mineral substances of that kind, 6 per cent of the norm value for precious metals of gold category and other precious metals of that kind and 6 per cent of the gross value for precious metals of diamond category and other precious stones of that kind. In Burundi, the royalties to be paid to the government were reduced under the new law to 4 per cent for basic metals, 5 per cent for precious metals, 7 per cent for precious stones and 2 per cent for other mineral substances. It is to be noted however that the issuance of an exploitation license automatically entitles the government to a 10 per cent share of the company. In Kenya, the government has recently increased royalties and under the new royalties regime, rare-earth minerals, which are classified as precious minerals and used to attract a royalty of 3 per cent, are now subject to a royalty of 10 per cent of gross sales. Coal and gold royalties have doubled to 8 per cent and 5 per cent, respectively. These newly adjusted royalties do not only exceed other royalties in the EAC by far, but are also above the African average.

The procedures for acquiring a mining license generally include the registration of a company, securing of the surface land rights, presentation of a business plan, financial statements, feasibility study, technical statement/ report, Environmental Impact Assessment and Environmental action plan. In

Uganda, additionally, a proposal on employment and training of Ugandans and a report on goods and services required is to be submitted.

While it takes about 50 days to be granted a license in Rwanda, including time required for registering a company and getting an Environmental Impact Assessment and so on, it is estimated that it takes on average six months in Tanzania. It can, as mentioned earlier, by law only take a maximum of two months in Burundi and it is estimated that it can take more than a year in Kenya.

Overall, as seen earlier, not all laws provide for transparent and similar applied procedures, since sometimes royalties to be paid to the government have to be negotiated in individual agreements, giving room to favouritism or unfair gain to government or the investor. The royalties to be paid, which were observable, do also differ between countries: 7 per cent on precious stones plus the 10 per cent share in the company in Burundi and 5 per cent on precious stones in Uganda. The time effectiveness does also vary a lot between countries: While it takes about 50 days to be granted an exploitation license in Rwanda, it can easily take more than one year in Kenya.

Challenges facing investments and recommendations

Upfront investment financing

Sectors requiring high capital investments are affected by the availability of capital and the ability of the capital market to provide adequate loans. This is a general challenge especially in the petroleum and gas sector but also for industrial mining. African companies and investors are more often constrained in their own in-house financial capacities, especially when comparing them with global players in the oil industry, which puts them at an obvious disadvantage. They are furthermore often restricted to the local capital markets, which are mostly underdeveloped and offer unfavourable loans, further worsening the situation. This is especially the case in the mining sector and affecting small and medium-sized mining businesses. In Uganda, for example, it remains very difficult for the national players, to raise the required US$82,000 for an investment license.

There is need for the respective governments to make deliberate efforts to make it easy for prospective investors to access financing through special arrangements with local and foreign banks. Additionally, the governments should come up with special incentives that are meant to encourage and attract local investments.

Human capital

Another major challenge in both sectors is the lack of know-how, technical knowledge and experience. Most hydrocarbon sectors in the EAC are very young, since economically viable sources have only recently been discovered, and there is not only a knowledge gap in the government which complicates policy design, institutional effectiveness, ability to negotiate favourable agreements and so on, but there is hardly any man-power equipped with the required skills to be employed in the sector. This is one of the major challenges for African businesses to newly enter this sector. Training in most countries, especially in oil and gas, is not provided and therefore the countries depend on external training, which is only accessible for few people as these courses are expensive. The inadequacy of human resources affects foreign investors and African investors alike, since expatriate personnel demand significantly higher wages and thus make the overall investment very expensive. Out of 33 companies active in the EAC only four are from Africa and only the Kenyan National Oil Company and a Tanzanian company are from within the EAC. The other two companies are Nigerian and South African. So far no big players emerged from the EAC, but the national oil and gas companies have a potential of becoming important players in their home countries. So far the lack of capacity and technical equipment has resulted in a dominance of other investors, and Africans for a great part remain unequipped to compete. The issue of lacking capacity is not only relevant in the hydrocarbons sector but also mining is affected by lack of sufficient mining engineers, geologists and metallurgists.

In trying to mitigate this situation, countries are putting up different measures. Rwanda's Mining Policy includes as a main objective the improvement of the mining sector knowledge, skills, and practices amongst others through the building of human capacity and expertise. The government of Uganda has planned to carry out specialised and general training of manpower and strengthening capacity of the institutions responsible for managing and safeguarding the energy and mineral resources. Besides a policy on mandatory employment of locals in the petroleum sector – an agreement is made between the government and the company, in which the positions to be filled with Ugandan nationals are defined, usually growing with time – this employment is furthermore coupled with a mandatory training of local workers, ensuring know-how transfer.

Infrastructure

A countries' infrastructure is also of great importance for investment decisions. Highly underdeveloped infrastructure like unpaved roads leading to the deposits makes the operations and export of the resource more costly, and the investment therefore unattractive. Big foreign investors often develop infrastructure necessary to facilitate easy accessibility but for domestic investors this becomes a challenge as it constitutes a significant part of the upfront investments.

Besides transportation, the energy sector plays a major role. Energy costs, which can be very high in the region, drive up the operational costs. Its availability is furthermore a must for any sort of industrialised exploitation, but not always a given in the EAC. Burundi, for example, has got a generation capacity of roughly 45 MW, which is not sufficient to support complex industrial mining activities. African and foreign investors are affected by this alike.

There are some infrastructure projects in the pipeline, which hopefully are going to significantly improve the current situation. Some of these initiatives include planned construction of several refineries together with the construction of an oil pipeline from Lamu to Juba, a pipeline from Lamu to Addis Ababa, a pipeline from Mtwara to Dar es Salaam, an extension of the Mombasa-Kampala pipeline to Kigali and a spur pipeline to join the Lamu-Juba pipeline to the existing Mombasa-Kampala pipeline. Another project is the East African Railway project, of which the commencement of works on the link Mombasa-Nairobi was launched in 2014. Much as there are several competing priorities, there has to be infrastructure investments focusing on providing the necessary supplies to the extractive industries.

Bureaucracy and issues of governance

Bureaucracy is an issue every organisation, public or private has to battle with. However high levels of bureaucracy that delay processes significantly are causing real challenges to investors. Obviously, mid- and long-term large investments may go over this hurdle while, for short and lower investment levels mainly coming from in-country and other African potential investors, this becomes unbearable as most of these are mainly looking for quick wins. The more offices and institutions involved in the process, the more complex a process becomes, which is why the institutional set-up is crucial in addressing this challenge. Corruption is yet another challenge that investors see themselves confronted with. While some countries in the EAC are known for extraordinary low levels of corruption, others acknowledge it as being a serious issue. High levels of corruption introduce an element of favouritism and obviously also increase the financial burden on the investor. Corruption is by definition hard to observe and therefore also hard to anticipate for investors. The positive effects of the non-discretionary and transparent attributes of the legal framework discussed earlier are jeopardised by corruption. In some countries, bribing is a known requirement to enter the sector, especially in mining. The remedy to this problem is a process requiring strengthening the good governance institutions. This is slowly happening. For example, to assist the investors in meeting all the requirements and to successfully go through the procedures, the governments of Rwanda and Tanzania have set up a One Stop Centre or One Stop Agency. All companies wishing to exploit hydrocarbons need to acquire approval from the Tanzania Investment Centre which is established under the Tanzania Investment Act of 1997, to promote, co-ordinate and facilitate investment in Tanzania. In Rwanda, investors also receive extensive assistance from the Rwanda Development Board. For investment levels exceeding US$100,000 for members of the EAC and COMESA, and US$250,000 for the ıⅽₒₜ of the countries, investors are eligible to apply for investment incentives.

Security

Most of the EAC's member states have seen a political crisis involving human tragedies in the past 30 years. Apart from the factual damages to human, physical and financial capital, this has to a certain extent also damaged the image and perception of the countries and the region in general. The east African region is seen as being very volatile and to a certain extent categorised as 'fragile'. Insecurity is a major factor hindering investments especially in sectors with long-term capital-intensive investments as is the case in the discussed sectors. Insecurity can exist in the form of general high crime rates, putting the physical well-being of employees at risk, but also in the form of political instability, which can erupt into full-blown internal conflicts. There were incidents where oil firms had to suspend ongoing operations over rising safety concerns. Apart from general crime, and internal instability, external conflicts are a major concern, since conflict crosses over national boundaries very swiftly, which is also the case in the Great Lakes region.

While each country is responsible for insuring peace and stability within its national borders, in which some have succeeded, regional efforts to stabilise the region as a whole have to be made. The integration of the EAC is one of the efforts that can be an effective mechanism of conflict prevention.

Information availability

Another challenge existing is the availability of information. This is an across–the-board problem for all potential investors. While some countries have gone far in terms of conducting the necessary studies on their resource availability, others are lagging behind. An investor will be more attracted to put his money in the exploitation of a resource when this resource has already been discovered and if its worth has been estimated as well. As has been mentioned previously, there are great differences between EAC partner states, bearing in mind that information accessibility does not only refer to the data which has been collected, or research which has been conducted; it also refers to the means through which they can be accessed by investors. The issue of access to information is also applicable when it comes to information on the legal and regulatory requirements and processes. In Burundi today, most data can only be provided in the form of hard copies. In this case, local or African investors might actually in some cases be slightly favoured since they are familiar with the processes in their home countries, speak the language and are physically present – being the reason most of the foreign companies do opt for partnerships with local companies that bring on board the local knowledge and ease in facilitation of especially administrative processes.

Some efforts are being undertaken by some countries to improve the accessibility of information. For example, the Kenyan government is planning to establish a National Data Centre and laboratory to enhance primary data acquisition, analysis and interpretation. In Uganda, information on mining opportunities are especially accessible through an open 'Modern Documentation Center' and an interactive cadastral map accessible via the Internet, which provides all information on licenses already awarded or still open. In Burundi, donors and the government are also going to create an electronic database, while Rwanda is currently working on establishing a project investment database, which will make identifying projects for potential investors much easier.

Apart from the lack of financial and technical capacity of African Investors and a slight advantage due to cultural proximity, it is safe to presume that the general challenges to investments in the EAC in the petroleum, gas and mining sector affect the local African and foreign investors almost equally.

In general, conducting of studies that shall facilitate availability of data and information is crucial and efforts should be undertaken to invest in this extractive industry.

Government initiatives to encourage African involvement

Specific government initiatives to encourage the direct involvement of Africans in the sector include the Tanzanian policy to take necessary measures to enable Tanzanians to participate in medium- and large-scale mining and to collaborate with stakeholders to eliminate obstacles hindering Tanzanians from buying shares in mining companies which are registered abroad. One of the steps undertaken by the government of Tanzania is an obligation of foreign investments in mining to have a minimum of 25 per cent local shareholding. This, with time shall create the culture and experience of local participation in the industry. The Tanzanian government does further also intend to take steps to allow Tanzanians to enlist their mineral rights on foreign stock exchanges to access capital and to facilitate small-scale miners to access markets for minerals, geological information, technical and financial services. One very aggressive policy favouring Tanzanian involvement is the discriminating price policy of the licenses which are cheaper for local companies than foreign companies.

In Rwanda, one of the Geology and Mining Department's mandates is the linking of local and international investors in the mining sector. This strategy is supposed to bypass the lacking technical and financial capacities of local investors by enabling them to profit from the international companies/investors' resources whilst also being involved in the sector, thus promoting greater future involvement of local investors. So far, there have been only 4 of such joint ventures in Rwanda, but the target set for 2015 under the Export Priority Action Plan is to have a total of 20 major joint ventures.

Kenya, with the intention of increasing local involvement, is currently contemplating to oblige all foreign mining companies to allocate 35 per cent of their shares to local investors and institutions. The proposal has however triggered opposition from executives in mining firms doing business in the country. This approach, much as it may result in more local participation in the industry, may not be sustainable, although every effort should be made by governments to create incentives that will attract local participation.

In Uganda, Africans or local investors are not favoured or deliberately encouraged. The government is however looking to encourage involvement in the downstream sector and to thereby create more positive effects and increase local involvement in this way. The employment policy for the petroleum sector states, for example, that the licensee, its contractors and subcontractors shall give preference to goods which are produced or available in Uganda and services which are rendered by Ugandan citizens and companies. Furthermore, oil and gas companies are mandated to employ at least a certain percentage of their staff as locals, which is normally agreed upon between the government and the company, and usually includes a percentage increase over time. Such an employment and training policy is also implemented in the mining sector. The same is being done in Tanzania, where the government requires mining companies to procure local goods and services and wants to promote Tanzanians to supply quality goods and services to the mining industry.

Some countries require companies active in their mining sector to be registered in the country. In Rwanda and Burundi, companies wishing to get involved in research and exploitation have to be headquartered in the respective countries. In Burundi, a specific agreement between the government and a mining company also includes a clause on the number of national employees. These agreements are however individually negotiated. Another incentive provided by the Burundian government to employ locals is a better tax deduction rate when more Burundians are employed, as has been mentioned in the preceding paragraphs.

Conclusion

Most governments are embarking on new strategies to either directly favour local investment or to increase the general involvement and benefitting from the sectors.

To encourage more African involvement however, policies and strategies need to be reoriented to address the challenges in the sectors focusing on enabling more citizens to contribute to the growth of their countries' economies. Since lack of technical capacity and lack of financial capacity have been the factors identified as constraining Africans most, this is where the intervention should first begin. To create technical knowledge and know-how, countries with relevant natural resources should reallocate their budget to create a well-educated work-force for these sectors. As regards financing, investors should be brought together and encouraged to pool finances thereby accessing more markets and realising better rates of return. This would for example work well in the mining sectors. Business forums and investment clubs should be created and encouraged.

Since the creation of a skilled labour force is a medium to long-term task, while the necessary capacity is being built, complex sectors like the petroleum and gas should be driven through the creation of joint ventures and public private partnerships, coupled with explicit employment roadmaps and training commitments.

Works Consulted

Internal government documents

Code Minier du Burundi, Government of Burundi, 2013.
Law on Mining and Quarry Exploitation, Government of Rwanda, 2009.
The Mineral Policy of Tanzania, Government of Tanzania, 2009.
The Mineral Policy of Uganda, Government of Uganda, 2000.
The Mining Act, Government of Tanzania, 2010.
The Mining Act, Government of Uganda, 2003.
The Mining Bill, Government of Kenya, 2013.
Mining Policy, Government of Rwanda, 2009.
National Energy Policy, Government of Kenya, 2013.
National Oil and Gas Policy for Uganda, Government of Uganda, 2008.
Oil and Gas Laws in Uganda; A Legislator's Guide, International Alert, May 2011.
The Petroleum (Exploration, Development, Production and Value Addition) Bill, Government of Uganda, 2010.
Petroleum (Exploration and Production) Act, Government of Kenya, 1984, Revised Edition 2012.
The Petroleum Exploitation and Production Act, Government of Tanzania, 1980.
US EIA data.
USGS Science for a changing world, '2011 Minerals Yearbook: Africa', http://minerals. usgs.gov/minerals/pubs/country/2011/myb3-sum-2011-africa.pdf.

13
Private Security
Stuart Doran

The global private security industry is by no means new, but its growth since the 1990s has been phenomenal, stimulated by economic liberalisation and the downsizing of government security services in the aftermath of the Cold War. By 2012, the sector was worth an estimated US$190 billion in global annual revenues, a figure expected to climb to US$240 billion by the end of 2017.[1] While much attention has focused on the Middle East and the rise of controversial mega-companies such as Blackwater, considerable growth has occurred in emerging markets. Africa is clearly no exception. British company G4S, for example, employs over 110,000 people across 29 African countries, making it the largest private sector employer on the continent.[2] But with its history of mercenarism and its continuing post-colonial preoccupation with liberation ideology, policy debate and academic study in Africa has centred on the ethics of private security and the need to create appropriate regulatory structures.[3] Necessary though the ethical debate is, it has predominated at the expense of other matters of importance. Relatively little is known about the industry from an economic perspective – about its economic impact in statistical terms or about the entrepreneurs that are spreading across the continent, both from bases in Africa and abroad.

The analysis that follows is an attempt to explore Africa's private security sector at the coal face, drawing on interviews with 31 private security companies (PSCs).[4] The sector – broadly defined here as providing goods and services in all areas related to human security and the protection of assets – is enormously diverse, ranging from manufacturers of technological solutions, to guarding services and armed response, through to logistical support for peacekeeping operations, and to the provision of maritime security on oil rigs or ocean-going vessels. (Private military companies (PMCs) associated with offensive military operations, such Eeben Barlow's Executive Outcomes, formerly active in Angola and Sierra Leone, are outside the remit of the survey.[5]) The selection of PSCs for this study is intended to underline such diversity, highlighting significant variegation between sub-sectors but also the common opportunities and challenges facing companies that are otherwise very different.

The same considerations apply to scale and ownership. Both large and smaller companies have been selected because this reflects important realities: large-scale players in Africa are relatively few in number and play a dominating role in certain sub-sectors and geographies, yet, more broadly, they cannot be considered in isolation from smaller PSCs, which are multiplying exponentially and are, frequently, beginning to expand internationally within Africa. In many ways, this kind of 'rhizomic growth' – where a multitude of new, smaller and largely hidden roots and shoots develop when systemic conditions are right – is perhaps where much of the real story lies. Around the larger organisms, an ecosystem has developed, sometimes in symbiosis with the preponderant structures and at other times filling gaps left by them. Some of these operations appear to be transitioning from medium to large-scale businesses, while others, particularly those involved in the provision of services such as training and other niche activities, have become highly mobile, with capacity to work in many countries and on many different projects despite relatively small budgets. It is not possible to accurately capture the dimensions of economic growth in the private security sector – or to point to its causes – without illustrating something of this biodiversity.

For similar reasons, a hard-and-fast definition has not been applied to the idea of 'African' ownership. Some companies that might typically be considered 'foreign' have become effectively 'African' in certain respects due to the sheer size of their local staff profiles or the importance of Africa to the company's business – or because of the extent of local acquisitions and the nature of their local partnerships. Swiss-registered and New York-listed Tyco International, for example, is the world's largest dedicated fire protection and security company with a presence in nearly 50 countries and is, in orthodox terms, a foreign direct investor in Africa.[6] Yet in its South African iteration through the ADT brand, it employs over 10,000 people, the largest in-country staff complement not only within the multinational ADT corporation but also within Tyco as a whole. Moreover, as ADT South Africa's Marketing and Strategy Director, Martin Ochien'g, explains, Tyco's international expansion within Africa is predicated on the 'judicious formation of local partnerships in the continent with an array of strong third parties who help deliver Tyco's services to its customers'.[7] The point is not that Tyco is 'African' in the established sense – as are most of the businesses surveyed in this study – but rather that it is a major player that is not entirely 'non-African' either. Tyco and a few other comparable organisations have been included on this basis and because their views provide useful comparisons with those tabled by companies that would generally be regarded as African.

In short, among more specific findings, this study underscores yet again that true economic growth is complex, multi-layered and organic – and that governments, where they are involved at all, must encourage rather than hinder the conditions that lead to such development. This is little more than a call for political leaders to recognise what works; to acknowledge that economic biodiversity creates wealth at all levels of society over time and that centrist policies – in Africa, so often associated with identity politics or elite interests – not only fail to do so, but positively retard broad-based growth.

Drivers and benefits of intra-African trade for PSCs

Domestic private security companies in Africa began to emerge and grow strongly in the 2000s for the simple reason that a demand existed. In South Africa, the best-documented case, the industry registered double digit growth prior to 2008, and while this has dropped back to below 10 per cent, the numbers continue to be striking.[8] In 2012, the industry was worth around ZAR50 billion or around 1.6 per cent of GDP.[9] In November 2013, there were 8,282 registered security service providers and nearly 440,000 registered and active security officers,[10] representing around 2.9 per cent of the total number of persons employed.[11] In Nigeria, an estimated 1,500–2,000 service providers were employing in excess of 100,000 people by 2005 – and, according to one observer, '[s]ecurity is now the second largest money-spinner in Nigeria, second only to oil and gas'.[12] In both cases, a growing private sector and middle class, combined with high crime rates and public security inadequacies, have stimulated and sustained demand for private security services.[13]

Feedback from PSCs shows that strong demand has also been the primary factor pushing private security providers to expand from a domestic base into Africa. MiX Telematics, a South Africa-based provider and manager of GPS tracking systems, has a presence in most African countries and cites the continent's 'unsaturated market', growing economies and relative lack of competitors as the major incentives for expansion.[14] Likewise, C-track, also a GPS/telematics business, notes a 'huge demand for products, safety and security',[15] while an East African employee of Warrior Security, a provider of manned guarding and related services in six countries (Tanzania, Sudan, DRC, Zambia, Kenya and Togo), speaks of 'increased demand and need' across Africa.[16]

In a number of cases, respondents point to indirect increases in demand, whereby foreign investors in African countries – from elsewhere in Africa and abroad – require goods and services. Guy Addison, Director of Altech Netstar International, another vehicle tracking operation, comments that 'clients are expanding their business into Africa and, as a result, require support'[17] – and Rory Steyn, the owner of an executive protection business, notes that many of his clients are operating in multiple African countries and his company is therefore seeking to grow with them.[18] C-track's experience has been comparable, with the company initially following BHP Billiton into a number of African countries and continuing to benefit from 'expats working in Africa'.[19] Similarly, Ochien'g comments that Tyco has 'followed global companies into sub-Saharan Africa – that has given us a foot in. But once we are in we've found opportunities that are local. We had known about these opportunities before, but have gained the necessary critical mass to exploit them once we're in'.[20]

These observations demonstrate that growth in Africa's private security sector sits on a bedrock of strong consumer demand in many domestic constituencies, but also that the demand-side equation is complex and cannot in practice be disaggregated from intra-African and international FDI. African PSCs are developing homegrown consumer bases, benefiting locally from FDI, and riding on the coat tails of other African companies and foreigners into new African markets. Meanwhile, largely foreign companies are following other foreigners into Africa and later branching off to form local partnerships. Through all this, African companies are increasing profits – another observation that respondents typically paired with cross-border expansion (the latter equals 'financial gain', as one put it)[21] – apparently without losing comparative advantage. Christian Bock, a director of Osprea Logistics, a major Pretoria-based vehicle manufacturer and provider of logistics solutions to peacekeeping missions, remarks that the company retains the advantage of 'regional knowledge' and is 'not totally foreign' when working in other African countries.[22] Scott Wilson, Export Manager for Centurion Systems, a manufacturer of access automation equipment, comments that being based in Africa 'means they are working in similar business climates in [other parts of] Africa'. To knowledge and connectivity are added the cost competitiveness advantages accrued by close market access. The same company asserts that 'it is easier to export to one's own backyard than further afield',[23] an observation used to explain the decision to trade in Africa, but one that applies with equal force as a disadvantage for those who are moving product from overseas.

Obstacles and challenges

'Africa' as a monolith does not exist and use of the term as a catch-all reveals more than it obscures – oft-quoted aphorisms that plead caution for those attempting to extract generalisations from such very different places, the more so in an industry as diverse as private security. Certainly, responses on the question of challenges and obstacles varied more than they did regarding the drivers of intra-African investment and involvement. Yet it is not a fool's errand. Sub-Saharan Africa (SSA), for all its rich heterogeneity, exhibits many continuities – cultural and otherwise – that run alongside the geographical. Such threads may not be omnipresent, but they are common nonetheless. In this sense, PSCs delivered few surprises when it came to outlining the difficulties associated with expansion in Africa. Nearly all problems identified were recognisably those for which African countries often rank poorly in the World Bank's 'Ease of doing business' listings and other similar indices. A frequent complaint related to bureaucracy and the drag created by excessive red tape. XFOR Security Solutions is a guarding and close protection business established in Kenya by British ex-military personnel and one that has grown rapidly, now employing over 1,000 people and expanding freelance operations into Uganda and Tanzania. The company's Communications Director, Aaron Kitchener, says that it is usually necessary 'to go through a third party' to establish a business and that government 'could offer more freely available advice about how to set up a company from scratch'. It could also 'modernise/digitise the company registration set up'.[24] Further downstream, Regal Ultra Security, a distributor of electronic security products, notes that import/export regulations are unnecessarily complex and have occasioned 'a need [for Regal] to have a well-trained export department and this adds to…company expenses'.[25] Altech Netstar, which avers to 'huge… numerous challenges' in working beyond South Africa's borders, singles out 'poor legal and regulatory environments' as one of their main headaches, part of which is the 'gap between what is written in the statutes and what is actually applied'.[26] Others specify the inefficiency of government machinery and the problems caused by variability (it is 'surprising…how everything takes so much time; the pace to get something done is very slow'; 'different tax laws' and 'different legislative requirements in each country').[27]

Of course, legal and bureaucratic millstones are not just about complexity and inefficiency. Laws and regulations are made by politicians with – lest we forget – politics in mind – and in Sub-Saharan Africa it is (as noted) the politics of identity and exclusion that dominate all too often. An ongoing fracas between South Africa's private security industry and the ruling African National Congress is a case in point. Already the most regulated on the continent, the industry has been presented with a draft legislative amendment which seeks to compel foreign firms to have a South African shareholding of at least 51 per cent. Reminiscent of Zimbabwe's notorious 'indigenisation and empowerment' laws, the amendment is reported to have its roots in a review of industry regulation ordered by the Minister for Intelligence Services in 2004, which was prompted by concerns about the 'intelligence' activities of private security companies and foreign involvement therein. Tabling the bill in February 2014, Police Minister Nathi Mthethwa lumped together the spectre of mercenarism, a foreign intelligence threat and human rights abuses:

[T]he line between private security companies (PSCs) and private military companies (PMCs) is increasingly becoming blurred…Equally private security companies are increasingly used in the field of intelligence. According to international research…private security companies are today used for a wide variety of intelligence tasks and there are numerous examples of such. International concern has also been growing about some of the large security companies who do not have a good record when it comes to human rights violations. As a developmental state, it will be irresponsible of us not to take seriously the above concerns and to ensure that our domestic legislation protects both our national and security interests.[28]

Industry has argued that the change will cause 'irreparable devastation of investor value', disinvestment and confusion across many parts of the economy given that 'private security' incorporates such a broad range of activities. Mthethwa has dismissed these concerns, telling parliament there was 'no evidence' that 'people will simply disinvest' with a change of ownership: 'Indications are that when the time comes, they will sell the relevant shares to comply with the law. Not closing down as we are led to believe... Private security companies, like any business, are driven by profit and nothing else'. Neither would there be job losses because 'provision of security service depends on supply and demand like any commodity in the market place. Change of ownership will not change demand'. It is this combination of economic illiteracy, paranoia and short-termism in South Africa's geographical north and the continent's past that has wrought so much ruin and desolation. Perhaps the most apposite commentary on the debate has come from opposition spokesman, Dianne Kohler Barnard, who derided the alleged threat to national security: 'There is no research, no proof; it's just a thumb-suck because xenophobia sounds good in the run-up to a general election'.[29] That such criticisms are unashamedly and persistently dismissed by the ANC as the rantings of 'whites' would tend to underline her point, along with the assertion that the politics of identity continue to overshadow rational economic debate. The salient lesson is not that white governments and colonial authorities were different – they were precisely the same at many points – but rather that Africa fails still to break free of this sterile and impoverishing cycle.

Corruption is another depressingly familiar gripe bracketed with government and bureaucracy by PSCs, and one which impinges on both African and foreign investors, small and large alike. Rory Steyn spoke not only of a generic problem, but of 'government intimidation', a phrase that brings to mind geographies where corruption has developed beyond customary 'fees' and 'taxes' and has become actively predatory.[30] Notably, the owner of a Kenya-based business similar to Steyn's also highlighted 'corruption' as prominent among 'many challenges'.[31] For some companies headquartered overseas, corruption is in some ways an even greater obstacle. Jim LeBlanc, co-Vice Chairman of Unity Resources Group, a multi-million dollar operation that offers a suite of security services including (inter alia), executive protection, crisis management, logistics, aerial surveillance and risk management, describes corruption as 'a huge issue', explaining that the United

States' Foreign Corrupt Practices Act (FCPA) and its UK equivalent are a 'big concern' for foreign companies such as his.[32] An identical point is made by Richard Leach, the CEO of a British-owned, Kenya-based risk advisory and manned guarding company that also operates in Ethiopia and Somalia.[33] The FCPA makes it illegal for US citizens and US-listed companies to bribe foreign officials and imposes heavy financial penalties and/or imprisonment on those convicted of contravening the statute.[34] The provisions of the UK Bribery Act are comparable.[35] Tom Callahan, Vice President of Government Affairs at PAE, a giant American logistics and facilities maintenance provider, remarks that his company has to be 'very sensitive' to the FCPA and steers clear of scenarios attended by any form of legal and reputational risk.[36] With an annual turnover of well over $1 billion and most of its work serving the US government, PAE is big enough – and has big enough friends – to remain clear of the corruption scrimmage, but it is perhaps unique in that regard. For others in the industry further down the food chain, there are tangible costs. LeBlanc comments that the hyper-vigilance required by anti-corruption legislation means that business is sometimes lost.[37] Thus, corruption is imposing costs on PSCs at different levels: opportunity costs on companies trading securities overseas (and it should be noted that these can include organisations that are otherwise African), direct costs to those prepared to make payments and costs passed down to the consumer.

Corruption, though, is not the most significant challenge cited by PSCs per se. Other 'software' problems are raised as equal obstacles to growth. These generally fall into two categories. Human resource deficits are one. Altech Netstar's experience is that the 'skillset is fine in SA, but [the equivalent] is not readily available in Africa'. Recruitment is therefore 'expensive'.[38] Independently, Tyco's Martin Ochien'g makes a similar observation. He says that skillsets in SSA 'often have to be complemented by an influx of experience from markets where these exist, especially when the work being delivered is of a complex nature'.[39] Also on the same page is Ephraim Kanga, the Chief Financial Officer (International Operations) of the Fidelity Security Group, the largest PSC in South Africa and one which has begun to expand into SSA (Swaziland and Zambia, with prospective operations in Namibia and Mozambique). He says a 'skills shortage', both for 'management and regular staff', is a major challenge and explains: 'Our industry relies heavily on human resources ... an unskilled/inadequate workforce negatively impacts our success in implementing business strategy'.[40]

A second category of 'software' vexation relates largely to cultural and language barriers. SBV Services, which dominates market share in South Africa for the cash-in-transit sub-sector (95 per cent of bank branches and 60 per cent of ATMs), finds that 'English is not common in business' in the other African countries where it works.[41] Companies are obliged to cobble together improvisations such as 'French translations online' or using employees with language skills – or seeking English speakers among their clients.[42] The need to negotiate widely divergent customs, including those of a religious nature, is another difficulty for PSCs.[43] Ironically, the raison d'etre of private security – insecurity and theft – was highlighted by some companies as having a negative effect on operations in some places. Warrior Security's Tanzanian interviewee flagged the 'theft of installed products' – presumably by insiders – as a problem and also reflected wryly on what he saw as another cultural challenge: 'Africans like to be safe, but don't like to pay', he said, explaining that 'so many people want service, but don't necessarily pay on time'.[44] Richard Schagen, the owner of a close protection and investigations outfit that operates in Mozambique, Zambia and Tanzania from a South African base, alludes to the same difficulty ('it can be difficult to be paid timeously')[45] as does Carlos Rega, the General Manager of a similar business with a footprint in Southern, East and West Africa.[46]

'Hardware' inadequacies of an infrastructural nature were the final significant type of handicap alluded to by PSCs working internationally in Africa. For tech-focused solutions providers such as C-track, a lack of local ICT infrastructure can hinder the distribution or effectiveness of otherwise high-demand products. GSM networks, for example, are not always available and this means the company's tracking devices 'don't always work'.[47] All three telematics companies interviewed cited variations in infrastructure as problem.[48] Pentagon, an Internet protocol security company, laments that 'travel in Africa is very expensive',[49] while NSA's Steyn pairs 'roads and flights' together as a recurrent challenge for his company.[50] Customs and borders – or 'barriers and boundaries' as one described them[51] – are the cousins of these terrible twins, and they have of course been repeatedly spotlighted in empirical studies on the hindrances to business in Africa conducted by the Brenthurst Foundation (TBF) and others.[52] Transport, communications and other infrastructural deficiencies are not a matter of economic theory; they are, as those on the ground testify, daily slowing or killing business on the continent.

Africa's diversity, referred to in the opening paragraph of this section, is customarily appropriated as a demonstration of the glass being half-full – namely, that while conditions for business might be poorer in some parts, they are considerably better in others. As a statement of fact, this is manifestly true. As an interpretive line, it is less so. It must not be forgotten the diversity is in itself, paradoxically, a shared encumbrance to businesses operating internationally within the continent and therefore a retardant to economic growth in all Sub-Saharan countries. Taken together, many of the obstacles identified by PSCs show that variability occurs so often and in so many different ways as to be, indeed, a common problem. In this sense, heterogeneity is not good but bad, be it in law, infrastructure – even culture and language. Diversity may be a fact of life, but it is also a matter of degree, the acuity of which continues to place Africa at a distinct disadvantage compared to the European Community, NAFTA and other regional trading blocs.

Solutions

With few exceptions – and in spite of the associations with espionage, 'regime change' and human rights abuses that tend to excite politicians – it is clear that most PSCs in Africa are engaged in legitimate and largely mundane activities. They are functioning as normal businesses, and their concerns generally match those of other businesses operating across borders in Africa. The solutions to their problems, by extension – and in their own words – tend to be unexceptional. *Ad oculus* – 'obvious on sight' – they may be to entrepreneurs, but the fact that such chronic, systemic challenges persist and that the solutions need to be repeated, suggests that *argumentum ad nauseam, argumentum ad infinitum* remains sadly necessary. Governments, too often, still don't get it.

At the most fundamental level, there needs to be a shift in attitude among many African governments and their bureaucracies. A mercantilist or Malthusian worldview, which renders economics a zero sum game fought over finite resources, remains pervasive.[53] In such a Darwinian universe, foreign businesses, be they from overseas or from elsewhere in Africa, become foes rather than friends, competitors seeking to 'steal' and 'pillage' rather mutual beneficiaries in the quest for wealth. The same 'us-versus-them' thinking is often evinced by elites in relation to their own populations. Until this changes, there will be little incentive to apply obvious solutions and African populations will remain poor.[54]

For those who are listening (and they do exist), few PSCs expect or want direct assistance, but express the hope that governments will create an enabling environment. A marked number of generic comments were made in response to a question about how governments could assist the industry. These highlighted:

- the need for 'policy consistency';[55]
- the centrality of macro-economic stability ('government needs to provide a stable economic system');[56]
- the need to 'drive economic growth and strengthen private sector investment';[57]
- the need for 'peace, stability and continuity';[58]
- the need 'to sort out the judicial system';[59] 'provide consistency in the laws and regulations';[60] ensure 'a more directed judiciary' (there being 'too many frivolous lawsuits that waste time and money').[61]

Other obvious remedies that emerge from the problems elucidated by PSCs include more aggressive efforts to fight corruption and the exigency of education and skills development.[62] It is one thing for governments to call for both FDI and value addition; it is another to provide the requisite skills base. 'Governments need to provide training programs to develop the skills of the people, so that employment can increase', says Wayne Botha, the owner of a private investigations company working in South Africa, Swaziland and Lesotho.[63] African governments must demonstrate a commitment to education equal to the almost religious zeal with which many Asian governments have approached the matter if they, too, are to move beyond resource dependence and toward specialisation and its attendant rewards.

The importance of regional economic integration is another axiom that issues from the reflections of PSCs on the practical difficulties created by variations in infrastructure, legal structures and the like, and by 'barriers and boundaries'. Stephen Karingi, Director of the Regional Integration, Infrastructure and Trade Division at the Economic Commission for Africa, remarks that 'individual African economies are small as markets…[M]arket integration through removal of tariff and non-tariff barriers is critical to creating a larger market space'.[64] There was some appreciation of the benefits of regional economic communities among the survey respondents who trade in security related goods,[65] but those involved on the services side were almost uniformly negative, bar one who said that SADC made visas easier to acquire.[66] Karingi comments:

> There is very low intra-African trade in services. Many services sectors remain closed…The logic that market integration should focus on goods first and services later is something to be challenged. Services sectors (security services for instance) can be both an input to production of goods or an enabler of the market environment that allows production to occur in the first place. In that sense, African countries should revisit the integration model…to put at an equal level the opening of goods and services markets. In other words, regional integration cannot be optimised in Africa, even if we build infrastructure and productive capacity, until we allow openness in the services trade regime. A new road or railway that cannot allow logistics services to be provided seamlessly across border (whether transport, insurance or security) cannot yield the maximum benefit possible to the countries being connected. In short, the opening of services trade in Africa is an imperative.

Cutting against conventional wisdom, Karingi believes that the impediments to regional integration in Africa are more bureaucratic than political. Drawing of a decade of experience in Africa's negotiations on trade and regional integration, he says 'political will is not a major issue in Africa's integration…The problem largely lies with the technocratic will…Africa's technocrats are not able to translate regional integration and continental visions to reality'. He sees such 'technocratic inertia' as rooted, firstly, in an inability to articulate ideas in the kind of practical terms that allow ministers of finance to allocate resources – and, secondly, in a false sense of patriotism 'whereby technocrats put national interests first and forget that regional integration is also about national interests'. Regional integration, he says, 'serves national interests better than [a] national approach to issues'.[67]

Politicians do, however, need to overcome pejorative attitudes in relation to PSCs, as they do the broader span of the identity politics ball and chain. Those who are serious about growth must recognise that PSCs are already an important component of many Sub-Saharan economies and that working with the industry, rather than against it, represents a crucial opportunity. In the South African context, for example, private security's contribution to GDP is approximately the same as that of agriculture. A government publication asserts that agriculture is a 'significant provider of employment' and a 'crucial sector...an important engine of growth for the rest of the economy' by virtue of its 'backward and forward linkages to other sectors'.[68] The same could be said of private security in view of the substantial numbers employed by the sector, many of whom have a low level of education, as well as the broad reach of the industry from manufacturing through to service provision and beyond. It should also be remembered that PSCs, in their appropriate forms, effectively provide the state with a developmental dividend by taking pressure off usually stretched government services (such as the police) and by affording security to people and their assets, without which economies cannot grow.[69]

With these factors in mind, policy makers should establish a positive dialogue with PSCs. Fidelity's Ephraim Kanga suggests governments should 'provide accessible information exchange forums to address investor concerns'.[70] This is another aspect repeatedly emphasised by business during TBF surveys over many years. Politicians often have strong views on the private sector, of elements thereof, and make decisions that have far reaching consequences, but rarely do they take the time to properly understand or engage with those who are on the ground. Garth Fuchs, CEO of DeltaOne International, a South African company that has provided security for some of the continent's most prominent politicians, articulates this sense of alienation, appealing for government to promote the interests of the industry's skilled operators 'instead of trying to prosecute [the] same under...the Foreign Military Assistance Act'.[71] Carlos Rega says that 'governments need to adjust the bias towards security companies in order to elevate their standing in the community'.[72] 'Government doesn't give a damn', was the way the export manager of one firm perceived attitudes on the other side of the fence.[73] This, evidently, has to change if a more beneficial relationship is to develop. It is critical that governments speak to business – and do it often – if they are to make informed choices. Formal and informal mechanisms should be created to lubricate dialogue with PSCs.

More sinned against than sinning it may be, but the industry also needs to play its part in this process. Collectively and individually, PSCs in Africa generally do a poor job at public relations. The non-response percentage for this survey – which represented a clear opportunity for companies to argue their value to African economies and to lobby government – was highest among the larger organisations – those who should be accustomed to the imperatives of PR.[74] Industry bodies, where they exist, likewise lack capacity and often even a willingness to engage on matters of core responsibility, comparing poorly with industry groups overseas. In SSA, there is nothing comparable with the Confederation of European Security Services (COESS), a group that carries out in-depth research into private security within the European Union, promotes standardisation within the industry and represents a vast membership in its dealings with government. COESS is formally recognised by the EU Institutions and, in its own words, 'builds and maintains strong partnerships with the relevant Directorates-General within the European Commission' and 'is the prime interlocutor for EU policymakers and policy advisors seeking industry know-how. For that reason, CoESS is systematically consulted on any EU policies and strategies, which may affect the industry's short-term or long-term interests'.[75] Much of this influence is derived from the organisation's ability to demonstrate, with comprehensive hard data, the economic importance of PSCs to the EU.[76] Africa's larger PSCs must take the lead in the formation of professional and well-resourced industry bodies, including one with continental scope, if they are to lobby more effectively and to more often avoid becoming collateral damage of SSA's political volatilities. Neither a siege mentality nor a shrug of the shoulders will suffice.

Outlook

PSCs are optimistic about the future of intra-African business for the sector. Ochien'g notes that different African countries represent different kinds of markets but that a 'growing middle class is a commonality', bringing with it 'increased middle class earnings and spending'.[77] He also refers to the fact that GDP growth in SSA is almost three times that of global GDP, a point picked up by URG's Jim LeBlanc, who stresses that Africa has slowed somewhat 'but is still doing better than the West' and that his company 'has services that people need in Africa'.[78] To be sure, the likelihood of continuing strong demand on the back of solid macroeconomic fundamentals, relatively high levels of insecurity (or declining levels of tolerance to insecurity among as upwardly mobile groups) and shortfalls in the capacity of government security services prompts a number of PSCs to use superlatives in relation to the prospects for further expansion in Africa.[79] Increases in FDI, as implied by its importance as a cross-border driver, were part of this optimism. Chris Beukes, the CEO of an executive protection company, states that prospects were 'definitely' positive because 'more British, French, American and Chinese companies are investing in Africa',[80] while another uses the same adjective and instances 'places like Luanda and Angola, where the Chinese are building the countries up'.[81]

At the same time, a number of respondents are careful to outline certain conditions and caveats to go with a generally sanguine view. Uneven socio-economic changes and political instability were two of the most common. Groups perceived as middle class in many countries outside of South Africa 'can't necessarily afford the products' and are 'not the same as the SA middle class', a security systems trader says.[82] Another agrees, affirming the growth of the middle class in South Africa but 'not necessarily in [the rest] of Africa'.[83] 'Poorer African countries are still poor', says the representative of a company that provides training and specialised protection services in South Africa, Uganda, Malawi and Namibia.[84] C-track's Chief Operating Officer, Franco Stoels, feels that the 'rich get richer, [the] poor get poorer; the guy on the ground gets nothing' and he 'doesn't think this is going to change any time soon'.[85] Ephraim Kanga perhaps sums up sentiment among those who sound a cautionary note. Growth potential for the sector is bright, he says, 'subject to certain critical factors (i.e. political stability, good governance, regional co-operation, etc.)'.[86]

This amalgam of optimism and a worldly wisdom borne through real experience of intra-African business shows itself in the counsel that PSCs offer to other companies seeking to expand from a domestic base into SSA. As Kanga puts it: 'Investment prospects exist; however, business in Africa is not for the faint-hearted'.[87] Of those who provided advice on expansion, 50 per cent referred explicitly to the need for thorough research. 'Do your homework', said one, and 'think twice'.[88] Others commented: 'Do your research first and thoroughly'[89]; 'visit the regions where you want your product [to sell and] talk to the local people'[90]; 'market research needs to be done on the ground level' – and be aware that 'this results in greater company expense'.[91] Using an appropriately military metaphor, the owner of a close protection company remarks: 'Reconnaissance is vital'.[92]

When non-explicit references are included, over 85 per cent of those who proffered advice referred in one way or other to the sine qua non of local knowledge. Where these responses were specific, awareness of Africa's diversity and the importance of reliable local partnerships were frequently underlined. Naivety was a danger to which South African companies were thought to be particularly vulnerable. 'Understand the place [you are going to]. It is not SA', says Centurion's Scott Wilson.[93] Do not use 'a one size fits all mentality', adds Guy Addison, the Director of Netstar International.[94] Ochien'g concurs:

> [D]on't take a Joburg mentality into the continent. It is more Eurocentric here with regard to standards and so on. Many companies have failed by taking a rigid system into other markets. Get to know local markets, take local partners. SA model replication is a problem.

Ochien'g says that the 'entrepreneurial attitude among Africans at a business partnership level' has meant that Tyco does not 'lack partners',[95] and others note that such strategies both circumvent problems and fulfil core requirements: 'find partner companies that already exist. Then merge skills, workers and costs. The culture, contacts and relationships then have a known quality'.[96] Such marriages must nevertheless be arranged judiciously, according to Pentagon: 'Don't just trust anyone. Be careful who you partner with'.[97] Beukes urges PSCs to 'do proper intelligence work on prospective partners' and, in the same vein, XFOR's Aaron Kitchener advises companies to 'find a trustworthy third party to deal with. Speak to other companies and find out who they used, who can be recommended. Networking is key for expansion'.[98]

With such due forethought and planning, the final ingredients to success for PSCs are as crucial as they are intangible, according to respondents such as Sonya Skipp, General Manager of iFacts, a human resources company specialising in pre-employment checks for the security industry in Southern and West Africa. She advocates 'thorough research', yet places considerable emphasis on the need for courage: 'Have the conviction to explore the possibilities that are out there and to discover what is viable. There are many opportunities in Africa'.[99] Ochien'g, again, comments that Tyco is 'selective' and 'cautious', but it does not eschew risk altogether, rather 'going where risks are balanced'.[100] To courage, others add tenacity. 'Patience' is vital, notes Addison; 'nothing comes quickly or cheaply'.[101] 'Be prepared for a long term commitment', opines Osprea's Christian Bock.[102] These are, in essence, the pioneering attributes that are underwriting (and have always done so) the successes of African entrepreneurs across all sectors. It is a spirit aptly captured by Rory Steyn: 'Don't have a negative perception of Africa', he says. 'Seek opportunities' – and 'get on with the job'.[103] To the extent that they are allowed and enabled to do so, Africa's entrepreneurs – which include the owners and operators of PSCs – can change the continent's fortunes.

Notes

1. Excerpts from Marketline global security services industry profile. See http://www. reportlinker.com/p0618805-summary/Global-Security-Services.html.
2. See G4S Africa factsheet (June 2012), http://www.g4s.co.za/~/media/Files/South%20 Africa/G4S%20Africa%20Fact%20Sheet%20-%20June%20updated.ashx.
3. See, for example, various papers by the Institute for Security Studies (ISS), including, among others, 'Conference report on the regulation of private security in Africa', Pretoria, April 2007; 'Private Security in Africa: Manifestations, Challenges and Regulation', ISS Monograph series no. 139, November 2007; and Sabelo Gumedze, 'The Regulation of Private Security in Africa', Pretoria, 2008.
4. Twenty-eight of these interviews were conducted telephonically and three respondents provided answers to questions via e-mail. One interview was terminated before completion. I am grateful to all who agreed to be interviewed; their names (where provided) appear in the footnotes.

5. The oft-used term 'private security and military companies' (PMSCs) has not been employed in this study, even though it would have been technically correct, because the overwhelming majority of those interviewed are engaged in non-military activities.

6. For figures, see http://www.tyco.com/ and http://www.tyco.com/about.

7. Interview with Martin Ochien'g, 21 February 2014 (with e-mail follow-up, 6 March 2014). Quotations are of notes made by interviewers during telephonic discussions and may at times represent a paraphrasing of original comments.

8. In 2007, the industry was estimated to be growing at 13 per cent per annum. For this and other figures illustrating the growth of the South African industry since the 1970s, see Anthony Minnaar, 'Oversight and Monitoring of Non-state/Private Policing: The Private Security Practitioners in South Africa' in 'Private Security in Africa: Manifestations, Challenges and Regulation', ISS Monograph series no. 139, November 2007, pp. 129–31. For reference to current growth figures, see interview with Steve Conradie, CEO, Security Industry Alliance, February 2013, www.securitysa.com/7654a.

9. Annual turnover for 2012 is quoted in Kim Imrie, 'Who Owns Whom: Investigation and Security Tracking Activities', May 2012, p. 1 (http://www.whoownswhom.co.za), and is set against a GDP of $383 billion (http://data.worldbank.org/country/south-africa) and an average exchange rate for the year of ZAR8.2 to the dollar.

10. E-mail from Tony Botes (Administrator, Security Association of South Africa), 10 February 2014.

11. This percentile is calculated from the figure of 15.2 million total employed persons quoted in 'Quarterly Labour Force Survey: Quarter 4, 2013', Statistics South Africa, p. vii.

12. Figures and quotation of 'a long-standing observer of Nigerian politics' cited in Rita Abrahamsen and Michael C. Williams, 'The Globalisation of Private Security: Country Report: Nigeria', January 2005, http://users.aber.ac.uk/rbh/privatesecurity/country%20report-nigeria.pdf.

13. Economic analyst Christ Hart has commented that 'the growth in the private security industry [in South Africa] has been underpinned by persistently high crime levels and decreasing confidence in the capacity and ability of the state to meaningfully improve physical security'. 2013 interview at http://www.securitysa.com/7654a.

14. MiX Telematics owns the well-known Matrix vehicle tracking company. Interview with Devan Delport, Business Development Manager, Matrix, 17 February 2014.

15. Interview with Franco Stoels, Chief Operating Officer, C-track, 17 February 2014.

16. Interview with Tanzanian employee, Warrior Security, 18 February 2014.

17. Interview with Guy Addison, Altech Netstar, 19 February 2014.

18. Interview with Rory Steyn, Executive Director, Nichols Steyn & Associates (NSA), 18 February 2014.

19. Interview with Franco Stoels, C-track, 17 February 2014.

20. Interview with Martin Ochien'g, Tyco International/ADT SA, 21 February 2014.

21. Interview with Dawn Matheson, Export Manager, Elvey Security, 17 February 2014.

22. Interview with Christian Bock, Co-director of Logistics, Osprea Logistics, 17 February 2014.

23. Interview with Scott Wilson, Export Manager, Centurion Systems, 17 February 2014.

24. Interview with Aaron Kitchener, XFOR Security Solutions, 3 March 2014. Sonya Skipp, General Manager of iFacts, a human resources company that specialises in pre-employment screening for the security sector (and which has a footprint covering South Africa, Zimbabwe, Zambia, Mozambique and Nigeria) likewise comments that governments should 'facilitate the…introduction of a new company into the country'. Interview, 5 March 2014.
25. Interview with Roy Nickrash, General Director, Regal Ultra Security, 19 February 2014.
26. Interview with Guy Addison, Altech Netstar, 19 February 2014.
27. Interview with Devan Delport, Matrix, 17 February 2014, and interview with Monique Ackermann, Human Resources Manager, ATM Solutions. The latter is a UK-owned company with a presence in Zambia, Namibia and South Africa.
28. Statement by Nathi Mthethwa to the National Assembly, 25 February 2014, cited at http://www.politicsweb.co.za/politicsweb/view/politicsweb/en/page71654?oid=553132&sn=Detail&pid=71616.
29. With the exception of Mthethwa's parliamentary statement, factual detail and quotations in this paragraph are drawn from 'Code red over limit on foreign firms', *Mail & Guardian*, 22 November 2013, http://mg.co.za/article/2013-11-22-00-code-red-over-limit-on-foreign-firms.
30. Interview with Rory Steyn, NSA, 18 February 2014.
31. Interview with Max Francis-Jones, Venture Risk Management, 18 February 2014. Venture Risk offers services in close protection, due diligence and logistics, among others.
32. Interview with Jim LeBlanc, Vice President (Americas), Unity Resources Group, 20 February 2014.
33. Interview with Richard Leach, CEO, Hybrid Solutions, 4 March 2014.
34. For an overview of the FCPA, see http://www.justice.gov/criminal/fraud/fcpa/.
35. See http://www.legislation.gov.uk/ukpga/2010/23/contents.
36. Interview with Tom Callahan, 17 February 2014. Figures were provided in the same interview.
37. Interview with Jim LeBlanc, Unity Resources Group, 20 February 2014.
38. Interview with Guy Addison, Altech Netstar, 19 February 2014.
39. Interview with Martin Ochien'g, Tyco International/ADT SA, 21 February 2014, and e-mail of 6 March 2014.
40. Fidelity employs over 30,000 people in South Africa (for comparisons with numbers employed by other PSCs, see Imrie, 'Who Owns Whom', pp. 5–7). Other major hindrances identified by Kanga include: 'Limited availability of affordable capital'; 'Poor in-country infrastructure'; 'Language barrier'; and 'Government policy of indigenisation'. Written response to questionnaire by Ephraim Kanga, Fidelity Security Group, 3 March 2014.
41. Interview with Angela Maciel, Office Manager, SBV Services, 17 February 2014. For figures on market share, see Imrie, 'Who Owns Whom', p. 8. For a company overview, see http://www.sbv.co.za/about.php.
42. Interview with Dawn Matheson, Elvey Security, 17 February 2014.
43. For example, one security training company, which wished to remain anonymous, cited language and 'how each country works' as two of the three major challenges (interview, 17 February 2014), while others commented that 'people relations can be difficult' or cited specifics such as the different landscape in Muslim countries. Interviews with Angela Maciel, SBV Services, 17 February 2014, and Scott Wilson, Centurion Systems, 17 February 2014.

44. Interview with Tanzanian employee, Warrior Security, 18 February 2014. Regal Ultra Security also pointed to theft, saying it was a 'common' problem 'especially in West and North Africa'. Interview with Roy Nickrash, 19 February 2014. Osprea's Christian Bock, working in a quite different sphere, testified that 'security issues' provided problems for the company. Interview, 17 February 2014.
45. Interview with Richard Schagen, owner, Assessed Threat Solutions, 3 March 2014.
46. Interview with Carlos Rega, General Manager, Magma Security Consultants, 3 March 2014. With a head office in South Africa, Magma operates in Angola, Mozambique, Botswana, Zimbabwe, Kenya and Nigeria. Kyle Condon, Managing Director of D&K Management Consultants (investigations, risk management, executive protection), who works in South Africa, Angola and Mozambique, advises PSCs hoping to expand into Africa, 'Do your research and get paid on time!' Written response to questionnaire, 5 March 2014.
47. Interview with Franco Stoels, C-track, 17 February 2014.
48. MiX Telematics/Matrix, for example, described Malawi's infrastructure as 'poor' and that in Kenya and Tanzania as 'better'. Interview with Devan Delport, Matrix, 17 February 2014. Also, interview with Guy Addison, Altech Netstar, 19 February 2014. The digital divide caused by ICT shortfalls also causes problems. iFacts' Sonya Skipp notes that her company's screening services are more problematic outside of South Africa: 'lack of [digital] databases and records' are among the biggest challenges as 'they tend to be paper-recorded and not automated', which 'makes finding the necessary info difficult'. Interview, 5 March 2014.
49. Interview with Edward van Trotenberg, Export Manager, Pentagon, 18 February 2014.
50. Interview with Rory Steyn, NSA, 18 February 2014.
51. Interview with Edward van Trotenberg, Pentagon, 18 February 2014.
52. See, for example, Greg Mills and Larry Swantner, 'Wings over Africa? Trends and Models for African Air Travel', Brenthurst discussion paper 4/2008; and Greg Mills, Jeffrey Herbst and Stuart Doran, 'Mobilising Zambia: A Strategy Report on Accelerating Economic Growth', Brenthurst discussion paper 2010/02.
53. For a recent discussion of the impact of this worldview on Africa's political economy, see Greg Mills, *Why States Recover: Changing Walking Societies into Winning Nations* (London, 2014).
54. A junior employee of Halogen Security, one of West Africa's largest manned guarding companies (principally Nigeria, with a lesser presence in Ghana), comments sagaciously on the need for a nation-building ethos in Africa: 'Governments need to continue working at bettering the people and the country'. Interview, 18 February 2014.
55. Interview with Jim LeBlanc, Unity Resources Group, 20 February 2014.
56. Interview with Halogen employee, Halogen Security, 18 February 2014.
57. Interview with Martin Ochien'g, Tyco International/ADT SA, 21 February 2014.
58. Interview with Roy Nickrash, Regal Security, 19 February 2014.
59. Interview with Max Francis-Jones, Venture Risk Management, 18 February 2014.
60. Interview with Guy Addison, Altech Netstar, 19 February 2014.
61. Interview with Christian Bock, Osprea Logistics, 17 February 2014.
62. An employee of Chubb Fire and Security, a major player in the South African and global security market, was one of those who made explicit reference to the first in terms of policy imperatives, singling out the need for governments 'to work at improving [problems related to] the levels of corruption'. Interview, 21 February 2014.

63. Interview with Wayne Botha, owner, EWB Private Investigations, 3 March 2014.
64. E-mail from Stephen Karingi, 4 March 2014.
65. Centurion Systems' Scott Wilson averred to the removal of tariffs afforded by SADC (interview, 17 February 2014), while C-track's Chief Operating Officer commented that SADC was 'a lot of help' as it 'promotes sales and exports' and 'assists in keeping prices low and competitive'. It is 'a good thing in these countries. Has many benefits'. Interview with Franco Stoels, 17 February 2014.
66. Interview with Martin Ochien'g, Tyco International/ADT SA, 21 February 2014. One other services-oriented company commented positively but did not point to a specific practical outcome beyond the utility of the SADC secretariat as 'a resource of information and research'. Interview with Angela Maciel, SBV Services, 17 February 2014.
67. E-mail from Stephen Karingi, 7 March 2014.
68. 'Economic Review of South African Agriculture, 2012/13', Department of Agriculture, Forestry and Fisheries, Pretoria, 2013, http://www.daff.gov.za/docs/statsinfo/EcoReview1213.pdf.
69. For example, Irene Ndung'u, speaking at a conference on the involvement of PMSCs in peacekeeping missions in Africa, observes that these companies 'have developed a greater capacity [than government] to deal with the demands of the dynamic security industry. They therefore fill what has become a security gap...[The] filling [of] this security gap had a positive outcome for human security as it had reduced risks to human security, and benefits associated with this ranged from employment opportunities to contributions to legitimate peace-building processes. In such cases PMSCs are able to contribute towards providing a space for states to develop'. See 'The Involvement of the Private Security Sector in Peacekeeping Missions', ISS, Nairobi, July 2010, http://psm.du.edu/media/documents/reports_and_stats/think_tanks/iss_conference_report_involvement_of_private_security_in_peacekeeping.pdf.
70. Written response to questionnaire by Ephraim Kanga, Fidelity Security Group, 3 March 2014.
71. Written response to questionnaire by Garth Fuchs, DeltaOne International, 7 March 2014.
72. Interview with Carlos Rega, Magma Security Consultants, 3 March 2014.
73. Interview with Dawn Matheson, Elvey Security, 17 February 2014. Matheson added that the South African government 'especially don't assist smaller companies with export'.
74. Among those who either failed make time or to respond to repeated requests for interview were G4S Africa's head office, Protea Coin, the Paramount Group and Kenya's KK Security, collectively representing a sizeable proportion of SSA's dominant PSCs. Securitas, another major multinational, terminated its interview after a few minutes.
75. See http://www.coess.eu/?CategoryID=175 and http://www.coess.eu/?Category ID=174.
76. See, for example, its publication 'Private Security in Europe – COESS Facts and Figures'. The most recent of these reports (2011) provides collective and disaggregated statistics on private security in 34 countries, including 7 outside the EU, and runs to 150 pages – http://www.coess.eu/?CategoryID=203. Another example of a well-organised international industry body is the International Stability Operations Association (ISOA). See http://www.stability-operations.org/. I am grateful to Jessica Mueller, ISOA Chief Operating Officer, for introductions to key members of the organisation.

77. Interview with Martin Ochien'g, Tyco International/ADT SA, 21 February 2014.
78. Interview with Jim LeBlanc, Unity Resources Group, 20 February 2014.
79. For example, among those who see prospects as unambiguously positive, terms such as 'very bright' and 'absolutely' and 'definitely' positive ('Africa = growth') were used. Respectively, interviews with Max Francis-Jones, Venture Risk Management, 18 February 2014, Guy Addison, Altech Netstar, 19 February 2014, and Devan Delport, Matrix, 17 February 2014.
80. Interview with Chris Beukes, CEO, TSU Protection Services, 17 February 2014. TSU also offers training and maritime protection services.
81. Interview with Dawn Matheson, Elvey Security, 17 February 2014.
82. Interview with Scott Wilson, Centurion Systems, 17 February 2014
83. Interview with Roy Nickrash, Regal Security, 19 February 2014.
84. Interview with anonymous PSC, 17 February 2014.
85. Interview with Franco Stoels, C-track, 17 February 2014. Richard Schagen surmises that the growth of the middle class in SSA 'will require a lot of time. It will not happen at the speed that people think...There is a lack of education hindering development and an increasing gap between "the haves and the have nots"'. Interview, Assessed Threat Solutions, 3 March 2014.
86. Written response to questionnaire by Ephraim Kanga, Fidelity Security Group, 3 March 2014.
87. Written response to questionnaire by Ephraim Kanga, Fidelity Security Group, 3 March 2014. Kyle Condon of D&K Management Consultants agrees, saying the outlook for PSCs in Africa '[d]epends on political stability'. Written response to questionnaire, 5 March 2014.
88. Interview with Devan Delport, Matrix, 17 February 2014.
89. Interivew with Aaron Kitchener, XFOR Security Solutions, 3 March 2014.
90. Interview with Dawn Matheson, Elvey Security, 17 February 2014.
91. Interview with Roy Nickrash, Regal Security, 19 February 2014.
92. Interview with Richard Schagen, Assessed Threat Solutions, 3 March 2014.
93. Interview with Scott Wilson, Centurion Systems, 17 February 2014.
94. Interview with Guy Addison, Altech Netstar, 19 February 2014.
95. Interview with Martin Ochien'g, Tyco International/ADT SA, 21 February 2014.
96. Interview with Angela Maciel, SBV Services, 17 February 2014.
97. Interview with Edward van Trotenberg, Pentagon, 18 February 2014.
98. Interviews with Chris Beukes, TSU Protection Services, 17 February 2014, and Aaron Kitchener, XFOR Security Solutions, 3 March 2014.
99. Interview with Sonya Skipp, iFacts, 5 March 2014.
100. Interview with Martin Ochien'g, Tyco International/ADT SA, 21 February 2014.
101. Interview with Guy Addison, Altech Netstar, 19 February 2014.
102. Interview with Christian Bock, Osprea Logistics, 17 February 2014.
103. Interview with Rory Steyn, NSA, 18 February 2014.

14
The Private Sector's Role in Africa's Water Infrastructure

David A. Rice

Water is a precious natural resource, vital for life, development and the environment. It can be a matter of life and death, depending on how it occurs and how it is managed. When there is too much or too little, it can bring destruction, misery or death. Irrespective of how it occurs, if properly managed, it can be an instrument for economic survival and growth. It can be an instrument for poverty alleviation, lifting people out of the degradation of having to live without access to safe water and sanitation, while at the same time bringing prosperity to all on the continent (Box 14.1).

Box 14.1 Water facts

- Less than 1 per cent of water on Earth is drinkable
- 1 in 3 people globally are water insecure
- 46 per cent of people on Earth lack piped water to their home
- 3,750,000 people die every year from water-related diseases
- An average American uses 176 gallons of water per day
- An average African uses 5 gallons of water per day
- 70 per cent of global water usage is devoted to agriculture

Source: Handshake, Vol. 1, May 2012, International Finance Corporation.

Less than 60 per cent of Africa's population has access to drinking water, while only 4 million hectares of new irrigation have been developed in Africa over the past 40 years, compared with 25 million hectares in China and 32 million hectares in India.

Africa's climate is characterised by extremes, from a humid equatorial climate at the equator, through tropical and semi-arid in the middle of the region, to an arid climate towards the northern and southern fringes. Sub-Saharan Africa has a relatively plentiful supply of rainwater, but it is highly seasonal, unevenly distributed across the region and there are frequent floods and droughts. Drought is the dominant climate risk in Sub-Saharan

Africa. It destroys economic livelihoods and farmer's food sources and has a significant negative effect on Gross Domestic Product (GDP) growth in one-third of the countries.

In Sub-Saharan Africa, access to sanitation is highly correlated with wealth and residence in urban areas. For example, in cities, 42 per cent of the poorest residents have access to improved sanitation facilities, while only 15 per cent of the poorest in rural areas have such access. This means the poorest 60 per cent of the population in Sub-Saharan Africa are largely denied the comforts and health benefits of a piped drinking water supply on premises, despite the fact that between 1995 and 2010, 221 million people gained access to an improved drinking water source, and 105 million were provided access to improved sanitation during this same period.

The Millennium Development Goal (MDG) number 7, Target 7c, calls on countries to 'halve by 2015 the proportion of people without sustainable access to safe drinking water and basic sanitation'.[1] To achieve this, Sub-Saharan Africa is estimated to require US$22 billion per year.

There are many factors that serve to undermine the African water sector, according to the World Bank. Among them are high hydro-climactic variability, inadequate storage, rising demand and a lack of trans-boundary rivers running across the region. Therefore, it's hardly surprising that the World Bank should conclude that 'developing large-scale infrastructure to manage water use and avoid conflicts is a huge challenge'.[2]

With current investment flows falling well short of that, at around US$8 billion per year, the Bank has focused a lot of attention on project preparation in order to help reduce the shortfall. 'The huge financing gap is not chiefly due to lack of financiers or money,' says the World Bank's head of water Mohamed El Azizi, but to the fact that there are 'few well prepared

---

Box 14.2   African water facts

- 322 million people in Africa gained access to an improved drinking water source since 1990
- The number of people with piped drinking water to the household increased from 147 million in 1990 to 271 million in 2010
- Despite an increase in drinking water coverage from 56 per cent in 1990 to 66 per cent in 2010, the population relying on unimproved drinking water source increased from 279 million in 1990 to 344 million in 2010
- In 2010, 115 million people directly draw on surface water to meet their drinking water needs
- To meet the MDG drinking water target 215 million people need to gain access by 2015

Source: Drinking Water Coverage Trends: The Snapshot of Drinking Water and Sanitation in Africa – 2012, http://www.wssinfo.org/fileadmin/user_upload/resources/Africa-AMCOW-Snapshot-2012-English-Final.pdf (p. 3).

projects to finance. When detailed project designs and feasibility studies are prepared, our experience is that funding is generally obtained', he says.[3]

Global investment firms like Goldman Sachs refer to water as 'blue gold'[4] – a whole new commodity that can be bought and sold on par with gold, oil and corn. But not everyone believes such partnerships will ultimately improve access to those most at risk – the poor. The fear is that – for a commodity with limitless demand and sharply diminishing supply – market distortions could ultimately deprive the needy of one of life's most critical resources.

Water sector governance

Professor Wangari Maathai, the first African woman to receive the Nobel Peace Prize, said that 'the global water crisis is a crisis of governance: manmade with ignorance, greed and corruption at its core'.[5]

Corruption in the water sector is reflected in the overall level of corruption in the country as a whole. For example, projects may be hard-wired to favoured companies who control market segments such as the supply of pipe that meets stringent technical specifications or investments in public supply can be steered to areas that are the source of political support rather than those that need it most. An effective strategy demands a shift in policy so that financial resources are allocated better to water resources, especially at the municipal level. The fear is that an increased water scarcity will escalate competition between business and local communities and could lead to conflict.

Poor governance is a major factor in water challenges, and common governance risks have contributed greatly to these problems. Readily identifiable and easily mitigated, substantial gains would be made if poor governance were addressed. Governance measures should be brought into donor procedures and approvals.[6]

African water legislation often consists of a disparate collection of laws and regulations developed over several decades, many dating back to colonial times, that are often overly complex and burdened by both redundancies in some areas and gaps in others.[7] Additional challenges include the existence of customary water law in which access is seen as a collective right and safeguarded by the tribal group despite modern laws. The policies that do exist are often developed without sufficient financing for implementation.[8]

Public-private partnerships are an important part of the solution, but governments need a clear blueprint on what policies are needed to create the right enabling environment. This means legislation is required in most places to ensure the effective functioning of the sector with regulation following the legislative framework to ensure proper management.[9]

The high political profile of water should be used to create more transparency for its operations. Public opinion, user associations and NGOs should be encouraged to monitor and publicise the activities of water organisations and expose corrupt practices. Likewise, private and public companies engaged in the water sector are urged to cooperate with public clients and other parties to develop methods for promoting ethical behaviour. Private participation contracts should be fully transparent, which will alleviate some of the concerns over granting the private sector a role in service provision.

In most countries, urban water services are provided by the municipality, a public or parasaital entity and by private operators contracted by the municipality under performance-management contracts.[10] The utility may be regional or even national in scope providing services to groups of municipalities, and self-regulation is most often used, usually via a performance contract with regulation provided by a network of stakeholders.[11]

Government should ensure that civil society groups as service providers, advocates, participants in planning processes and watchdogs are supported. Overall, effective water governance depends not only on how much financing can be mobilised but also on the extent to which these resources are managed and allocated efficiently, effectively and sustainably by recipient institutions across the sector.[12]

Advancing the role of the private sector in the provision of water-related services won't be easy. Some leading stakeholders, including policy makers, believe that water should be valued as an economic good and ensure that all have access instead of only some. But in its efforts to ensure this, government policies have met with limited success. A core challenge for government is attempting to balance the commercialisation of the water sector and provide the constitutional right of access to water; the complexity of such a task makes this nearly impossible and leads rather to the contradictions, tensions and injustices we see in the reality of water provision.

Box 14.3   The Dublin principles

1. Fresh water is a finite and vulnerable resource, essential to sustain life, development and the environment
2. Water development and management should be based on a participatory approach, involving users, planners and policy makers at all levels
3. Women play a central role in providing, managing and safeguarding water
4. Water has an economic value in all its competing uses and should be recognised as an economic good

Source: "Dublin Statement on Water and Sustainable Development," International Conference on Water and the Environment.

Water development and management should be based on a participatory approach, involving users, planners and policy makers at all levels. The participatory approach involves raising awareness of the importance of water among policy makers and the general public. It means that decisions are taken at the lowest appropriate level, with full public consultation and involvement of users in the planning and implementation of water projects.[13]

Multilateral donor commitment to water in Africa

The international community, especially multilateral donors like the World Bank and African Development Bank (AfDB), are critical sources of funding and other forms of support. The amount of capital required, the fact that governments control access to water and to water-related services and the sheer complexity of the issues involved necessitate a prominent role for these institutions, even as enablers of private sector involvement in the sector.

The bank, as set up to promote sustainable economic growth and reduce poverty in Africa, has become a financing stalwart on the African continent: between 1967 and 2012, it lent around US$98 billion.[14] The increased sector focus is due to a greater recognition about the importance of the water sector and the role it plays in the socio-economic development of the continent, as well as greater visibility of the sector within the bank.

To date, the AfDB has focused its lending exclusively on public sector entities. However, the AfDB is keen to increase its exposure to projects that involve private sector participation. Despite having US$2.1 billion of exposure to the water sector across 71 projects and 42 countries, the AfDB's lending to date has been exclusively focused on public sector entities, although it is keen to increase its exposure to projects that involve private sector participation.[15] These projects will be funded under the AfDB's Private Sector Window. To be eligible for funding, the project sponsor must be incorporated in an African country and is expected to take a minimum 30 per cent equity stake in any project.

Water supply and sanitation (WSS) have become a priority for the AfDB only over the past decade and a half. The majority of AfDB's lending has always gone to infrastructure, but between 2000 and 2010 the AfDB committed US$340 million per year to drinking water and sanitation initiatives, with lending in this area peaking at US$700 million in 2010.

Most water supply and sanitation projects in Africa are technically feasible but are not bankable. This is a challenge that we are taking on and are working on increasing both feasible and bankable projects in the sector. The changing face of Africa's water infrastructure landscape is leading the African Development Bank to adopt new strategies in order to support the sector.[16] This broadening of the bank's mandate is natural, given its pre-eminent position as a lender to the water sector in Africa. AfDB is now perhaps the financing institution with the largest staff dedicated to WSS for Africa.

Along with lending volumes, the nature of the AfDB's activities in the sector has also changed. Lending initially focused on urban projects, but with the launch of the Rural Water Supply and Sanitation Initiative (RWSSI) in 2003, the bank's support for rural projects increased from less than 15 per cent of the WSS portfolio to 42 per cent by 2012, during which time it has contributed to access to drinking water for 66 million people and improved sanitation for 49 million people. The AfDB has also shifted away from stand-alone projects to a more programmatic approach taking into consideration the cross-sector nature of water.

This formed the rationale for the establishment of the African Water Facility (AWF), an institution that provides grants and technical assistance to bring innovative water projects to market. For every €1 it has invested, the facility has attracted €30 in follow-up investments, and its leverage capabilities are such that it expects to pass the €1 billion threshold in terms of raised capital this year.

Ensuring adequate allocations for the water sector remains a challenge. Other infrastructure like energy, roads and health are often prioritised by governments. This is not specific to AfDB; the bank, together with the African Ministers' Council on Water (AMCOW) and other partners, is continuously working to raise the visibility and importance of the sector. The bank's current exposure to the water and sanitation sector amounts to US$2.1 billion, accounting for 7.5 per cent of the bank's total lending portfolio. Looking ahead, WSS represents 15 per cent of the bank's 2014–2016 indicative lending program, although this figure is likely to change as governments' priorities change (Table 14.1).

Crucially, AfDB is investing a lot of time and effort into developing new funding mechanisms. The investment gap, together with the recognition that the sector cannot reach any meaningful targets if it only relies on concessional funding, has created a greater acceptance of the idea of market finance. The bank has therefore set up the Africa50 vehicle to implement transformational infrastructure projects.

Table 14.1 Largest donors to water and sanitation infrastructure in Sub-Saharan Africa (per cent)

Source	Hard	Soft
World Bank	22	16
European Union	14	23
AfDB	12	–
Germany	8	13
France	7	–
Japan	–	6
Canada	–	5
26/21 others	37	37

Source: Infrastructure Financing Trends in Africa: ICA Annual Report 2012.

It is also working on a variety of non-lending activities, all geared towards enabling actors in the sector to access new sources of finance, be it commercial loans or private sector contributions through Public-private-partnerships (PPPs). Initiatives include running shadow credit ratings of high-performing utilities to alleviate commercial banks' concerns about the sector's risks; working with partners such as the African Water Association's Water Operators' Partnership to identify utilities that are making positive performance improvements; providing expertise on various levels of private sector intervention across urban and rural water infrastructure (from service contracts right through to full concessions); and undertaking tariff surveys and studies on water regulation.

Commercial opportunities in water

Regional or global economic policies, such as the development of the internal market in Europe, NEPAD in Africa, or privatisation conditionalities of the World Bank, create new business opportunities that encourage national and international commercial expansion. Liberalisation and privatisation in other countries provide an opportunity for a state to encourage expansion by key companies in that sector, whether private or public, as a way of developing national dominance in a regional or international market.[17]

In most cases, World Bank funding and its conditionalities are critical in creating the conditions for neoliberal restructuring in the water sector. As water Transnational Corporations (TNCs) are withdrawing from developing countries, national public utilities and firms from developing countries seems to be filling the space.

The existing structures of the public sector affect what is possible. Scale and size are clearly significant: larger city, regional and national entities are more able to expand commercially than municipal operators. If the water services of South Africa had vertically integrated structures, with bulk supply as part of the municipal distributors, the large regional or national companies would not exist. While scale and size are influential, regional or national scale does not inevitably lead to commercial expansion.

By 2016, annual expenditure in the traditional water sector is projected to grow to US$770 billion, with growth primarily in the water supply and sanitation sector. This figure is comparable to expenditures in other utilities: global expenditures in the natural gas sector amount to around US$770 billion and in the electric utility sector at US$1.5 trillion. In developing countries, expenditures on water-related infrastructure and services are between US$65 and US$75 billion annually. If the MGDs related to water are to be met, annual investments of US$180 billion will be required until 2025.[18]

In principle, most countries have more than enough water to supply their populations' growing needs and maintain environmental sustainability.

The challenge is found in identifying ways to integrate decisions on water management into the full set of economic choices a country needs to make. Governments, as well as businesses across a diversity of sectors including agriculture, power generation and manufacturing, understand the value of access to water to maintain operations.

Investors, both public and private, lack a consistent basis on which to make economically rational investment decisions and therefore the will to invest in the sector. The fundamental lack of clarity on the economics of water resource management limits informed policy making on a country-wide basis. Most households in African cities (70–90 per cent), and virtually all poor households, deal with their own waste by building latrines or septic tanks themselves or by hiring others to do so. This implies high growth potential for water utilities in these countries, although the socio-economic characteristics of each country will largely mitigate development. The coverage of rural household water and sanitation connections across all given countries is materially low, and non-existent in some instances, again implying substantial growth potential for water utilities.[19]

Small-scale private entrepreneurial providers of water and sanitation (including vendors), otherwise known as alternative service providers (ASPs), are important actors to take into account in governance assessments, particularly due to their role in reaching the poor and un-served. ASPs offer the advantage of working in low-income areas that are difficult to reach with pipe networks and they operate without subsidy and dependence on the public purse. By being responsive and innovative, they are often an easier, quicker and less expensive way of reaching the poor with improved services.[20]

Sector practitioners have come to realise that with the exclusion of the smaller providers and vendors, privately operated utilities provide only a small portion of the world's water supply and even less of sanitation, 5–10 per cent at most. A World Bank report found 10,000 small-scale service providers in a limited sample of 49 countries.

Over time, Africa has therefore developed its own utility models and is finding that efficiency and consumer responsiveness depends less on whether the utility is private or public and more on the local context, the quality of regulation and the nature of their contracts. The question is less about whether international companies should gain access to local markets and more about how both public and private operators can better provide service to the un-served and particularly to the poor and the marginalised.

Private-sector participation in water by number of projects has expanded threefold during the past decade. With an average of 50 projects and US$2– US$3 billion in investment commitments per year, 535 water projects benefitting from private participation have reached financial closure during the past ten years. During this period, more than 55 per cent of water PPPs were signed by private firms originating from low and middle-income countries.[21] However, Sub-Saharan Africa has the lowest level of PPP activity in this space with only 15 projects totalling investments of only US$180 million in 13 countries, the majority of which were utility management contracts.[22]

In government, the time between when a resource constraint appears and when it shows up on the bottom line is much longer than the time it takes for a corporation to register the same result. The corporate world has greater impetus to act because it will be affected more quickly. Companies are increasingly becoming more and more interested and willing to participate in discussions about making progress on water-related development in poor countries. However, making the link between water and the economy is essential. What makes these partnerships successful is when there is a good national champion on the corporate side and a very strong commitment from the government.

In 2010, the total number of urban water and sewage utilities operated by the private sector reached a record high of 257 in 35 countries including 10 in Sub-Saharan Africa. Most of these are based on concession arrangements. Given current trends, the number of urban water and sewage utilities operated by the private sector in low- and middle-income countries should be roughly 300 within the next five years. However, there is a school of thought that feels involving the private sector in such a basic service as water is controversial, but water can be a business.[23]

Box 14.4 Private water services in Uganda

The IFC recently supported the government of Uganda to successfully tender the expansion and management of water services for the town of Busembatia to the domestic private sector. Crucial to the success of the project was the fact that the traditional public-private partnership transaction advice provided by IFC was complemented by a range of activities that addressed some of the key challenges faced by the domestic private sector, such as access to credit.

The project worked with local private operators to increase their ability to access finance from local banks and also with financial institutions to help them understand the risks faced by small town water operators and develop risk mitigation strategies.

While the transaction was small in scale, the project also helped the government to facilitate the management of water public-private partnership contracts by developing a 'generic' management contract for use of privately managed piped water systems that will ensure consistency in contract administration and management.

In addition, training was provided to representatives of the government and private operators in order that all signatories to the contract understood their obligations within the 'generic' management contract. The operator has also committed to maintain tariffs at its current, government threshold tariff.

Source: 'Public-Private Partnership Impact Stories – Uganda: Small Scale Infrastructure Provider Water Program', International Finance Corporation.

'It is unreasonable to expect private operators to transform, in a few years, a loss-making, subsidy-dependent water company incapable of maintaining its asset base. It is even more unreasonable to expect them to transform into a profit-making company capable of financing new investments, without a tariff increase to reward the capital investment'.[24]

Private sector participation and investment in the water sector is not a substitute for sector reform and regulatory oversight, which is invariably a prerogative of the government. For the private sector to produce strong results, its public sector counterpart, the regulator, needs to be equally empowered. Local sensitivities and the specific technical and economic conditions of each operation require careful and continuous adaptation.[25]

The Calvert Global Water fund engages in advocacy and policy work to promote 'thorny issues' around access to clean water and establishing guidelines for companies in how they deal with their water use.[26] 'We see a tremendous convergence between global sustainability challenges and an investment opportunity in water', said Ellen Kennedy, manager of environment, water and climate change at Calvert Investments, which manages a high-profile water fund.

A similar fund, the Equinox Water Fund, has also taken on the challenge, and grown from US$10 million in value in 2006, when Manchester Capital created it, to about US$20 million today. But not everyone is welcoming private investment in water, especially when it means companies getting involved at the utility level, or in the actual distribution of water to people, especially the poor.[27]

The Boston-based Corporate Accountability International, or CAI, sent a letter to World Bank President Jim Yong Kim demanding that its banking arm, International Finance Corp, stop investing in privately held water companies.

The organisation claims the funds rarely meet their development goals and, in the end, undermine the democratic control and governance of public water systems.

'I think they are well intentioned', said Shayda Edwards of CAI. 'The intention is probably to support access but the problem is that instead of investing in access, they are actually investing in the private water funds that essentially are furthering "commodification"'.[28] A CAI report, 'Shutting the Spigot on Private Water,' claimed that private investment often hurt access to water, especially for the poor. The World Bank disputes the findings and stands behind a paper it produced in 2010, which supports private investment, finding that private operators can improve efficiencies and reduce waste of the resource. Calvert also responded to the CAI report, stating that 'there is a legitimate concern over the privatization of water and one of the ways we address that is to try to instill the human right to water in all our company dialogues and encourage companies that we hold to make a policy statement to the human right to water'.[29]

Box 14.5   Political economy of private investment in infrastructure

- Investors have at times reneged on contractual obligations
- Appropriate pricing of basic services
- Financing operating and maintenance costs and mitigating non-market risks
- PPPs are vulnerable to public perception that the private counterparty profits disproportionately
- Governments often fail to put PPP obligations on their balance sheets
- Solvency II and Basel III pose difficulties for commercial banks to issue long tenures on bank loans making the development of local financial markets more important
- Development agencies often do not want to directly promote national commercial interests and development agencies may also be concerned over private investors neglecting to align with development objectives.
- Incentives to motivate private investment to achieve development objectives should be built into projects
- Privatisation of infrastructure should be carried out only if there is private sector interest to invest
- Cost recovery by investors should not become unaffordable for the poor
- PPPs may need to be financially viable in the short to medium term, but should lead to long-term development impacts
- Risk sharing should not disproportionally burden the private sector, resulting in further indebtedness of host country governments when projects fail

Source: Public-Private Partnerships for Urban Water Utilities: A Review of Experience in Developing Countries, World Bank, Washington DC.

Africa offers one of the strongest future opportunities for growth and investment worldwide. Water is a hugely controversial issue, especially as many countries face negative implications from climate change and pollution/water contamination. Water efficiency and management is critical, as major users like agriculture consume more and more of the available resources. This is made even more controversial by the fact that 70 per cent of water diverted for irrigation is lost in the process due to inadequate infrastructure such as poor storage and leaky distribution systems.

Public-private partnerships in water

The World Bank's Public-Private Infrastructure Advisory Facility found that in a sample of 1,200 water and energy utilities in 71 developing and transition countries, there was no systemic change in residential prices as a result of a PPP in the water sector. In 6 African countries, 2.5 million people are already being served by the private sector. The Research has found the following: 54 per cent increase in connections per worker, 18 per cent increase in water sold per worker and a 41 per cent increase in hours of service per day.

Twenty-four million people have been connected to piped water through PPP projects since 1990.[30]

Figures from the database of the Public-Private Infrastructure Advisory Facility are instructive in this respect. They show that, of 238 African infrastructure projects undertaken between 2000 and 2009, the telecom sector witnessed 97 projects in 37 countries; transport 57 projects in 19 countries; energy 69 projects in 27 countries; and water just 15 projects in 13 countries.

Most often overlooked are the small and often informal enterprises that fill the demand for water and sanitation services from households beyond the reach of public WSS infrastructure. These households are composed of the poorer customers in small cities, peri-urban and remote areas of most developing courtiers. Alternative service providers provide services to up to 60 and 70 per cent of urban populations, giving access to water through private supplies such as wells, public stand posts, water kiosks, informal distribution networks, tankers and small-scale vendors.[31]

In the vast majority of African countries, user fees and debt financing are not a realistic means to fund service delivery alone and government and donor support will be required in most cases for the foreseeable future. However, government policies can help align industrial behaviour with the broader objectives of an efficient sector. In the US, for example, the Environmental Protection Agency creates incentives for the commercial sector to adopt more efficient practices to conserve natural resources. Entrepreneurs and financiers need transparency to benchmark new technologies and understand where innovations can create value. In some cases, water cost curves will be so steep that the country is exposed to share increases in the marginal cost of water for relatively small changes in demand. In these situations, countries run out of obvious options to tackle the water supply-demand gap, and innovation becomes critical.

'Water is absolutely challenging for the private sector', said Gad Cohen, deputy managing director at InfraCo Africa, a private company that pools capital from bi-lateral and multi-lateral development finance institutions to leverage private capital for investment in African infrastructure. Cohen said there is sensitivity on the part of governments to relinquish something to the private sector that is viewed as so fundamental. Furthermore, around ten years ago some governments tried to bring in more efficiency and increased tariffs and it was 'politically explosive' with the cost equation as the biggest issue.[32]

Developing infrastructure that potential customers can ultimately afford to pay for is problematic. The political economy of private investment in water is complex, requiring a number of critical issues and concerns to be addressed in order to be successful such as those identified in figure 14.1. Cohen says that in the power sector tariffs have been gradually increased to allow the private sector to play a role but he adds that 'associated income-producing activities' make these tariffs affordable. In the case of water, 'you have a sector where governments do not want to relinquish control and where you have a fundamental issue that, for project to be effective, they will need a lot of concessionary/grant money to make them affordable' (Interview with Gad Cohen).

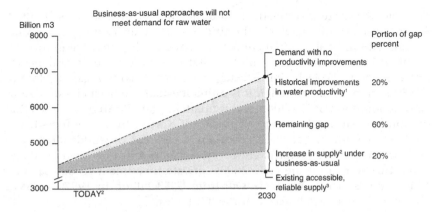

Figure 14.1 Raw water demands

[1]Based on historical agricultural yield rates from 1990–2004 from FAOSTAT, agricultural and industrial effiiciency improvements from IFPRI

[2]Total increased capture of raw water through infrastructure buildout, excluding unsustainable extraction Current 90%-reliable supply does not meed average demand

[3]Supply shown at 90% reliability and includes infrastructure investments scheduled and funded through 2010.

Source: OECD Promoting Private Investment for Africa's Infrastructure.

Jane Jamieson, a senior infrastructure analyst with IFC, says there's no lack of the kind of pragmatism that's required, meaning governments will frequently provide subsidies in order to keep prices low. Consumers are often willing to pay the extra amount if only they can be guaranteed water access. The poor are often served by unregulated operators and thereby end up paying more.[33]

Box 14.6   Principles for private sector participation in infrastructure

1. Provisions or decision-making: cost-benefit analysis, risk allocation and contingent liabilities
2. Enabling institutional environment: transparency, procurement, competitive environment on equal footing and easier access to financing
3. Goals, strategies and capacities: stakeholder consultations, private sector participation, stronger administrative capacity, monitoring contacts, coordination across jurisdictions
4. Implementation: expectations on private sector performance, regular consultations between private and public entities, due diligence, simplified award criteria, provisions for future tariffs, dispute resolution
5. Responsible business conduct: combat bribery, dialogue with affected communities, abide by environmental and human rights standards

Source: Kate Baliss, UNDP Policy Research Brief No. 3, January 2007.

The role of private investment in African infrastructure has been limited. According to a study on water by the Africa Infrastructure Country Diagnostic, the annual financial requirement for infrastructure in Sub-Saharan Africa is about US$93 billion a year for both capital expenditures and maintenance. However, only US$45 billion is being mobilised, leaving a gap of close to US$50 billion a year, although it is estimated that inefficiencies of various kinds amount to US$17 billion of this financing gap. It can be assumed that the funding gap would also be significant if North Africa were included to provide a continental scope.[34] Less than 4 per cent of worldwide private investment in infrastructure went to Sub-Saharan Africa between 1990 and 2003. However, since the early 2000s, private investment in Sub-Saharan Africa's infrastructure has increased: from US$3 billion in 1997 to US$12 billion in 2009, mostly directed at the ICT sector.

A number of recent studies put the annual water supply and sanitation investment, and operation and maintenance requirements at between

---

Box 14.7   Public-private partnerships in water: keys to success

- Participation of grassroots organisations
- Involving elected officials and local councils
- Ensuring women and marginalised groups and the poor are active
- Responsive channels for consumer/user complaints, recourse and appeal
- Raising awareness of inequities
- Strengthen alternative providers of services, particularly in difficult-to-reach neighbourhoods
- Improving monitoring and access to information
- Decentralisation to local governments
- Involvement of NGOs and user associations
- Clear and consistent authority for governance and oversight
- Emphasis on rural access to water and sanitation
- Transparency and accountability
- Stronger financial management
- External performance audits
- Integrated water and sanitation plans into poverty reduction strategies
- Modern information technology tools and data capture methods
- Appropriate pricing of water assets and tiered user fees for household, commercial and industrial use
- Clear plans for conflict resolution
- Harmonise best practices
- Develop indicators and tools to track progress
- Incentives for alternative service providers
- Emphasise public-private partnerships

Sources: Task Force on Financing Water for All: Enhancing Access to Finance for Local Governments; Financing Water for Agriculture, World Water Council, Global Water Partnership and the 4th World Water Forum.

US$18 and US$29 billion annually. According to the best estimates, only about US$8 billion is being mobilised through tariffs, domestic taxes and government subventions as well as transfers from development partners. As public sector funds are insufficient to cover resource requirements, there is a need for collaboration and strong involvement of the private sector as implementers, financiers and providers of services. A World Bank study found that out of the more than 260 contracts awarded since 1990, 84 per cent were still active at the end of 2007, and only 9 per cent had been terminated early.[35]

Widespread decentralisation reforms across Africa over the past decade have greatly facilitated civil society participation. In line with the principle of subsidiarity, many local governments on the continent have now assumed responsibility for implementing rural water supply projects. Likewise, many municipalities are outsourcing water services delivery to public and or private utilities. This has enabled new participatory approaches to be undertaken, although both government and community representatives continue to need orientation and training with such new approaches to service delivery.

In many cases, private operators have improved operational efficiency, quality of service and access to water and sanitation services. The main findings were that PPPs have proved effective through (1) improved quality service, (2) improved operational efficiency, and (3) dispersed impact on tariff levels. The area demonstrating mixed results was the equitable expansion of coverage.

Case study: Rand Water

Rand Water (RW) – originally named the Rand Water Services Board – was formed in 1903 under its own statute as the first bulk supplier of potable water in South Africa, with responsibility for providing water to the old mining industry and towns on the Witwatersrand. Over the years Rand Water has grown and remained the biggest water board in South Africa – 15 times larger than its nearest equivalent, and the largest public water utility in Africa, and one of only a handful that is privately owned.

Rand is the largest bulk water utility in Africa and one of the largest in the world, providing potable water to more than 11 million people and in an area beyond 18,000 km². Rand's primary reach includes metropolitan and local municipalities, mines and industries primarily in Gauteng, parts of Mpumalanga, the Free State and North West provinces in South Africa. Rand operates a vast network including over 3,000 km of pipelines, two combined pumping and purification stations, four booster pumping stations and various enclosed reservoirs. Rand Water draws water from catchments, purifies it for human consumption, and then supplies it to municipalities that then supply it to consumers or individuals. Since the 1990s, the World

Health Organization has rated RW's water quality as in the top three in the world.

The primary function of RW is the abstraction, purification and distribution of bulk potable water. For abstraction RW draws 99 per cent of the raw water it uses from the Vaal dam, which is fed by the Vaal and Wilge rivers. Since there are not sufficient water resources in Gauteng, a series of water transfer schemes have been necessary. These transfer schemes rank amongst the most sophisticated in the world. Rand is also involved in Bulk Sanitation services, working with the Department of Water and Environmental Affairs (DWEA) to ensure standards and meet the challenges throughout their area of operation.

RW has been experiencing commercial growth, with surplus growth per year for the majority of this period consistently over 30 per cent. As RW is not supposed to make a profit, such surplus is justified and used as capital for new infrastructure works and to pay off RW's debt; RW refers to such surplus as 'not profiteering but recovering cost of capital' (Public is as Private Does: The Confused Case of Rand Water in South Africa, Municipal Services Project, Occasional Papers No. 15). While profits have gone up, RW's number of employees has been decreasing slowly since 2000.

Rand has a proven track record and profitable history, making it more attractive for investment. Its strong success and growth through South Africa, and the benefits they have provided outside of the workplace to communities and their employees, has helped it maintain a motivated, diverse and competent workforce and has remained a leader in its sector.

Since the mid-1990s, RW has slowly been expanding its activities beyond bulk potable water supply. With the acceptance of the Water Services Act in 1997, RW is now legally becoming involved in the full cycle of water services, including bulk water supply and retail water, bulk and retail sanitation and resource protection. In pursuit of this strategy, RW has both expanded the geographical area of its bulk water supply and expanded beyond bulk water supply into other activities in South Africa and in other countries.

In terms of its role as a public utility, RW argues that it has a role in meeting the socio-economic needs of South African society. This role RW sees as different to the one played by the private sector via CSR. In a position paper prepared by RW for the World Summit on Sustainable Development (WSSD) in 2002, RW said 'it can be argued that although the private sector can bring efficiencies in certain areas, if equitable considerations are to be also served in a financially sustainable manner, then there should also be a role for public water providers – particularly in terms of improving access to basic water and sanitation services to the poor'. This assumes that public providers automatically consider equity issues, which is not always the case.

Rand Water's commercial ambition is to provide their services and expertise throughout the region. In many ways, South Africa is an economic leader on the continent, especially in the southern region, and the performance of companies in the country is comparatively advanced and often looked to as a model for companies in other areas to follow. For example, after the end of Apartheid, South Africa's newly elected government inherited huge services backlogs with respect to access to water supply and sanitation. About 15 million people were without safe water supply and over 20 million without adequate sanitation services. The government thus made a strong commitment to high service standards and to high levels of investment subsidies to achieve those standards. Since then, the country has made satisfactory progress with regard to improving access to water supply: It reached universal access to an improved water source in urban areas, and in rural areas the share of those with access increased from 66 per cent to 79 per cent from 1990 to 2010. South Africa also has a strong water industry with a track record in innovation, and Rand remains a leading company in this area.

Rand's policies have helped them to maintain their position as a leader, to scale their business and to both expand their profit and provide a social impact as well. One of the ways that Rand Water maintains this leading position as a highly regarded water services company is through substantial investments in research, training and knowledge in partnership with the Water Research Commission. It serves as the country's water centred knowledge 'hub' leading the creation, dissemination and application of water-centred knowledge, focusing on water resource management, water-linked ecosystems, water use and waste management and water utilisation in agriculture. Rand is also one of the founders of the Water Institute of Southern Africa (WISA), a professional association, and keeps its members abreast of the latest developments in water technology and research through its national and international liaison, links and affiliations.

For South African companies like Rand, NEPAD has been a significant factor, both as a regional economic policy creating new markets, and as a driver of the South African government's wish to see its own companies exploit the opportunities of those markets. To be self-financed, they look for profit-making opportunities, and with primary activities regulated, non-core activities seems to be the place for such profit-making. With money made available from DWAF and other national government bodies to municipalities to enable them to fund and contract for all sorts of activities, the road has been paved for public water utilities to engage in other activities for profit-making or at least on a cost-recovery basis.

Rand Water Services (Pty) Ltd

In 2005, Rand Water launched Rand Water Services (Pty) Ltd (RWS) as a subsidiary company of Rand Water. The initiative came from the Engineering Division, which in the late 1990s had little in the way of major infrastructural projects, leaving it with underutilised personnel. Instead of laying people off, the division wanted to turn to other activities to 'keep people' for 'capacity to do outside work'. In February 2000, RWS was registered with the Registrar of Companies. What seemed to have held up the full establishment of the Pty until 2005 was partly fear by RW management of the reaction of the unions to its formation – that they might see it as a form of privatisation.[36]

Initially RWS was to focus on East and Southern Africa, although it was 'to pursue commercial water- related projects in South Africa outside RW's 31 areas of service and in the broader African continent including the Indian Ocean islands and the Middle East'. The key focus areas for RWS are local municipalities (providing advisory services and technology), such as a Ghana management contract, bottled water, setting up of a water infrastructure fund, strategic relations, management contracts, capacity-building mandates, consulting and advisory mandates, procurement contracts and development facilitation transactions in Africa.[37] Because commercial activities are 'unknown territories', RWS aims to engage via partnerships and joint ventures in these activities so as to obtain more expertise and to spread the risk in business initiatives. In this regard, RWS is targeting municipalities by establishing PPPs.

While the initial idea was clearly that RWS would draw on the capacity and skills of staff within RW, and that RW and RWS would give each other preferential treatment, practical issues soon emerged including human resource constraints, union resistance, and erosion of political support in South Africa as campaigners complained that RW shouldn't be attempting to serve the needs of Ghana while so many South Africans were still lacking clean water.

Unhappiness with a contract in Ghana was particularly acute. As one interviewee indicated, '[N]ow that we won the contract we are actually in deep trouble'. This 'deep trouble' refers to the lack of skills that RW is experiencing itself: '[We] need to give [RWS] the technical support; [we] don't have it. That's why we are recruiting overseas. The people we're sending to Ghana at this stage are four people – all four that should have come from [RW]. We have managed to find one... The other three positions, all the technical positions, we're out trying to recruit. And it is costing us an arm-and-a-leg'.[38]

One of the most positive responses about RWS was that it would raise the visibility of RW in the market and internationally with the World Bank, British government, European governments, Asian governments and other African governments. To this end, RW was keen to 'share what it has learnt' with other African utilities, including through the development of 'public-public partnership models'.

In support of NEPAD, RW states that Africa's development should be led by Africans, with RW as an African utility in a good position to provide leadership: 'We believe we should help to build efficient and effective utilities to promote service delivery for Africa and that such utilities should be owned in Africa' (Public is as Private Does: The Confused Case of Rand Water in South Africa, Municipal Services Project, Occasional Papers No. 15). RW also raises the 'fear' that 'if RW is not allowed to pursue operational activity in support of the development of Africa, then private water companies from Europe and North America will undertake this work. The implication of this is that it will limit the development of African skills, it will limit the employment of African people, and will serve to repatriate profits out of Africa' (Public is as Private Does: The Confused Case of Rand Water in South Africa, Municipal Services Project, Occasional Papers No. 15) although RW did enter joint ventures with private firms from Europe and North America.

In the midst of criticism, RW stated that because in South Africa it is a public utility, it should be distinguished from traditional private water companies, and thus cannot be accused of furthering water privatisation when it bids for contracts in other African countries. Except for the obvious profits to be made and to be applied to RW's primary activity, RW also proposed that going into Africa will help it to deal with its perceived overcapacity in terms of skills – with the added benefit that the skills are to be used for Africa's development. RW thus wants to export its expertise (Lushaba 2005), but interviews with local authority officials in RW's area of supply indicated their unhappiness with RW going into other parts of Africa; they argued that if RW has such overcapacity of skills these should be used to strengthen the capacity of South African local authorities which face major problems due to the lack of technical skills. Their opinion is 'why sign a twinning agreement with Lilongwe Water Board in Malawi while Delmas or Emfuleni local municipality in South Africa – RW's own customers – urgently need help?'

The majority of projects RWS pursues outside of South Africa are sourced through international tenders, by responding to invitations to collaborate from potential partners, and by supporting other African water utilities through MOUs. A summary of some of RWS' international work includes:

- An MoU was signed with Swaziland Water Services Cooperation (SWSC) for collaboration on broader water sector issues. SWSC appointed Rand Water to assist them in preparation for ISO accreditation of their laboratory. The project was completed successfully within time (July 2011) and budget (R30,000)
- The DRC requested assistance from the South African government in 2007 to improve water supply in the Katanga Province. Visits to the DRC culminated in the signing of the Bi-national Agreement between SA and DRC on 20 June 2011, in Lubumbashi (DRC) with a project value of R22 million. The project entailed a variety of design and installation of new equipment as well as on-the-job-training to maintenance personnel.
- The Botswana water utility appointed Rand Water to assist in design and implementation of business systems. The project commenced in April 2012 with a value R486,000 and was used as a spring board to launch the Rand Water product offerings in Botswana.

Rand Water has also used multilateral funded pan-African programs to enter new markets, using its advantages as the most advanced African provider of such services. For example, the African Development Bank's WOP program was launched on August 2011. 490.000 EUROS was provided as a grant by the ADB acting as trustee for the African Water Facility (AWF). Under this program, Rand Water was awarded to mentor the River State Water Board in Nigeria and engaged in similar efforts in Kenya and Ethiopia.

RW's support activities in Africa are done on a cost-recovery basis and are mostly project-based. It has been involved in such activities with Swaziland, Mauritius and Zambia. These activities typically involve assistance with technical skills and are funded externally. For example, in 2004, the New Business Development department in collaboration with the Scientific Services division conducted training and a development needs analysis assessment at the Central Water Authority in Mauritius.[39] In 2002, RW was contracted by the International Water Association to hold two workshops with the Water and Sanitation Association of Zambia involving training aimed at the top management of newly established commercial water utilities. Topics covered included customer relations, billing system, reducing costs and regulation.

By July 2005, five South African water utilities had already signed twinning agreements with countries in East and Southern Africa,[40] with RW having two such contracts – in the DRC and Malawi – and discussions ongoing with Kenya. RW provided the DRC with capacity development, operations management, technical assistance and rehabilitation of infrastructure.[41] It has already provided capacity-building for a team of senior management from the DRC on water treatment process and technology. To support additional work, RW and the DRC are attempting to secure donor funding from the World Bank, EU, African Development Bank and the Development Bank of Southern Africa.

The RW agreement with Malawi proved that in the short term both parties share ideas and information, and transfer skills, while the medium- to long-term plan is for specific areas of cooperation to be project-driven, with a focus on issues of governance, water demand management, revenue management, policy issues and infrastructure development.[42] RW sees more opportunities in Malawi in the future since Malawi is also starting its institutional reforms for the water sector.[43]

Many of RW's other activities in Africa – commercial, support and capacity-building – are based on political policies and finance from governments, aid agencies and donors, through conventional procurement. The objectives and economics of some of the commercial and support contracts – for example, constructing or advising on conventional engineering projects, or training – may not be more problematic than any other procurement contract. Some of the contracts, however, are highly problematic, in their political objectives, in their economic impact and in their commercial impact on RW. The Ghana-contract is a clear example of this, and the Disi water-project is an example of a BOT model that has proved very damaging elsewhere in the world.

The kind of skills RW believes it can share with the rest of Africa include its strong engineering and water quality management backbone, as well as its focus on customer service and efficiency and water demand management practices. However, it defines 'water demand management' as 'the potential to save and use water in a manner that acknowledges it as a scarce resource and to increase the revenue potential from water sales by governments'.[44]

Key challenges to intra-African investment in water

Cross-border investing in water utilities across Africa is very limited, although further privatisation of public water infrastructure and service provision presents the best opportunity to improve and expand water access to the millions who have unreliable access or no access at all. A number of key challenges prevent this type of intervention, despite the efforts of regional, continental and international multilateral institutions and funders, and the growing interest among a sub-set of global investors and foreign companies with deep expertise in the industry. The primary challenge is the reluctance of governments to privatise the links in the water supply chain that present the best commercial potential, which would also provide the greatest benefit to the public.

Countless obstacles face companies seeking to expand in Africa, and deter the growth of intra-African trade and investment. For many, including Western investors and others with a means to invest within Africa, much of this has been perception. Unstable economies and political systems, massive inflation, corruption and other problems have led many Africans to make their investments outside of Africa in more established and stable economies, and where risk is seen as less. These risk factors, coupled with an often undertrained work force/shortage of skilled labour, lack of education and high overhead costs due to lack of infrastructure also commonly deter investment within Africa.[45]

In terms of water infrastructure, the ownership of water resources is a major issue, but in many countries the ownership is still unclear and many simple methods to purify or decontaminate water are unavailable. Africa also faces a situation of economic water scarcity, and current institutional, financial and human capacities for managing water are lacking. The situation is exacerbated by competition for public funding between sectors, and heavy public debt burdens in most countries. And while provision of clean water and the ability to expand and improve access across the continent have remained a major focus of many individuals, governments, and organisations worldwide, a significant amount of funding in this area has not been for investment at all, but rather charity.

Many initiatives have emerged, including some leading non-profits such as water.org, which are backed by significant investors, celebrities, and others worldwide. And despite this attention, the impact of charitable donations will never equal the benefits of being able to provide consistent clean water without aid. While even simple education can provide a tremendous impact at a rapid rate, especially in terms of improved healthcare, potential investment to expand water infrastructure provides an actual solution. This includes permanent answers to many of the problems facing this industry in Africa, and significant social and community benefits across greater overall areas and massive populations.

Additionally, in Africa, financing is insufficient and the institutional capacity to absorb what is available is limited. The danger of slippage to already made progress against the MDG on water and sanitation is real. Most countries within the continent are falling short to sustain Water Sanitation and Hygiene (WASH) commitments, with over 80 per cent of countries reportedly falling significantly behind the trends required to meet their defined national access targets for sanitation and drinking water. There is insufficient domestic financing for WASH overall with particularly serious shortfalls for sanitation. This is exacerbated by difficulties in spending the limited funds that are received.

Chief among the barriers preventing intra-African trade in the water sector are the predilection of governments to maintain complete control over their public water systems. In most countries, urban water services are provided by the municipality, a public or para-public utility and by private operators that are contracted by the municipality under performance contracts. In some cases, the utility may be regional or even national in scope, providing services to a group of municipalities.

In RW's case the institutional reform in the water sector in South Africa raised questions about the future of water boards, leaving water boards 'needing' to reposition themselves. By gaining experience in retail water contracts, for example, water boards can position themselves to become vertically integrated companies and act as regional water distributors, thus ensuring their continued existence.

What seems particularly significant in determining whether a public sector operator expands, either for commercial purposes or for developmental solidarity, is the senior management of the public sector operator. The corporatisation of public utilities prepares them for application of principles and practices of private sector management, leading to a greater focus on financial sustainability and the tendency to want to engage in commercial activities. Another challenge Africa faces is lack of coordination among authorities, stemming from an unclear definition of roles and responsibilities, coupled with lack of harmonisation of laws and policies related to environmental management. Inadequate staffing in government departments that handle environmental issues is another factor in the downward trend in environmental sustainability in some countries within the continent.

Private sector providers operate under performance contacts that can be upgraded to include requirements for transparency such as clear lines of responsibility, responsiveness to the public and service quality standards. These performance criteria are set into contacts that can be made available to the public and used in ensuring downward accountability. In all such cases, disclosure requirements also need to be included into performance contracts, including public disclosure of investment plants, management contracts, rate-setting information, and financial and operational performance information.

To enter the water market, entrepreneurs and financiers need transparency to benchmark new technologies and understand where innovations can create value. In some cases, water cost curves will be so steep that the country is exposed to share increases in the marginal cost of water for relatively small changes in demand. In these situations, countries run out of obvious option to tackle the water supply-demand gap, and innovation becomes critical.

Notes

1. WSP, 'Getting Africa on Track to Meet the MDGs on Water and Sanitation: A Status Review of 16 African Countries', AfDB, AWCOW, EUWI, UNDP, WSP-Africa, Nairobi, Kenya (2006).
2. 'Africa's Infrastructure: A Time for Transformation', World Bank.
3. 'Developing Africa's True Water Potential', *Global Water Intelligence* (Vol. 15. No. 3, March 2014).
4. 'Water as a Commodity: Can Investors Boost Access to This Critical Resource?' http://www.theguardian.com/sustainable-business/water-access-commodity-human-rights?CMP=twt_gu.
5. 2008 Global Corruption Report: Corruption in the Water Sector, Transparency International.
6. UNDP, 'Water Governance for Poverty Reduction' (2004).
7. SDC, AAAS, UN-Habitat, COHRE (2007), *Manual on the Right to Water and Sanitation*.
8. Gordon McGranahan and David Satterthwaite, 'Governance and Getting the Private Sector to Provide Better Water and Sanitation Services to the Urban Poor', Human Settlements Discussion Paper Series (International Institute for Environment and Development, 2006).
9. Global Water Partnership, 'Dialogue on Effective Water Governance,' Stockholm, Sweden (2002).
10. Merra Mehtaand Dinesh Mehta, 'Financing Water and Sanitation at Local Level,' Draft Synthesis Paper, WaterAid UK, 2007.
11. Eugenia Ferragina, M. Marra and D.A.L. Quagliarotti, 'The Role of Formal and Informal Institutions in the Water Sector', Plan Bleu, Sophia Antipolis (2002).
12. Judith Rees, James Winpenny and W. Alan Hall, 'Water as a Social and Economic Good', TEC Background Papers, No. 12, Global Water Partnership (2008).
13. S. Tremolet and J. Halpern, 'Regulation of Water and Sanitation Services, Getting Better Service to Poor People', GPOBA Working Series Paper 8, Washington, DC (2006).

14. www.afdb.org/en/projects-and-operations/.
15. Interview: Mohamed El Azizi, Vice-President of Water, African Development Bank.
16. 'Developing Africa's True Water Potential'.
17. Vivien Foser et al., 'Africa Infrastructure Country Diagnostic Descriptive Manual: Water Supply and Sanitation Performance Indicators', World Bank, Washington, DC (2006).
18. Water Aid, 'Local Millennium Development Goals Initiative: Local Government and Water and Sanitation Delivery', London, UK (2008).
19. Global Credit Rating Co., Africa Water Utility Regional Comparative, Utility Creditworthiness Assessment Report (December 2009).
20. GWP, 'Integrated Water Resources Management', TAC Background Paper No. 4, 2000.
21. Handshake, *International Finance Corporation* (Vol. 1, May 2012).
22. Phillippe Martin, *Public-Private Partnerships for Urban Water Utilities: A Review of Experiences in Developing Countries*, World Bank.
23. OECD, 'Private Sector Participation in Water Sector Infrastructure', OECD Investment Division, France (2008).
24. 'Water PPPs', Handshake, Issue #1, International Finance Corporation.
25. WSP-AF, 'Rural Piped Supplies in Ethiopia, Malawi and Kenya: Community Management and Sustainability', Nairobi, Kenya (2002).
26. Infrastructure Investor Africa Intelligence Report. Sector Focus: Water.
27. Charting our Water Future: Economic Frameworks to Inform Decision-Making, 2030 Water Resources Group.
28. Interview, Shadya Edwards, Director of Water Campaigns, Corporate Accountability International.
29. 'Why Investing in Water Could be a Good Thing', Copy Carbon, http://copy-carbon.com/water-article/.
30. Public-Private Partnerships for Urban Water Utilities: A Review of Experience in Developing Countries, World Bank, Washington DC.
31. T. Maluleke, T. Cousins and S. Smit, 'Securing Water to Enhance Local Livelihoods, Community Based Planning of Multiple Uses of Water in Partnership with Service Providers', CARE, RSA (2005).
32. Interview: Gad Cohen, Deputy Managing Director, InfraCo Africa.
33. Interview: Jane Jamieson, Senior Infrastructure Analyst, International Finance Corporation.
34. Foser et al., 'Africa Infrastructure Country Diagnostic Descriptive Manual', World Bank, Washington, DC (2006).
35. Martin, *Public-Private Partnerships for Urban Water Utilities*.
36. RW Board September 2000:136; RW Executive Committee February 2001:127.
37. *Aquavita* 9th issue 2005b:7.
38. Interview: Anonymous Rand Water executive.
39. *Aquavita* 6th issue 2004b:2.
40. *Aquavita* 4th issue 2004.
41. *Aquavita* 3rd issue 2004:10.
42. *Civil Engineering* 2005:23.
43. *Aquavita* 7th issue 2004:2.
44. *Traders Africa* 2004.
45. Handshake, *International Finance Corporation*.

15
Transport and Logistics Sector

Mark Pearson

As part of the *Africans Investing in Africa* series, this chapter looks at the opportunities and challenges in the transport and logistics sector. This is a very large and strategic economic sector, and the companies interviewed were mainly in the road transport and logistics sectors. Most freight moved between African countries is moved by road as, apart from South Africa, the railway sector in Africa has been allowed to decline so that rail, typically, accounts for less than 5 per cent of the volume of goods transported in Africa. Volumes of cargo moved by air are insignificant compared to that which travels by road within Africa and by ship to and from the rest of the world, although this air cargo is important and has a high value, such as diamond and gold exports and urgent replacement parts for industrial machinery, or are time sensitive, such as cut flowers and vegetable exports to Europe. Although there used to be regular ferry services and cargo carriers on Africa's major water ways, water transport in Africa has declined to almost non-existent except on sections of major rivers such as the Congo and the Nile.

Transport and logistics are a major challenge to doing business in Africa, with the associated challenges being poor reliability, long transit times and high costs. This is partly to do with geography. Distances within and between African countries are, to the most part, vast and surface transport costs are a function of distance. It is also partly to do with poor infrastructure. Distances are vast and, because national economies are under-developed and small and because population centres are far apart, it is often the case that there is not enough traffic using the transport infrastructure (roads, ports, railways, airports, etc.) to realise a positive return on investment. This means that there are usually insufficient funds generated from the infrastructure to pay for its maintenance and further improvement. However, although there is nothing that can be done about distance and solving the infrastructure constraint is a long-term issue, a lot can be done to reduce costs by improving the efficiency of transport and transit procedures and regulations that govern transport.

Other factors that result in high costs in Africa are trade volume imbalances, which typically result in 75 per cent empty return hauls, and delays at terminals and border posts, which result in poor equipment utilisation and high fixed costs.

Globalisation has changed the way business is done. The way goods are manufactured in the modern world is a process of assembly from many specialised manufacturers located in many parts of the world rather than one company in one location manufacturing the majority of component parts and manufacturing the final product from these component parts. This fundamental change in the manufacturing process means that global value chains need to be as efficient as possible if producers are to compete on a global scale. An efficient global value chain is dependent on an efficient transport and logistics system.

The World Bank's Doing Business Survey measures how easy it is to do business in various countries and regions of the world and ranks the ease of doing business according to a number of parameters. According to the latest Doing Business survey, Africa as a region ranks as the worst performer in transport and logistics.

The World Bank's Logistics Performance Index shows that a trade supply chain is only as strong as its weakest link and that by removing unnecessary obstacles, governments can contribute to an environment that encourages entrepreneurs to look beyond their own borders for business opportunities.

Exporting out of Africa typically involves an exporter signing a contractual agreement with the overseas buyer. The exporting company prepares all required documents and gets them approved by the relevant authorities such as customs and other border agencies; gets a letter of credit from a commercial bank; arranges for the goods to be packed and transported from the warehouse to the port; pays port fees and handling costs and gets a bill of lading; and then has the goods loaded onto the ship. Full payment to the exporter is often only after presentation to the bank of the bill of lading.

Importing is similarly complex, and this is usually why importers and exporters (all over the world) hire freight forwarders and customs clearance agencies. The importing company prepares and obtains all required documents and submits them to the relevant authorities; obtains an import letter of credit from a commercial bank (subject to the availability of foreign exchange); completes the necessary documents for clearance of goods out of the port once the goods are off-loaded from the ship and gets these documents approved; pays all handling fees; arranges for the goods to be bonded and transported to a neighbouring country (where appropriate) which means that transit documentation must be completed and approved; and completes all customs clearance documentation for the country of destination.

The general trade pattern between Africa and the rest of the world has not changed much since the 1960s, when most African countries attained independence from the European colonial powers, and it is still the case that Africa, in general, exports almost all it produces in an unprocessed or semi-processed, unfinished, form and mainly imports finished manufactured goods. What has changed is where goods from Africa go to and where imports come from, with China and the rest of Asia replacing Europe as Africa's main trading partner. There is relatively little trade between African countries, although South Africa has made significant inroads into the rest of Africa in recent years, and Africa is very much a minor player in terms of global value chains. The trade volume balance with the rest of the world is typically 80:20 and Africa's container depots are full of empty containers, waiting to be picked up and taken back to Asia, Europe and America.

A note on methodology

Africa is heterogeneous and conditions vary by region and country and even within countries so it is always difficult and dangerous to characterise business practices, constraints and opportunities as African. For the purposes of the study, African companies are those companies that have traded and/ or invested across multiple geographies in Africa and have a strong African component. Large trucking companies in South Africa, Zambia and the DR Congo, freight forwarding companies, shipping companies and railways are examples. This means that the companies themselves are very varied in all ways.

Because of this, a case study methodology was used in which a number of companies in the logistics and transport sectors that were defined as African according to the criteria outlined earlier were identified and were asked to complete a structured questionnaire either in writing or through a verbal interview or both. The chapter, therefore, reflects responses from selected companies on a case-by-case basis, although it must be said that there was a strong thread of commonality in the responses of the companies contacted.

In order to ensure that companies were as candid as possible, an undertaking was given to respondents that their answers and comments would not be attributed to them, and where they are, the permission of the company has been obtained.

Main trade and logistics challenges in Africa

The main concern of the transport and logistics companies taking part in the study was corruption, and the corruption spoken of was seen as being endemic and across the board. As corruption, in the broader sense of the word and not only referring to the practice of demanding bribes to perform services that should be performed in the normal course of duty of border agency officials in particular, was a cross-cutting theme, it is dealt with under the sectors discussed.

Customs and border clearances

For the companies that participated in the survey, customs and the bureaucracy surrounding customs was the major constraint to doing business in the transport and logistics sector and a deterrent to investing further in the sector. There is a general feeling that, although government and the customs services are seemingly making efforts to improve customs and remove unnecessary bureaucratic delays, not enough is actually being done on the ground. There is also a common feeling amongst businesses that customs and government officials often do not actually want to make customs more efficient than it is as this will reduce the potential to rent seek – there is more money to be made by unscrupulous officials in administering chaotic systems than in efficient systems.

It is also the case that many countries have invested significantly in electronic clearance systems; yet even when these systems are in place, it is still necessary to present paper documents to border officials when crossing the borders and to suffer delays that most transporters and logistics companies consider unnecessary.

Despite this, there have been attempts by both the private sector and governments to improve systems through automation and computerisation. For example, DHL has invested significant amounts of money in Nigeria with the construction of its own clearing facility at the airport in Lagos, Nigeria, and has about 29 customs officials, plus other officials from other border agencies, stationed in the facility dealing exclusively with DHL business. Nigeria has introduced the latest version of the UNCTAD-supported customs management system – the Automated System for Customs Data(ASYCUDA World) – and has chosen to pilot it at a number of sites, with one of the pilot sites being the DHL facility.

Implementation of ASYCUDA World has not gone as smoothly as would have been hoped for, but it must be said that Nigeria would not be the only country to experience teething problems with ASYCUDA World. Zimbabwe introduced ASYCUDA World in the last quarter of 2011 and within three months, in December 2011, the Shipping and Forwarding Agents' Association of Zimbabwe claimed that ASYCUDA World had significantly slowed down clearance processes, with funds being locked in prepayment accounts and turnaround of declarations taking up to two weeks instead of the normal three hours. In April 2013, scores of car imports were left stranded at Beitbridge Border Post after Zimbabwe's vehicle clearance system went offline for eight hours.

In January 2014, Bruce Kaemba, President of the Zambian Customs Clearing and Freight Forwarding Agents Association, stated that the recently introduced ASYCUDA World customs system by the Zambia Revenue Authority was acting as a barrier to trade rather than as a facilitator. Kaemba said that the slow pace at which ASYCUDA World connected to the Internet had forced clearing agents to submit entries to customs in the night when there was no traffic. Kaemba said clearances were taking a week and the failure of ASYCUDA had forced customs at Chirundu (the border post between Zambia and Zimbabwe and the second busiest border post on the North South Corridor) to give special deliveries to importers. This means that importers can bring their cargo into Zambia without paying for it there and then but at a later date. The risk associated with this is that importers being given special delivery might default and fail to pay for the goods, resulting in loss of revenue to the Revenue Authority.

ASYCUDA World is a web-based system that is totally dependent on connectivity of the borders to the Internet and the majority of customs departments in Africa seem to have a challenge maintaining consistent connectivity at the required band-width. However, private sector companies in the transport and logistics business are not convinced that the challenges in introducing an efficient and reliable customs management and clearance system are only because of technical difficulties and there are recorded instances where the break in connectivity is not as a result of any technical problems but involves a human factor. For example, the border between Zimbabwe and Zambia at Chirundu is, and has been since 2009, a one-stop border post and operations rely on good Internet connectivity. Although investments have been made in upgrading connectivity, there are numerous instances where Internet power was disconnected manually. In fact, it is true to say that for at least one year after the one-stop border post at Chirundu was opened, officials at the border post took measures to ensure that the Chirundu border did not operate as a one-stop border post. There were many reasons for this, including the fact that the one-stop border procedure, as it was designed, did not capture 'round-tripping' arrangements but, instead of trying to address this issue, border agencies referred back to the old, tried and tested, systems and, in the process, ensured the new procedures did not work. Maybe one lesson to learn from this is that not enough effort is put into 'change management' issues when these new systems, aimed at improving efficiencies, are introduced.

However, not all the blame for inefficient clearance through national borders in Africa can be placed at the door of government and the public sector. A June 2013 World Bank book entitled *Why Does Cargo Spend Weeks in Sub-Saharan African Ports? Lessons from Six Countries*, by Gael Raballand, Salim Refas, Monica Beuran and Gozde Isik, indicates that private-sector behaviour can also be a factor contributing to transport and logistics inefficiencies. A common assumption holds that the private sector (terminal operator, customs broker, owner of container depots, shipper) has an interest in reducing the amount of time cargo sits in ports. However, the data in this report shows that the bulk of port delays come from transaction and storage time rather than poor handling or operational issues.

The report suggests that importers in Sub-Saharan Africa often have strong incentives to use ports as storage areas. At Douala port in Cameroon, for example, the port – not external storage facilities – is the cheapest option for an importer storing goods up to 22 days. This causes congestion and inefficient use of port space. In addition, terminal operators, who earn large revenues from storage, also benefit from long waits and have little incentive to reduce dwell time. The introduction of privately operated Container Freight Stations in Mombasa, which handle more than half the Kenyan import containers, has succeeded in decongesting the port, but has added to costs and transit time – the CFS operators are selling storage and handling fees.

The research done by the World Bank also shows that companies may use long dwell times as a strategic tool to prevent competition, similar to a predatory pricing mechanism. Incumbent traders and importers, as well as customs agencies, terminal operators and owners of warehouses, see a benefit to long cargo dwell time because it generates additional profits by acting as a strong barrier to entry for international traders and manufacturers.

These findings by the World Bank are contested by some of the operators who contributed to this study. Their view is that most ports try to discourage storage in ports and penalise importers keeping goods in the ports to encourage a faster turn-around. The problem may be attributable to some importers using containers and ports or depots as a cheaper storage option than a warehouse or because the importers lack their own warehousing space.

Security

The security situation for a number of companies in the transport and logistics sector is a concern and affects investment decisions in African countries.

In many countries in Africa, there are security problems on the roads and especially at night. In Nigeria, for example, there are gangs (sometimes referred to as 'area boys' but, whatever the term used, they are a modern form of highway bandits) that set up road-blocks on roads between cities and stop vehicles, commonly using boards with nails or spikes in them put across the roads, and exhort cash and valuables from drivers and passengers who have no option but to stop at these impromptu road blocks. The police are not able to address this issue in a way that is satisfactory to the travelling public or business. There are some Nigerian press reports that claim that the police themselves are involved with the 'area boys', but even if this is true the highway bandits move positions regularly so unless the entire road is patrolled continuously and regularly it is difficult to see how the police could address this unlawful activity with the resources it has.

One way to address this issue is through investments in other forms of transport. For example, partly because of the security situation on the roads in West Africa, and because of the need to run an overnight service for their customers, DHL has invested in a fleet of nine aircraft based at Murtala

Muhammed International Airport in Lagos which it uses to service 22 cities overnight in West Africa. DHL still has a road fleet, but this is now reserved for delivering over-sized parcels mainly for the oil and gas industries and travelling by day.

Security of transit is a major concern for transporters along a number of major African transport corridors and in a number of African countries and highway bandits are not unique to Nigeria. When referring to moving cargo on the Beira Corridor a transporter is quoted[1] as saying:

There is a serious security problem with trucks entering the Munhava area of Beira port.

The Munhava access route is the only entrance used by trucks entering the port to load and offload. This is an extremely high crime area with drivers being harassed by third parties while entering and departing the port. The road is in a poor condition and is congested so vehicles have to slow right down. The criminal elements gather in this area and stop the vehicles by engaging the rear axle park brake on the fuel tankers or jumping onto the vehicle itself. They then demand money from the drivers (approx. US$5 to US$10). Should the driver fail to pay over the cash, he is then pulled from the vehicle and beaten. The driver is then thrown under the truck while a member of the group enters the truck and steals the personal effects, radios, money, tools etc from the vehicle. If the drivers overnight within the Port, they are harassed by parties again. If the driver leaves the vehicle to submit documents, they enter the vehicle using duplicate keys. As you know, keys for trucks are not unique. If you are travelling along this road with fertilizers or wheat, then you need an armed guard.

There are many anecdotal tales of extortion of truck drivers and theft from trucks such as the story told about a goat that was already dead being thrown under a moving truck in DR Congo and the driver of the truck stopped by a crowd on the road demanding compensation for the goat to robbers jumping onto slow-moving trucks from above as they make their way up the escarpment from Chirundu in the Zambezi valley through road cuttings into the hillside and off-loading cargo, such as sacks of grain, as the truck is moving.

One result of the lack of opportunity and poor education services in African cities is the proliferation of groups of youths and children on Africa's city streets. In some cities, they get organised and pose a safety threat to transport operators and their clients. This, in turn, means that transporters need to put in place security measures to counteract these threats and this raises the costs of transport and logistics to the client. The unemployed youths that are a feature of African cities are also often recruited as 'rent-a-crowd' to take part in demonstrations and bouts of ethnic, religious and political violence in the cities.

There are also a number of areas in Africa where security is affected by the activities of Muslim extremists, such as Al Qaeda and its off-shoots such as Boko Haram that exerts influence in the north-eastern Nigerian states of Borno, Adamawa, Kaduna, Bauchi, Yobe and Kano, where states of emergency have been declared, and al Shabaab in Somalia and northern Kenya, whose activities have affected the way firms do business, and have affected investment decisions, especially in East Africa. At the end of 2012, after African Union troops drove rebels out of Somalia's Kismayu port, the level of piracy off Somalia was reported to go down. This, in turn, resulted in more cargo vessels being routed through Mombasa as some shippers had been re-routing their ships away from Mombasa because of the threat of piracy.

Piracy, which is most prevalent off the coast of Somalia and in the Gulf of Guinea, has driven up the costs of shipping and transport through higher insurance costs, private security guards and extra fuel and has affected trade with Africa as shippers divert ships away from areas where pirates operate, if at all possible.

Regulation and legislation

As a general rule, transport and logistics companies regard regulation of, and legislation dealing with, the transport and logistics sectors as, probably at best, inadequate and, at worst, a major deterrent to operational efficiency and investment in the sectors.

The fees, permits, taxes, levies and other revenue raising activities imposed by authorities along transport corridors are included in transport charges to customers. The costs to users are legitimate business expenses and are therefore deductible from income taxes, thereby nullifying the revenue effect to government. The effects of such institutional charges are skewed as they increase revenue for some countries For example, South Africa raises about ZAR176 million per annum[2] in 'taxes' on transporters and this has the knock-on effect of increasing costs in destination countries.

The levels of permit charges imposed by the authorities in a specific country can skew the competitiveness of that country's carriers when competing with operators in neighbouring countries. As an example, in SADC, if a carrier is to be able to register as a carrier in another country (and so be able to pick up a back-load on return) the carrier needs to buy an SADC permit. Permit charges vary per SADC country. In Zambia, the cost of the SADC permit is US$40 per annum per truck/trailer combination for all SADC countries; for Zimbabwe, the permit charge is US$150.00 per annum per truck/trailer combination per SADC country; and for South Africa the permit charge is US$700.00 per annum per truck/trailer combination per SADC country. When the cumulative costs of permit fees, levies, cross-border charges, tolls and other institutional costs become significant, they contribute to a switch in the usage of corridors towards the lowest cost route between ports and inland areas sometimes irrespective of the distance and time factor. In addition, when the accumulated cost of all government levies, taxes, fees, permits and so on are significantly higher in one country than in another, there is an incentive for companies to establish in the country with the least punitive tax regime. Botswana and Zambia are attractive investment destinations for South African companies as well as being good locations from which to do business for regional transporters in SADC.

'Good' legislation in the transport industry is necessary to protect infrastructural investments, improve safety and govern operations of industry players but, as far as road transport is concerned, the sector is largely unregulated (as opposed to deregulated). A lack of regulation can:

- improve competition, with small and large operations competing, but this also compromises service quality and safety as maintenance is deferred so as to lower operational costs;
- allow other government agencies to dictate transport policy (such as revenue authorities licensing transit vehicles to reduce illegal imports but also restricting back loads); and
- allow countries to license foreign trucks as a protectionist measure and restrict commercial presence of foreign trucking companies.

Regulation can assist in law enforcement (such as withdrawing a carrier's licence for overloaded vehicles). The current situation throughout most of Africa, as regards legislation of the road transport sector, could be characterised as benign neglect and there are a number of examples of legislation governing the transport and logistics sector that actually reduces the efficiency of the sector:

- In Kenya, the Kenya Revenue Authority (KRA) licenses trucks to operate either inside or outside of Kenya. A truck that is licensed to operate outside of Kenya can only take loads from a destination in Kenya to another country and pick up a backload from another country to a Kenyan destination (if it is a licensed carrier in the country outside of Kenya). The truck cannot pick up a backload from within Kenya to a Kenyan destination. KRA has this legislation in place ostensibly to limit smuggling but this restricts the efficient use of the national trucking fleet which could arguably be worth more to the economy than the amount of smuggling this legislation stops.
- The Nigerian Postal Service (NIPOST) is a government-owned and -operated corporation, responsible for providing postal services in Nigeria but also manages Courier Regulatory Services. The Nigerian Postal Services Act regulates the postal services and, under the act, a courier company needs to apply for a license from the Minister. NIPOST functions as both operator and regulator in the postal service industry. It would be

extremely difficult for any organisation to regulate itself as it is unlikely to enforce or create rules that threaten its position in the market and favour its competitors.

- In South Africa, anyone that transports goods by road on a commercial basis across the border requires a Cross-Border Road Transport Permit. Private sector companies question the necessity of having to obtain a Cross-Border Road Transport Permit or of supporting the Cross-Border Road Transport Agency (CBRTA) which manages the licensing system. Given that the cost of obtaining this permit has recently increased by over 60 per cent, which is seen by many in the industry as both arbitrary and unjustified, the benefits and costs of this permit system and the necessity of the CBRTA are being questioned afresh.
- In some Nigerian cities (including Lagos and Abuja) there have been bans imposed on the use of motorcycles on selected major roads. The main reason for this appears to be to control *Okadas* (motorcycle taxis) that are considered to be a traffic hazard, and the riders themselves are associated with theft, robbery and even kidnapping. However, because of the traffic congestion in Nigeria's cities (which was the reason for the rise in popularity of *Okadas* in the first place) the ban on motorcycles has resulted in creating difficulties in getting parcel deliveries to firms in the cities (as even motorcycle fleets belonging to courier companies are banned from using these routes) as well as for people getting to and from work.

The level of competition in the road transport sector in Africa varies by region, with southern Africa probably having the highest levels of competition and the least affected by cartel operations. However, nowhere in Africa is there a full road transport cabotage[3] system (the transport of goods or passengers between two points in the same country by a vehicle registered in another country) in operation. Although this would, if operated correctly, maximise the efficient use of the continent's road transport fleet, it would almost certainly not be supported by the road transport operators as it would introduce a level of competition that would most probably put all but the biggest operators out of business. The 'third country rule' is also extensively applied, prohibiting hauliers from one country to pick up loads in another country for delivery to a third country – for example, a Namibian truck returning empty from South Africa to Namibia cannot carry goods from South Africa to Botswana.

Another way to reduce costs of transport in Africa, in this case air transport, would be the liberalisation of air services. African Ministers responsible for civil aviation adopted the Yamoussoukro Decision in 1999 and, in doing so, committed 44 African signatory countries to deregulate air services, and open regional air markets to transnational competition. The decision was endorsed by heads of states and governments at the Organization of African Unity, and became fully binding in 2002.

One of the provisions of the Yamoussoukro Decision is to allow fifth freedom rights, which is the right to fly between two foreign countries with the flight originating or ending in one's own country. For example, fifth freedom rights would allow Kenya Airways to originate a flight from Nairobi, fly to Lagos, drop off passengers and cargo in Lagos, pick up new passengers and cargo in Lagos and take them to Dakar, drop off passengers and cargo in Dakar, pick up new passengers and cargo in Dakar and return to Nairobi and terminate the flight. Ten countries have not signed or completed proper ratification of this decision, and many others that are signatories have not implemented it. Most countries in Africa have now closed down their national carriers and opened up to foreign operators. This has reduced the costs of air travel and air freight and has made air services more efficient, safer and more competitively prices. However, with the introduction of fifth freedom (and possibly higher freedoms – there are nine freedoms of the air), air services would be even more efficient than they are now.

These examples show that there is a need for governments to consult a lot more widely with the private sector and other stakeholders than is currently the situation. Government also needs to separate itself from the regulator and to also regulate its own activities.

Legacy issues and social and cultural issues

Most businesses spoken to did not consider legacy issues (such as a colonial hang-over) as a major challenge to either the way they do business or investment decisions. There were instances where governments have a deliberate policy of indigenisation and so will give preferences to business owned and managed by nationals of the country concerned. However, businesses participating in the study were generally of the opinion that there was enough business to ensure that these preferences did not seriously affect the operations of the larger established businesses. There were also reported cases of indigenous firms getting government business as a result of preferences but then sub-contracting the business on to a larger company which was not eligible to bid for the business from government directly.

Most of the larger companies are very selective about whom they do business with. Some companies are reluctant to do business with African governments at all as they are perceived to be slow to pay and the process of procurement of services and award of tenders is not always as transparent as it could be.

If 'failed states' could be considered as legacy issues which, in the case of some African 'failed states', seems reasonable to do as governance was failing pre-independence, then legacy issues have a big impact on the way transport and logistics companies make investment decisions and do business. In some African 'failed states', police and the army are not paid salaries on a regular basis and even seem expected to 'live off the land' and raise money for their upkeep and survival through doing their job, which is to police the roads and control banditry. Companies interviewed were adamant that they had zero tolerance on paying bribes and that any employee caught paying a bribe faced instant dismissal. In situations where in order to pass through a roadblock or pass through a border post there is no option but to pay the police or army an un-receipted amount, then the choices facing the transporter would be to either pay the amount demanded (which presumably would constitute paying a bribe) or seek protection higher up the chain of command (which implies paying a bribe, or exchanging favours, at a different level) or simply not doing business in that country.

Cultural and language barriers affect the rate and level of inter-African investments, and these factors increase the challenge of establishing a business in a new country and a new market, which is not unique to African investors investing in other parts of Africa and is probably the case in all parts of the world. Xenophobia and a lack of trust of other nationalities or groups or tribes are by no means unique to Africa.

After the challenge of becoming established, in terms of registering the business, getting communications established, opening bank accounts, securing premises and recruiting staff has been done, there is then the challenge of insinuating the business into the local business community. Some of the larger companies do this through the established Western approach of advertising, sport sponsorship (such as football and rugby teams), product launches, recruiting influential people onto the board of the local company and hosting dinners and parties and other social gatherings where local dignitaries are invited.

There are also Africans investing in Africa that establish themselves by using links and contacts within their own ethnic groups in a foreign country as the base from which they build their business. For example, because of the way Africa was divided up by the European powers, there are a many ethnic Somalis in northern Kenya simply because the borders were drawn that way. The number of Somalis now in Kenya has increased substantially as a result of internal conflict within Somalia so that Somalis are now a dominant business force in Kenya. As documented in a Chatham House Briefing Paper by Farah Abdulsamed, the success of Somali businesses in Kenya, and in particular in the Nairobi district of Eastleigh, has not only attracted more Somali investments from Somalia itself but also from Somalis based in the Middle East and other parts of the world. A large number of Somalis in Eastleigh are employed in the import and export business and this business relies on access to finance through the *hawala* system rather than formal banking or state interventions such as letters of credit. Somali business people can capitalise on a global network of kinsmen amongst the diaspora with whose help they are able to import goods from all over the world. Using the port of Mombasa and Eldoret airport as the main hubs goods are transported within Kenya and other countries in eastern and central Africa.

Availability of human capital

Companies considered the availability of qualified human capital in the higher levels of management to be a challenge. One of the effects of the economic slow-down in Europe and the USA in particular, coupled with improved job opportunities in Africa, is that there has been an increase in young, qualified Africans returning home and entering the African job market, with one benefit of this being a rising middle class in African cities and formalisation of the labour force which contributes to increasing capital availability through pension funds and so on. Although the quality and availability of locally skilled professionals has improved in African countries with higher economic growth rates, companies employing these skilled staff, mainly into middle management posts, consider the staff costs, in terms of wages and associated costs, to be expensive. In addition, there is still a shortage of human capital required to fill senior management positions and some specialist skills and still the need to bring in highly qualified expatriate staff.

Infrastructure

As has been recorded time and time again, a lack of infrastructure in Africa, including in the transport, electrical power, water and ICT sectors, is a major deterrent to economic growth. It is recognised that the global economy relies on an efficient international logistics chain that can connect markets, people, businesses and countries.

Transport and logistics firms recognise the constraint imposed on their businesses as a result of a lack of infrastructure and a number of companies, such as DHL, Maersk, Grindrod, Imperial Logistics and small individual African investors, have already invested in infrastructure. DHL has, amongst other things, invested in a new Hub and Gateway in Nigeria and has a dedicated fleet of aircraft to service its clients in Africa.

APM Terminals, a member of the Maersk Group, has invested in a new container terminal at Apapa in Lagos, Nigeria. In February 2013, APM Terminals announced that it had opened a new road and rail serviced container freight station (CFS) 4 km inland from Mombasa port. Maersk has also invested in 22 new 4,500 TEU (twenty foot equivalent) container vessels, at a cost of US$2.2 billion, to serve customers on the Far East to West Africa trade. The WAFMAX vessels carry more than twice as much cargo as most other ships calling at ports in West Africa and were designed to improve Maersk Line's service offerings to customers while overcoming the current capacity constraints in the major West African ports and terminals, given that West Africa ports are not deep-water ports.

Bolloré Africa Logistics, according to the *Economist* magazine,[4] handles nearly all of Africa's cotton and cocoa, as well as much of its coffee, rubber and timber, which accounts for $2 billion of the Bolloré group's $10 billion annual revenues. Bolloré has invested in the port of Abidjan in Côte d'Ivoire, and this has resulted in reducing the handling time of containers in the port from eight days to two. Bolloré has also invested in the port of Freetown in Sierra Leone.

Grindrod has invested in other parts of Africa from its South African base in freight services and trading and in shipping in Mozambique. In January 2014, Grindrod Freight Services announced the establishment of a leasing joint venture with the Pembani Remgro Infrastructure Fund (established in 2012 as a partnership between former MTN CEO Phuthuma Nhleko and Remgro to invest equity in long term infrastructure projects across the African continent) to provide innovative and cost effective leasing solutions to the African rail industry. In shipping, Grindrod is a shareholder in the Maputo Port Development Company[5] (MPDC) which, together with Mozambique's ports and railways company (CFM – Portos e Caminhos de Ferro de Moçambique), Dubai Ports (DP) World and local partners, has already invested over of US$300 million into MPDC and a further US$838 million will be invested in the port by the consortium. Grindrod has also invested in, and operates, dry bulk terminals in Maputo handling coal, magnetite, iron ore and motor vehicles. Grindrod has stated that it is actively looking for investment opportunities in port and rail operations in Africa.

The Board of Directors of Grindrod is reported to have approved ZAR1.6 billion (about US$160 million) in new investments in Africa from 2014 to 2016. All the projects are aimed at creating new or replacement infrastructure in Sub-Saharan Africa, allowing Grindrod to better service trade flows on the continent. Grindrod have said that they will remain focused on developing infrastructure to use the opportunities they have to leverage that infrastructure to be a supplier of choice for logistics solutions.

Imperial Logistics has a large fleet of trucks operating in 14 African countries. Imperial also has international freight forwarding and courier capabilities, with offices and agents in all major centres in southern Africa, specialising in air and ocean freight forwarding, rail and road forwarding, direct express and customs clearing.

Moving to smaller investors, Farah Abdulsamed provides an insight into Somali businesses and investments in Kenya. Amongst the businesses Somalis have invested in is the trucking sector. According to the research done by Abdulsamed, in the past 17 years, over ten Somali trucking companies have been formed in Kenya. With an initial capital investment of around $5 million each these now show substantial annual profits of around US$20 million. Leading companies such as Awale, Tipper Freighters, Dakawe and Ainu-Shamsi Transporters own hundreds of trucks each. There are also many individually owned and run truck companies operating with 2–6 trucks, and this growing sector plays a very significant role in the Kenyan transport market. As has been noted elsewhere, the combination of ready access to finance through clan networks and the quick and cheap movement of capital through the *hawala* system are at the core of Somali business success.

Solutions

Given the many challenges faced by Africans investing in Africa, one may have thought that these African companies would not be willing or keen to invest in other African countries and would prefer instead to invest in economies where it is perceived to be easier to do business and where the investment is more secure. Companies did not, in general, think that returns on investments were higher in Africa than other locations and high returns were not one of the reasons given for investing in Africa. The main reasons given were:

- The investors knew Africa and how Africa worked and Africa was their home. Some South African firms accept that there was a steep learning curve from 1994, when, after democratic elections took place in South Africa, South African companies were able move into other African countries, but now South African companies are aggressively pursuing market opportunities in almost all other regions in Africa.
- Clients in other parts of the African continent, and in some cases, the rest of the world, needed to do business in Africa so the motivation to invest further in Africa is to provide a global service for the companies' corporate clients and expand global networks.
- Companies are always optimistic and seem to always believe that business will get better and business opportunities will improve and that, when they do, those businesses that are already established in the market will have an advantage over new entrants. Bolloré, for example, expects to lose money on serving the remote ends of its 'vital corridors', but believes maintaining the network will put it in a better position to bid for supplying lucrative projects such as iron ore mines in DR Congo, oil fields in Sudan, gold fields in Tanzania and gas pipelines in Nigeria. In West Africa, DHL's backbone business is supplying the oil and gas industry, and they have invested heavily in ensuring that they have the capacity to handle this sector. But they also fully understand that the world is changing rapidly and see their presence in the West Africa market as an advantage in diversifying into new sectors and connecting new companies as these opportunities emerge.

Most companies are somewhat wary of recommending government interventions and believe that governments need to put their own houses in order and reduce corruption within and by governments and generally improve their own levels of accountability and transparency before they can start to improve the legal and regulatory environment within which the transport and logistics companies operate. However, perhaps ironically, by improving customs management systems, introducing self-regulation systems, automating weighbridges and moving to paperless systems, governance at national and regional levels would improve as there would be less opportunity for government officials and border agencies to rent-seek and to divert tax payments into informal payments.

There are examples of good governance such as at the port of Durban, where the parastatal port authority and customs administration put pressure on the private sector to reduce delays by taking a stick and carrot approach – the stick being the application of prohibitive charges for storage and enforcing storage limits and the carrot being the option to pre-clear cargo. This reduced both clearance times and dwell times and so made the port a lot more efficient.

Companies do accept that government has a role to play in establishing the legal and regulatory environment and, in the case of road transport, some of the areas governments could address include the following.

Regulation and legislation

Private sector operators in the transport and logistics sectors are, in the main, in favour of a liberalised transport market in Africa, with liberalisation of the carriage of international road freight, introduction of international regulatory mechanisms and regional harmonisation of road traffic legislation. At the regional level, the following regulatory environment would greatly assist to make transport and logistics more efficient and significantly contribute to making African businesses more competitive so that they could be more meaningfully included in regional and global value chains:

- Regional Customs Bond. The present systems force a transporter to take out customs bonds as security for customs duty for each country traversed and to retire the bond at each border before taking out another bond for the next country and so on. This inefficient system unnecessarily ties up the equivalent of millions of US dollars in customs bonds. Some regional organisations, such as COMESA, have regional bond systems in place and it is not clear why these are not taken advantage of to a much greater extent than is currently the case.
- Regional Transit Management System. Because many African countries are land-locked, management of goods in transit is an important trade facilitation instrument which, if not implemented appropriately, results in excessive delays for transporters and losses to governments as goods in transit may get diverted to customers that are in countries which ostensibly the goods are supposed to be transiting through.
- Implementing a harmonised regional third-party vehicle insurance scheme such as the ECOWAS Brown Card or the COMESA Yellow Card.
- Implementing harmonised standards for fitness of vehicles, such as smoke emissions, vehicle registration standards, training of examiners, bus overloading and so on.
- Self-Regulation of Transporters: Many of the region's transport delays can be attributed to bureaucratic delays caused by the need to check on

compliance (such as customs inspections, weighing trucks, document checks at police road blocks, etc.). These delays can be reduced through the introduction of a transporter accreditation system in which a transporter undertakes to comply with a specified package of regulations. In doing so the transporter would be exempt from the usual compliance checks. There would, however, need be a system of spot checks which would also apply to accredited transporters and if an accredited transporter was caught contravening the regulations he would face severe penalties and lose his accredited status.

- Overload Controls: Given the high costs of transport throughout Africa it is not difficult to understand the economic attractiveness of overloading vehicles to reduce the unit cost of transport to an importer. However, vehicle overloading not only significantly accelerates the rate of deterioration of road pavements but, when coupled with inadequate funding for road maintenance, contributes significantly to poor road conditions and high transport costs. Some regions have standardised axle load limits and a maximum Gross Vehicle Mass (GVM) and, in some cases, such as the East African Community, have regional legislation that enforces compliance with these regulations. However, even in the East African Community, not all countries comply with these regulations and the standards are not enforced. If the GVM is set at 48 tonnes for road transport (which is the case for some African countries) instead of 56 tonnes for a seven-axle interlink (or horse with double semi-trailer), then the cost of transport per tonne increases by about 25 per cent.
- Reduce the bureaucracy at borders by implementing internationally benchmarked customs processes supported by a Coordinated Border Management system, implementing in full the Revised Kyoto Convention (RKC) at national level, and introduce a paperless clearing mechanism, with pre-clearance of Authorised Economic Operators an option available to transports, importers and exporters.
- Ensure that trade facilitation is an integral and important part of national customs services' mission statements, backed up by key performance indicators (KPI) to allow verification of how well they are doing.
- Implement as many clearance functions 'behind the border' as possible and so improve border efficiencies by utilising effective risk management, deferred duty payment systems and periodic entry procedures. This reduces waiting times at the border and also the number of agencies that require a physical presence at the border.

Some companies interviewed also suggested tax incentives should be given to potential investors in the transport and logistics sector, but no details are available.

Companies were also keen to improve security but this will require a host of interventions implemented over a long period of time.

Infrastructure

Although it is clear that the bigger transport and logistics companies are investing heavily in their own infrastructure, such as in Inland Container Depots, CFSs, container terminals, ships, truck fleets and railways, there is still a need to invest significantly more than is being invested currently into the common transport infrastructure.

The World Bank's 2009 study, *Africa's Infrastructure: A Time for Transformation*, argues that that the poor state of infrastructure in Sub-Saharan Africa cuts national economic growth by two percentage points every year and reduces productivity by as much as 40 per cent. To close the infrastructure gap with other parts of the world, meet the Millennium Development Goals and achieve national development targets in Africa within ten years, an annual spending of US$93 billion would be required.

In the past, governments in Africa have been almost wholly responsible for the provision of infrastructure, which has traditionally been regarded as a public good. However, it is clear that the public sector, on its own, cannot meet the demand for new infrastructure or maintain existing infrastructure and needs input from the private sector. There are, however, a number of challenges facing the private sector for them to finance a nation's or region's transport infrastructure partly, in the case of roads, because the traffic volumes on the roads are not usually sufficient to recoup investments fully through a user pays system; partly, in the case of railways, because railway companies are parastatals with high debt-equity ratios and the railway sector not being liberalised.

Conclusion

African transport and logistics companies did not consider that being African had many advantages over new foreign entrants. Local companies had local knowledge and were familiar with the way business was done in their country or region but new foreign entrants could quickly acquire this expertise either by hiring qualified local staff or by going into a joint venture with a local company. Being a local company can even have disadvantages over international or foreign companies owing to inferior access to finance and because multinationals often work through global contracts in which one multinational is contracted to provide services to all national offices.

Apart from corruption, transport and logistics operators taking part in the study considered the major constraints to doing business and investing in their sector as being: the high levels of inefficiencies and bureaucracy surrounding customs; security of their staff and their equipment; and poor and inadequate regulation of the sector, coupled with inappropriate legislation.

Most businesses spoken to do not consider legacy issues (such as a colonial hang-over) as a major challenge to either the way they do business or investment decisions.

Ethnic and cultural links are important for the success of some groups, such as the Somalis, who have access to finance through the *hawala* system and a global network of kinsmen amongst the diaspora with whose help they are able to import goods from all over the world.

Companies also considered the availability of qualified human capital in the higher levels of management to be a challenge.

A lack of infrastructure in Africa, including in the transport, electrical power, water and ICT sectors was considered to be a major deterrent to economic growth.

There is a strong sense that the African private sector, and in particular Africans investing in Africa, have a major role to play in improving efficiencies in the transport and logistics sectors, both in terms of improving infrastructure and in terms of improving the regulatory and administrative aspects of the sector. Given the many challenges faced by Africans investing in Africa one may have thought that African companies would not be willing or keen to invest in other African countries. However, there are major investments taking place by Africans in other African countries in the transport and logistics sector, the main reasons given for this being familiarity with the environment and an abiding sense of optimism that things would get better.

Going forward, the businesses taking part in the survey wanted to see government first putting their own house in order (meaning that governments should address the levels of corruption within government systems) before they could start to improve the legal and regulatory environment within which the transport and logistics companies operate. The companies did, however, appreciate that by improving customs management systems by, among other things, pre-clearing as much as possible; introducing self-regulation systems based on harmonised vehicle and safety standards; harmonising implementation of overload controls and automating weighbridges; using regional customs bonds and transit management systems; and moving to paperless systems, governance at national and regional levels would improve as there would be less opportunity for government officials and border agencies to rent-seek and to divert tax payments into informal payments.

Although it is clear that the bigger transport and logistics companies are investing heavily in their own infrastructure, such as in Inland Container Depots, CFSs, container terminals, ships, truck fleets and railways, there is still a need to invest significantly more than is being invested currently into the common transport infrastructure. What is needed for the private sector to play a more active part in financing infrastructure would be a mechanism that is able to allow private sector investments in the transport and logistics infrastructures in Africa.

In conclusion, there is a strong sense of optimism in Africa's future and, especially in the transport and logistics sectors, Africans are keen to invest in Africa, while still being very aware of the challenges and relative insecurities of these investments.

Notes

1. This is a complaint that was registered under the COMESA-EAC-SADC TradeMark Southern Africa Programme's Non-Tariff Barrier Monitoring and Reporting Mechanism. The complaint number is NTB-000–606, and it was registered by the Federation of Eastern and Southern Africa Road Transporters Association (FESARTA). See http://www.tradebarriers.org/active_complaints/page:2.
2. CBRTA Financials (2004–2012).
3. In theory, the South African Cross-Border Road Transport Agency (CBRTA) can issue cabotage permits to foreign hauliers on application, but the fee is considered to be very high by transporters.
4. http://www.economist.com/node/12432456.
5. http://www.grindrod.co.za/Company/49/Maputo-Port-Development-Company.

Other Sources Consulted

Abdulsamed, F. (2011). 'Somali Investment in Kenya'. http://www.chathamhouse.org/sites/default/files/public/Research/Africa/bp0311_abdulsamed.pdf.

Business Day. 'PcW Shows Demand for Logistics Services in Africa'. http://www.bdlive.co.za/business/trade/2013/10/31/pwc-study-shows-demand-for-logistics-services-in-africa.

Cross Border Road Transport Agency website: http://www.cbrta.co.za/.

Economist. (2008). Logistics in Africa – Network Effects. http://www.economist.com/node/12432456.

Engineering News. (2014). 'Grindrod to Raise Capital for R10bn Infrastructure Project Pipeline', 27 February. http://www.engineeringnews.co.za/article/grindrod-to-raise-capital-for-r10bn-infrastructure-project-pipeline-2014-02-27.

Pearson, M. (2013). 'Financing Infrastructure through Innovative Strategies in Africa'. *GREAT Insights* (Vol. 2, No. 4. May–June). http://www.ecdpm.org/Web_ECDPM/Web/Content/Navigation.nsf/index2?readform&http://www.ecdpm.org/Web_ECDPM/Web/Content/Content.nsf/0/51E02684D712101AC1257B7500402F52?OpenDocument.

Porée, Nick. (2014). Harmonised Road Transport Regulatory System for the ESA Region and Associates (draft), February. TradeMark Southern Africa.

The Post Online. http://www.postzambia.com/post-read_article.php?articleId=43609.

Rabelland et al. (April 2012) 'Why Does Cargo Spend Weeks in Sub-Saharan African Ports? Lessons from Six Countries, World Bank.

Reuters. (2013). Africa Investment – From FDI to AIA: Africans Investing in Africa. http://www.reuters.com/article/2013/08/08/africa-investment-idUSL6N0G92SW20130808.

This Day Live. (2013). Maersk: Nigeria's Import Will Grow in Second Half of Year. http://www.thisdaylive.com/articles/maersk-nigeria-s-import-will-grow-in-second-half-of-the-year/158884/.

World Bank. Trading across Borders. http://www.doingbusiness.org/data/explore-topics/trading-across-borders/why per cent20matters.

——. Transforming Africa's Infrastructure. http://web.worldbank.org/WBSITE/EXTERNAL/COUNTRIES/AFRICAEXT/0,,contentMDK:22386904~pagePK:146736~piPK:146830~theSitePK:258644,00.html.

16
Tourism and Travel
Terence McNamee and Daniella Sachs

The travel and tourism industry has evolved over the past six decades into one of the world's most significant economic sectors, contributing 9.5 per cent (US$7 trillion) to global GDP, 5.8 per cent of all exports globally (US$1.1 trillion) and 4.5 per cent of total global capital investment (US$652 billion).[1] The United Nations World Tourism Organisation (UNWTO) estimates that international tourism arrivals have expanded at a constant average rate of over 5 per cent annually (despite severe interim economic downturns) from 25 million arrivals in 1950 to 1,087 million arrivals in 2013. The growth of the industry has not only outpaced that of financial and business services, but also transport and manufacturing.[2] The tourism sector is moreover the biggest employer globally providing 1 in 11 of all jobs (nearly 266 million jobs) and is the principal foreign exchange earner for 46 out of 49 developing countries.[3]

Tourism has proved to be an important catalyst for economic growth, especially in developing countries. Not only does the sector contribute to job creation, but it also acts as an entry market for a wide range of businesses, ranging from SMEs to multinational corporations. Part and parcel of investments in tourism have been dramatic improvements in infrastructure (roads, airports, energy) to support the industry directly and indirectly, as well as trickle-down improvements ranging from better healthcare facilities to improved security. Emerging regions such as Asia and the Pacific have successfully harnessed the economic development potential of tourism, and increased their contribution to global arrivals by 16 per cent over the past 20 years to now comprise 47 per cent of the global total. The African continent is severely under-performing in comparison, capturing a mere 5 per cent of the market share of global tourism.

Although the Tourism Action Plan of the New Partnership for Africa's Development (NEPAD) recognises that tourism is 'one of the sectors with the most potential to contribute to the economic regeneration of the continent, particularly through the diversification of African economies and generation of foreign exchange earnings',[4] in reality very few African countries have prioritised tourism at a political level,[5] and the catalytic effect of tourism on economic development is grossly under-appreciated in most parts of the continent. This is despite its inclusion as a strategic pillar of economic growth in most countries' National Development Plans, as well as in the myriad of donor-funded tourism policies and master plans that have been completed.[6] Ministries of Tourism in Africa, often understaffed and under-funded, are rarely accorded sufficient weight in government policy making circles, and as a result, 'they often get in the way of tourism growth'.[7] In sum, there is a marked disconnect between government rhetoric and policy documents on the one hand, and actual support for the sector at ground level on the other.[8]

Perhaps one of the biggest hurdles to the effective prioritisation of tourism in many African countries is the complexity of the industry, which comprises a broad range of activities that go beyond the common perception of tourism being limited to holiday activities only. The World Tourism Organisation has defined tourism as 'the activities of persons traveling to and staying in places outside their usual environment for not more than one consecutive year for leisure, business and other purposes'.[9] According to the World Bank, tourists to Sub-Saharan Africa can be divided into four main groups depending on the purpose of their visit. Leisure tourists constitute the first group, and they make up approximately 15 per cent of the market, while business travellers constitute about 55 per cent of arrivals (subdivided into 30 per cent traditional business and 25 per cent small business or traders). The third group is comprised of people visiting friends and relatives (VFR), and although data on these tourists is not collected by all countries, it is estimated to represent 30 per cent of arrivals. The last category termed 'other' includes sports tourism, visits for medical treatment, incentives and attendance at meetings or conventions (MICE).[10]

Tourism is not only complex at the market level but also at the sectoral level, because, as Mathieson and Wall (1982) emphasise, it is 'a system with an originating area (the market or demand element) and a destination area (the attraction or supply side) with a travel component linking the two'.[11] Tourism at both the originating and destination area comprises a series of sub-sectors, which range from the services employed by a tourist to book a holiday to the transport required to reach his/her destination. At the destination level, it includes the accommodation and excursion/activity providers as well as a range of interlinking supply sectors such as fisheries, agriculture, forestry, and manufacturing, which supply fresh produce and goods to the hospitality industry.[12]

These strong inter-sectoral linkages are reflected in the tourism industry's higher-than-average economic and employment multipliers. According to the World Economic Forum (WEF), US$1 spent on travel and tourism generates US$3.2 in total economic output (this includes indirect and induced impacts), in contrast to every dollar spent in the economy as a whole, which generates on average only US$2.7 in total economic output. In addition, research has shown that for every US$1 million spent in travel and tourism, US$701,000 in income is generated, which exceeds the income generated for automotive manufacturing, communications, chemicals and mining.[13] Furthermore, a recent study in Zambia found that a US$250,000 investment in this sector can generate 182 full-time jobs – up to 50 per cent more jobs than a similar investment in agriculture or mining.[14]

Although, tourism's multi-dimensional, multi-faceted, and multi-sectoral features are responsible for its catalytic development impact, they are also partly responsible for the African governments failing in their support and prioritisation of the industry. Because the sector is consequently regulated by more than one ministry or parastatal, it is thus often 'a victim of multi-tiered and horizontal overlaps, resulting in poor co-ordination'.[15] If other departments, such as Finance, Trade, Home Affairs and Transport, are routinely taking the most critical decisions affecting the sector,[16] it is no wonder that Africa is failing to realise both the economic development impacts of tourism, as well as its own tourist potential. This is despite the fact that it has many natural advantages (in terms of the extraordinary diversity of wildlife, environment and people) over other regions such as Asia and the Pacific, which have nevertheless performed much better.

Box 16.1 New visa laws in South Africa set to damage tourism

Africa's tourism investment profile

South Africa, the success story of tourism growth and development in Africa, has not been immune to poor government coordination. The Department of Home Affairs' new immigration regulation requirements for an unabridged birth certificate for minors, as well as the provision for in-person collection of biometric data, are forecast to have a significant detrimental impact on tourism in the country. According to the Tourism and Business Council of South Africa, the new regulations may cause the country to lose 270,000 international tourists and consequently 21,000 jobs annually, costing South Africa R9.7 billion.

Yet Africa's continuing laggard performance should not obscure the real opportunities on the horizon. The continent's much-vaunted economic growth since 2000 has seen disposable incomes increase across the continent, producing a rise in domestic inter- and intra-regional travel. The World Bank estimates that more than 10 million people are already 'traveling across international borders every year within Africa for shopping, medical needs, sports, religious gatherings, business meetings and conferences, and visiting friends and relatives'.[17] The UNWTO, furthermore forecasts that tourism arrivals will increase to 77 million by 2020 (compared with just over 30 million in 2010), and that approximately 50 million (65 per cent) of these arrivals will be intra-regional travellers.[18]

Consequently, South Africa's state-owned national development finance institution, the Industrial Development Corporation (IDC), has identified hotel development to be one of the most lucrative investments in the fast growing economic nodes of West and East Africa, where hotel infrastructure remains grossly inadequate in filling the burgeoning market demand, with less than 10 per cent of the region's hotel rooms meeting international standards. Confidence in Africa's tourism investment potential is further borne of the fact that Africa was the only region whose tourism sector grew during the global financial crisis, and since 2008 it has increased – albeit off a low base – faster than the global average.

To capitalise on this growing trend, global hotel chains 'are poised to invest hundreds of millions of dollars in Africa to meet the rising demand from both international tourists, business travellers, and the continent's own fast growing middle class'. According to HVS's Africa Hotel Valuation Index, this has produced a 33 per cent increase between 2009 and 2013 in the average value of hotel rooms in US dollar terms across the continent. In addition, the 2014 annual survey of international hotel chains' development intentions and activities in Africa has revealed that since 2010 the number of hotel deals signed and confirmed (although not necessarily under construction) has increased by 84 per cent, showing a compound annual growth rate of 13 per cent from 2010 to 2014. Moreover, the 27 hotel chain survey respondents reported a total of 215 new hotels with almost 40,000 rooms in their 2014 Sub-Saharan Africa development pipelines.[19]

In contrast to international trends, South African hospitality brands have been slow to enter the African hospitality market. Norman Basthdaw, the New Business Development Manager at Sun International, explains that South African hospitality brands, specifically in the four and five star market, cannot compete with the well-established international brands who have rolled out across Africa.[20] It is significant that the two largest South African hotel chains that successfully fore-fronted local expansion into Africa have both sold out to big international brands. The leading global hospitality company Marriott International, Inc recently acquired Protea Hotels while Sun International Limited have sold their five star hotel stake in five African countries to Minor International Plc, one of the largest hospitality and leisure brands in the Asia Pacific region.

Box 16.2   Mantis collection bucking the trend

Traditionally a five star leisure and wildlife tourism group, the privately owned South African Mantis Collection has done a 180-degree about-turn with their African expansion strategy. Graham Moon, CEO of Mantis Development, explains that the company's strategy is simply to capitalise on the growth of tourism demand in Africa that is being built on the back of the resource and commodity drive into the continent by big multi-national oil, gas and mining companies like BP, Shell, Rio Tinto and so on. To do so, they have not only elected to focus on the business travel segment of the market, but have moreover developed a strategic joint venture with the well-known Australian Staywell Group. Together they plan to roll out not the luxury business hotels one would expect from Mantis, but rather the three and four star Park Regis and Leisure Inn Brands, to fill the critical market gap for more affordable accommodation in East and West Africa.

Although South African hotel chains are struggling to catch the lucrative wave of African tourism expansion, their leisure safari counterparts have been steaming ahead. Both Wilderness Holdings Limited and AndBeyond, two of South Africa's largest luxury experiential travel and safari companies, have been operating with a pan-African investment strategy since their respective inceptions. Wilderness currently has 61 safari camps and lodges operating in eight SADC (Southern African Development Community) countries,[21] with a further nine destinations marketed in four countries, including two camps in the Democratic Republic of the Congo and future plans to expand to East Africa. AndBeyond, in contrast, expanded first to East Africa in 1995, followed by the SADC region, and currently operates 33 lodges and camps located in seven countries.

While Wilderness attribute their pan-African strategy to the passion of the founders to 'protect and promote the remote and wild places of Africa', Les Carlisle, AndBeyond's Group Conservation Manager, explains that on a practical business level a pan-African investment strategy not only enables a safari company to take advantage of the myriad diverse wildlife attractions that Africa has to offer, but is moreover critical to building resilience and maintaining business viability in Africa. Unlike the more durable business travel segment of the market, leisure tourism is highly discretionary, therefore any political, security or economic hiccup has a major impact on tourism arrivals. A key example is Kenya, where arrivals have plummeted not only due to the threat of Al Shabab, but also due to uncompetitive market pricing resulting from the value added tax (VAT) the state levies on tourism operators and conservation fees.[22] AndBeyond is able to weather the collapse of the industry because the company's pan-African strategy enables them to make significant returns across destinations, thereby cross-subsidising their failing Kenyan investment until the market picks up again. As for other Kenyan companies with far more limited 'land under influence' and resources, their existence is becoming more precarious, deeply constrained as they are especially in terms of their scope for expansion.

Obstacles to tourism growth

Even though investment into Africa's tourism industry has increased at a rapid rate over the past four years, tourism companies express frustration at the vexing 'brakes on growth' experienced across Africa. Studies commissioned in SADC countries routinely cite the same macro constraints on tourism growth – from major infrastructure gaps and unreliable power supplies to ever-rising transport costs – which the Box on Malawi clearly demonstrates. African investors, in contrast, have honed in on a number of obstacles generated at a governmental regulation level which they consider to be the greatest impediments to investment, namely, land tenure and asset security, opaque tax regimes, limited and expensive air access, and perception issues.

Box 16.3   Obstacles hampering tourism growth in Malawi

Malawi, long ago dubbed the 'warm heart of Africa' due to its rich cultural heritage and outstanding natural endowments, should have a burgeoning tourism industry. However, growth in high-yield, long-haul international leisure tourism has been slow and faltering over the past 15 years. In addition, the country has witnessed a further decline in regional and low-budget backpacker travellers, owing to the opening-up of competing markets (such as Mozambique and Mauritius) and the escalating health risks and fears surrounding bilharzia in Lake Malawi. Several factors have been put forward by both government and private sector for Malawi's poor performance, which echo the situation in many other African countries, namely:

• poor multi-sectoral coordination;
• inadequate supporting infrastructure and services (e.g., poor roads, erratic power and water supply, weak visitor-handling facilities, limited marketing promotion);
• high costs and limited direct air services;
• underdeveloped products and services (e.g., depletion of wildlife due to poaching, lack of visitor-friendly heritage sites);
• limited access (through weak facilitation) to land for tourism development (how it is accessed, what tenure is available, what land uses are permitted, and whether investors are treated fairly and consistently are all key questions);
• onerous red tape and bureaucracy that stymies new investment;
• failure of private sector investors to proceed with planned projects, which 'to some extent was linked to the absence of dedicated tourism investment incentives';
• lack of access to finance (especially for local small enterprises); and
• varied levels of quality service delivery (e.g., limited supply of skilled labour, underinvestment in tourism facilities).

All of these have been important contributing factors to explain Malawi's under-performance in tourism. Interviews with several key private sector officials reveal, however, that the greatest constraints to growth are in some respects more systemic and institutionalised, namely, successive administrations' failure to prioritise the country's tourism sector and integrate it into the country's economy, and its governing structures.

Source: Adapted by the authors from Terence McNamee, 'The Warm Heart of Africa 2014–2064: Transforming Malawi into a Top Tourism Destination', *PACE Report 01/2014* (Johannesburg: The Brenthurst Foundation, 2014).

Land tenure and asset security are two of the greatest factors inhibiting investment in many African countries. Often, there is either insufficient land use planning and onerous legislation, or legal processes and tenure can be challenged at will. Thus, there is the perception that in Africa 'everything is rented even if you own it, for it can all be taken away in the blink of an eye when the political situation changes or you fall out of favour with the ruling party'.[23] Land security in wildlife areas and national parks is equally tenuous, for 'in Africa, there are no guarantees that they will not develop a factory next door to your luxury safari camp'.[24] One only has to look at the oil drilling in the Murchison Falls National Park in Uganda, or the uranium mining being conducted in the Selous UNESCO World Heritage site in Tanzania, to see that these fears are not exaggerated.

Box 16.4 West Africa investment climate

One of the single largest obstacles to intra-African tourism investment in West Africa is investment security. However, this hesitancy of foreigners to invest in West Africa's high-risk business environment has not in fact inhibited the growth of hospitality in the region. In contrast, in its absence, a strong local investment growth model has developed. In emerging destinations, tourism development is normally spearheaded by foreign investors, with the inevitable result that the industry is subject to high levels of economic leakages and low economic returns for the host country. In West Africa, this model is different, as the big hotel chains are by and large entering the market as hotel management companies, with the local private sector investors owning the assets.

The opaque tax structure and legislation within many African countries is deemed to be a further hindrance to investment growth. Various shady dealings often accompany the murky depths of tax regulations that can see small, 10-room facilities paying more taxes than 500-bed hotels in certain destinations. Protectionist tax regimes also have considerable economic impact on the viability of business operations and industry competitiveness. In Namibia, for example, the government charges 20 per cent withholding tax on management fees to non-Namibian service providers,[25] which results in companies having to pay their staff an extra 25 per cent. This elevated cost is in turn passed on to the consumer through higher room rates, thereby heightening investor risk in what is already a non-competitive leisure tourism destination. Protectionist import duties (on building materials and furnishings) have a similar impact in elevating room rates in Nigeria to cover the high cost of hotel development, which is upward of US$400,000 per room for a mid-market hotel (double the world average of US$200,000). This results in an inhibitory investment environment where 40–50 per cent equity contributions may be needed in addition to collateral of 1.5–2 times the loan amount.[26]

According to the World Bank, the exorbitant costs of flights to and within Africa combined with limited air access are further severely constraining the continent's competitiveness and international demand for African tourism.[27] African flights are not only on average 50 per cent more expensive than global norms, but are also only serviced by 4 per cent of the world's scheduled seat capacity. With less than 15 per cent of those seats devoted to flights that connect African regions,[28] the deficit is further inhibiting the growth of inter-regional trade and travel. Government protectionism of national tax-funded airlines is cited as the key inhibiting factor to the growth of low-cost carriers (LCCs) within domestic travel markets, thereby impeding the implementation of the 1999 Yamoussoukro Decision to liberalise African aviation with an open air policy, and stimulate the competitive free flow of private capital in the industry which would reduce airfare costs.[29]

Box 16.5   Low-cost carrier investment

Low-cost carriers (LCCs) have an important role to play in the economic growth of tourism, and specifically business tourism across Africa. With 38 per cent of passengers flying for the first time in Fastjet's first six months of operation in Tanzania, Africa's first LCC has not only demonstrated that more affordable ticketing structures (60–70 per cent cheaper than traditional flights) can create a new valuable multi-segment travel market of burgeoning middle class and VFR travellers, but, moreover, that new LCC airline routes, such as Fastjet's link between Dar es Salaam, Tanzania, and Harare, Zimbabwe, have the added benefit of enhancing cross-regional trade, which has been hampered by a legacy of bad infrastructural linkages. According to Justin Glanville, Fastjet's South Africa Commercial Manager, the low cost of airline tickets and new regional route linkages that are attracting these traders has already had a significant knock-on-effect in creating a new demand in Tanzania for two, three and four star hotel accommodation.

Despite the uncompetitive airfares and hotel room rates, many countries in Africa would still struggle to build a leisure tourism base due to the legacy of conflict and the perception of instability that still haunts them, inhibiting both tourism demand and investor attraction. One such example is Madagascar, a country with an undeniable, extensive and rich product base for tourism, yet which has few, if any, established operators or top end tourism establishments.[30] It will therefore take even longer to develop confidence in the possibility of a leisure tourism industry in West Africa, whose product offerings are virtually unknown in contrast to those of Madagascar. However, companies like AndBeyond and Wilderness Holdings are already eyeing out future opportunities and are waiting for the political, economic and tourism situations to improve before they throw their dice.

Solutions

Identifying *what* the obstacles to successful tourism are is one problem; explaining *how* to overcome them is quite another. What can be clearly ascertained from the earlier list of constraints to African private sector investment across the continent is that these obstacles are neither insurmountable nor financially draining for emerging economies with small asset bases to smooth over. In fact, it is governments and regional blocs themselves that are the key to improving and enhancing investments in African tourism, through the creation of a stable enabling environment for the private sector to operate within. According to economic analysts and investment institutions, an enabling tourism investment environment should comprise the followings key aspects that increase industry competitiveness and decrease capital start-up costs:[31]

- clear supportive policy frameworks;
- ease of doing business;
- clear and transparent regulatory requirements;
- timely application processing;
- financial incentives (capital reduction incentives, operating cost reduction incentives or indeed capital mobility incentives);
- tax waivers (starting up income tax reprieves, import duty waivers); and
- favourable labour practices.

Box 16.6   Costa Rica's effective use of incentives

In the mid 1980s, tourist arrivals to Costa Rica had been stuck around 400,000 for several years – not paltry for a country of its small population and size, though far from the numbers which champions of the industry in government believed Costa Rica could achieve. This condition of stasis led the government to launch a series of generous fiscal incentives to accelerate growth in the sector, including tax credits for investments in tourism, income tax exemptions and the tax-free importation of equipment. Critically, these incentives were designed in such a way that they helped companies compete, and did not allow them to be privately profitable by shielding them from market competition. Partly as a consequence of these incentives, a true 'cluster' – where economics of scale, efficiency gains and innovations are realised – developed. Not everyone in Costa Rica was pleased that tourism was privileged to enjoy such generous incentives, and indeed by the early 1990s they had to be discontinued.

By that time, however, arrivals had more than doubled – today the figure is more than 2 million – and the sector had gained an irreversible momentum. Growth continued even after the incentives were phased out, and public policy was able to shift focus towards a more promotion-oriented strategy built around intensive marketing and brand development. Part of the reason growth continued unabated was the frequent and intense consultations and cooperation between the private and the public sectors that occurred. This became the norm, rather than the exception, even though they sometimes occurred on an informal basis. Of singular importance was the shared understanding of tourism policy's clearly defined aim – to promote the development of the sector and increase arrivals – and government's palpable commitment to support private initiative rather than replace it. Perhaps above all, the experience from Costa Rica demonstrates conclusively that tourism cannot thrive unless governments and the private sector work together in 'planning tourism infrastructure, promotion and financing'.

Source: Adapted by the authors from Jorge Cornick, 'The Development of Tourism in Costa Rica', in Terence McNamee, 'The Warm Heart of Africa 2014–2064: Transforming Malawi into a Top Tourism Destination', *PACE Report 01/2014* (Johannesburg: The Brenthurst Foundation, 2014).

Although tourism in Africa represents a powerful development path, its growth potential will not be realised unless it is 'integrated into each country's economy and government structure and seen as a benefit by everyone, from the president, to the ministers, to the general population'. Zimbabwe has recently become a good example of top-level prioritisation, where tourism investment is given such high development precedence that projects are fast-tracked to the President's office for approval.[32] This proactive approach has included the liberalisation of air travel in the country with the launch of the LCC FlyAfrica and is leading to increased tourism development and investment in the country. It has moreover been an influencing factor in the General Assembly of European Council on Tourism and Trade deciding to unanimously award Zimbabwe 2014's 'Top Tourism Destination in the World'.[33]

If government's role is to enable investment and increase industry competitiveness, then the role of the Regional Economic Communities (RECs) is surely to foster intra-African investment. Private sector investors do not believe that SADC's Regional Tourism Organisation of Southern Africa (RETOSA) has done much to foster interregional tourism development.[34] Even SADC's Transfrontier Conservation Areas, which were supposed to be powerful catalysts for tourism development, have very little outcomes to measure despite the large amounts of donor funding that they have consumed.

In this regard, the Economic Community of West African States (ECOWAS)[35] has steamed far ahead of SADC and other regional bodies in successfully boosting intra-regional tourism linkages though their combined issuing of an ECOWAS Passport (facilitating ease of travel between West African states) and the liberalisation of affordable and accessible air travel (facilitating the affordability of movement between states). ECOWAS achieved this by supporting the development of ASKY, a private sector cost competitive airline based in Togo, with a 40 per cent stake owned by Ethiopian Airlines, as well as by spearheading the creation of enabling bilateral agreements within West and Central Africa to open up the skies to ASKY.[36] With its major hub in Lomé, Togo, ASKY's network currently covers 23 destinations in 20 countries of West and Central Africa, operating 174 multi-stop flights a week with an average of 10,000 passengers.[37]

In the context of Southern and Eastern Africa, only Tanzania and Zimbabwe have foregone protectionism to facilitate the implementation of open sky policies, enabling not only the growth of LCCs in their countries, but also creating valuable inter-regional trade routes between them. As ECOWAS has so clearly demonstrated, regional blocs, as well as NEPAD (which is in the process of re-initialising its African tourism programme), have an important role to play in setting up intra-government communication channels, and facilitating the implementation of the Yamoussoukro Decision, thereby opening up the skies of Africa to enhanced trade, tourism and economic growth.

Key lessons

Tourism growth in Africa can happen in a variety of ways depending not only on the stage of tourism life-cycle a particular country is in, but also on what type of tourism market they have and are targeting. The different segments of the tourism industry described in this chapter (notably leisure, business, VFR and other) create different opportunities for different growth trajectories. When it comes to the development of tourism, what is evident is that governments cannot take a short-term view or planning strategy. As Derek de la Harpe emphasises, the key to building a sustainable tourism economy is for 'governments to look 20 years to the future and start planning how to get there, not taking short term decisions without considering long terms impacts'.[38] There are key lessons to be drawn from past experiences, both within Africa and from successful tourism growth stories outside of Africa, which could help reshape the current environment and make it more conducive to current and future tourism development.[39]

- Tourism must become a pillar within the economy and be integrated into its key structures for the sector to grow significantly. Successful tourism is impossible if there is not strong support for the sector at the highest levels of government.
- Devising ways to make it easier, more efficient and more affordable to travel to a country is the most urgent requirement for growth – such as encouraging the entry of LCCs, streamlining procedures and improving the most critical entry/exit facilities.
- Successful and sustainable tourism in an underdeveloped country requires major improvements and additions to its infrastructure over the long term, but this deficit is relatively unimportant in the short term.
- There is considerable scope for tourism development by better utilising and exploiting existing resources. This requires a deeper understanding of the key selling points of the country which already exist, and greater flexibility by government in deciding how staff and resources are used.
- In leveraging a country's most vital existing assets, no effort should be spared in protecting them. More robust approaches to protecting natural

environments and key wildlife areas are essential, not least because environmental damage is often irreversible.

- One should not overprescribe the targeting of high-end or low-end, backpacker or business traveller. Although examples of narrowly focused approaches, such as Rwanda's, have proven successful, there is an element of unpredictability to tourism development: the sector is likely to evolve in ways that were not anticipated at the outset of reforms, just as the habits and needs of international tourists have changed. Today's backpacker could one day be tomorrow's banker – with a family, wanting to re-live his youth, but this time in luxury.
- Corruption is antithetical to tourism growth.

Key action steps

- **Future planning.** It is imperative, therefore, that those emerging countries in Africa that are developing a tourism industry off the backs of their valuable mineral, oil and gas resources start planning now for their future diversification into the different tourism segments.[40] This is important not only because a mono-tourism industry is not economically sustainable, but also because the creation of a new leisure tourism destination on average takes a minimum of ten years to develop as a significant point on the tourist map.
- **Cross-sectoral funding.** Governments need to take a more holistic and in-depth view of the industry, and of its different potential segments and products. This will enable the woefully underfunded tourism ministries to harness and unlock cross-departmental funding for the development of valuable cross-sectoral supply chain industry linkages and spin-off effects. For example, the development of niche coffee agri-tourism product offerings in Uganda would not only help to diversify the product market, but would also promote local agriculture, build pro-poor local economic development opportunities, as well as serve to promote global exports for Uganda's private sector coffee industry.
- **Offer strong incentives.** There is a clear need for stable, durable and attractive incentives for capital investments in the tourism sector. These incentives should be devised to enable private companies to become more competitive and the tourism sector to achieve (as it did in Costa Rica) 'cluster economies', as opposed to incentives that 'produce private rents without social benefits'. Establishing the right set of incentives requires, firstly, thorough consultation with the private sector, to identify which are most likely to generate new activity and investment. A range of new measures might be considered, including, but not limited to:
  - extending duty-free and surtax-free status to renovations and upgrading existing developments (the need to continually upgrade and refresh properties is the *sine qua non* of successful tourism);

- incentives for companies to invest in training by, for example, offering double rebates on any monies spent on training (perhaps with provisions to protect such companies from losing staff to companies that do not spend on training);
- where exchange controls are in place, for companies that generate forex from tourism, a provision to retain 100 per cent of foreign exchange earned; elsewhere, liberalising the capital and current accounts.

  Whichever incentives are devised, African governments could examine in greater detail the experience of countries like Costa Rica where the introduction of incentives to invest in tourism proved highly successful. Importantly, the incentives should not last forever, but rather be discontinued once they have fulfilled their role.

- **Establish a high-level public-private forum/committee for tourism.** Successful tourism requires not only regular consultation between government and the private sector, but mechanisms that enable the private sector to have a role in defining policy and action, whether through participation in working groups or membership on tourism boards/councils that are empowered to make decisions. This body ought to include the relevant government ministers and permanent secretaries along with captains of industry to facilitate better cooperation, fast track reforms and build unity of purpose and vision. This new high-level public-private forum/committee for tourism should have a clearly defined mandate to prioritise key actions and be empowered to progress them through to implementation. Given the high-level nature of the body, from the private sector side membership should be limited to owners and general managers.
- **Conduct market research.** There is currently a gap in in-depth sector research and statistics on the various multi-faceted market aspects of the tourism industry in emerging destinations in Africa.[41] Such research would be highly valuable in guiding both the effective implementation of government tourism growth strategies[42] and in enhancing the promotion of potential and future private sector tourism investment opportunities.[43]
- **Develop an international standard hotel school.** There is an acute shortage of qualified hospitality staff across Africa, including especially middle management and senior management staff, which is a significant impediment to growing African tourism businesses. Many hospitality training institutes are underfunded and not fit for the purpose, and can – at best – only produce junior-level staff. In most countries there are no government resources to fund a school – or even send tourism students to another country to study – in order to meet the needs of the industry for qualified staff. One option would be to enlist the support of donors to finance scholarships overseas for middle to senior managerial staff. A more preferable option would be to engage with donors on the establishment of an institution similar to the Luxembourg-funded centre in Laos;

or alternatively partner with a foreign institution willing to set up a satellite school in the respective country.

* **Ringfence and reinvest.** Revenue raised from taxation on tourism offerings should, through clearly defined legislation, automatically be deployed back into the sector.
* **Improve tourism's PR.** Traditional marketing techniques (trade shows and poorly funded overseas representatives) should be reduced in favour of a consumer-facing PR campaign utilising social media and tourism journalists. It has been nearly 20 years since Costa Rica created an ambitious promotion strategy ('Cost Rica – No Artificial Ingredients'). The extraordinary success of that message is testament to what can be achieved, provided the message aligns with reality. Even with all their limitations, African countries have an incredibly rich and diverse tourism product to offer *right now* – but it requires a new message to capture the attention of the global tourism market

Future outlook

The future outlook for tourism world-wide is impressive, with international tourist arrivals expected to increase by 3.3 per cent year on year from 2010 to reach 1.8 billion by 2030. Of these 1.8 billion arrivals, 1 billion (57 per cent) are forecast to reach the shores of emerging economies, like Africa.[44] This positive outlook is, however, dependent on the successful diversification of the African tourism product base and destination map.

Related to this point, the World Bank has highlighted the critical importance of 'first movers' in establishing new destinations. 'Targeting areas of high potential also enables destinations to focus promotion activities on one or two iconic attractions, to pilot key and delicate policy reforms for land and air transport, and [to] create appropriate institutions with coordinating mechanisms in a contained setting' (Christie et. al. 2014: 117).

It is evident from this research that the 'first movers' in the development of tourism in emerging African economies are the big multinational resource and commodity companies. With their exploration activities, they are the actors paving the way for the development of business tourism in the most remote parts of Africa. The promotion of business tourism off the back of resource extraction has many benefits for African economies for, although business tourism receipts are significantly lower than leisure tourism receipts per traveller, it is not discretionary travel and thus is not as affected by external shocks, lack of infrastructure, lack of competitiveness or high prices.

It is not as easy to create new destinations for leisure tourism, and leisure travel in emerging areas will thus more than likely grow off the back of business travel. However, there is also the opportunity to take advantage of the leisure tourism industry's 'first movers', who are adventure and experience-seeking tourists. In the 1980s, Asia was at the forefront of tourism expansion; it was the exciting new frontier to be explored and uncovered. In the

2000s, it has developed into a popular family holiday destination. The only unexplored territory left in a world colonised by tourism is Africa. One of the most important attractions that draws these tourists to the continent is the myriad wildlife experiences that are uniquely and endemically African. However, with 50 per cent of wildlife in Africa already destroyed in the past ten years, the future of even these 'first movers' may be tenuous.

Not only is the lion already extinct in eight countries, and the elephant in eleven countries in Africa, but the rhino, the African wild dog, the cheetah and the gorillas may soon follow suit.[45] Conservation of wildlife and preservation of species across the continent is therefore integral to the future tourism development of new destinations in Africa. As a result, these governments need to ensure that they mobilise the top-end eco-tourism providers as the 'first movers' of the industry. Not only do they require little infrastructure to develop, but the high value of the tourism product they create has the ability to help fund both conservation efforts as well as community development efforts in the rural areas abutting national parks.

It has been stated in this chapter that aviation has a critical role to play in the shaping and development of tourism on the continent. According to the World Bank, the intra-African aviation market is forecasted to grow at 10 per cent in the short term and at over 8.5 per cent in the medium term. However, as the region's economies become more intertwined, demand for intra-African connectivity may even exceed this forecast.[46] The 'first movers' that will open up African skies for intra-regional travel are the LCCs. As Justin Glanville of Fastjet points outs, the demand is already there for travel; all they need to do is create the supply to fulfil that demand.[47]

The future may soon see the aviation industry overcoming road, rail and freighting infrastructure obstacles to intra-African trade tourism, especially as new affordable routes are created to link previously isolated countries across the continent. Adrian Hamilton-Manns predicts that in the near future there is a distinct possibility that low cost cargo planes will start to follow low cost passenger planes, transporting people and goods across Africa. Once they do, trade tourism revenues will more than likely exceed corporate and leisure travel revenues combined.

What this demonstrates is that one of the greatest assets Africa has for future tourism growth and investment is the infancy of its economy. Graham Moon believes that inefficiency, poor government policy, legacy issues and corruption all serve to create a fertile breeding ground for entrepreneurs, as it has done in both India and China. 'When an economy is fully developed opportunities decrease, because the environment is so exceedingly complex that it is difficult to do anything inspirational', he states. It is the uncertainty in Africa that breeds economic growth, and creates business opportunities, as can be seen in the earlier description of the future potential development of the LCC model. Thus, he wisely advises African tourism companies to follow in the footsteps of the LCC companies by not looking to recreate what the big international brands are already doing in Africa but rather to look at the space around the established market that has already been cornered; to look for where the market is not covered and the real opportunities lie. 'Go in with your eyes wide open', he concludes, 'the experience of Africa is impossible to beat, the opportunities are huge, if you understand the minor hurdles that you need to beat to reach them'.[48]

Notes

1. World Travel and Tourism Council Report, 'Travel and Tourism: Economic Impact 2014 Africa,' 2014.
2. World Travel and Tourism Council Report, 'The Comparative Economic Impact of Travel & Tourism,' 2012; WEF, 2013: 67.
3. WTTC, 2014: i; Honey, 1999: 9; Honey and Kranz, 2007: 16; Spenceley, 2008: 6; Markovic, Satta, Skaricic and Trumbic, 2009: 18.
4. Nepad, 2005: 4.
5. Moseketsi Mpeta, Interview, 13 August 2014.
6. ACET, 2014: 155.
7. Nepad, 2005: 11, 16; ACET, 2014: 153.
8. Moseketsi Mpeta, Interview, 13 August 2014.
9. WTO, 1995: 1.
10. Christie et al., 2014: 61.
11. Cited in Dowling and Fennell, 2003a: 1.
12. Inskeep, 1991: 15, 387; Ashley and Haysom, 2008: 130.
13. WEF, 2013: 66–68.
14. Christie et al., 2014: 32
15. Nepad, 2005: 11.
16. Nepad, 2005: 11, 16.
17. Christie et al., 2014: 2
18. UNWTO, 1999.
19. Ward, Adepoju, 2014: 2.
20. Norman Basthdaw, Telephonic interview, 22 August 2014.
21. Wilderness Holdings Limited Integrated Annual Report 2014–15.
22. Kenya is the only East African Community state that is levying VAT, which means that local players are losing out to neighbouring countries as visitors seek better deals.
23. Adrian Hamilton-Manns FlyAfrica, Sandton, 14 August 2014,.
24. Les Carlisle, Interview, 2014.
25. Namibia has a lack of human resource capacity especially at the five star management level, so luxury lodge providers are forced to bring in expat staff to build capacity at the local level.
26. Christie et al., 2014: 6.
27. World Bank, Africa Region Tourism Strategy Annexes, V3.0. October 2011, p. 40.
28. Ibid., p. 39.
29. IDC 2012, 29; ICAO/ATAG/WB Development Forum, Montreal, Canada, 24–26 May 2006, 'Implementation of the Yamoussoukro Decision: Progressing or Stalled?'
30. Les Carlisle, Interview, 2014.
31. Moseketsi Mpeta, Interview 13 August 2014; Nepad, 2005: 10, 16; ACET, 2014: 154; Christie et al., 2014: 12–15, 35.

32. Adrian Hamilton-Manns, Interview, 2014.
33. ECTT, 2014, Internet.
34. Les Carlisle, Interview, 2014; Derek de la Harpe, Interview, 2014; Graham Moon, Interview, 2014; Justin Glanville, Interview, 2014; Adrian Hamilton-Manns, Interview, 2014; Dr. Mohamed Harun, Interview, 2014.
35. Economic Community of West African States (ECOWAS).
36. W. Shadare, 'How to Harness Africa's Potential, by ECOWAS President', Inform Africa, 2011, http://www.informafrica.com/politics-africa/how-to-harness-africa%E2%80%99s-potential-by-ecowas-president/ (accessed 18 August 2014).
37. ASKY, 2014. 'Network.' Website: http://www.flyasky.com/asky/en/Corporate/Important-figures/Important-figures/Network-87.aspx (accessed 19 August 2014).
38. Derek de la Harpe, Interview, 2014.
39. T. McNamee, 'The Warm Heart of Africa 2014–2064: Transforming Malawi into a Top Tourism Destination', PACE Report 01/2014 (Johannesburg: The Brenthurst Foundation, 2014), pp. 61–62.
40. It is further imperative to understand how the different segments of the leisure market interact and influence the development timeline, so that the right segment is targeted at the right time. Generally, in any new remote destination, it is the adventure experience seekers who will forge the way, opening up the path to other segments of the leisure tourism industry.
41. Perret and Smith, 2014: 10; Christie et al., 2014: 5.
42. Christie et al., 2014: 5.
43. Perret and Smith, 2014: 10.
44. UNWTO, 2014: 2.
45. Les Carlisle, Interview, 2014; Derek de la Harpe, Interview, 2014; African Conservancy; WWF.
46. Christie et al., 2014: 38.
47. Justin Glanville, Interview, 2014.
48. Graham Moon, Interview, 2014.

Other Works Consulted

2014 African Development Bank Group. http://tourismdataforafrica.org/.
Adrian Hamilton-Manns FlyAfrica, Sandton, 14 August 2014.
The African Center for Economic Transformation. (2014). '2014 African Transformation Report: Growth with Depth', ACET, Accra, Ghana.
Christie, I., Fernandes, E., Messerli, H. and Twining-Ward, L. (2014). 'Tourism in Africa: Harnessing Tourism for Growth and Improved Livelihoods'. Agence Française de Développement and the World Bank, Washington, USA.
City Lodge Hotels Limited, 'City Lodge Hotel Group Integrated Report,' 2013. 33–35.
Derek de la Harpe, Wilderness Safaris, Rivonia 25 July 2014.
Ernst & Young. (2014). 'EY's Attractiveness Survey, Africa 2014: Executing Growth'. Johannesburg, South Africa.
European Council on Tourism and Trade. (2014). 'Informations about World Best Tourist Destination Award'. http://ectt.webs.com/besttouristdestination.htm (accessed 20 August 2014).
Graham Moon, Mantis Collection, Bryanston, 6 August 2014.
Justin Glanville, Fastjet Randburg, 12 August 2014.
Les Carlisle Meeting, Sandton, 23 July 2014.
Moseketsi Mpeta, IDC, Sandton, 13 August 2014.

NEPAD, AU/NEPAD TOURISM ACTION PLAN. (2005). New Partnership for Africa's Development, African Union, Nigeria.

Perret, S. and Smith, T. (2014). 'African Hotel Valuation Index', HVS. London, UK.

UNWTO (United Nations World Tourism Organization). (2010). *UNWTO Tourism Highlights*, 2010 Edition. Madrid: UNWTO.

Ward, T.J. and Adepoju, D. (2014). 'Hotel Chain Development Pipelines in Africa', W Hospitality Group. Lagos, Nigeria.

World Tourism Organisation. (1999). *Tourism 2020 Vision*. Madrid: WTO.

———. (2014). 'UNWTO Tourism Highlights, 2014 Edition'. UNWTO, Madrid, Spain.

World Travel Organisation. (1995). Collection of Tourism Expenditure Statistics, Technical Manual no. 2.

Index

CPSIA information can be obtained at www.ICGtesting.com
Printed in the USA
LVOW03*1800290515

440448LV00002B/2/P